The Legal Recognition of Sign Languages

Full details of all our publications can be found on http://www. multilingual-matters.com, or by writing to Multilingual Matters, St Nicholas House, 31–34 High Street, Bristol BS1 2AW, UK.

The Legal Recognition of Sign Languages

Advocacy and Outcomes
Around the World

Edited by
**Maartje De Meulder,
Joseph J. Murray and
Rachel L. McKee**

MULTILINGUAL MATTERS
Bristol • Blue Ridge Summit

DOI https://doi.org/10.21832/DEMEUL4009

Library of Congress Cataloging in Publication Data
A catalog record for this book is available from the Library of Congress.
Names: De Meulder, Maartje, editor. | Murray, Joseph J., editor. | McKee,
   Rachel Locker – editor.
Title: The Legal Recognition of Sign Languages: Advocacy and Outcomes Around
   the World / edited by Maartje De Meulder, Joseph J. Murray and Rachel L.
   McKee.
Description: Bristol; Blue Ridge Summit: Multilingual Matters, 2019. |
   Includes bibliographical references and index.
Identifiers: LCCN 2018060942| ISBN 9781788924009 (hbk : alk. paper) | ISBN
   9781788923996 (pbk : alk. paper) | ISBN 9781788924030 (kindle)
Subjects: LCSH: Deaf—Legal status, laws, etc. | Sign language—Law and
   legislation.
Classification: LCC K638 .L44 2019 | DDC 346.01/3087—dc23 LC record available
at https://lccn.loc.gov/2018060942

British Library Cataloguing in Publication Data
A catalogue entry for this book is available from the British Library.

ISBN-13: 978-1-78892-400-9 (hbk)
ISBN-13: 978-1-78892-399-6 (pbk)

Multilingual Matters
UK: St Nicholas House, 31–34 High Street, Bristol BS1 2AW, UK.
USA: NBN, Blue Ridge Summit, PA, USA.

Website: www.multilingual-matters.com
Twitter: Multi_Ling_Mat
Facebook: https://www.facebook.com/multilingualmatters
Blog: www.channelviewpublications.wordpress.com

The policy of Multilingual Matters/Channel View Publications is to use papers that
are natural, renewable and recyclable products, made from wood grown in
sustainable forests. In the manufacturing process of our books, and to further
support our policy, preference is given to printers that have FSC and PEFC Chain of
Custody certification. The FSC and/or PEFC logos will appear on those books
where full certification has been granted to the printer concerned.

Typeset by Nova Techset Private Limited, Bengaluru and Chennai, India.
Printed and bound in the UK by Short Run Press Ltd.
Printed and bound in the US by Thomson-Shore, Inc.

This book is dedicated to the campaigners, both deaf and hearing, who have worked for the betterment of deaf people's lives, through numerous campaigns around the world, some of which are chronicled in this volume.

Contents

Contributors

Austria

Franz Dotter (1948–2017) trained as a school teacher in German and maths at the University of Salzburg, Austria, but instead of teaching he continued his academic studies. He was a formal linguist (habilitation on iconicity in syntax, 1990) and in 1996, he founded the Centre for Sign Language and Deaf Communication at University of Klagenfurt (https://www.aau.at/gebaerdensprache-und-hoerbehindertenkommunikation) and led its team until his official retirement in 2013. It is to this day the only such centre at an Austrian University. Franz Dotter collaborated with and hired Deaf colleagues, was an outspoken ally of the Austrian Deaf community and his approach to anything he did in the field of sign languages was one of justice and equal rights.

Lukas Huber serves as General Secretary of the Austrian National Association of the Deaf since 2001. He is one of the key figures in the Austrian disability movement with special focus on Austrian Sign Language policy work and promoting knowledge about the rights, culture and language of deaf people. He also is a deaf advocate for human rights and accessibility issues. He was a co-author of the alternative report on the implementation of the UN Convention on the Rights of Persons with Disabilities in Austria on the occasion of the first State Report Review, published in 2013. He is also a board member of the Klagsverband since 2009. The Klagsverband is a litigation Association of NGOs Against Discrimination. Since 2015, he has been chair of the Lower Austria Association of the Deaf.

Helene Jarmer can do anything but hear! Since 2001, she has been President of the Austrian National Association of the Deaf. She was a member of the National Council of the Austrian Parliament and speaker of people with disabilities for the Austrian Green Party from 2009 to 2017. Born in 1971, Helene Jarmer lost her hearing at the age of two after a car accident. She studied education (summa cum laude) and worked as a lecturer at the University of Vienna and the University of Graz. Helene Jarmer enjoys art, travelling and languages.

Verena Krausneker is a sociolinguist at the University of Vienna, Austria, where she has been a lecturer and researcher since 2002. Her main research focus is on language policies and sign language rights, especially in Deaf education. From 2001 to 2007 she served as board member of the Austrian Deaf Association. From 2009 to 2015 she served as an expert for the World Federation of the Deaf. Her latest research project produced an overview of bimodal bilingual education in Europe (www.univie.ac.at/map-designbilingual), including insight into curricula and laws that support bilingual-bicultural education in 39 countries.

Catalonia

Marta Bosch-Baliarda is a hearing sign language linguist and interpreter who has worked as a trainer for sign language interpreters and sign language teachers. She has been involved in the Deaf community since 1998 and was an active member of the Platform LSC Now! during the legal recognition campaign for LSC. She is currently a research assistant with TransMedia Catalonia, a research group working on audiovisual translation and media accessibility from the Autonomous University of Barcelona. She is doing her PhD on sign language accessibility and interpretation on TV. She has a teaching position on intervention for the deafblind within the vocational training program for communication support workers.

Menchu González is a deaf speech therapist, LSC teacher and special education teacher for the Deaf. She holds a master's degree and is a specialist in the Deaf community. She has been a member of the LSC department in the Federation of Deaf People of Catalonia (FESOCA) (1991–1996) during the campaign towards Resolution 163/IV on the promotion and dissemination of Catalan Sign Language and was involved in the Catalan Sign Language Law campaign as an independent professional. She has been a teacher in a deaf school since 1995 and was involved in the working groups in the Department of Education (Catalan Government). Since 2014, she has been head of the language policies department of FESOCA.

Maria-Josep Jarque is a hearing sign language linguist who worked as a trainer for sign language interpreters and sign language instructors. She has been involved in the Deaf community since 1994 and during the legal recognition campaign for *llengua de signes catalana* (Catalan Sign Language, LSC), supported Platform LSC Now!'s actions from within academia. Currently, she is an adjunct professor at the University of Barcelona where she conducts research on LSC structure and LSC teaching in deaf education from a cognitive–functional perspective. She collaborates with the Department of Education (Catalan Government) in the development of the LSC curriculum and resources for intervention in sign language communication problems.

Belgium

Maartje De Meulder has a cross-disciplinary academic profile. She is a language policy scholar with an interest in sign language policy and planning, sign language rights, family language policy, multilingualism and sign language maintenance and revitalization. She is also interested in aspects of sign language interpreting and in discourses around the implementation of inclusive education for deaf learners. She was co-editor of *Innovations in Deaf Studies* (2017, Oxford University Press) and has published in journals covering language policy, applied linguistics and human rights. She is a beneficiary of a 'MOVE-IN Louvain' Incoming Post-doctoral Fellowship, co-funded by the Marie Curie Actions of the European Commission.

Thierry Haesenne is deaf and has a master's degree in Romance languages and literature, a master's in translation (English to French) and a postgraduate diploma in legal interpreting. He has co-written the report on the feasibility of the recognition of French Belgian Sign Language (LSFB) and was part of the first governmental advisory committee on LSFB. He has worked as a LSFB researcher at the Institut Libre Marie Haps between 2002 and 2014 and is now a full-time lecturer in the LSFB unit at the Louvain School of Translation and Interpreting (UCLouvain).

France

Yann Cantin is a deaf historian, university lecturer at Paris 8 University and specializes in the historical lives of deaf people. Another of his research focuses is the origins of sign language before de l'Epee's arrival. He has published two books: *Dictionnaire biographique des grands sourds en France* (2017, with Angélique Cantin) and *La communauté sourde de la Belle Epoque* (November 2018).

Florence Encrevé (PhD in history) is a hearing associate professor in linguistics (including deaf history and French Sign Language interpreting) at the University Paris 8 (France) – research team 'Sign Language and Gestuality' (Laboratory UMR 7023) – and a qualified LSF (Language des Signes Française)/French interpreter. Her main publication is *Les sourds dans la société française au XIXe siècle. Idée de progrès et langue des signes [Deaf in French Society in the 19th Century. Idea of Progress and Sign Language]* (Grâne, Créaphis, 2012).

Marie-Thérèse L'Huillier (research master in linguistics) is a deaf research engineer in CNRS's UMR 7023 Laboratory (she specializes in linguistic resources of LSF). She was also the youngest women activist in 1975, in the first deaf mobilisation in France. Her main publication is *Les représentations des sourds vis-à-vis des interprètes hier et aujourd'hui [The Representations of the Deaf vis-à-vis Interpreters Yesterday and Today]* (December 2014).

Italy

Carlo Geraci is director of research at CNRS, Institut Jean-Nicod, Paris and member of the Department of Cognitive Science at the École Normale Supérieure in Paris. Since 2011, he has directed the Sign Language Group at the CNRS, Institut Jean-Nicod, which helped to found. He has wide interests in sign language linguistics, from grammatical descriptions and formal approaches, to psycholinguistics, sociolinguistics, typology, language planning and signing avatars. He mainly works on French sign language, Italian sign language and tactile Italian sign language.

Humberto Insolera is a sign language activist who has worked and collaborated with several organizations mostly related to protecting the rights of deaf people. Since 2007, he has worked as a lecturer of deaf studies at Ente Nazionale Sordi, the main Italian Deaf Association, where he is also member of the observatory on accessibility. At the international level, he has been member of Board of the European Union of the Deaf (EUD) and since 2013 became its vice president. He has also been appointed chair of the accessibility working group and part of the expert group on human rights for the World Deaf Federation of the Deaf.

Iceland

Júlía Guðný Hreinsdóttir is a Sign Language Program director at the Communication Center and the principal instructor in Icelandic Sign Language at the University of Iceland and the Centre. From 2011 to 2017 she has been a substitute in the Language Council for Icelandic Sign Language. The president of Iceland invested her with the Order of the Falcon on June 16th 2011 (right after the legislation) for work for the Icelandic Sign Language and struggle for rights. Among other things she is presently participating in the European Prosign project working on a professionally-oriented competency framework for sign language teachers and on ITM and CEFR such as curriculum guide, revision of courses, teaching materials etc.

Ari Páll Kristinsson, PhD, is Research Professor and Head of Language Planning Department at the Árni Magnússon Institute for Icelandic Studies in Reykjavik. He was previously Director of the Icelandic Language Institute (1996–2006), Language Consultant at the Icelandic Broadcasting Service (1993–1996), Chairman of the Icelandic Linguistics Society (1995–1997, 2013–2015), Chairman of the Icelandic Place Names Committee (1998–2006) and Vice Chairman of the Icelandic Sign Language Council (2011–2015). His publications include works on the Icelandic language and language use, language management, language ideologies, language planning and policy studies, and language use in the media.

Valgerður Stefánsdóttir has been the CEO of the Communication Centre for the Deaf since the centre was founded in 1990. From 2011 to 2017, she was chairman of the Language Council for Icelandic Sign Language. Stefánsdóttir was a teacher at the Deaf School for 13 years. Her educational qualifications include a BEd (special education teacher), an MA in educational research specialising in the interaction between the Icelandic and Icelandic Sign Language communities, and she is currently working on a doctoral theses on Icelandic Sign Language within the field of linguistic anthropology.

Ireland

John Bosco Conama is director of the Centre for Deaf Studies (Trinity College, University of Dublin) and former chairperson of the Irish Deaf Society. He was the co-chair of the Irish Sign Language Recognition Campaign. He holds an MLitt in social policy (Trinity College Dublin) and a PhD in equality studies (University College Dublin). Dr Conama was involved in establishing the first certificate level course for Deaf people organised by the Equality Studies Centre, University College Dublin. He was awarded Language Ambassador of the Year 2015 by Leargas/Erasmus + for his work on the promotion and preservation of Irish Sign Language. His recent publications have focused on Deaf people in society and social policies affecting Irish Sign Language.

Korea

Seung-Il Byun (deaf) was a 17-year-old student at Jeonbuk Deaf School when he learned about human rights violations and became interested in the recovery of human rights for the deaf. In 2005, Seung-Il Byun was elected president of the Association of the Deaf in Korea. He was re-elected twice more and continued his presidency until 2015. As president, he achieved the eligibility of deaf people to obtain a driver's license, and the expansion of subtitles and sign language interpretation in broadcasts. Seung-Il Byun was the initiator and driving force of the KSL legislation.

Sung-Eun Hong (hearing) was born in Germany and studied sign language studies at the University of Hamburg. After her PhD, she became a researcher at the Institute of German Sign Language in the DGS (Deutsche Gebärdensprache)-Corpus Project. After she moved to South Korea with her family, she was involved in numerous Korean Sign Language-related research projects such as the KSL Legislation Project and the KSL Corpus Project. Currently, Sung-Eun Hong gives lectures at the Korea National Welfare University and works on the KSL Dictionary Project of the National Institute of Korean Language.

Mi-Hye Lee (hearing) began learning KSL at the Korean Association of the Deaf in Jeonbuk when she was a freshman at university. After completing volunteer work in the Deaf community, she was employed by Social Welfare Services for the Deaf in the Jeonbuk province. Mi-Hye Lee has also worked as a sign language interpreter and sign language lecturer at Hanil University from 1998 to 2005. From 2005 to 2015, Mi-Hye Lee was employed by the Korean Association of the Deaf. As the Secretary General, she coordinated the KSL legislation campaign. Mi-Hye Lee currently teaches at various universities.

Hyunhwa Lee is a hearing Child of Deaf Adults (CODA) and her mother tongue is Korean Sign Language (KSL). She is deeply rooted in the Deaf community not only because of her family environment, but also because of her previous employment at the Korean Association of the Deaf. She has participated in diverse research projects such as the KSL Legislation Project and the KSL Corpus Project, and has worked as a sign language lecturer. Currently, Hyunhwa Lee is employed at the National Institute of Korean Language, which also develops sign language policies based on the KSL Act. Furthermore, Hyunhwa Lee is in charge of the KSL–Korean/Korean–KSL Dictionary compilation.

Malta

Marie Azzopardi-Alexander is a professor in the Institute of Linguistics and Language Technology at the University of Malta and is coordinator of the Maltese Sign Language research project. Her work on the Maltese Sign Language Dictionary started over 20 years ago and will be published online by the end of 2018. She was actively involved with the Maltese Deaf community in the journey towards the official recognition of Maltese Sign Language.

Karl Borg was born deaf. He met other Deaf persons at the special unit for deaf children when he was 3 years old. However, he completed his primary and secondary education in a mainstream school without an interpreter and supported by his family. He works as a draughtsman. He started to attend the Deaf club at the age of around 20. He served as a member of the board of the Deaf Association for 15 years, was secretary and also president. He has taught Maltese Sign Language (LSM) for many years and contributes to the work on the LSM Dictionary. He was involved in the discussions that led to the passing of the Maltese Sign Language Recognition Act. Karl is married and has two children.

Dorianne Callus was born deaf. She attended mainstream school without an interpreter, supported by her family. She works as a bank clerk. She started going to the Deaf club where she learnt Maltese Sign Language at the age of 16. She was a member of the board of the Deaf Association for

12 years and president for 2 years. She has taught Maltese Sign Language (LSM) for many years and has been a long-time contributor to the work on the Dictionary project. She was involved in the discussions that led to the passing of the Maltese Sign Language Recognition Act. Dorianne is married and has two children.

Keith Callus was born deaf and is a native user of Maltese Sign Language. He was a board member of the Deaf People Association Malta from 2012 to 2014. He has represented Malta at a number of international events including the European Union of the Deaf General Assembly in Dublin and 'Multilingualism and Equal Rights in the EU' held at the European Parliament. Keith was involved in the Maltese Sign Language Dictionary project and has contributed to other research projects related to LSM. He is married and has two children.

Steven Mulvaney was born deaf to Deaf parents and has been involved in the Deaf People's Association all his life. He has been the president of the Deaf People Association (Malta) since 2012 and has represented Malta at the European Disability Forum in Brussels, EUD general assemblies in Dublin and Athens and the 2018 World Deaf Day celebrations in Rome. He is an activist and was involved in the discussions that led to the passing of the Maltese Sign Language Recognition Act. He contributed to the organisation and presentation of the EUD meeting in Malta in 2017. He is married and has a child.

Alison Vere is a Maltese Sign Language interpreter and researcher. She was introduced to sign language thanks to a Deaf friend at primary school in Manchester, UK. She gained a BSc in Deaf studies (BSL interpreting) from the University of Bristol's Centre for Deaf Studies and an MA in linguistics from the University of Malta's Institute of Linguistics. She was a board member of the Deaf People Association (Malta) from 2012 to 2016.

Annabelle Xerri lost her hearing at the age of 6. She graduated with a BComms with psychology and is currently reading for her master's in disability studies. She became an activist in 2013 when she met the Deaf community for the first time and began to learn Maltese Sign Language. She became a member of the board of the Deaf Association almost immediately. She uses social media consistently to raise awareness about the Deaf. She has participated in discussions regarding the Maltese Sign Language Law. She was appointed Chairperson of the Council set up by ACT XVII. Ms Xerri received the Queen's Young Leaders' award in recognition of her work. She is married and has a child.

Loran Ripard Xuereb was born deaf and is a native user of Maltese Sign Language. He is a draughtsman. He has been a lifelong member of the Deaf People Association since he was at school, practically all his life. He

xviii The Legal Recognition of Sign Languages

was elected as a board member of the Association in 2014. He has represented Malta at a number of European level events (mainly with the European Union of the Deaf and the European Union of the Deaf Youth) and contributes to ongoing LSM (Il-Lingwa tas-Sinjali Maltija, Maltese Sign Language) research, particularly to the Dictionary and to resource creation at the University of Malta's Institute of Linguistics and Language Technology. He is an activist and was involved in the discussions that led to the passing of the Maltese Sign Language Recognition Act.

New Zealand

Victoria Manning gained a master's in mental health counselling at Gallaudet University in 1996, before becoming involved in human rights and disability policy. She was a key government adviser on the development of the NZSL Bill 2002–2006 and while working at the Human Rights Commission Victoria she led the inquiry into NZSL. The resulting report, 'A New Era in the Right to Sign' (2013), helped to establish a new service supporting early acquisition of NZSL and the NZSL Board. A highlight of her career was representing disabled New Zealanders at the United Nations for New Zealand's first examination of its progress under the Convention on the Rights of Persons with Disabilities in 2014. Victoria was awarded a Queen's medal in 2015 for services to the Deaf and disabled communities. Victoria is the General Manager–Strategy at Deaf Aotearoa and the inaugural chairperson of the NZSL Board.

Rachel Locker McKee is an associate professor in the School of Linguistics and Applied Language Studies at Victoria University of Wellington, New Zealand. Professional involvement in the Deaf world as a sign language interpreter in New Zealand and the USA led to an academic career in applied linguistics. Rachel, together with husband David McKee, have established teaching programmes in New Zealand for interpreters, Deaf New Zealand Sign Language teachers and second language learners of NZSL. Research publications span description of NZSL grammar and lexicon, sociolinguistic variation, interpreting studies and language policy for sign language users.

USA

Joseph J. Murray is Professor of American Sign Language and Deaf Studies at Gallaudet University. He is co-editor of *Deaf Gain: Raising the Stakes for Human Diversity* (2014, University of Minnesota Press) and *In Our Own Hands: Essays in Deaf History 1780–1970* (2016, Gallaudet University Press). He has served as guest editor of two issues of *Sign Language Studies*; in 2015 on sign language rights and in 2016 on Deaf history. Dr Murray has published in the fields of Deaf history, deaf studies, language planning and language rights.

Brazil

Ronice Müller de Quadros is a professor and researcher at the Federal University of Santa Catarina and researcher at CNPQ (National Council for Scientific and Technological Development) with research related to the study of sign languages. Professor Quadros works with longitudinal and experimental data from deaf children and bimodal bilingual hearing people and the Libras Corpus Research Group. She coordinates the consolidation of the National Libras Inventory, which includes several subprojects for the composition of the Libras documentation, with funding from CNPQ and the Ministry of Culture.

Marianne Rossi Stumpf is a professor of postgraduate studies in linguistics at UFSC (Federal University of Santa Catarina, Brazil). Her field of research concerns analysis of phonological, morphological, syntactic, semantic and pragmatic aspects of Brazilian sign language through the 'SignWriting' system. She is the coordinator of the group developing the online academic signs glossary of the Letras Libras graduate course, focused on developing the Libras lexicon (www.glossario.libras.ufsc.br). She completed her postdoctoral studies at the Catholic University of Lisbon during from 2013 to 2014 and has given lectures at various national and international conferences. She has written various book chapters and edited and published several books.

The Netherlands

Richard Cokart is a linguist and works as a researcher at the Dutch Sign Centre specializing in sociolinguistics and sign lexicography. He studied psychology at Gallaudet University and sign linguistics at the University of Amsterdam and subsequently received his master's degree in general linguistics from the University of Amsterdam.

Trude Schermer has been active in de the field of sign language research since 1979. She studied general linguistics at the University of Amsterdam and experimental psychology at Northeastern University in Boston. She received her PhD from the University of Amsterdam for her thesis on Nederlandse Gebarentaal (NGT). The main focus in her work is on sign lexicography, sociolinguistics and equal opportunities for deaf people. Since 2001, she has been the director of the Dutch Sign Centre (www.gebarencentrum.nl), the national centre of expertise for NGT and sign lexicography, which maintains and develops the largest online NGT dictionary and produces multimedia sign language materials.

Corrie Tijsseling is a native signer of NGT with experience in advocacy work, both on a national (Dovenschap) and an international (World Federation of the Deaf) level. She studied philosophy and the history of education at Utrecht University and received her PhD for her thesis on the meaning of deaf education for the Dutch Deaf community. As well as her position as research coordinator at GGMD (Geestelijke Gezondheidszorg en Maatschappelijke Dienstverlening), an organization for mental healthcare and social counselling for deaf people, she also works as a senior researcher at Kentalis, an organization providing education and care for people who are limited in hearing and/or sight and/or language.

Eva Westerhoff is the former president of the National Association of the Deaf in the Netherlands (Dovenschap). She is also the founder and former president of the National Association of Teachers of Dutch Sign Language. She currently works as an inclusion and accessibility consultant with a focus on ICT. As well as this, she still volunteers for Dovenschap and the National Association of People with a Disability in the Netherlands (Iederin) working on the implementation of the UN Convention on the Rights of Persons with Disabilities.

Turkey

Deniz İlkbaşaran received her PhD in communication from the University of California, San Diego (UCSD). She is currently a postdoctoral researcher at UCSD, jointly appointed at the Mayberry Laboratory for Multimodal Language Development and the Padden Lab at the Center for Research in Language (CRL). Her research interests include the literacies, mobilities and technologically mediated communication practices of deaf people, sign language acquisition, history of deaf education, and sign language planning and policy in Turkey.

Okan Kubus received his PhD from the Institute for German Sign Language and Communication of the Deaf at the University of Hamburg in 2016. He has been a visiting professor at the same department in 2017 and 2018. He is a freelance lecturer, interpreter and researcher. He works currently on sign linguistics, psycholinguistics and sign language interpreting. He is also interested in sign language planning regarding Turkish Sign Language (Türk İşaret Dili –TİD).

Scotland

Lilian Lawson was Director of the Scottish Council on Deafness (SCoD) from 2000 to 2013 and led SCoD's campaign for legal recognition of British Sign Language (BSL) in Scotland. Over the years, she has been involved in many significant developments: the foundation of (what now is) the Scottish Association of Sign Language Interpreters; of the Council for the Advancement of Communication with Deaf People; and the development of a course to train teacher-trainers of British Sign Language tutors in Scotland. She is co-author of 'Words in Hand', a structural analysis of the signs of British Sign Language (1980). In 2016 and 2017, she received honorary doctorates from Heriot-Watt University and the University of Edinburgh.

Frankie McLean originally trained in biomedical sciences, but has worked in social work and the voluntary sector for a number of years – as a practitioner and a manager – and has been involved in a wide range of work and projects in a variety of roles, including strategic-level and policy work with the Scottish Government and others. He is also a qualified practice educator and a British Sign Language speaker from birth. McLean is currently a senior manager responsible for operations, services and projects at Deaf Action, a Scottish voluntary organisation, and is also a lecturer at Queen Margaret University, Edinburgh.

Rachel O'Neill lectures in deaf education at the University of Edinburgh where she teaches teachers of deaf children. She previously taught deaf children and young people in Greater Manchester. Her research includes a study of the school achievements of deaf pupils, the online reading skills of deaf and hearing young people and changing attitudes to British Sign Language. She is currently investigating a new undergraduate degree at the School of Education for people fluent in BSL who want to become primary school teachers. Rachel is the UK editor of *Deafness and Education International*.

Wales

Rob Wilks is a Deaf qualified solicitor of England and Wales, and a lecturer at the University of South Wales, teaching employment and equality law through British Sign Language. He is currently completing a PhD with the University of Leicester exploring the possible solutions to the conflict between equality law (which categorises Deaf people as disabled) and the Deaf identity. His research interests include Deaf people and the legal system, sign language interpreting in the legal system, criminal justice for Deaf people, sign language recognition, the UN Convention on the Rights of Persons with Disabilities, critical disability theory and Deaf legal theory.

Japan

Soya Mori is a senior researcher at the Institute of Developing Economies (IDE-JETRO) in Japan. From 2017 to 2018, he was a visiting research scholar at the University of California, Berkeley. He was born Deaf and is a professional and pioneer in the research of 'disability and development' in Japan. He conducted several international research projects and published articles and books on the Philippines, India and Kenya. He is also a sign linguist and conducts research in several sign languages in these countries. He was the first Deaf president of the Japanese Association of

Sign Linguistics. He earned his BA and MA degrees in economics from Waseda University in Japan.

Atsubumi Sugimoto is Associate Professor at Tokyo International University, Japan. He is hearing and earned his master of political science degree from Waseda University. He first learned about the French judicial systems, but he met minority language speakers in France and changed the subject of research to language rights. He is one of the few constitutional scholars on language rights in Japan. He has published on Japanese language policy and specifically on the right for immigrants to learn Japanese and the rights of deaf sign language users.

Chile

Maribel González is an educational psychologist and a postdoctoral research fellow at the 'Lengua, Educación y Cultura Sorda' [Language, Education and Deaf Culture] laboratory at the Department of Psychology of the Pontificia Universidad Católica de Chile. Her current research focuses on the role of Deaf pedagogy in the generation of collaborative and intercultural practices for Deaf education. She obtained her PhD in social sciences at the Centre for Deaf Studies of the University of Bristol. Maribel González coordinates the Interdisciplinary Network for Deaf Education (RIESOR) and participates in diverse projects to support the development and strengthening of Deaf students' education.

Juan Luis Marín is a Deaf teacher and activist. He is a teacher in a Deaf school in Santiago and is also part of the research group 'MOVIMIENTO 42' focused on Chilean Sign Language research. Juan Luis Marín is the president of the social organization called 'Centre for Deaf Educators of Chile' (CES) and a member of the board of directors of the Instituto de la Sordera [Institute of Deafness]. He has a BA in pedagogy and is also a licensed primary school teacher (licence obtained at the Universidad de Los Lagos in Chile).

Andrea Pérez is a teacher of Deaf students. She works at the Special Education Unit of the Chilean Ministry of Education and is part of the research group 'MOVIMIENTO 42' focused on Chilean Sign Language research. She has a BA in special education, hearing and language disorders of the Universidad Metropolitana de Ciencias de la Educación (UMCE), and a master's in integration of persons with disabilities at the University of Salamanca. Andrea Pérez also works as a Chilean Sign Language interpreter, and has created and led different projects related to the improvement of Deaf education at a national level.

Camila Villavicencio is a Deaf teacher and activist. She is part of the research team of the 'Lengua, Educación y Cultura Sorda' [Language, Education and

Deaf Culture] laboratory at the Department of Psychology of the Pontificia Universidad Católica de Chile. In the laboratory, she works on a research project aimed at promoting Deaf students' acquisition of Spanish as a second language. Camila Villavicencio obtained a BA in primary school education at the Universidad Católica Silva Henríquez (UCSH) in Chile. She is currently a vice president of the AMOMA (A mover las manos) foundation where she works as a Chilean Sign Language instructor.

Norway

Paal Richard Peterson is deaf and head of the sign language department at the Norwegian National Broadcasting Company (NRK). He has been involved with the NRK since 2014 and is also one of the sign language news anchormen. He is educated as a political scientist and in his thesis focused on deaf people's participation in politics on four levels: media, voting, organisations and actions. From 2006 to 2010, he was general secretary of the Norwegian Association of the Deaf. From 2010 to 2014, he was a senior adviser in the Ministry of Government Administration. One of his most important tasks was the employer's responsibilities for inclusion in the labour market.

Arnfinn Muruvik Vonen is a general linguist and a professor in the Section for Sign Language and Interpreting, Department of International Studies and Interpreting, OsloMet – Oslo Metropolitan University. He is hearing. He has a broad interest in language and languages, including grammatical structure as well as language in education and language policy. From 2011 to 2015, he was Director General of the Language Council of Norway, a government agency working to implement national language policy. During his period in office, work on Norwegian Sign Language policy found its place as an integral part of the activities of the Council.

Introduction: The Legal Recognition of Sign Languages: Advocacy and Outcomes Around the World

Maartje De Meulder, Joseph J. Murray and Rachel L. McKee

This volume presents the first comprehensive overview of the types and impacts of national laws recognizing sign languages, and the advocacy campaigns leading up to these laws. While most campaigns emerged in the late 1990s, they and their outcomes have only recently become the object of documentation and analysis, and a discussion of these developments that allows for comparative reading is long overdue.

This book contains 18 studies of countries in Europe, the USA, South America, Asia and New Zealand. The chapters set sign language legislation within their national context of language policies and the status of other minority languages in that country, showing patterns of intersection between language ideologies, public policy and deaf communities' discourses. Each chapter describes a deaf community's expectations and hopes for legal recognition and the type of sign language legislation achieved. The strategies used in achieving passage of the legislation, including coalition building and negotiations with governments and other stakeholders, as well as an account of barriers confronted and surmounted (or not) in the legislative process are discussed. Each chapter summarizes the legislation (or proposed legislation) and analyses its implementation, including policy gains and the role of language management bodies.

Interest in sign language rights is increasing among academic researchers and within deaf communities. In 2016, the World Federation of the Deaf (WFD) issued a 'Position Paper on the Language Rights of Deaf Children' (Murray *et al.*, 2016) and the theme of the 2019 quadrennial WFD Congress in Paris is 'Sign Language Rights for All'. Claims to sign language rights (usually educational) through complaint and litigation have been made in various countries; for example, the USA (Siegel, 2008), Belgium (Murray *et al.*, 2018) and Australia (Komesaroff, 2007, 2013) (see also Snoddon, 2009). Academic interest in sign language rights has primarily focused on the human right to language (Jokinen, 2000; Siegel, 2008), the right of deaf children and their parents to sign language (Humphries *et al.*, 2012, 2013; Kushalnagar *et al.*, 2010; Paul & Snoddon, 2017; Snoddon & Underwood, 2017) and the right to education in sign language (Hult & Compton, 2012; Tapio & Takkinen, 2012), although this right has again become contested (Knoors & Marschark, 2012). Family (sign) language policy is a growing area of academic interest (McKee & Smiler, 2017; Pizer, 2013). The volume also appears at a turbulent time in which the increased legitimation and institutionalization of sign languages coincides with changes in medical technology and educational practices that threaten the vitality of sign language communities (McKee, 2017).

Case studies of the codification of sign language rights have only recently become the object of academic scrutiny, e.g. in New Zealand (McKee, 2007, 2011; McKee & Manning, 2015; Reffell & McKee, 2009), Austria (Krausneker, 2013); England (Batterbury, 2012; Gulliver, 2003; Turner, 2003), Scotland (De Meulder, 2015, 2017), Ireland (Conama, 2010), the USA (Reagan, 2011), Spain and Catalonia (Quer, 2012), Langue des signes québécoise (LSQ) in Canada (Parisot & Rinfret, 2012), Italy (Geraci, 2012), Finland (De Meulder, 2016) and Brazil (de Quadros, 2012). There also have been two special issues of *Sign Language Studies* on sign language planning and rights (Quer & de Quadros, 2012; Murray, 2015a) and various book chapters on sign language policy and planning (e.g. Quer & de Quadros, 2015; Wilcox *et al.*, 2012). In 2010, the first comprehensive overview of sign language legislation in Europe was published (Wheatley & Pabsch, 2010, updated 2012), identifying any piece of legislation that explicitly mentions the word(s) 'sign language' (constitutions, laws on disability access, broadcasting, anti-discrimination legislation, laws recognizing the profession of sign language interpreters and language laws, etc.). Accounts of the status of sign languages in EU Member States also exist (e.g. Krausneker, 1998, 2000, 2003, 2006, 2009; Ladd *et al.*, 2003; Leeson, 2004; Timmermans, 2005), while the first international overview of sign language laws was by Reagan (2010).

Laws Recognizing Sign Languages

Languages are commonly recognized as a national language, an official language, a working language, a regional language or a minority language. Sometimes recognition occurs in combinations; for example, the national and official language can be identical, the national or official language can be a minority language and a country can have more than one national and/or official language. Whereas the status of national language often carries symbolic status, that of official language often has many practical implications (Coulmas, 2013), though commonly, the terms are undefined (Spolsky, 2009). Generally, an official language is the language used by government to communicate with citizens, and likely also the language used or required to be used in institutions such as schools and in government mass media (Spolsky, 2009).

In contrast to the recognition of most spoken languages, the recognition of sign languages does not always lead to one of the statuses above or the language's inclusion in language legislation or a constitution. The laws covered in this volume rarely confer one of these statuses. Chapters in this volume follow the distinction made by De Meulder (2015) between constitutional recognition, recognition in language legislation, Sign Language Acts, Sign Language Acts including 'other means of communication' and recognition by means of legislation on the functioning of the national language council.

Some sign languages are recognized as a minority language; for example, British Sign Language (BSL) in Scotland or Finnish Sign Language and Finland–Swedish Sign Language in Finland. This recognition is nonetheless not equivalent to the recognition accorded to the spoken minority languages in these countries (Gaelic and Sami respectively) (Lawson *et al.*, Chapter 4, this volume; De Meulder, 2016). The Korean Sign Language Law recognizes Korean Sign Language as 'the official language of Korean deaf people'. 'Official' in this case merely means that KSL is granted status as a language; it has no legal implications.

Because of the dual category perception of deaf signers as users of a minority language and people with a disability it is relevant to distinguish between explicit and implicit recognition. Explicit recognition refers to legislation that recognizes sign language in dedicated language laws. Implicit recognition refers to legislation that implicitly acknowledges the use of sign language via measures addressing disability access. An example of implicit recognition is the Americans with Disabilities Act in the USA (Murray, Chapter 7, this volume), which provides for American Sign Language (ASL) interpreting services.

Sign Language Recognition as Language Policy and Planning

We observe that sign language laws have elements of all four kinds of language planning: status, corpus, acquisition and attitude planning. Notably, aspirations for acquisition planning in the context of sign language legislation are concerned not so much with expanding the existing number of signers, but rather with ensuring that deaf children can acquire sign language, through the provision of sign language classes for parents, siblings and grandparents of a deaf child (Ireland) or by stating a more general right for deaf children and their immediate family to learn and use a sign language from the time a child is identified as deaf (Iceland). These measures stem from the fact that most deaf children are born into non-signing families, meaning that intergenerational transmission is permanently fragile and has been historically impeded by institutionalized pressure against the use of sign language. Currently, a revived focus on exclusive use of spoken language associated with infant cochlear implantation is observed to be jeopardizing deaf children and their parents' access to sign language (Humphries *et al.*, 2012). Those countries which have not achieved acquisition rights note this lack as a particular failure of existing legislation.

An additional focus concerns achieving instrumental measures that enable deaf people to access and participate in everyday domains of civil society. In most, if not all cases, this access is provided through the provision of sign language interpreting services, which Murray (2015b) has argued can be seen as a form of status planning. Such instrumental rights have often resulted from disability-related legislation, demonstrating the 'dual category status' (De Meulder & Murray, 2017) of deaf people's campaign for sign language recognition, which invoke both language and disability rights.

Dual Category Status: Influence on Campaigns and Legislation

Dual category status refers to deaf signers being seen and claiming intersectional rights as both a linguistic minority and a group of people with a disability (De Meulder & Murray, 2017; Murray, 2015b). One consequence of this claim to intersectional rights is that in several countries, sign languages have been granted linguistic status and deaf signers given linguistic rights in disability laws, such as in Chile (González *et al.*, Chapter 8, this volume), France (Cantin *et al.*, Chapter 9, this volume), and Turkey (İlkbaşaran & Kubus, Chapter 5, this volume). In this framework, sign language is sometimes grouped with 'other communication methods' such as lip-reading, sign supported speech, note-taking, cued speech, hearing aids and braille (e.g. Korea).

In many cases sign language legislation has a hybrid basis, blending language and disability claims. The LSM *(Il-Lingwa tas-Sinjali Maltija)* Act, for example, declares Maltese Sign Language to be an official language (although it is not constitutionally recognized as English and Maltese are), yet also states that LSM is an 'endorsement for equal opportunities'. Indeed, the Act is considered part of the Equal Opportunities (Persons with Disabilities) Act and the Malta National Disability Policy pursuant to the obligations emanating from the UN Convention on the Rights of Persons with Disabilities (UNCRPD). Another consequence of the dual category status is the use of 'needs'-based language in legislation, with rights being made dependent on 'need'. Art. 3 of the law in Iceland, for example, states Icelandic Sign Language is the first language 'of those who rely on it' and that 'anyone who has need of sign language' shall have the opportunity to learn ISL. (Art. 4 on 'Icelandic braille' uses the same needs-language while there is no such language for Icelandic.) We will return to the issue of dual category status in the closing chapter.

A critical factor in the development of the most recent cases of sign language legislation has been the adoption of the UNCRPD in 2006, which states that the acquisition and use of sign language is crucial to realize the human rights of deaf people, and obliges State Parties to protect these rights in domestic laws (for a legislative history of the articles that mention the status of sign languages, see Meereboer *et al.*, 2018). The UNCRPD, although a disability human rights instrument, is now the only legally-binding international instrument in place to monitor states' actions on sign language rights. In many countries, UNCRPD ratification has placed recognition of sign language more firmly on the political (disability) agenda; for example in Korea, Chile and Malta. These implications are also seen in countries such as the Netherlands and Italy, where explicit legal recognition is still ongoing.

Campaigns: Influences, Strategies and Opportunities

Sign language recognition legislation has been on the agenda of numerous deaf associations around the world as far back as the 1980s, but has only become a widespread political priority since the late 1990s. State-level recognition of American Sign Language (ASL) began in 1979, and the Swedish Parliament recognized Swedish Sign Language as a language to be used in bilingual education in a 1981 Parliamentary decision. The WFD used the concept of recognition in a resolution passed by the World Congress in Helsinki in 1987 (World Federation of the Deaf, 1993). This has been reinforced over the years in national, regional and international congresses and meetings. On a European level, in 1985, the British Deaf Association initiated the establishment of the European Community Regional Secretariat (ECRS, now called the European Union of the Deaf, EUD), through which a European campaign for the recognition of sign languages led to the adoption of the first European Parliament resolution on sign languages in 1988, reiterated in 1998. These resolutions have been instrumental for the first steps towards legal recognition in EU countries. For a more detailed account of the turn towards linguistic human rights discourse, and the role of the WFD, EUD, and national deaf NGOs, see Murray (2015b).

International networks have been instrumental for recognition processes and campaigns in many countries, with many chapters attributing inspiration for their campaigns to contact with international and extranational sources of activism. Campaigners have looked towards other countries' sign language laws and minority laws. Visits to WFD Congresses, EUD special events, and the first (1989) and second (2002) Deaf Way festivals in Washington, DC are among such events mentioned in several chapters. The resolution from a 2010 European Union of the Deaf conference on sign language recognition was used as a tool by Maltese campaigners, boosted by a presentation from an EUD staff member on a visit to Malta. The Icelandic law was influenced by developments in other Nordic countries, with advice from the Nordic Deaf Council proving helpful for the Icelandic campaigners. Countries often draw upon examples of sign language legislation from abroad, with New Zealand (and sometimes Hungary and Finland) named as a primary example of high status recognition. One reason these specific countries are chosen is that their laws are available online in English (as stated in Conama, Chapter 1, this volume).

Some sign language campaigners cited other (sign and/or spoken) minority language legislation as models. The Catalonian LSC (Catalan Sign Language) Law was modelled on the Aranese language minority law. The New Zealand Sign Language Act mirrors aspects of the Maori Language Act, which in turn references Welsh and Irish language acts before it. The Sami Language Act in Finland was a model for the Sign Language Act in that country (although there are considerable differences in outcomes) (De Meulder, 2016). Articles in the sign language acts of Sweden, Iceland and Finland all served as examples for the campaign for the Norwegian Sign Language (NTS) provisions in the expected Norwegians Language Bill (Vonen & Peterson, Chapter 12, this volume).

Campaigns are often conducted in broad-based coalitions that include national organizations of deaf people, grassroots deaf people, deaf leaders and academics, particularly sign language researchers. In a few cases, schools using a bilingual education model serve as sites for support and resources to campaigners, such as in Brazil and Catalonia. Lobbying for sign language legislation sometimes serves as an impetus to bring multiple deaf organizations into a temporary nationwide coalition in support of the common cause of recognition (e.g. Chile and France). At times, these coalitions have been developed separately from existing national organizations of deaf people (e.g. Flanders) or developed alongside the national organization (e.g. Ireland).

Common campaign strategies included rallies, marches and demonstrations, as well as meetings with legislators and public bodies responsible for disability issues (e.g. Malta and Chile). Only rarely did campaigners work with minority language communities in their countries, although some laws were inspired by such communities. Some strategies were inspired by protest methods common to particular national settings, such as the one-man protest in Korea. Other strategies used were press conferences (e.g. Malta), petitions (e.g. Austria, Flanders and Iceland), filing legal complaints (e.g. Chile and Iceland), use of social media (e.g. the Facebook group in Scotland) and use of specific symbols such as the turquoise ribbon in Austria. In the closing chapter, we will discuss barriers and challenges in the campaigns.

Structure of the Book

This volume includes 18 chapters arranged in four different parts, each addressing one aspect of sign language recognition legislation. The first part, 'Recent Sign Language Laws', discusses sign language laws in Ireland, Korea, Malta and Scotland, which were passed between 2015 and 2017. Since it is too early to discuss implementation, these chapters discuss the campaigns leading up to the laws, and gaps between the laws and deaf community expectations. The second part, 'Implicit Legal Recognition', discusses five cases (Turkey, Japan, USA, Chile and France) of 'implicit recognition' that for different reasons fall outside the five categories De Meulder (2015b) distinguished. The third part, 'Ongoing Campaigns towards Explicit Legal Recognition', includes chapters about the Netherlands, Italy and Norway, three countries which have not yet achieved explicit legal recognition but have ongoing campaigns to achieve this recognition. The fourth and final part, 'Implementation of Sign Language Laws', focuses on advocacy but especially discusses implementation of sign language laws adopted between 2005 and 2011 (New Zealand, Iceland, Brazil, Catalonia and Belgium) or constitutional amendments recognising sign language (Austria), with specific attention to sign language management bodies.

The first part, 'Recent Sign Language Laws', begins with Chapter 1 written by John Bosco Conama about the most recently passed sign language law at the time of writing this volume: the Irish Sign Language Act (2017). The chapter focuses on the intersection between the legislative process and the campaign for ISL recognition, and on how ISL is legislatively managed in comparison with English and Irish. In Chapter 2, Sung-Eun Hong, Hyunhwa Lee, Mi-Hye Lee and Seung-Il Byun discuss the campaign that led to the adoption of the Korean Sign Language Act (2016). They discuss the campaign's aims, strategies and challenges, and the shortcomings of the Act. This theme is continued in Chapter 3 about the Maltese Sign Language Act (2016), written by Marie Azzopardi-Alexander, Karl Borg, Dorianne Callus, Keith Callus, Steven Mulvaney, Alison Vere, Annabelle Xerri and Ripard Xuereb Loran. They describe how the legal implications of the declared 'official status' of LSM remain unclear, and discuss the hybrid character of the legislation, blending language and disability rights. The final chapter in this section, Chapter 4, written by Lilian Lawson, Frankie McLean, Rachel O'Neill and Rob Wilks discusses the British Sign Language (Scotland) Act (2015). In the absence of a UK-wide recognition of BSL, Scotland remains the only nation in the UK so far to legally recognize BSL. The authors describe the context which enabled this to happen, and how the ambiguous influence of charities 'for' deaf people affected progress towards legal recognition of BSL.

In the second part, 'Implicit Legal Recognition', the authors discuss other legislative opportunities that are not sign language laws, constitutional measures or general language legislation. In the first chapter of this section (Chapter 5), Deniz İlkbaşaran and Okan Kubus discuss the legal recognition of Turkish Sign Language (TİD), which materialized in a climate of increased political interest in disability rights and academic interest in sign language. TİD was legally mentioned for the first time in the Disability Act (2005) and was recognized in a 2006 law on 'the implementation of the Turkish sign language system'. The authors discuss the gains this legislation presented, as well as factors that had a negative impact on status planning and actual implementation. In Chapter 6, Soya Mori and Atsubumi Sugimoto discuss progress and problems in the campaign for sign language recognition in Japan. The chapter is an interesting account of the apparent difficulties in determining a national sign language in Japan, due to competing language ideologies, and how this has an impact on the legal recognition of Japanese Sign Language. Chapter 7 on American Sign Language by Joseph Murray describes a case of a sign language without legal status recognition on the national level, but with widespread state-level recognition, particularly related to acquisition planning. This acquisition planning has been widely successful and ASL has been institutionalized as a part of language learning in US higher education. One of the two chapters from South America is about Chile (Chapter 8), and is written by Maribel Gonzalez, Andrea Pérez, Juan Luis Marín and Camila Villavicencio. Chilean Sign Language (LSCh) was legally mentioned for the first time in the 2010 Law on people with disabilities 'as the natural means of communication of the Deaf community'. The chapter gives an overview of the three major periods in the pathway towards implicit recognition and barriers confronted in the process, primarily challenges with establishing successful nationwide coalitions of deaf organizations, lawsuits replacing coordinated lobbying work and lack of deaf capacity building, which has stymied the inclusion of deaf people's views in the political process. The last chapter in this part (Chapter 9) is about France, written by Yann Cantin, Florence Encrevé and Marie-Thérèse L'Huillier. French Sign Language (LSF) was recognized by a law on the rights of people with disabilities in 2005, which in turn provided for the amendment of the Education Code which authorized LSF teaching. In the chapter, the authors trace the emergence of this recognition starting in the 1830s, the conditions for its success and the gap between *de jure* and de facto status of LSF.

The third part of the book, 'Ongoing Campaigns towards Explicit Legal Recognition', discusses the cases of the Netherlands, Italy and Norway. These countries all have implicit recognition in place; for example, the right to sign language interpreting services free of charge, or the right to education in sign language, often provided in educational or disability legislation. Nevertheless, they are all still advocating for

explicit legal recognition, and they all discuss current legislative proposals to achieve this aim. Each chapter explicitly mentions UNCRPD ratification as one of the factors that facilitates this process. Chapter 10,
about the Netherlands, written by Richard Cokart, Trude Schermer,
Corrie Tijsseling and Eva Westerhoff, describes the various attempts
that have been made towards explicit legal recognition of Nederlandse
Gebarentaal (NGT). They discuss the current law proposal and compare it with the legal status of Frisian, a regional minority language in
the Netherlands. Carlo Geraci and Humberto Insolera, in Chapter 11,
review the debate around the Bill recognizing Italian Sign Language
(LIS) as discussed by the Italian Senate during the XVII legislature. The
legislative session ended, however, before the Bill could be discussed in
Parliament. This is one of the chapters that explicitly examines arguments by policy makers and legislators in favour of and especially
against legal recognition of a sign language. In the final chapter of this
section, Chapter 12, Arnfinn Muruvik Vonen and Paal Richard Peterson
discuss sign language policy in Norway, which is most clearly formu-
lated in the domain of education. Despite this implicit recognition of
NTS, an NTS Act was seen as a symbolic measure that could strengthen
and develop these already existing rights. The government argued
against a separate NTS Bill, but included NTS in a proposal to prepare
for a Language Bill in Norway that would cover all languages in the
country, including NTS, and added NTS to the responsibilities of the
Language Council of Norway. This chapter is also one of the chapters
that notes the loss of vitality of sign language, simultaneous with the
strengthening of legal measures.

The final part, 'Implementation of Sign Language Laws', discusses six
cases. Chapter 13 is about the constitutional recognition of Österreichische
Gebärdensprache (ÖGS) in Austria, and written by Franz Dotter (who
sadly passed away during the writing of this book), Verena Krausneker,
Helene Jarmer and Lukas Huber. While constitutional recognition is presented as the most 'prestigious' form of recognition, there often is a significant gap between *de jure* and de facto recognition. In Austria, a
so-called 'legal reservation' restricts or limits any implementation of the
constitutional recognition. Continuing this theme, in Chapter 14 Rachel
McKee and Victoria Manning discuss implementation of the NZSL Act,
a well-documented example of sign language legislation compared to
most other cases in this book. While making NZSL an official language
signalled societal recognition of NZSL users, this status-raising action did
not progress their practical rights or resolve language-based inequities.
Their chapter also discusses the establishment of the NZSL board as an
implementing body presenting new strategic opportunities to use the law
as a lever to push for stronger instrumental rights. Icelandic Sign Language
(ITM) was recognized in 2011 in language legislation that also regulates
the status of Icelandic. In Chapter 15, Valgerður Stefánsdóttir, Ari Páll

Kristinsson and Júlía Guðný Hreinsdóttir chronicle the campaign for legal recognition of ITM, which is the only indigenous minority language in Iceland and the first language of about 250 deaf people in the country. They discuss the progression through the Icelandic Parliament, and expectations of recognition expressed by key people in the ITM community, based on interviews with one former deaf member of parliament as well as six presidents of the deaf association. Despite the strengths of the legislation (and its often serving as an example for other sign language legislation) they argue that in important language domains (education, administration, legal settings), ITM is still associated with disability and impairment, and they highlight the gap between *de jure* and de facto status of ITM. The Libras Act, which legally recognised Brazilian Sign Language in 2006, is the second case from South America in the book (Chapter 16) and written by Ronice Müller de Quadros and Marianne Rossi Stumpf. They discuss the campaign leading up to the legislation, and also consider implementation of the Libras Law in higher education contexts, highlighting how implementation must be expanded to include bilingual education in other educational settings. Also, this chapter interestingly discusses how the Libras Law has led to tensions around ownership of Libras. In Chapter 17, Maria Josep Jarque, Marta Bosch-Baliarda and Menchu González discuss the legal recognition and regulation of Catalan Sign Language (LSC) by Law 17 of 2010. In Catalonia, language policies constitute a complex and central political issue, but the authors argue that the multilingual language policy approach of the Catalan government provided the appropriate sociolinguistic context for the passage of a sign language law within a language rights model (as opposed to Spain, where the sign language law is based on an accessibility model). They also point to the new Statute of Autonomy that was passed in 2005 as an important sociopolitical factor in the passage of the law, because it boosted the Catalan identity and right to self-determination. They further discuss the establishment of the Catalan Sign Language Social Board (paralleling Catalan and Aranese boards). The sixth and final chapter in this part (Chapter 18), by Maartje De Meulder and Thierry Haesenne, discusses the legal recognition of the sign languages of Belgium. French Belgian Sign Language (LSFB) and Flemish Sign Language (VGT) were recognized in 2003 and 2006 respectively, in separate sign language laws. Just like Catalonia, Belgium is an interesting case for sign language policy and planning scholarship because of the specific context with 'twinned monolingualism', which puts limits on the nature and scope of sign language recognition. The authors discuss the campaigns leading up to the laws, and argue that they are an example of a typical 'Belgian compromise' that allows for an agreement without unsettling the status quo but also without granting any rights. This chapter also discusses in detail the establishment and challenges with the operation of the implementation bodies, namely the LSFB and VGT governmental advisory committees. In the closing chapter (Epilogue), we reflect on the evidence and themes presented in the chapters.

Author Positionalities

Each chapter in this volume outlines developments for a sign language community in a specific national context; in most cases, these events have not been previously documented in a synthesized form, and thus authors have drawn on a variety of knowledge sources, including direct observation, to give an account of progress in their respective countries. It is critical then, that each chapter is authored by writers who are participant-observers in the campaigns that they document. It was an editorial requirement that at least one co-author of each chapter be a deaf person, to ensure that an insider perspective informs the account for each country. A collaborative approach to writing these case studies also reflects the reality that advancing sign language claims has entailed collaboration between deaf community leaders, deaf and hearing academics, and political allies from outside deaf networks. The campaigns featured in the book were often publicly led by national deaf associations representing a grassroots membership, supported by researchers and other allies of the sign language community. Internationally, the disciplines of linguistics, applied linguistics and Deaf Studies, in particular, have supported research and teaching or training that have contributed to empowering deaf communities and, in turn, facilitated status change for sign languages (e.g. McKee & Manning, Chapter 14, this volume, as in many countries), and many authors' backgrounds reflect these affiliations.

Contributing authors write from the perspectives of academics, policy advisors and language/community activists, depending on the context (Gorter, 2012), and indeed, many hold more than one of these positions. Their 'embedded' positionalities had some specific implications for producing this work; during the writing period, some authors were so busy with political actions in progress that time to write was scarce, while others had to revise between drafts to reflect unfolding progress towards recognition. Sign language communities are numerically small, and it is a common fate for those who have leadership capacity (especially the deaf authors in the volume) to negotiate many demands on their time and attention. Completion of their contributions to the book amid ongoing advocacy is thus an accomplishment that the editors acknowledge with gratitude.

In line with the legal recognition of sign languages being a recent development in language planning and policy, which is still taking shape, numerous chapters are the first of their kind and contemporaneous accounts of a national situation. Thus, authors had to draw on diverse and often primary sources, including interviews and/or personal communication with key players involved in the campaign (Turkey, Iceland, Chile and

Catalonia), desk research (study of policy documents, government reports, laws, surveys and media sources) (most chapters) and direct involvement in relevant events (again, most chapters). Furthermore, we note that collaborative writing between language researchers and language activists is in itself a method of jointly producing new knowledge about a political story, as authors potentially bring differing details and interpretations to reflecting on the trajectory of events in their country.

The call for chapters for this book was circulated via social media, deaf academics networks and emails to people with a known interest in the field, and we received many more abstracts than expected, indicating that this topic resonates with a tremendous amount of work currently being done worldwide, by a growing network of language activists and academics who identify with this purpose. We hope that collating their work into a shared volume generates an appreciation of commonalities in their positionality and strategies, and offers participants comparative perspective on progress across their diverse national contexts which can energize and inform further work.

About the Use of deaf/Deaf

Researchers working with deaf communities have sought to highlight the fact that deaf people are not merely people with different audiological status, but also people who use sign language and have been seen to create cultural communities within their larger societies. For the past four decades, researchers used the term 'deaf' to signify people with a hearing loss who do not sign and 'Deaf' to mean members of a sign language using community. A number of researchers are currently moving away from the practice of using the term 'Deaf' for signing deaf people and 'deaf' for non-signing deaf people, instead preferring to use only 'deaf'. They see this dichotomy as an oversimplification of what is an increasingly complex set of identities and language practices, which are impossible to represent with a simplified binary (Kusters *et al.*, 2017). In the Introduction and Epilogue of this volume, the editors have followed this practice of only using 'deaf' to refer to individual deaf people. Individual chapter authors were informed about this current practice and then given the choice to use only 'deaf' or also 'Deaf'. Some decided to continue to use capitalized 'Deaf' in some instances, with reasons ranging from adhering to earlier practice to acknowledgement of the wishes of deaf communities in their countries, in which 'Deaf' is still widely used.

References

Batterbury, S. (2012) Language justice for sign language peoples: The UN Convention on the Rights of Persons with Disabilities. *Language Policy* 11 (3), 253–272.

Conama, J.B. (2010) Finnish and Irish Sign Languages: An egalitarian analysis of language policies and their effects. PhD thesis, University College Dublin.

Coulmas, F. (2013) *Sociolinguistics*. Cambridge: Cambridge University Press.

De Meulder, M. (2015a) A barking dog that never bites?: The British Sign Language (Scotland) Bill. *Sign Language Studies* 15 (4), 446–472.

De Meulder, M. (2015b) The legal recognition of sign languages. *Sign Language Studies* 15 (4), 498–506.

De Meulder, M. (2016) Promotion in times of endangerment: The Sign Language Act in Finland. *Language Policy* 16 (2), 189–208.

De Meulder, M. (2017) The influence of deaf people's dual category status on sign language planning: The British Sign Language (Scotland) Act (2015). *Current Issues in Language Planning* 1–18.

De Meulder, M. and Murray, J. (2017) Buttering their bread on both sides? The recognition of sign languages and the aspirations of deaf communities. *Language Problems & Language Planning* 41 (2), 136–158.

De Quadros, R. (2012) Linguistic policies, linguistic planning, and Brazilian Sign Language in Brazil. *Sign Language Studies* 12 (4), 543–564.

Geraci, C. (2012) Language policy and planning: The case of Italian Sign Language. *Sign Language Studies* 12 (4), 494–518.

Gorter, D. (2012) Minority language researchers and their role in policy development. *Language, Culture and Curriculum* 25 (1), 87–100.

Gulliver, M. (2003) BSL OURS. Proposing a concept of ownership. MA thesis, University of Bristol.

Hult, F.M. and Compton, S. (2012) Deaf education policy as language policy: A comparative analysis of Sweden and the United States. *Sign Language Studies* 12 (4), 602–620.

Humphries, T., Kushalnagar, P., Mathur, G., Napoli, D.J., Padden, C., Rathmann, C. and Smith, S.R. (2012) Language acquisition for deaf children: Reducing the harms of zero tolerance to the use of alternative approaches. *Harm Reduction Journal* 9 (1), 1.

Humphries, T., Kushalnagar, R., Mathur, G., Napoli, D.J., Padden, C., Rathmann, C. and Smith, S.R. (2013) The right to language. *Journal of Law, Medicine and Ethics* 41 (4), 872–884.

Jokinen, M. (2000) The linguistic rights of sign language users. In R. Phillipson (ed.) *Rights to Language: Equity, Power and Education* (pp. 203–213). Mahwah, NJ: Lawrence Erlbaum Associates.

Knoors, H. and Marschark, M. (2012) Language planning for the 21st century: Revisiting bilingual language policy for Deaf children. *Journal of Deaf Studies and Deaf Education* 17 (3), 291–305.

Komesaroff, L. (2007) Denying claims of discrimination in the Federal Court of Australia: Arguments against the use of native sign language in education. *Sign Language Studies* 7 (4), 360–386.

Komesaroff, L. (2013) *Disabling Pedagogy: Power, Politics, and Deaf Education*. Washington, DC: Gallaudet University Press.

Krausneker, V. (1998) Sign languages in the minority languages policy of the European Union. MA thesis, University of Vienna.

Krausneker, V. (2000) Sign languages and the minority language policy of the European Union. In M. Metzger (ed.) *Bilingualism & Identity in Deaf Communities* (Vol. 6) (pp. 142–158). Washington, DC: Gallaudet University Press.

Krausneker, V. (2003) Has something changed? Sign languages in Europe: The case of minorised minority languages. *Deaf Worlds* 19 (2), 33–46.

Krausneker, V. (2006) *Report on the Protection and Promotion of Sign Languages and the Rights of their Users in Council of Europe Member States: Needs Analysis*. Strasbourg: Council of Europe.

Krausneker, V. (2009) On the legal status of sign languages: A commented compilation of resources. *Current Issues in Language Planning* 10 (3), 351–354.

Krausneker, V. (2013) Österreichische Gebärdensprache ist annerkannt. In V. Vetter and R. de Cillia (eds) Sprachenpolitik in Österreich (pp. 127–141). Bestandsaufnahme 2011. Peter Lang Verlag.

Kushalnagar, P., Mathur, G., Moreland, C.J., Napoli, D.J., Osterling, W., Padden, C. and Rathmann, C. (2010) Infants and children with hearing loss need early language access. *The Journal of Clinical Ethics* 21 (2), 143–154.

Kusters, A., De Meulder, M. and O'Brien, D. (eds) (2017) *Innovations in Deaf Studies: The Role of Deaf Scholars.* Oxford: Oxford University Press.

Ladd, P., Alker, D., Batterbury, S., Gulliver, M., Turner, G.H. and Krausneker, V. (2003) An agenda for change: Principles and guidelines for policy making and research in deaf-related areas. *Deaf Worlds* 19, 66–77.

Leeson, L. (2004) Signs of change in Europe: European developments on the status of signed languages. In P. McDonnell (ed.) *Deaf Studies in Ireland: An Introduction* (pp. 172–197). Coleford: DougMcLean.

Mereeboer, S., Mereeboer, K. and Spijkers, O. (2018) Recognition of sign language under international law: A case study of Dutch Sign Language in the Netherlands. *Netherlands Yearbook of International Law 2017* 411–431.

McKee, R. (2007) The eyes have it! Our third official language – New Zealand Sign Language. *Journal of New Zealand Studies* 4–5, 129–148.

McKee, R. (2011) Action pending: Four years on from the New Zealand Sign Language Act. *VUW Law Review* 42 (2), 277–298.

McKee, R. (2017) Assessing the vitality of New Zealand Sign Language. *Sign Language Studies* 17 (3), 322–362.

McKee, R. and Manning, V. (2015) Evaluating effects of language recognition on language rights and the vitality of New Zealand Sign Language. *Sign Language Studies* 15 (4), 473–497.

McKee, R. and Smiler, K. (2017) Family language policy for deaf children and the vitality of New Zealand Sign Language. In J. Macalister and S.H. Mirvahedi (eds) *Family Language Policies in a Multilingual World. Opportunities, Challenges and Consequences* (pp. 30–55). London: Routledge.

Murray, J.J. (ed.) (2015a) Special Issue: Language Planning and Sign language Rights. *Sign Language Studies* 15 (4).

Murray, J.J. (2015b) Linguistic Human Rights Discourse in Deaf Community Activism. *Sign Language Studies* 15 (4), 379–410.

Murray, J.J., Kraus, K., Down, E., Adam, R., Snoddon, K. and Napoli, D.J. (2016) *WFD Position Paper on the Language Rights of Deaf Children.* https://2tdzpf2t7hxmggqhq3 njno1y-wpengine.netdna-ssl.com/wp-content/uploads/2017/01/WFD-Position-Paper-on-Language-Rights-of-Deaf-Children-7-Sept-2016.pdf (last accessed 27 January 2019).

Murray, J.J., De Meulder, M. and le Maire, D. (2018) An education in sign language as a human right? The sensory exception in the legislative history and ongoing interpretation of Article 24 of the UN Convention on the Rights of Persons with Disabilities. *Human Rights Quarterly* (40), 37–60.

Parisot, A.-M. and Rinfret, J. (2012) Recognition of Langue des Signes Québécoise in Eastern Canada. *Sign Language Studies* 12 (4), 583–601.

Paul, J.J. and Snoddon, K. (2017) Framing Deaf children's right to sign language in the Canadian Charter of Rights and Freedoms. *Canadian Journal of Disability Studies* 6 (1).

Pizer, G. (2013) Bimodal bilingual families: The negotiation of communication practices between deaf parents and their hearing children. In M. Schwartz and A. Verschik (eds) *Successful Family Language Policy: Parents, Children and Educators in Interaction* (pp. 203–221). Dordrecht: Springer.

Quer, J. (2012) Legal pathways to the recognition of sign languages: A comparison of the Catalan and Spanish Sign Language Acts. *Sign Language Studies* 12 (4), 565–582.

Quer, J. and de Quadros, R. (eds) (2012) Special Issue: Language Planning and Policies for Sign Language. *Sign Language Studies* 12 (4).

Quer, J. and Müller de Quadros, R. (2015) Language policy and planning in Deaf communities. In A. Schembri and C. Lucas (eds) *Sociolinguistics and Deaf Communities* (pp. 120–145). Washington, DC: Gallaudet University Press.

Reagan, T. (2010) *Language Policy and Planning for Sign Languages* (Vol. 16). Washington, DC: Gallaudet University Press.

Reagan, T. (2011) Ideological barriers to American Sign Language: Unpacking linguistic resistance. *Sign Language Studies* 11 (4), 606–636.

Reffell, H. and McKee, R. (2009) Motives and outcomes of New Zealand sign language legislation: A comparative study between New Zealand and Finland. *Current Issues in Language Planning* 10 (3), 272–292.

Siegel, L.M. (2008) *The Human Right to Language: Communication Access for Deaf Children*. Washington, DC: Gallaudet University Press.

Snoddon, K. (2009) Equity in education: Signed language and the courts. *Current Issues in Language Planning* 10 (3), 255–271.

Snoddon, K. and Underwood, K. (2017) Deaf time in the twenty-first century: Considering rights frameworks and the social relational model of Deaf childhood. *Disability & Society* 32 (9), 1–16.

Spolsky, B. (2009) *Language Management*. New York: Cambridge University Press.

Tapio, E. and Takkinen, R. (2012) When one of your languages is not recognised as a language at all. In J. Blommaert, S. Leppänen, P. Pahta and T. Räisänen (eds) *Dangerous Multilingualism – Northern Perspectives to Order, Purity and Normality*. Basingstoke: Palgrave McMillan.

Timmermans, N. (2005) *A Comparative Analysis of the Status of Sign Languages in Europe*. Strasbourg: Council of Europe.

Turner, G.H. (2003) Government recognition and £1 million boost for British Sign Language. *Deaf Worlds* 19 (1), 74–78.

Wheatley, M. and Pabsch, A. (2010) *Sign Language Legislation in the European Union (I)*. Brussels: European Union of the Deaf.

Wheatley, M. and Pabsch, A. (2012) *Sign Language Legislation in the European Union (II)*. Brussels: European Union of the Deaf.

Wilcox, S., Krausneker, V. and Armstrong, D.F. (2012) Language policies and the Deaf community. In B. Spolsky (ed.) *The Cambridge Handbook of Language Policy* (pp. 374–396). Cambridge: Cambridge University Press.

World Federation of the Deaf (1993) *Report on the Status of Sign Language*. Helsinki: World Federation of the Deaf.

Part 1

Recent Sign Language Laws

1 'Ah, That's Not Necessary, You Can Read English Instead': An Analysis of State Language Policy Concerning Irish Sign Language and Its Effects

John Bosco Conama

Introduction

The Irish Sign Language Act[1] (hereafter the ISL Act) was signed into law on 24 December 2017 (Figure 1.4). At the time of writing, it is too early to assess the actual impact of the Act on current national language policies. In light of this, the chapter focuses on how ISL is legislatively managed in the shadow of the dominant language English and a lesser used language, Irish (*Gaeilge*). Irish and Irish Sign Language (ISL) bear no direct relation to each other, though the common public often wonders if they are related or even the same language. Irish is constitutionally recognised as the national and first language of Ireland. In terms of state support, it holds a far advanced position compared to that of ISL. Yet within the jurisdiction of the Republic of Ireland, both Irish and ISL are de facto subordinate to English.

While English and Irish are constitutionally recognised languages in Ireland, English, by default, is regarded as the standard, dominant language that requires no specific legislation (Darmody & Daly, 2015). Yet *Gaeilgeorí* (Irish speakers) found it necessary to seek specific legislation to bolster their linguistic rights supporting access to public services in their chosen language. This support materialised in the form of the Official Languages Act 2003. Despite this Act and the national cultural affinity for Irish, *Gaeilgeorí* continue to express dissatisfaction with regard to how public officials treat them linguistically (Nic Shuibhne, 2001; Watson, 2016).

The public often perceives official language policy in Ireland as having a dominant focus on the revival and maintenance of Irish (Atkinson & Kelly-Holmes, 2016; Conama, 2010), and political attempts to enhance the status of Irish are often met with a general antipathy (Darmody & Daly, 2015). Despite the official image of Ireland as a bilingual nation, and even an emerging popularised image of Ireland as a multilingual nation, the reality is that monolingualism remains solid on the ground (Mahon, 2017). Public servants do display monolingual behaviours and attitudes when dealing with language issues (Rose & Conama, 2017; Ni Drisceoil, 2016; Walsh, 2012). In contrast to this, during the ISL recognition campaign, members of the public often expressed disbelief when learning ISL had not yet been bestowed official status. While it is difficult to pinpoint the reasons to explain this surprising contrast, it is possible that the experience of learning Irish in schools has left a negative legacy for many people (Devitt *et al.*, 2018), while ISL is associated with a positive emotional feeling.

The campaign for ISL recognition demanded the recognition of ISL as the third official language of Ireland (see Figure 1.1), and also referred to ISL as Ireland's second indigenous language, alongside *Gaeilge*. Speakers of other (non-indigenous) languages such as Polish or Chinese can avail of online public services such as state social security information[2] and employment rights, to a limited extent. However, public services are not legally obliged to provide such access since there is no enforcing legislation to demand this. Public officials often see requests of ISL users to extend linguistic access to ISL as irrational (Conama, 2010). Indeed, public services

Figure 1.1 Campaign boards from an ISL rally in Dublin, September 2015
Photo credit: Maartje De Meulder.

often resort to the 'solution' of making English text available for Deaf[3] ISL users, rather than producing video translations in ISL (Conama, 2010).

Campaigners for state recognition of ISL (led by the Irish Deaf Society with the author as its main representative) have successfully drawn upon such differing treatments, resulting in the successful passage of the Bill seeking the recognition of ISL.

In Ireland, in order to get a parliamentary bill passed, if it is proposed by the *Seanad* (the Upper House), it has to undertake 10 stages – five stages in each House (upper and lower). At each stage, a bill is minutely scrutinised and debated before the final vote, giving politicians and government officials the opportunity to propose amendments and mould the legislation. The ISL Bill went through the five stages of legislative recognition in both houses of the *Oireachtas* (Irish Parliament), culminating in the signing of the legislation by the President of Ireland.

Campaign to have ISL Recognised

For brevity and convenience, the following sections distinguish between the legislative process and the campaign; however, both were deeply interwoven.

In looking back, there is no specific watershed or historical milestone that can be regarded as the starting point for the campaign for ISL recognition, but an incremental path can be observed from the establishment of the Irish Deaf Society, the national Deaf-led organisation, in 1981, and its development of international connections to the World Federation of the Deaf (WFD) and the European Union of the Deaf (EUD). The international aspects of the campaign include the WFD's resolution in 1991 calling on national associations to pursue the official recognition of sign languages and the successful resolution on sign languages brought forward by an Irish Member of the European Parliament in 1988. Given Ireland's vicinity to the UK, there is regular exposure to the UK media, and the Deaf community in Ireland have regularly watched stories of the campaigns for signed language rights in the UK. Paralleling this exposure there has been an increase in the number of Deaf people entering universities and who were beginning to adopt a critical perspective on (life) issues of language identity as highlighted by O'Connell (2017) and Conama (2010).

The rationale behind the campaign for the ISL Act can be linked to an international desire to protect and promote signed languages, ensuring such languages can be enjoyed by future generations. This is not unique to Ireland; De Meulder (2015) and the Council of Europe (2003) have identified the preservation, protection and promotion of signed languages as the most important reasons behind campaigns for the legal recognition of signed languages. Additionally, the transmission of signed languages and their aligned cultures almost always takes place on a 'horizontal' basis[4] (Hill, 2015: 197), which entails a significant risk to the survival and sustainability of ISL, and is one of the factors that has necessitated a campaign for the official recognition of ISL. The steady decline of the number of Deaf children in the residential schools and the wide dispersal of deaf children in mainstream education inevitably erodes the 'natural' base for producing and sustaining the number of signers.

McKee and Manning (2015) and Johnston (2006) have outlined the potential threats and risks to the traditional basis of signed languages in other countries such as New Zealand and Australia. It is not unreasonable to envisage a similar situation for ISL (for a discussion see Leeson & Saeed, 2012). Following on from this analysis, brief comparative parallels can be seen between the desire to have ISL and Irish properly resourced to ensure their sustainability.

Campaign strategies

From the initial drafting of the ISL Bill in 2009, the Irish Deaf Society (IDS) followed two main strategies. The first one was collaboration with Senator Mark Daly of *Fianna Fáil* (a centrist and nationalist political party) (Conama, forthcoming). For the upper house of the Irish parliament in certain categories candidates have to seek nominations from the registered civil society groups in order to stand for the *Seanad* election. Senator Daly sought the IDS' nomination and was successful, and was committed to raise any concern the IDS wanted to highlight. The second one was the set-up of the cross-community group within the Irish Deaf community, facilitated by the IDS. This group included various national organisations ranging from Deaf youth to interpreters, and was created with the purpose of presenting a strong, cohesive, community response to the issue of recognition and deflect any potential criticism that the community was not united on this topic. This group advised the IDS representatives collaborating with Senator Daly.

The IDS also availed use of social media platforms such as Facebook and Twitter to keep the community informed about the campaign's developments. On Twitter, the campaign used the hashtag #yestoISL (see Figure 1.2). The 'Irish Sign Language Recognition Campaign' Facebook page has over 3,000 followers, and offered members of the community an opportunity to query and debate issues in relation to the campaign. In addition, this proved to be a useful information outlet encouraging members to take active roles in the campaign at a local level (see Lawson *et al.*, Chapter 4, this volume, for how Facebook has been used in the campaign for the Scottish BSL Act).

The campaigners also disseminated a leaflet with 10 reasons to recognise ISL (Figure 1.3).

Paralleling the initial legislative work on the ISL Bill, the IDS launched a separate campaign asking local authorities to pass a standard motion calling on the government to recognise ISL. The campaign not only

Figure 1.2 #yestoISL tweet and tag campaign
Credit: Haaris Sheikh.

engaged with local governments, but also with local media. In 2012, Monaghan County Council became the first local authority to pass such a motion after one of its councillors visited an ISL photography exhibition at a local gallery and decided to propose a motion. When reflecting upon this motion, the IDS realised the huge potential impact that could take place at a local level. The campaign continued, reaching completion with Waterford County Council becoming the 48th and final local authority to pass the motion. The level of coverage in local media appeared to show the success of putting forward this motion at a local level.

Development of the Bill

Originally, Senator Daly (a member of the parliamentary opposition) proposed that a government representative should take responsibility for tabling the Bill (Senator Mark Daly, pers. comm., 2011). However, attempts to get the government to table the Bill and initiate the process failed, though no clear reason was given for this reluctance. Separately, and paradoxically, given the reticence to take responsibility for the Bill, government Senator Cáit Keane, who had been working on sign language issues previously,[5] proposed a motion calling on the respective governments of each nation in the British Isles to recognise their signed languages. This motion was passed in Glasgow in October 2012 (British-Irish Parliamentary Assembly, 2012).

Figure 1.3 Ten reasons to recognise ISL
Credit: Haaris Sheikh.

Senator Daly engaged a legislative draftsman to draw up the Bill, in consultation with IDS representatives. Their initial work entailed examining several pieces of legislation on signed languages and drew chiefly upon those from New Zealand (see McKee & Manning, Chapter 14, this volume), Hungary and Finland, which were available online, in English. It was initially agreed to provide a draft general bill rather than creating a specific version of the Bill, as this would allow for it to be scrutinised, discussed and amended through the parliamentary process, as described previously. The Bill was presented for the second time in 2013, with the first version of the Bill having been withdrawn for some unknown reason in 2009.

Despite the government motion in Glasgow in October 2012 acknowledging Irish Sign Language, the second attempt to have ISL recognised in Irish legislation in 2013 also failed, with the government of the day rejecting the 'Recognition of Irish Sign Language for the Irish Deaf Community Bill' at the second stage of *Seanad Éireann*. While the vote was close, the Bill was defeated by three votes. The rejection was rationalised by the then Minister for Disability, Kathleen Lynch TD as follows:

> We do not want to see scarce resources, particularly at this time of extremely scarce resources, used without the service being put in place. We need to put the service in place before we put the legislation in place. That is what we have done in other areas and that is what we would like to do in this regard. (*Seanad Éireann*, 22 January 2014)

Minister Lynch did not define 'services' in her speech, but among the community it was taken that she may have been referring to sign language interpreting services.

In February 2016, a general election was called, resulting in a political quagmire. As a consequence, after 70 days of negotiation, a minority government was formed with the biggest party relying on the main opposition party for support and the continuation of the government in the absence of an overall majority. The arrangement became known as the 'confidence and supply agreement'.

This created an opportunity for the ISL recognition campaign to re-table the Bill in July 2016, however the Bill was severely curtailed during the negotiation process (which is briefly explained below).

Description of the ISL Act and its Origins

The original version of the Bill that was created in 2011 contained more than 30 clauses, covering the provisions mentioned below, but also including the establishment of statutory targets regarding the accessibility of television programming and regulation of ISL interpreters, Deaf interpreters and ISL teachers with the establishment of an Irish Sign Language Council to ensure standards for interpreting and teaching ISL. Furthermore, it included a legal requirement to provide ISL classes for parents of Deaf children, and provisions to make sign language interpreting services, when accessing public services, available free of charge for the users of ISL.

The ISL Act that was eventually adopted in 2017, contains 11 clauses covering the recognition of ISL and the right to use it, ISL users' statutory rights to access public services,[6] the setting up of an accreditation and registration scheme for ISL interpreters and vague references to children's rights in education. While 'access' is not defined in the Act, it can be assumed it means access through the provision of sign language interpreting services. It also has become possible to use ISL in legal proceedings, with the provision of access to civil cases an especially important change. The most useful part of the Act is the review of the Act in 2020 and every five years subsequently. A Deaf human rights officer in Denmark remarked on the inclusion of this review mechanism, as she observes that such a review mechanism is largely absent in most SL legislation (Jenny Nilsson, pers. comm., 28 February 2018; note the Scottish BSL Act as an exception to this trend, see Lawson *et al.*, Chapter 4 in this volume).

After the Bill passed the second stage in the *Seanad*, the Irish Deaf Society was advised by Senator Daly to get a proper legal adviser, and it successfully procured a law expert (a barrister) from PILA (Public Interest Law Alliance). This barrister proved a very useful asset for advice on technical legal issues. In spite of having independent legal advice, due to political manoeuvrings a number of decisions were made without being cleared with the IDS and its legal expert. This put IDS at a serious disadvantage. For example, the IDS campaigned for a separate and stand-alone clause in the Act recognising ISL as a language in its own right, aligned with cultural features appropriate to the language and 'not just a vehicle for accessing information' (Clare Daly, 14 December 2017, *Dáil Eireann Debates*). This clause was not accepted and IDS was left facing the reality that a rare opportunity for the recognition of ISL lay before them, with no real option but to accept the amended clause (see below) that describes the right to use ISL as a native language and the obligation on the state to make services accessible as a result.

> 3(1) The State recognises the right of Irish Sign Language users to use Irish Sign Language as their native language and the corresponding duty on all public bodies to provide Irish Sign Language users with free interpretation when availing of or seeking to access statutory entitlements and services. (Irish Sign Language Act 2017)

From July 2016, the Bill was reintroduced and passed through the second stage in the *Seanad*. In order to get through the next stages in the parliament, it underwent more scrutiny and was intensely debated through a series of negotiations. The negotiations became multifaceted and were widened to include civil and public servants, parents' organisations and the interpreters' bodies, which made it more complicated to reach a consensus. The private sector was deliberately exempted from this legislation. Indeed, it became apparent to the IDS that many original clauses would not be accepted by the government because of the potentialities of incurring charges on the exchequer (i.e. increased expenditure). In light of the government's strong 'pro-business' stance, it was deemed necessary to remove any likely imposition of increased taxes on the private sector. The exclusion of the private sector was counterbalanced by a 'voucher system' under the 'Support for access to events, services and activities for users of Irish Sign Language' clause that would allocate a certain number of interpreting hours each year to ISL users that they may use to make events accessible, even if the organisers are not providing access.

On foot of legal advice, the IDS decided it was important to have the language recognised and in order to safeguard the recognition, agreed to a form of 'horse-trading'. An example of this can be seen in the removal of the clause referring to the proposed ISL council to monitor

Figure 1.4 (From left to right) Senator Mark Daly, Eddie Richmond (IDS CEO), Brendan Lennon (Deaf Hear), Fr Gerard Tyrell (chaplain), Lianne Quigley (IDS Chair) and Dr John Bosco Conama

implementation of the Act resulting in some implementation responsibility being given to an existing state service, the Sign Language Interpreting Service (SLIS). The political climate was such that the establishment of a new quango introducing charges on the exchequer would not be tolerated. The SLIS is not, in a strict sense, a monitoring body, but was given responsibility for establishing a register for 'competent' interpreters.

There is an anecdotal sense of consensus among community stakeholders that the Act is imperfect, as it has not incorporated a number of relevant clauses, including references to culture and clauses regulating sign language teachers that were removed after a series of negotiations. The government side held the view that such clauses referred to topics that can be regulated voluntarily outside of the Act; however, there are widespread concerns over the ease of setting up ISL courses and offering students phoney certifications on the completion of courses. The ease with which this can be done potentially deprives competent and qualified ISL teachers from the economic benefits of their qualifications and their language. With regard to the reference to culture, the sanitation of culture from the Act reinforces the belief that ISL is merely a communication tool.

Within the ISL Act, there is a clause referring to the education of Deaf children in sign language:

5. The Minister for Education and Skills shall –

(a) establish a scheme for the provision of Irish Sign Language classes to –

(i) the parents, siblings and grandparents of a child who is deaf, and

(ii) other persons who serve in loco parentis or as a guardian to a child who is deaf.

However, this clause is not clear cut because the second part refers to a review of the Special Needs Assistants Scheme[7] (a type of communication support worker for children with disabilities) and the need for this to be completed before the Minister can be advised by experts about the educational rights of Deaf children.

While acknowledging that the Act is not perfect, and that it is still too early to assess its impact on the status of ISL, it is possible to carry out an analysis of the position of ISL (prior to the recognition of ISL) with that of Irish at present. The analysis will centre on four themes: (1) *regulation* relating to the current legislations and policies governing the language usage; (2) *propagation* referring to actions of spreading and promotion of the usage of languages; (3) the languages' *relationship with the majority language, English*; and (4) the *sustainability* of ISL.

Current Analysis of ISL

Regulation

Before the enactment of the ISL Act, ISL had not had specific legislation regulating its use in service provision. The only specific reference to ISL was found in the Education Act (1998), under the support services section. The Education Act regulates the education system and was the first comprehensive piece of legislation on education for many decades. Prior to this legislation, the State left the responsibility of regulating schools to the Church (Inglis, 1998). Prior to the ISL Act, the government had assured on several occasions that ISL had been sufficiently recognised by this Education Act. Conama (2010), however, suggests that the inclusion of ISL in the Act is not an act of recognition but a mere acknowledgement of the existence of the language. This is exemplified by the absence of positive rights for ISL users, and the inclusion of the language in a section that contains various support services such as psychological assessments, speech therapists and technological assistance.

Moreover, the acknowledgement is further qualified by including 'or other sign language' in the same sentence as ISL, although this term is not defined (Conama, 2010). The Minister for Education and Science justified this qualification by saying it avoided the impression of exclusiveness (*Dáil Debates*, 1998).[8] However, the rhetorical claims of ISL being de facto recognised have not been matched on the ground (Conama, 2013; Leeson & Saeed, 2012; O'Connell, 2017). There are a number of statutory instruments that implicitly acknowledged the existence of ISL; for instance, the statutory instrument obliging the Gardaí (police) to make reasonable attempts to get an interpreter when a Deaf person is being formally questioned.[9]

As with Irish, with the actions of private citizens to progress aspects of state use of the language, parallels can be seen in how ISL has been approached. In a number of situations, private citizens (parents of deaf children for instance) have taken the Department of Education to the courts to vindicate their children's rights to be educated in ISL. Most have opted for out of court settlements given the complicated interpretation of educational clauses in the Constitution (e.g. see *Irish Times*, 28 February 2006).[10] Such settlements, although they offer resolutions in particular cases, mean that individual parents as the litigators are the main beneficiaries of any of the outcomes, and the terms are not automatically extended to any and all parents of deaf children.

Propagation

Moving on to examine the propagation of ISL, it does not currently have the same capacity as Irish or English to further propagate. Governmental policy advice exists on how Deaf children should be educated (NCSE, 2011), but this has not been fully implemented to date. On examination of the respective websites of schools for Deaf children, there is no explicit language policy adopted by all schools catering for Deaf children, though all of them adopt implicit communication policies. Conama (2010) suggests that these schools emphasise the individual needs of each child according to communication needs rather than adopting a language policy that is based on one or more chosen language.

The predominance of communication policy-type statements in deaf education exemplifies the lack of distinction between communication and language in the minds of many educational policy makers. The ISL home tuition scheme,[11] though not widely publicised, refers ISL teachers to work with families in their homes, introducing families, and not only the child, to ISL (CIDP.ie 2009). The purpose of the scheme is to facilitate early language acquisition by deaf children. The establishment of this scheme came about as a result of determined lobbying by two hearing parents (Conama, 2010). For some, such a scheme suggests implicit recognition of ISL by the government; however, the scheme is poorly structured and poorly remunerated, and as a result its tutors are not highly motivated to take on tasks (Kevin Mulqueen, pers. comm., 28 May 2018). This points to the recognition it being of a cynical tokenistic nature. Despite that, the Minister for Education reported to the parliament that there were 205 families (with 228 children) participating in the scheme (*Dáil Debates*, 4 October 2016).[12]

There are hundreds of evening classes for learning ISL in the adult education sector; however, given the large and uncoordinated number of agencies providing ISL classes, there is no reliable or accurate figure of the number of class participants. Even though classes exist, true propagation is really limited to the education system, a situation that is a cause of concern for its survival. The sustainability of ISL will be discussed below.

Relationship with the majority language English

Both Irish and ISL are de facto subordinate to the majority language English. Even so, Irish laws are produced in both Irish and English and despite the dominance of English in everyday life, the Irish language version of legislation has precedence when both texts conflict in terms of meaning (Forde & Leonard, 2013: 75).

Walsh (2012) identifies the poor quality translations of websites and materials by many agencies as further proof that public agencies believe that these languages can be literally translated, and that there is no need to involve proper translation expertise. There is also a strong belief among public servants that there is no serious demand for Irish translation, yet this belief exists despite a failure to provide services in Irish. Walsh (2012) claims that most Irish speakers have been conditioned by their experiences of dealing with public agencies to use English in order to get their needs met without adding an additional layer of inconvenience to their interactions.

Walsh (2012) lists a number of problems, as mentioned above, that can be comparable to the experiences of ISL users when interacting with public services in the majority language.

Other related pieces of legislation exist that could influence language governance for ISL; these include the Disability Act 2005 and equality legislation. In spite of their existence, these legislations have proven to be ineffectual given that they are of a benign nature without strong, easily enforceable rights, and do not afford avenues for further ligation based solely on the grounds of language. In dealing with public agencies, ISL users continue to have frustrating experiences (Conama, 2010, CIB, 2017). It will be interesting to see how the ISL Act fares in this regard.

Interestingly, Walsh (2012) detected a distaste among Irish speakers for the '*cúpla focal*' (few words) approach used by public officials, underpinned by a strong belief among Irish people that possessing a few words is sufficient to declare their ability to speak Irish, and that in order to provide services it is enough for public officials to brush up their Irish rather than hiring native or fluent Irish speakers. For many ISL users, however, anecdotally at least, the goodwill shown by public agencies that offer to cover the cost of interpretation and by its staff willing to learn a few signs or knowing some signs, are much appreciated. ISL users have viewed this as something to be actively supported (Conama, 2010). Conama (2010) also notes that there seemed to be an unwillingness among public agencies to include ISL translations on their websites, despite the presence of other non-indigenous languages. Such unwillingness was based on a common belief that there was no demand for such a service and that the majority of ISL users can read English instead (Conama, 2010). These similarities match the factors that were identified by Walsh (2012) for Irish speakers.

English is the language associated with the educational system, as it is associated with employment opportunities and social mobility. ISL, by comparison, has no meaningful public status. Therefore, the relationship between the Deaf community and educational service providers displays an asymmetry in terms of power (Conamá & McDonnell, 2001). Inevitably, the asymmetrical power structures generate the presence of linguistic imperialism in the regulation of ISL, with the imperialism coming from English as the dominant language (Rose & Conama, 2017). Conama (2010) states that in such circumstances, language attitudes and beliefs are internalised, as is the belief that to learn English is to better one's career prospects and increase one's ability to partake in the majority society. The use of English is often seen as a bone of contention for the Irish Deaf community, with many people regarding a lack of fluency in English, instead of linguistic imperialism, as a serious barrier to their societal participation. Yet this fails to problematise the power afforded to English when compared to that afforded to ISL or Irish, and the monolingual-centred expectation that people should be using English.

Sustainability of ISL

The preservation and sustainability of ISL is always a lively topic within the Irish Deaf community, but there has not been much academic scrutiny into this area. There are exceptions, however, with Leeson and Saeed writing:

> We can add that with the advent of moves toward mainstreaming for a majority of deaf and hard of hearing children, with small clusters of children attending 'partially hearing units' across the country, the potential for destabilisation of ISL is significant, leading to additional, educational policy-led fragmentation of ISL and increased variation, not just in terms of region but in terms of a cohort by cohort shift. (Leeson & Saeed, 2012: 52)

Leeson and Saeed (2012) echo concerns expressed by Johnston (2006) that such changes would make it necessary to reposition Auslan (Australian Sign Language) as an endangered or threatened language. They believe the reduced number of people with access to ISL and Deaf culture would put ISL in grave danger. It is hard not to agree with those concerns. The gradual decline in enrolments in residential schools for the Deaf in Ireland (Ryan, 2008), the clearly documented struggle to fill social and cultural organising committees with the community (Conama, 2005; Ladd, 2003[13]) and the prevalent discourse among practitioners in the early intervention arena where they provide downgraded descriptions of the benefits of using ISL, highlight threats to the sustainability of ISL. In contrast, the ISL Act might offer some form of counterbalance as it has generated more public attention on the language, and has made the presence of ISL felt.

Discussion and Concluding Remarks

Having outlined very briefly how Irish Sign Language, Irish and English are interacting, it is clear that English as the dominant language has an impact upon the bearing of both ISL and Irish. As discussed, a number of analyses show that even if they have an ability to speak Irish, citizens would avail themselves of public services in English as to do so is considered to be faster and more effective (Walsh, 2012). In contrast, such an ability to speak or write English is not prevalent among many Deaf ISL users, so their access would not be as comprehensive as that of Irish speakers. This point of differing abilities to make contextual language choices is often lost on public servants when it comes to a demand from ISL users to have information translated into ISL. The first part of the title of this chapter exemplifies such an attitude.

From the outset, it can be seen that legislation does not seem to be able to tackle monolingualism in order to ensure that the public are served bilingually or multilingually. English is not just the dominant language, but has a lot of bearing on psychological well-being and philosophical outlooks. Both ISL and Irish have been affected negatively, and both are often regarded as backward languages and obsolete in current times (Darmody & Daly, 2015; Rose & Conama, 2017).

With regard to regulation and propagation, Irish is far more advanced in terms of resource allocation and national attention, and although its sustainability is often questioned (e.g. Ó hIfearnáin, 2013), its intergenerational transmission leaves it better positioned than ISL. O'Raigain (2007) points out that the Irish language, despite its low usage in society, always has a strong ethnocultural value which provides a basis of Irish identity. The designated Gaeltacht areas provide a stable foundation, as does the growing number of 'new' speakers outside the Gaeltacht (O'Rourke & Walsh, 2015). Such opportunities have the potential to consolidate the levels of intimacy and identification. It is often argued that public attitudes, and the willingness of users to speak or sign the languages in public, are crucial factors to the survival and sustainability of languages, as exemplified by the statement that 'if the language is seen as an important part of one's identity, individuals are more likely to speak it and be interested in its survival' (attributed to Edwards, 2010 quoted in Darmody & Daly, 2015: 1). This highlights how language users can internalise the low status of a language, but that it is possible to internalise and embrace societal respect for a language that will promote an interest in its use and sustainability.

Notes

(1) https://beta.oireachtas.ie/en/bills/bill/2016/78/. (24 January 2019).
(2) For example: https://www.welfare.ie/en/Pages/General-Information-and-Links.aspx and https://www.workplacerelations.ie/en/Publications_Forms/Other_Language_Publications.html. (24 January 2019).

(3) While I accept and agree that the definition of d/Deaf are anthropologically and politically contested, I prefer to follow the resolution by Canadian Cultural Society of the Deaf (CCSD) with the aim to 'indicate that ASL and Deaf culture are the birth-right of every Deaf individual by virtue of their having been born Deaf or become Deaf in childhood, whether or not they have been exposed to it' and not to use this term to identify or adjudge individuals based on their audiological or educational backgrounds. (https://www.deafculturecentre.ca/Public/Default.aspx?I=299&n=The+Lower+Case+%22d%22+or+Upper+Case+%22D%22 (accessed August 2017)) (Conama, forthcoming).

(4) It is an accepted convention that 95% of Deaf children who have potential to be ISL users are born to non-ISL using hearing families therefore language and culture could be said to be transmitted 'horizontally', as opposed to 'vertically' down a family line.

(5) Cáit Keane sat on the board of the Model School for the Deaf (a project working on the establishment of a preschool emphasising bilingual delivery). The project folded in the early 2000s. Therefore, she was an excellent person for liaising with on several issues concerning ISL.

(6) In the ISL Act, the term 'public body' refers to anybody that is chiefly funded by the government, ranging from public health services to adult education services. The private sector is not included.

(7) The review was completed and published on 30 May 2018, which was too late for analysis in this chapter. See http://ncse.ie/wp-content/uploads/2018/05/NCSE-PAP6-Comprehensive-Review-SNA-Scheme.pdf. (28 August 2018).

(8) *Dáil Éireann*, Volume 493, 3 July, 1998 Education (No. 2) Bill, 1997: Report Stage.

(9) Statutory Instrument 119/1987 – Criminal Justice Act 1984 (Treatment of Persons in Custody in Garda Síochána Stations) Regulations 1987.

(10) Coralan, M. (2006) Signing case to be taken against State. *The Irish Times* p. 4.

(11) For more information on this scheme, see: http://www.deafeducation.ie/irish-sign-language-home-tuition-scheme/. (August 2017).

(12) http://oireachtasdebates.oireachtas.ie/debates%20authoring/debateswebpack.nsf/(indexlookupdail)/20161004~WRH?opendocument#WRH01200. (August 2017).

(13) Ladd focuses on the British context but many of his analytical findings are similar and can be applied to the Irish situation.

References

Atkinson, D. and Kelly-Holmes, H. (2016) Exploring language attitudes and ideologies in university students' discussion of Irish in a context of increasing language diversity. *Language and Intercultural Communication* 16 (2), 199–215.

CIB (Citizens' Information Bureau) (2017) *Information Provision and Access to Public and Social Services for the Deaf Community*. Research Series. See http://www.citizensinformationboard.ie/downloads/social_policy/Deaf_Community_Research_Rpt_Feb2018.pdf (accessed March 2018).

Cidp.ie. (2009) See http://www.cidp.ie/wp-content/uploads/2013/12/Education-Policy-Paper-August-2009.pdf (accessed 25 January 2019).

Conama, J.B. (2005) 'Potential of the Centre for Deaf Studies (CDS): Its role in enhancing social justice for the Deaf community: A personal observation'. *Deaf Worlds* 21 (2).

Conama, J.B. (2010) Finnish and Irish sign languages: An egalitarian analysis of language policies and their effects. Doctoral dissertation, University College Dublin.

Conama, J.B. (2013) Situating the socio-economic position of Irish Deaf community in the equality framework. *Equality, Diversity and Inclusion: An International Journal* 32 (2), 173–194.

Conama, J. and McDonnell, P. (2001) *Newsletter 10 – Irish Sign Language*. See https://www.ucc.ie/archive/publications/heeu/Newsletter/April2001/news10irishsignlanguage htm.htm (accessed 16 October 2017).

Conama, J.B. (forthcoming) 35 years and counting! An ethnographic analysis of sign language ideologies within the Irish Sign Language recognition campaign. In K. Annelies, G.E. Mara, M.H, Erin and S. Kristin (eds) *Sign Language Ideologies in Practice*. Mouton de Gruyter/Ishara Press.

Council of Europe (2003) *PACE – Recommendation 1598 (2003) – Protection of Sign Languages in the Member States of the Council of Europe*. See http://assembly.coe. int/nw/xml/XRef/Xref-XML2HTML-EN.asp?fileid=17093&lang=en (accessed 24 January 2019).

Dáil Éireann debate – Thursday, 14 Dec 2017. See https://www.oireachtas.ie/en/debates/ debate/dail/2017-12-14/43/#spk_428 (accessed 24 January 2019).

Darmody, M. and Daly, T. (2015) *Attitudes towards the Irish Language on the Island of Ireland*. Dublin: Economic and Social Research Institute.

De Meulder, M. (2015) The legal recognition of sign languages. *Sign Language Studies* 15 (4), 498–506.

Devitt, A., Condon, J., Dalton, G., O'Connell, J. and Ní Dhuinn, M. (2018) An maith leat an Ghaeilge? An analysis of variation in primary pupil attitudes to Irish in the growing up in Ireland study. *International Journal of Bilingual Education and Bilingualism* 21 (1), 105–117.

Forde, M. and Leonard, D. (2013) *Constitutional Law of Ireland*. A&C Black. Dublin

Hill, J.C. (2015) Data collection in sociolinguistics. In O. Eleni, B. Woll and G. Morgan (eds) *Research Methods in Sign Language Studies: A Practical Guide* (pp. 193–205). John Wiley & Sons, 2014.

Inglis, T. (1998) *Moral Monopoly: The Rise and Fall of the Catholic Church in Modern Ireland*. Dublin: University College Dublin Press.

Johnston, T.A. (2006) W(h)ither the Deaf community? Population, genetics, and the future of Australian Sign Language. *Sign Language Studies* 6 (2), 137–173.

Ladd, P. (2003) *Understanding Deaf Culture: In Search of Deafhood*. Clevedon: Multilingual Matters.

Leeson, L. and Saeed, J.I. (2012) *Irish Sign Language: A Cognitive Linguistic Account*. Edinburgh: Edinburgh University Press.

Mahon, Á. (2017) Derrida and the school: Language loss and language learning in Ireland. *Ethics and Education* 12 (2), 259–271.

McKee, R.L. and Manning, V. (2015) Evaluating effects of language recognition on language rights and the vitality of New Zealand Sign Language. *Sign Language Studies* 15 (4), 473–497.

NCSE (2011) *NCSE Policy Advice Paper: The Education of Deaf and Hard of Hearing Children in Ireland*. National Council for Special Education. See http://ncse.ie/wp-content/uploads/2014/09/DeafEducationReport.pdf (accessed 16 October 2017).

Ni Drisceoil, V. (2016) Antipathy, paradox and disconnect in the Irish state's legal relationship with the Irish language. *Irish Jurist* 55, 45–74.

Ó hIfearnáin, T. (2013) Family language policy, first language Irish speaker attitudes and community-based response to language shift. *Journal of Multilingual and Multicultural Development* 34 (4), 348–365.

O'Connell, N.P. (2017) Teaching Irish Sign Language in contact zones: An autoethnography. *The Qualitative Report* 22 (3), 849–867.

O'Rourke, B. and Walsh, J. (2015) New speakers of Irish: Shifting boundaries across time and space. *International Journal of the Sociology of Language* 2015 (231), 63–83. See https://www.degruyter.com/view/j/ijsl.2015.2015.issue-231/ijsl-2014-0032/ijsl-2014-0032.xml (accessed June 2018).

Rose, H. and Conama, J.B. (2017) Linguistic imperialism: Still a valid construct in relation to language policy for Irish Sign Language. *Language Policy* 1–20.

Seanad Éireann debate – Wednesday, 22 Jan 2014. See https://www.oireachtas.ie/en/ debates/debate/seanad/2014-01-22/12/#spk_265 (accessed 24 January 2019).

Shuibhne, N.N. (2001) The European Union and minority language rights. *The Human Rights of Linguistic Minorities and Language Policies* 3 (2), 61–77.

Walsh, J. (2012) Language policy and language governance: A case-study of Irish language legislation. *Language Policy* 11 (4) 323–341.

Watson, I. (2016) The Irish Language and the media. In *Sociolinguistics in Ireland* (pp. 60–80). Palgrave Macmillan: UK.

2 The Korean Sign Language Act

Sung-Eun Hong, Hyunhwa Lee, Mi-Hye Lee and Seung-Il Byun

Introduction

In 2016, the Government of the Republic of Korea enacted the Korean Sign Language Act. Through the adoption of this Act, Korean Sign Language (KSL) gained legal recognition as the language of deaf people of South Korea. The aim of the Korean Sign Language Act is to improve the quality of life and guarantee the linguistic rights of deaf people and Korean signers. The Act also raises awareness of KSL and promotes KSL research. The authors of this chapter were all involved in the KSL legislation process. The first two authors participated in the KSL Legislation Research Project (2013), which was funded by the Ministry of Culture, Sports and Tourism and had the aim of discussing the KSL Bill. The last two authors were the respective initiator and coordinator of the campaign that successfully ended in the adoption of the KSL Act. We start the chapter by describing the monolingual society in Korea and the Framework Act on Korean Language, which is essential because the KSL Act was based on it. After giving general information on deaf people in Korea, we describe the campaign, its aims, the campaign's main activities, the challenges and strategies. We end the chapter by summarizing the KSL Act and discussing its shortcomings.

Korea as a Monoethnic Monolingual Society

The origins of the Korean people are far from clear and studies show that it is rather unlikely that the Korean people are racially homogeneous (Song, 2012). Nevertheless, Koreans regard themselves as a homogeneous ethnic group. Although the number of immigrants is increasing rapidly, the concept of being a homogeneous ethnic group is deeply embedded within Korean society and influences the way Koreans look at other cultures and languages. Korea has been a largely monolingual society since the 7th century (Song, 2012). In fact, most speakers of Korean are Koreans. The congruity of speech community and nation is higher than that of most ethnic groups in the world (Coulmas, 1999: 408 cited in Song, 2012).

Since the beginning of the 20th century, Korean has been influenced by languages such as Japanese and English. The first half of the 20th century was the most dramatic era in the history of the Korean language, due to the Japanese occupation which threatened its survival (Kim, 2012). During occupation, Japanese became the teaching language in Korean schools. Korean was at first treated as a foreign language, but later on disappeared from the curriculum. Japanese was not only the official language in education, but also in areas such as administration, police and the military. The Japanese also closed down all newspapers that were published in Korean. Towards the end of the Japanese occupation, Koreans were also forced to adopt Japanese names (Song, 2012). Due to this history, the Korean government has run language purification campaigns for more than 30 years in which loanwords from Chinese, Japanese and English were officially banned. It was a declared aim to establish the use of a 'pure' Korean (Brenzinger & Yang, 2018). Despite such campaigns, Korean was continuously influenced by foreign languages, especially English. At the same time, the demand for learning Korean is rapidly increasing all over the world, as the international status of Korea is rising owing to the growing popularity of Korean soap operas, K-pop and fashion (this phenomenon is called 'Hallyu', the Korean Wave). Therefore, it is expected that the Korean language will disseminate further in the future.

Although the languages used in Korea are becoming more diverse, there is no explicit language policy guiding this new multilingual reality. The language policy of the Republic of Korea was for the Korean language only. However, there is a policy to support foreign language education (e.g. Multicultural Family Support Act (enacted 2008) and Act for Promotion of Special Foreign Language Education (enacted 2016)) and to cultivate talented people with special foreign language skills. But the legal position of the Republic of Korea on foreign languages stands in support of education only.

Framework Act on Korean Language (2005)

There have been two decrees on the national language in Korea since the government was established in 1948: the Law on the Exclusive Usage of Hangeul (1948) and the Law on the Promotion of Culture and Art (1972). These two decrees have been merged into the Framework Act on Korean Language (2005). It includes new policies for the promotion and development of the Korean language and was promulgated in January 2005. The Framework Act on Korean Language defined Korean as the official language of the Republic of Korea and Hangeul as unique alphabetic letters used for writing the Korean language. The Framework Act on Korean Language can be seen as the legal basis of South Korea's language planning and policy. The designated institutions overseeing the Framework Act on Korean Language are the Language Policy Department of the Ministry of Culture, Sports and Tourism, and the National Institute of Korean Language (NIKL). The NIKL was established in 1991 and is seen as a milestone in South Korea's language planning and policy. Indeed, for the first time in South Korea's history, there was now a central government agency designed specifically to address language planning and policy issues or concerns (Song, 2012).

The Framework Act on Korean Language requires the Minister of Culture, Sports and Tourism to draw up actions plans (known as Basic Plan) through the NIKL once every five years and to implement them in specific language planning/policy areas (Song, 2012). The Minister is also required to submit a biennial report on implemented language policies or measures to the Parliament, which is known as the Enforcement Decree. The purpose of the Framework Act on Korean Language is to enhance the quality of the cultural lifestyle of Korean speakers, and contribute to the development of Korean ethnic culture. The Act does so by fostering people's creative thinking through encouraging the use of the Korean language and establishing the foundation for the development and conservation of the Korean language. This is done by addressing the following issues (Song, 2012): orthographic norms and reforms, the use and teaching of Hanca 'Chinese characters', purification of Korean (i.e. replacement of Sino-Korean words with native Korean ones, or Japanese and English loanwords with native or Sino-Korean ones), production of authoritative Korean dictionaries, Korean/language education in schools (in particular, production of Korean language textbooks), digitization/ computerization of Korean (including the development of digitized Korean corpora, web-based Korean (monolingual or bi/multilingual) dictionaries, etc.), linguistic reunification of North and South Korea and so-called 'internationalization of Korean' (e.g. Korean as a foreign or heritage language). Although the Framework Act on Korean Language primarily focuses on Korean, its Basic Plan mentions KSL (as well as braille) as a special Korean language.

Status of Deaf People and KSL in South Korea

Korean deaf people live within the Korean hearing society but have their own identity, language and culture. The Korean Association of the Deaf was established over 70 years ago and is well organized, with branch offices in the cities and provinces. The Act on Welfare of Persons with Disabilities (1998) as well as the Enforcement of the Anti-Discrimination Against and Remedies for Persons with Disabilities Act (2008) provides sign language interpreters for deaf people in public settings such as broadcasting, administration of justice, education and work. This is done by financing sign language interpreter centres where deaf people can request an interpreter. This service is administered by the Association of the Deaf and has the function of giving deaf people the services they need in order to participate in a hearing society. Deaf people in Korea are still considered as disabled people, who need to be rehabilitated and treated for auditory dysfunction; for example, by having a cochlear implant. Korean society is only slowly realizing that deaf people have their own language and identity. Currently, deaf people have only limited access to education, resources, employment, public institutions, information and community participation.

The sign language of deaf Koreans was first officially documented in 1913 when the first public deaf-blind institution was established (Won & Kang, 2002). Due to the Japanese occupation, KSL (as well as Taiwan Sign Language) was influenced by Japanese Sign Language (Fischer & Gong, 2011). Although the deaf schools in Korea mainly used the oral education method, students and teachers also used signs. In the 1990s, there was great interest by hearing people in learning sign language. Many private and public institutions offered sign language classes. Research on sign language can be dated back to the 1980s when mostly university students began to undertake master's theses relating to Korean Sign Language (Hong, 2008). In 1999, the Korean Sign Language Research Association was established and since 2002 it has been possible to study sign language interpretation at college or university level. Currently there are two universities and one college offering degrees in sign language interpretation. Since 2005, the NIKL has started to fund sign language research. This was a result of the Basic Plan of the Framework Act on Korean Language, which mentions KSL and braille as special Korean languages. The equalization between sign language and braille shows how insufficient the understanding of sign language was at the time. The NIKL treated sign language as a manual form of Korean and not as an independent fully-fledged language with its own structure and grammar. However, over the last 10 years, the NIKL has financed the production of several KSL dictionaries.

The Campaign for the KSL Act and its Aims

The core campaigners

The main campaigner and initiator of the campaign in order to achieve the legal recognition of KSL was the 7th President of the Association of the Deaf in Korea, Seung-Il Byun (deaf). Byun was the Association's president from 2005 until 2015, and already had experience with human rights advocacy. When Byun travelled to Finland in 2005, he was introduced to the legal recognition of Finnish Sign Language and this inspired Byun to fight for the same rights in Korea.

The campaign for the KSL Act started in 2008. This was an advantageous starting point since the Republic of Korea was about to ratify the

UN Convention on the Rights of Persons with Disabilities. The UN Convention included non-discrimination against persons with disabilities, and full and effective participation and inclusion in society of persons with disabilities. Byun was involved in the legislative process of the Convention as a member of the Korean delegation and able to observe closely the law-making process. This experience made him realize how important it was to enshrine rights in law to advocate for the legal recognition of KSL. Byun found an effective fellow campaigner in Mi-Hye Lee (hearing), the Secretary General of the Association of the Deaf. She coordinated the campaign and made sure that Byun's original aims did not get lost during the long campaign process. The initiators organized diverse campaign activities, contacted Congressmen and Congresswomen and built a network in order to start the legislation process. Byun and Lee stayed in office until February 2015. In March 2015 Dae-Seob Lee was elected as the new president of the Association of the Deaf. He continued the campaign and the KSL Act was enacted in 2016.

Campaign activities

From 2008 onwards, the campaign for the legal recognition of KSL was the main objective of the Association of the Deaf, and became a priority in the branch offices in the cities and provinces as well as the subgroups of the Association of the Deaf, such as the Deaf Youth Group, Deaf Women Group and Deaf Senior Citizen Group. The campaign used the slogan 'Sign language is a language', which used to be a slogan for a general campaign against discrimination of deaf people led by the Association's former President, Sin-Ki Ju. In September 2008, the Association of the Deaf established a KSL Legislation Committee consisting of hearing and deaf persons and lawyers. The KSL Legislation Committee's main task was to review domestic and international legislation and policies, and prepare a draft of the legislation.

The campaigners organized numerous activities to support and promote the KSL Act, of which the main activities were as follows:

- Mass rally: On 1 June 2012, a mass rally was organized. About 1000 deaf people from all over the country joined the event. Prominent deaf people spoke to the crowd and demanded the legal recognition of KSL. There were also representatives from other associations of disabled people, who came and spoke to show their support for the demands of deaf people.
- Hundred-day-one-person-protest relay: On 3 June 2012, the campaigners started a one-person protest relay in which every day one person would carry a protest poster around their neck and demonstrate in public for the rights of deaf people. The one-person protest is a common protest method in Korea. In this case, the poster contained

deaf people's demands such as language rights, the right to an adequate education, access to information, etc. This activity endured for one hundred days and was done nationwide; that is, on one day someone would stand in Seoul and the next day someone else would stand in another city. In Seoul, the one-person protest was done in front of the National Assembly and at the Gwanghwamun Square, in the centre of Seoul and often used for political demonstrations because of its historical importance. Figure 2.1 shows Byun, the initiator of the campaign doing the one-person protest on the first day of the relay.

- Protest march: On 6 October 2012, due to the International Deaf Day, the campaigners organized a protest march with the slogan 'Sign Language is a language'. About 200, mostly young deaf people, participated in the march, which started in Insadong, a touristic location in the centre of Seoul, and ended in Seoul Central Station. This activity was organized with the help of the Young Deaf Group within the Association of the Deaf.

These activities had two significant effects. On the one hand, they demonstrated the importance of legal recognition of KSL to hearing people. On the other hand, they raised awareness and support for recognition of KSL within the deaf community. The campaigners wanted the deaf community to actively participate during the whole legislation process and to fight for their rights. In this regard, the activities were successful. The campaign was supported not only by deaf people, but also by children of deaf adults (CODAs), hearing KSL signers and KSL interpreters. The campaigners achieved uniting the KSL community for the purpose of the legal recognition of KSL.

Outcomes of the campaign

Language rights for deaf people in South Korea

The main goal of the campaigners was the legal recognition of KSL as an official language of deaf people. Until then, deaf people only had access to information in Korean or Hangul. Through the legal recognition of KSL as their official language, deaf people should have the opportunity to receive information in KSL, which would improve their quality of life. As mentioned above, sign language interpretation services were covered by other laws already. Therefore, it was the goal of the campaigners to claim language rights for deaf people, which they considered a part of human rights, including the right to choose the language in which one wants to communicate. Deaf people in Korea use sign language as their preferred language, but neither the language itself nor the choice to use it was protected by law. The campaigners wanted KSL for deaf signers to have the same status as Korean for Korean speakers, as provided by the Framework Act on Korean Language. Therefore, they stated, KSL should become the

Figure 2.1 Byun, with the one-person-protest-poster around his neck standing in Gwanghwamun Square

official recognized language of deaf people in Korea. Although equal status between Korean and KSL was the main goal, because of the monolingual mindset in Korea the campaigners believed it would be unrealistic to demand that KSL would receive status as an official language of Korea.

The campaigners' decision to advocate for a language act was also met by concerns over whether the NIKL, which would be the institution to carry out the Act, would accept KSL as an independent language and not as a manual form of Korean, as they had done in the past. Therefore, some members of the KSL Legislation Committee argued that a language act would not make any sense because the NIKL would not be able to change their attitude towards KSL. They thought it might be better to give up the idea of a language act and aim for disability legislation and deal with the Ministry of Health and Welfare instead of the NIKL. There was no guarantee that the Ministry of Health and Welfare would understand that KSL was an independent language, but at least disability legislation would improve the living environment for deaf people in general and no sign language policy would be better than a wrong sign language policy. Nevertheless, the campaigners decided to pursue a language act because the core goal was to secure the language rights of deaf people and to get legal recognition for KSL.

A faster option to achieve this goal might have been to demand a revision of the Framework Act on Korean Language. This Act did not include KSL in the legislative text but mentioned KSL in the Basic Plan as a special Korean language. The campaigners could have lobbied to include KSL in the legislative text and ask for the same language rights as speakers of Korean. In fact, some members of the Congress advised following this path, but the campaigners decided to advocate for an independent language act despite the prospect that it would take much longer. The decision was based on the fact that the identity, social background and culture of deaf KSL signers is different than that of hearing Korean speakers, and the campaigners did not believe that a revision of the Framework Act would consider the special needs and circumstances of KSL users.

The KSL Act: A law of deaf people, by deaf people, for deaf people

Besides the fact that the campaigners wanted a language act, it was of great importance to them that the law was initiated and demanded by deaf people. In the past, laws concerning deaf people were written by hearing experts, not by the people who would be affected by those laws. The KSL Act was initiated and conducted by deaf people themselves. The campaigners actively mobilized the deaf community during the whole legislative process, demonstrating that deaf people demanded language rights and had a close interest in determining how their demands were reflected in the law. However, there were worries among the deaf community as to whether deaf people would really benefit from the KSL Act. For example, some of these concerns were related to the KSL Teacher Qualification Certificate, which was described in the Enforcement Decree of the KSL Act. There were worries that the new rules would disadvantage deaf KSL instructors and benefit only hearing KSL instructors. Although the campaigners were able to allay concerns by clarifying this issue, there still was an underlying fear among deaf people that they would not get their due rights. It was obvious that the deaf community had suffered from oppression by hearing people in the past and they remained cautious that hearing people might usurp control over their own matters.

Strengthening KSL within the deaf community

Another aim of the KSL Act was to strengthen the status and identity of KSL within the deaf community. In the past, the deaf community used to identify themselves by using KSL. Only a minority of deaf children acquired sign language from their parents, and most learned KSL in deaf schools from their peers (since the curriculum in deaf schools usually did not contain KSL classes or use it as a medium of instruction). Deaf schools were an important place where KSL would be passed on to the next generation and where deaf students could be among their peers, using KSL. In 1994, however, the Ministry of Education adopted an educational inclusion approach, which favoured disabled and non-disabled students learning in the same classes. As a result, more deaf students began attending mainstream schools, while the proportion of deaf students with additional disabilities increased in schools for the deaf (Choi, 2009). At the time of writing, deaf schools are silently vanishing in Korea. The Ministry of Education's 2012 report of special education stated that 70% of deaf children of school age attend a mainstream school. This change of educational setting leads to a loss of fundamental sign language pools, along with all their cultural aspects, because often deaf children have only hearing peers at school. Furthermore, it also means that a good portion of deaf students have to follow a class without a sign language interpreter (sign language interpreters are only provided in college and university) and instead have to follow the class only by lip-reading and the use of their remaining hearing ability. Disregarding the fact that deaf students are in an absolutely insufficient learning environment, this class situation forces students to adapt to spoken language only and this also influences their use of sign language out of school. Deaf students attending mainstream schools instead use Signed Korean, a visual-manual code of Korean, rather than KSL. Deaf students graduating from mainstream schools usually have higher academic degrees than deaf students graduating from deaf schools. This might be because mainstream schools prepare students better for the College and University Entrance Exam. Academic degrees are seen as very prestigious in Korea and this led to the phenomenon that Signed Korean gained more prestige within the deaf community. A motivation for the KSL campaign was therefore to reinforce the language identity of the deaf community. The campaigners wanted to strengthen the status of KSL not only in hearing society, but also in the deaf community.

Strategies and Challenges within the Campaign

KSL as a curriculum subject in hearing schools

Besides strengthening KSL's status in the deaf community, the campaigners also wanted to enhance its status in hearing society. They hoped a language act for KSL would raise appreciation for the language and thus change the perception of deaf people in society for the better. For this reason, the campaigners wanted KSL to become a compulsory curriculum subject in hearing schools. This would ensure that every student in Korea would come in contact with sign language and in this way increase the number of KSL users. Although the deaf community strongly supported this point, the campaigners decided to give up this goal, because introducing KSL as a compulsory school subject would need much more effort and time. Korea is extremely sensitive on the issue of education and schools. The whole school system can be seen as preparation for a single college entrance exam, determining which university students can get into. Since only graduates of the top universities are considered by future employers, the competition is extremely fierce and this exam is given the utmost importance in the Korean education system. Any attempt to introduce a new subject such as KSL into the curriculum would encounter many objectors within and outside of the Ministry of Education, Science and Technology.

Law making process: From a bottom-up to a top-down strategy

The Association of the Deaf initiated the legislative process by establishing the KSL Legislation Committee, who wrote the draft legislation. The usual way to make a law in Korea is to find a Congressman or Congresswoman who is willing to submit the bill in the National Assembly. At the beginning of the legislative process the campaigners actively looked for Congressmen and Congresswoman and contacted them, but it was hard to find an appropriate political advocate for legal recognition of KSL. Later on, some members of the Congress approached the campaigners, because introducing bills to the National Assembly is counted as their duty as a Congressman/Congresswoman and because they knew the campaigners had a bill ready in their hands. But in both cases the campaigners did not have the feeling that the legislative process would be fruitful, because the members of the Congress did not seem to understand the core motivation of the KSL legislation.

Fortunately, the campaigners found helpful advice from policy makers involved in the Anti-Discrimination Against and Remedies for Persons with Disabilities Act (2008). One very important piece of advice from them was to make sure that the KSL legislation became a national task, because once this was the case, the question was not if this issue would be implemented, but how and to what extent it would be. In order to make the KSL legislation become a national task, it was important that this issue was included in the party platform of the elected president. All political parties were willing to include pledges for people with disabilities, but the challenge was to promote the KSL legislation as an issue that was supported by all people with disabilities. People with other disabilities were not very interested in the language rights issue, as seen in an unpublished survey conducted by the Association of Persons with Disabilities among people with disabilities. The survey identified the priorities of people with disabilities, and the KSL bill was very low on the ranking. The campaigners knew that the Association of Persons with Disabilities could only claim 12 requests to the presidential platform. Therefore, it was necessary to canvass for the KSL issue to the board of the Association of Persons with Disabilities. Much effort and time was spent on explaining to them why deaf people needed KSL legislation. The campaigners explained that deafness is an invisible communication disability which affects every area of life because deaf people have only limited access to information. They further explained that deaf people use a language that is different from the language used by persons with other disabilities, and that is why deaf people sometimes cannot benefit from support services for disabled people.

Fortunately, the Board of the Association of Persons with Disabilities was convinced and the KSL bill was included in their official request to the presidential platform. This was one of the most important milestones towards achieving legislation. After the campaigners persuaded the policy makers of the Association of People with Disabilities to support the KSL legislation, this issue became one of 12 official pledges that were included by all parties participating in the presidential election. After President Park Geun-Hye confirmed the KSL legislation as a national task, the issue was no longer a matter for the Association of the Deaf or Association of People with Disabilities. It was a national matter and the Ministry of Culture, Sports and Tourism was in charge of preparing the legislative process. The campaigners then supported the process by providing the Ministry with all materials (previous drafts, statistics, survey results, literature, etc.) concerning KSL. Although the legislation originated in a bottom-up campaign, it turned into a top-down movement after the KSL bill became a national task. This strategy was essential for the accomplishment of the KSL Act.

Terminology: Suhwa versus sueo

The campaigners and the ministry responsible for the KSL law faced the problem of terminology for referring to the language. There were slightly different expressions for deaf, similar to the English terms deaf versus hearing impaired. The most discussed term, however, was the term for Sign Language, which has had many different labels. The most widely used term with the longest history was 'suhwa' (수화). A relatively new expression was 'sueo' (수어), in which the first syllable of the Chinese characters means 'hand' and the second syllable means 'language', whereas the second syllable of the traditional term, 'suhwa', means 'words'. Because the second syllable in 'sueo' means 'language', the term was used more recently among many young deaf people and also some linguists. The question now was which term to use for the KSL Act: the traditional term 'suhwa' or the rather new term 'sueo'? The Association of the Deaf conducted two surveys among their members and staff about the terminology issue. The first survey was done online in March 2013, with 131 deaf and 168 hearing people responding: 41% voted for 'suhwa' and 59% voted for 'sueo'. The second survey was conducted in paper form and/or in face-to-face communication within the Association of the Deaf in June 2013: 48% of 1423 interviewed persons preferred the term 'suhwa' and 52% preferred the term 'sueo'. After a public panel discussion and a public hearing, the lawmakers decided to use the term 'suhwa eoneo' (수화언어), which can be translated as 'suhwa language'. It was also decided that the abbreviation of this expression would be 'sueo' consisting of the first and last syllable of the above official term, which means that the new term 'sueo' was favoured over the traditional term 'suhwa'. The terminology issue accompanied the whole process of legislation and was controversial among the deaf community, making it hard for the campaigners to take up an official position.

Unexpected delays in the legislative process

It was originally planned to submit the bill during President Myung-Bak Lee's term, but when the campaigners decided to make the legal recognition of KSL a national task, they waited until after the next presidential election. Moreover, the campaigners were confronted with delay of the legislation because of two unexpected events in South Korea. One was the sinking of the MS Sewol on 16 April 2014, which cost the lives of 304 crew members and passengers, mostly secondary school students. The second one was the Middle East Respiratory Syndrome (MERS) outbreak in May 2015, followed by an assembly ban and official closure of schools and institutions. The ferry disaster and the effort to shed light on the tragedy led to a crippling of the operation of the National Assembly and the complete halt of the law-making process. This did not just concern the KSL bill but also four other bills, which were stuck in the process for over a year. The MERS outbreak, with all its ensuing complications, delayed the KSL legislation for another six months.

The KSL Act

The significance of the Act lies in its provision of legal grounds for KSL policies. Table 2.1 shows the key details of the Act, which consists of 20 articles in four chapters:

Table 2.1 Key points of the Korean Sign Language Act (Jung, 2016: 156)

Article	Details
2	KSL shall be the official language of Korean deaf people.
4	The government and municipalities shall establish and implement policies that facilitate deaf people's use of KSL; for example, policies on education, dissemination and promotion of KSL.
6 7	A KSL Development Plan shall be established every five years for development and preservation of KSL, and enforcement plans for the KSL Development Plan shall be established and implemented every year.
9	A survey on deaf people's KSL environment shall be conducted every three years.
10	KSL studies, including standardization of KSL vocabulary, shall be conducted, for which a specialized organization shall be designated.
11	The government and municipalities shall encourage the use of KSL as a language on par with spoken Korean in Deaf education as the medium of instruction, and set necessary policies for early acquisition of KSL.
12	A KSL education support system shall be established for deaf people and their families.
14	Projects that promote KSL through mass media, develop the KSL curriculum and teaching materials, and foster KSL teachers, shall be carried out to disseminate and promote the use of KSL.
15	A KSL competency test system shall be established and implemented to enhance and assess KSL capabilities.
6	The government shall provide sign language interpretation to deaf people and foster sign language professionals to facilitate deaf people's access to public facilities, public events and judicial proceedings as required.

It is worth noting that the Basic Plan (called the KSL Development Plan above) is to be established every five years (Article 6). This plan is more or less envisaged as an implementation plan and includes both status planning and corpus planning aspects: improvement of the KSL environment, KSL studies, professional vocabulary standardization, education in and dissemination of KSL, fostering career development of KSL professionals by establishing the KSL Teacher Qualification Certificate, computerization of KSL by investing in KSL content on the Internet and increasing barrier-free access for deaf people on the Internet, and exchange and research of inter-Korean sign language, that is, the sign language of South and North Korea.

The KSL Act and the Enforcement Decree of the KSL Act are available in English on the English homepage of the Ministry of Government Legislation (www.moleg.go.kr/english/) as well as on the English homepage of the National Law Information Center (www.law.go.kr/eng/engMain.do).

Role of the NIKL

The NIKL is in charge of establishing this Basic Plan and is also responsible for its implementation. The NIKL collaborates with the

Association of the Deaf and is tasked with initiating and coordinating diverse research projects resulting from the Basic Plan. Currently, the NIKL is managing research projects such as the KSL Corpus Project, KSL Dictionary Project, KSL Grammar Project and KSL Teaching Material Project. The NIKL deals with issues such as the KSL language policy and gives policy advice on KSL to public institutions. The campaigners and deaf community wanted to establish an independent Sign Language Research Institute, similar to the NIKL. Due to budget problems and equity with other policies, this point could not be realized in the KSL Act. Instead, the NIKL has set up a department, the Promotion Division of Special Languages, which is in charge of all KSL-related issues.

Shortcomings of the KSL Act

The KSL Act contains many details in the Basic Plan such as the implementation of a survey on the use of KSL, promotion of KSL, a KSL competency test, etc. Although the deaf community and the campaigners are very happy about the enactment of this law, there were also a few things that did not meet the expectations of the community.

Sign language acquisition in deaf education

Sign language acquisition in deaf education was a very urgent and desired goal for the campaigners. The insufficient education of deaf students is seen as the root of the main barrier that deaf people face throughout life. The KSL Act contains regulations concerning the education of deaf people (Article 11). It says that deaf students should be given an environment in which to improve their proficiency in KSL and it should be ensured that KSL is used at schools as an instruction and learning language equal to Korean. While the designated ministry for this provision is the Ministry of Culture, Sports and Tourism, issues concerning education in Korea are usually handled by the Ministry of Education, Science and Technology. This article, therefore, can be understood as a recommendation and it will need far more time and effort to implement KSL in deaf schools.

Coordination between the Ministry and local government

The KSL Act also determines issues relating to sign language interpretation services, such as the training of sign language interpreters. Currently, local governments provide funding for sign language interpretation. The actual enforcement of the law, therefore, depends on cooperation between the KSL-related ministry and the municipal institutions. There is no active and systematic collaboration between the Ministry of Culture, Sports and Tourism and local government. Therefore, it is questionable whether local governments will be financially able and willing to enforce the KSL Act adequately. Furthermore, the Basic Plan states that the Ministry of Culture, Sports and Tourism evaluates implementation by local governments every year. This ensures that it is possible to check if the KSL Act is implemented effectively. On the one hand, the annual evaluation is valued highly, but on the other hand the Basic Plan does not provide a budget for the local governments and does not determine staff that should be responsible for implementation. Local government(s) have a limited understanding of what needs to be provided or evaluated in relation to KSL. The NIKL is aware of this problem and is trying to appoint a department in local government, and to establish a network between the local governments and the Promotion Division of Special Languages (NIKL), which is in charge of KSL-related issues.

KSL teacher qualification

The KSL Act contains promotion of KSL teacher development (Article 14). The enforcement decree of the KSL Act determines the qualification requirements in detail (required hours of training, required exam, etc.) in order to gain a KSL teacher qualification certificate. In Korea, KSL is taught by hearing and deaf people. Since KSL instructors (no matter if they are hearing or deaf) have never been systematically trained before, there were no guidelines that could be adopted in the KSL teacher qualification program. The lawmaker therefore adopted the systematic training course of hearing teachers teaching Korean as a foreign language. Teaching Korean to foreigners is different from teaching KSL to Koreans. Not only are the target language and target group different, but many KSL instructors are deaf. Unfortunately, this important issue has not been considered sufficiently and this makes the KSL teacher qualification program not really suitable for deaf people. Many subjects that have to be taken to get the KSL teacher qualification certificate are not offered in KSL, because currently no hearing academics can teach in KSL and as of yet there are no deaf academics with the required qualifications. Also, there are no KSL-based teaching materials yet. For now, deaf KSL signers thus have to study for a KSL teacher qualification in their second language, Korean. Actually, deaf people are used to these circumstances; if they attend higher education (college or university) in Korea, they always rely on a KSL interpreter and they also use textbooks in Korean. But the KSL teacher qualification is provided for in the KSL Act, a law that recognizes KSL as the official language of deaf people. The deaf community considers it ironic that the implementation of the KSL Act will not be in KSL and will therefore disadvantage them. The NIKL is aware of this situation and is carrying out a research project with the aim to develop KSL-based teaching materials. The NIKL also aims to offer deaf people the opportunity to take the exam for a KSL teacher qualification in KSL.

Distinction between KSL and signed Korean

Some sign language linguists regret that the KSL Act does not distinguish between KSL as a fully-fledged and independent language and Signed Korean, which is an artificial sign system. But this distinction was not added on purpose because the campaigners did not want to exclude anybody from the deaf community. It is now the responsibility of the NIKL to make sure that the distinction is made when research projects are carried out (see Chapter 6, Mori & Sugimoto, this volume, for a similar debate in Japan).

Conclusion

This chapter has discussed the process of achieving the KSL Act from the perspective of the campaigners. We have described the aims and activities of the campaign, the content of the KSL Act, challenges and allies in the law-making process and difficulties in its implementation. The KSL Act secures the language rights of the deaf community. KSL is now the official language of deaf people and has the same status to deaf people as Korean has to hearing people in Korea. The legal recognition of KSL might not show immediate influence on the lives of deaf people, but it is an important milestone on the way to equal rights for deaf people in Korea.

References

Brenzinger, M. and Yang, C.Y. (2018) Jejueo in South Korea. In C.A. Seals and S. Shah (eds) *Heritage Language Policies around the World* (pp. 185–198). New York: Routledge.

Choi, S.K. (2009) Deaf education in South Korea. In D. Morres and M. Miller (eds) *Deaf People Around the World: Educational and Social Perspectives* (pp. 88–97). Washington, D.C.: Gallaudet University Press.

Coulmas, F. (1999) The Far East. In J.A. Fishman (ed.) *Handbook of Language and Ethnic Identity* (pp. 399–413). Oxford: Oxford University Press.

Fischer, S. and Gong, Q. (2011) Marked hand configuration in Asian sign languages. In C. Rachel and H. van der Hulst (eds) *Formational Units in Sign Languages* (pp. 19–41). Berlin/Bosten: De Gruyter Mouton.

Hong, S.E. (2008) *Kongruenzverben in der Koreanischen Gebärdensprache [Agreement Verbs in Korean Sign Language]*. Hamburg: Signum.

Jung, H.W. (2016) Korean Sign Language policies: Trends & outlook. International Conference, 'Sign Language and Social Communications, 7 September 2016', National Institute of Korean Language and Korea Deaf Association, Seoul.

Kim, S.J. (2012) Preservation policies for the Korean language – History and problems. International Conference 'Protecting and Revitalizing Native Languages in an Era of Globalization 21–22 November 2012', National Institute of Korean Language, Seoul.

Song, J.J. (2012) South Korea: Language policy and planning in the making. *Current Issues in Language Planning* 13 (1), 1–68.

Won, S.O. and Kang, Y.J. (2002) 수화교육개론 *[Introduction to the Sign Language Education]*. Seoul: Press for Society and Information of the Deaf.

3 The Road to Maltese Sign Language Recognition

Marie Azzopardi-Alexander, Karl Borg, Dorianne
Callus, Keith Callus, Steven Mulvaney, Alison Vere,
Annabelle Xerri and Loran Ripard Xuereb

Language and Language Policy in Malta

Malta is located in the middle of the Mediterranean Sea close to Sicily in the north and between Tunisia, Libya and Greece in the west, south and east, respectively. It is the smallest, but most densely populated country within the European Union (EU), with a population of 460,297.[1]

Malta is a bilingual country: the Constitution recognises Maltese as the national language and Maltese and English as official languages. Thus, both Maltese and English are used in legal and official documents and both languages are taught in primary and secondary schools. Maltese is also one of the official languages of the EU, which Malta joined in 2004. Most of the population of the Maltese islands speak standard Maltese or a dialect of Maltese. They also speak English to different degrees and often codeswitch between English and Maltese, particularly in informal settings. A good number of Maltese people consider English to be their primary written language, although they are usually literate in Maltese too (Vella, 2013: 539; Pace & Borg, 2017: 75). A good working knowledge of written and spoken English is necessary to advance in secondary and tertiary education, and Deaf students recognise the need to be literate in both Maltese and English to participate in post-secondary education and employment (Portelli, 2017: 32).

Maltese Sign Language – known as LSM from *Il-Lingwa tas-Sinjali Maltija*, the Maltese version of the name since 2001 – (see Azzopardi, 2001) became an official language in Malta in March 2016. This means that technically, a Deaf person[2] has a right to official documentation in LSM and the right to be taught LSM in school. However, only two years after LSM receiving official status in Malta, it is too early to say whether this status is legally equivalent, *de jure* and de facto, to that of English.

LSM has several varieties and is a rapidly developing language (Azzopardi-Alexander, 2018). No empirical research has been done yet, but lexical variation is observed between generations of Deaf people; younger signers often borrow from British Sign Language and American Sign Language, and other sign languages they are exposed to, for example by meeting deaf tourists or attending conferences. Home signs are also used in some contexts.

Maltese Sign Language

Deaf education and the history of Maltese Sign Language

Very little if anything is known about the use of sign language before the establishment of a unit, within a mainstream primary school, for deaf children in 1956, which may have been the first time deaf people met on a regular basis (Azzopardi-Alexander, 2018). The unit consisted of a few classrooms in a mainstream school and students were taught vocational subjects, through a predominantly oral-aural approach (Galea, 1991). Before the establishment of the deaf unit, deaf children simply stayed at home or went to school with hearing peers without much educational benefit. There were never any deaf residential schools in Malta, probably because the population of deaf children was so small. The Deaf authors of this chapter report that some families used home signs to communicate, some of which survive in the current vocabulary of the Deaf community. The first known document on LSM is a report by Llewellyn-Jones (1986), and an account of the available evidence about LSM is made in Azzopardi-Alexander (2018). Maltese teachers of the deaf adopted the oral-aural approach originating from their UK training, until one teacher came back from self-funded training, and was able to use signing along with speech in her teaching. However, few teachers have the opportunity to become proficient signers. Currently, all deaf children in Malta attend mainstream schools; there is no other option.

LSM is rapidly developing in terms of its lexicon to meet the demands of deaf learners who access the school curriculum through interpreters across all educational levels, and to interpret the daily news bulletins on TV. Also, deaf people are increasingly participating in various events, from local meetings, to international seminars and conferences (Azzopardi-Alexander, 2018: 280–282).

Teaching Maltese Sign Language

The Institute of Linguistics at the University of Malta set up LSM courses in 1995. The courses started as a result of collaboration between Deaf people and hearing professionals. This led to the teaching of sign linguistics and subsequently to research on LSM at the University of Malta.

The LSM courses triggered awareness about LSM as a language in its own right, independent of the official spoken languages, Maltese and

English. Deaf adults began to sign more openly in public, whereas for many years they were not comfortable doing so. This was probably influenced by a few children having been sent to residential schools for the Deaf in the UK, who then returned to Malta and used British Sign Language in public, which encouraged more public use of LSM by the community. When Deaf signers started to interpret the news on TV in 2000, this increased appreciation of LSM as a language among the hearing population. Since 1995, around 120 hearing students per year enrol for a 14-week long introductory LSM course, and around 30 take a 14-week long intermediate level LSM course at university. These courses form part of the Institute of Linguistics and Language Technology's Linguistics programme, where sign linguistics has been taught since 1998 and where most research on LSM originates. An additional 40 students enrol in evening courses at the vocational college (Malta College of Arts, Science and Technology) and at the Department of Education.

Maltese Sign Language interpreting

In 2001, Maria Azzopardi (now Galea), a University of Malta graduate in linguistics who had learnt LSM and sign linguistics, was hired by the Deaf People's Association of Malta to work as a sign language interpreter. Subsequently, a small number of graduates succeeded each other in this role. However, until 2013, there were only three full-time interpreters in Malta for 200 Deaf people. At the end of 2013, the Association was no longer able to employ the interpreters. Eventually, Dr Justyne Caruana, the Parliamentary Secretary for Disability, took the initiative to employ interpreters through the local government agency for Support Services. Caruana would also be a key person in the process towards the Maltese Sign Language Recognition Act (see below, 'The first draft of the bill').

Currently, there are five full-time interpreters in Malta, but they had not received any formal training locally. A Postgraduate Diploma in Maltese Sign Language Interpreting started in October 2018 (see below, 'Sign language interpreters'). Three freelancers fill in where it is not possible for the full-timer interpreters to cope with the requests and where funds can be found. Students at university, for example, can request funds for interpreting where the full-time interpreters cannot provide the service.

The development of research on Maltese Sign Language

Research on LSM was initiated by a small group of hearing researchers working with the Deaf community. The development of the language was hastened by work on the LSM dictionary and the lexicon continues to grow (Azzopardi-Alexander, 2003, 2004, 2015, 2018). This development can be traced through the first studies on LSM documented in

D'Amato (1988) and Porter (1995), and later in Azzopardi (2001), Azzopardi-Alexander (2009), Fenech (2002), Galea (2006, 2014), Mifsud (2010), Vere (2014) and others.

Research is also refining available tools to encode LSM in written form that should enable scaffolding for literacy for Deaf children in the future. The use of Signwriting (http://www.valeriesutton.org/) has been adopted, since Deaf signers learn to read it very quickly (http://www.signwriting.org/symposium/). One such work is that of Galea (2008), which gives Deaf people access to the Christmas Story from the synoptic gospels through signwriting.

First Steps towards a Sign Language Law

The National Association for the Deaf (now the Deaf People's Association of Malta) was founded in 1972 by teachers and parents, with no direct involvement of deaf adults. The above-mentioned Deaf Unit was the place where the Deaf community was first formed. Some of the former students of the unit went on to become committee members of the Association. The opening of the Deaf Club in 1982 raised their awareness and they soon started to lead the Association with some help from hearing people, usually parents. The Deaf Club was instrumental in the start of the Deaf Pride movement in Malta.

The Deaf People Association (Malta) has been a full member of the European Union of the Deaf (EUD) since 2005 and sends representatives to annual meetings and other events, offering an opportunity to learn about developments for Deaf citizens in larger EU Member States. On 19 November 2010, the EUD and a deaf MEP, Adam Kosa, organised a conference at the European Parliament entitled 'Implementation of Sign Language Legislation' resulting in the signing of the Brussels Declaration by representatives of all National Associations of the Deaf in the EU and Iceland, Norway and Switzerland. The Deaf People Association (Malta) also signed the declaration. The Brussels Declaration provided the Association with a much-needed tool, as it calls upon the EU and its Member States to recognise the national sign languages on an equal footing with the respective spoken languages of the Member States.

In October 2012, Malta's ratification of the United Nations Convention on the Rights of Persons with Disabilities (UNCRPD) and the Optional Protocol placed LSM recognition firmly on the national disability agenda. A three-year deadline was set by the National Commission for Persons with Disability to officially recognise LSM in the Maltese Constitution (KNPD, 2013: pp. 16ff). It must be noted, however, that there is serious misunderstanding reflected in official reports of the Commission, with basic LSM courses described as equivalent to training in interpreting (CRPD Malta, 2014 – Article 21: 122, p. 28).

The result of UNCRPD ratification was that the three main political parties contesting the 2013 General Election included a promise to recognise LSM as an official language in their election manifestos.

In 2013, the EUD's Policy Officer visited Malta as the main speaker at a seminar on sign language legislation organised by the Deaf People Association (Malta) and the EUD. This again triggered awareness about the need for LSM legislation. The Minister and Shadow Minister for Disability were present at the seminar, and pledged to work towards sign language legislation. The Minister for Disability, Coleiro Preca, indicated that she would discuss the Deaf Association's proposal for a '*Deaf Office*' that would serve Deaf persons needing to access government services in LSM. Coleiro Preca assumed the Presidency of the Republic of Malta in April 2014 and Justyne Caruana was appointed as Parliamentary Secretary for Disability.

Drafting the Law: A Journey

The first draft of the bill

During her 2013 visit, the EUD Policy Officer presented a copy of the book on sign language legislation in the European Union (Wheatley & Pabsch, 2012) to the Dean of the Faculty of Law, Professor Kevin Aquilina. In October 2013, in his professional capacity, Aquilina offered to draft a bill with the recognition of LSM as a principal objective. This is one way laws are initiated in Malta. Aquilina met representatives of the Deaf People's Association, the National Commission for Persons with Disability (KNPD), the Disability Studies Unit and the Institute of Linguistics of the University of Malta to discuss the possibility of a bill. After the meeting, he sent a draft to those present to invite feedback. The draft went beyond language legislation, to address the needs of deaf and hard of hearing people who do not use sign language. It included the recognition of LSM and the right to be educated in sign language.

Unfortunately, because of the disruption to the interpreting service at the time, which required the urgent attention of the Deaf Association, their representatives could not immediately give feedback on this draft. However, it was superseded by a bill presented to Parliament by the newly appointed Parliamentary Secretary for Disability, Caruana, herself a lawyer. When she was appointed, she started drafting various laws relating to disability. She was not aware of the draft proposed by Aquilina, and did not consult the Deaf Association or any other deaf representatives. The first reading took place in March 2015 and the Deaf community found out about it by chance. However, they decided to be pragmatic and support the Caruana Bill, since it addressed the Deaf community's major concern: the right to their sign language through recognition. Moreover, there was no realistic hope of making significant changes to the Bill.

The Deaf Association immediately requested a meeting with Caruana in March 2015. At the meeting, the Deaf Association raised several concerns, mainly regarding the composition of the Sign Language Council as proposed in the Bill (see below, 'The Maltese Sign Language Council'). They argued that the Council should have seven members instead of the proposed five, and that the majority, including the chairperson, should be Deaf. They also asked for funds to be assured, including a paid full-time executive officer, and that the Deaf Association should be consulted regarding selection of members, and that the Council should be considered an authority on matters related to LSM just like the Maltese Language Council.[3] While there was verbal reassurance from Caruana that there would be more Deaf members on the Sign Language Council than provided by the Bill, their request, to specify 'at least three' deaf members on the Council, in practice, was not accepted. Their first meeting did not result in any improvement to the Bill.

In a meeting lobbying the Opposition Members of Parliament after the first reading, the Deaf Association was assured of the Opposition's support in requesting revisions to the proposed legislation. This was the start of six months of intense discussions about the Bill with key activists within the Deaf Association, including the authors of this chapter, as well as other stakeholders.

In November 2015, the EUD's Vice President, Dr Humberto Insolera, met Caruana at a Council of Europe conference in Dublin. The authors consider subsequent progress towards LSM recognition to be, in part, a consequence of this meeting. Following the conference, Insolera tweeted that LSM would be recognised by the end of the year (Insolera, 2015).

A main point of discussion was, again, Deaf membership of the Council. The Deaf Association requested that the proportion of Deaf members be increased to 51% or more, and that all Council members be nominated by the Deaf Association. Furthermore, the Association again requested that the Bill include funding for the Council to be able to achieve the objectives of the law. There was no commitment to make any changes to the Bill at the meeting. However, after further discussion with one of the participants during a separate meeting, Caruana increased the number of Deaf Council members to 'at least two' (see Article 9(2) of ACT XVII, 2016[2]).

Since Caruana was very welcoming of the Deaf representatives at the meetings and assured them repeatedly that all would be well, to this day some Deaf campaigners think that all the proposals were accepted. During the writing of this chapter, it has become clear from discussions among the authors, that few members of the Deaf Association actually *read* the text of the Act (available in Maltese and English). It appears the legal language made it hard for them to access the text, and there was a lack of interpreters at the time. In fact, the Maltese Sign Language Act (Act XVII, 2016[2]) specifies only two and not three deaf members on the Council.

Caruana emphasised at her meeting with the deaf representatives that there could be three or even more in practice, and in fact there could even be an all-Deaf Council. However, the Deaf representatives felt that future administrations might prefer to keep to the two required by the Act.

Metamorphosis: Bill becomes Act becomes Law

The Sign Language Act was finally passed in Parliament on 16 March 2016, witnessed by most of the authors of this chapter, together with other campaigners. On 24 March 2016, it was signed by the President and became the Maltese Sign Language Recognition ACT No. XVII of 2016 – 'An ACT to provide for the setting up of the Maltese Sign Language Council, and for matters ancillary or consequential thereto.' (hereafter, 'the Act'). It requires additional work to amend the Constitution to enable LSM to be recognised on a par with English. The Act is considered part of the Equal Opportunites (Persons with Disability) Act and the Malta Natioanl Disability Policy, pursuant to the obligations emanating from the UNCRPD (see below, 'Provisions of the Maltese Sign Language Recognition Act').

Provisions of the Maltese Sign Language Recognition Act

Maltese Sign Language becomes an official language to enable access and inclusion

The Act consists of 11 articles. Article 1 lists the title and basic principles, namely 'the consolidation of human rights, equal opportunities and linguistic rights'; Article 2 defines important terms. These include '(D)eaf community' defined as

> (a) the distinct linguistic and cultural group of people who have a hearing impairment and who use Maltese Sign Language as their first or preferred language;
> (b) people who have a hearing impairment and who identify with the group of people referred to in paragraph (a);

and 'Maltese Sign Language' defined as

> the visual and gestural language that is the first or preferred language in Malta of the distinct linguistic and cultural Deaf community'.

Article 3 (1) states:

> The Republic of Malta recognises Maltese (S)ign (L)anguage as an expression of culture and endorsement for equal opportunities and inclusion. The purpose of this Act is to promote and maintain the use of Maltese Sign Language by declaring Maltese Sign Language to be an official language of Malta and empowering the making of regulations setting competency standards for the interpretation of Maltese Sign Language.

One could assume that deaf people would have the same right to use LSM as English speakers have to use English. In practice, this would be extremely difficult even in the long term, unless everyone in Malta learnt LSM. Therefore, in Malta as in most other countries, the important factor to implement this right is the availability of sign language interpreting services. Without those services, access through LSM is inevitably limited, even where the Act provides for it. For example, the current number of interpeters is insufficient to provide full access to education.

Article 3 (2) states:

> The guiding principle of this Act is that the Deaf community should be consulted on matters relating to Maltese Sign Language including the promotion of the use and development of Maltese Sign Language.

Consultation has not been extensive so far. This is partially due to resource constraints, with a small number of activists doing key tasks, a problem also found in other sign language communities (see Introduction, De Meulder, Murray and McKee, this volume).

Article 4 states:

> Maltese Sign Language is declared to be an official language of Malta and the Government of Malta shall promote through all possible means the widest use of Maltese Sign Language in all government information and services, education, broadcasting, media, at the law courts, and in political, administrative, economic, social and cultural life.

The meaning of LSM as an official language of Malta and how this relates to the status of English as an official language remains unclear. The only way to test this might be through a lawsuit. Claims for the same rights that English speakers have could be limited by 'reasonableness' as set out in the Equal Opportunities (Persons with Disability) Act 2000, specified as 'not imposing a disproportionate or unjustifiable burden'. Indeed, Article 5 states that 'The obligations under this Act are subject to such limits as circumstances make reasonable and necessary in terms of the Equal Opportunities (Persons with Disability) Act if all reasonable measures and plans for compliance with this Act have been taken or made.' However, the onus for the implementation of the Sign Language Act is on the Maltese Sign Language Council nominated by the Minister for the Rights of Persons with a Disability. The Council is responsible for making any recommendations to achieve the goals of the Act.

The role and responsibilities of the Maltese Sign Language Council

The major instrument for implementation of the Act is the Maltese Sign Language Council (Article 7). The responsibilities, summarised from the Act (and often using the same phraseology) include: advising the

Minister in all matters related to sign language; supporting the development of LSM and research related to and enhancing its recognition and expression; promoting 'the dynamic development of such linguistic characteristics as identified by the Maltese Deaf community'; in consultation with the Deaf community, adopting a suitable linguistic policy backed by a strategic plan and ensuring these are 'put into practice and observed in all sectors of Maltese life'; evaluating and coordinating the work done by others and fostering cooperation through a consensual plan; seeking to obtain financial resources locally and overseas to strengthen its activities; prescribing and establishing regulations about the standards of competency for interpreters and keeping a register of recognised LSM Interpreters; and undertaking such other activities as may be assigned to it by the Minister.

The Council is composed of a maximum of five members, appointed by the Minister for the Rights of Persons with a Disability. The chairperson is appointed after consultation with the National Commission for Persons with a Disability (Article 9 (1)). At least two of the members of the Council 'shall be persons belonging to the Deaf community'; another member is chosen in consultation with the Minister responsible for education (Article 9 (2)).

Article 9 (2) states that 'The members shall be appointed from amongst persons who are knowledgeable in matters relating to sign language, ancillary services, public service procedures, education or in other areas related to signing'. This means it is possible to appoint members who are unrelated to Deaf people or sign language, and simply know something about matters related to public service procedures or to education (a service that is ancillary to the use of sign language), but unrelated to sign language. Article 9 (4) even permits the chairperson to be a hearing public officer if recommended by the National Commission, although, naturally, one would not expect this to happen.

The Council members are appointed for three years and the Act details what happens should a member resign or be removed from office (Article 9 (5) to (7)).

Article 9 (8) asserts that necessary resources are provided – however, no financial specification is made and Article 8 (g) declares the obligation of the Council to seek to obtain the required financial resources. There is ambiguity as to whether Articles 9 (8) and 8 (g) are contradictory if one considers finance as a primary resource. After all, even coverage of stationery and postage, let alone awareness campaigns, seminars and other events, require financial resources.

The Council has now sent its first written report to the Minister as required by the Act (Article 10 (1) (a) and (b)).

The Council 'shall ensure that persons or organisations that are representative of the interests of the members of the Deaf community' are consulted on the content of the report (Article 10 (2) of the Act).

Presumably, this includes parents of deaf children who are below the legal age of 18 and possibly these children too in the presence of their parents, as well as professionals who work with deaf people or on LSM.

The report must be tabled to the House of Representatives eight weeks after the Minister receives the report or if the House is not in session, at the following session. The Committee will discuss the report and it may be included in any report related to the Equal Opportunities (Persons with Disability) Act 2000 or in reports on progress made related to the UNCRPD (Articles 10 (3) and 11).

The Maltese Sign Language Council

The LSM Council is critical for the implementation of the Sign Language Act. The Council was officially established on 1 November 2016. The Act can only take effect if the LSM Council works and delivers in consultation with the Deaf community. Council decisions need to be first recommended to the Minister, who can then follow up (or choose to ignore) the Council's recommendations. Recommendations might refer to education or interpreting service delivery that are a priority to the Deaf community, policymaking or other changes to the law. The Council needs to collaborate with other entities in order to fulfil its role (Article 8 (h) states it has 'to co-operate with persons, bodies and organisations in the disability sector'). It both makes recommendations to the Minister and monitors the Minister's progress in activating the recommendations. In order to develop a language policy and planning, the Council sees different priorities. It considers it necessary to increase awareness of LSM in the hearing community. It needs to study the status of LSM and to research best practice elsewhere in sign language legislation (e.g. Scotland, see Chapter 4, Lawson, McLean, O'Neill and Wilks, this volume) and in the provision of services (e.g. in Iceland with a similar population to Malta, see Chapter 15, Stefánsdóttir, Pall Kristinssin and Hreinsdottir, this volume).

The formation of the Maltese Sign Language Council is crucial in ensuring the Act has more than symbolic value. Another crucial factor is how the Council responds to demands from stakeholders, for example, the Deaf community and parents of Deaf children.

The Deaf Association recommended a number of potential Council members to the Parliamentary Secretary. Initially, three Deaf persons were appointed to the Council; two from the Deaf Association's list – one of whom was appointed Chairperson – and one other. Several months later the other members were appointed: one parent of a young Deaf adult and one other person who had no connection with Deaf people.

The Council may not be able to publicise what it has accomplished yet. The minutes and the first report have now been submitted. Once they are tabled in Parliament, they should be accessible to the public. This report will show the Council's recommendations and how they want to see the

Act implemented or improved. Council membership is voluntary with a token remuneration for the meetings attended. This means that the time members can spend on Council-related work is limited, although they have to cope with high expectations from the Deaf community. Nevertheless, they have a great deal of voluntary work experience and understand the limitations. The work of the Council would be facilitated further if there were at least one paid Council member or secretary.

Hopes and Aspirations of the Deaf Community

Sign language interpreters

Deaf Association representatives and the larger Deaf community in Malta have repeatedly emphasised the importance of quantitively and qualitatively efficient sign language interpreting services to improve their quality of life (e.g. *Independent*, 2014). Qualified interpreters are the key to access and therefore to inclusion. The reference to interpreting in the Act is in Articles 3 (1) and 8 (i) 'regulations setting competency standards for the interpretation[4] of Maltese Sign Language' and in keeping a register of recognised LSM interpreters, both roles entrusted to the Council. In October 2017, the Parliamentary Secretary for Disability agreed to fund the first postgraduate course for interpreter training. The course started in October 2018 and the first group of graduates are expected to complete their training by September 2020.

LSM teachers

An increase in the number of LSM teachers is another outcome many Deaf people hope to see from the Act. LSM teacher training is important to extend the learning of LSM as widely as possible. The purpose of the Act is 'to promote and maintain the use of Maltese Sign Language' (Article 3 (1)) and the government declares through the Act that it will 'promote through all possible means the widest use of Maltese Sign Language'. This implies the facilitation of its teaching in all ways and at all levels possible. The Council has already discussed the possibility of providing for LSM teacher education with the Institute of Linguistics and Language Technology. Meanwhile, the two LSM tutors have been provided with professional development throughout the last five years.

Television

Since LSM is now an official language, the Council plans to make recommendations to ensure that TV, digital media and broadcasting are accountable to sign language users too. At present, the only regularly signed programme on national television is a five-minute summary of the daily news, mainly by Deaf persons and sometimes by hearing interpreters. In the past, a popular live talk show/current affairs pro-gramme called *Xarabank* (Bus) was shown with in-vision LSM interpret-ers, but this has been stopped owing to lack of funds. Political broadcasts also often feature in-vision LSM interpreters, but Deaf people would like to enjoy greater access to a wider range of TV programmes.

Maltese Sign Language in public services, the workplace and entertainment

Public services could be brought in line with the Act to increase acces-sibility for Deaf people. One way of doing that would be to make it man-datory for a percentage of frontline workers in hospitals, health and emergency services to attend LSM tuition. The required competence would need to be ensured through regular refresher courses. This is one way in which the Act could be implemented without relying on interpret-ers becoming available.

The Deaf community hopes that in the workplace, managers and frontline staff in major companies will be trained in Deaf awareness and that some employees could take part in further training, including learn-ing LSM.

The Maltese Sign Language Act should in fact provide for the imple-mentation of access to leisure activities through LSM on the Council's recommendation in Article 4, which considers the use of LSM in 'social and cultural life'.

LSM in education

The very early introduction of LSM in the homes of deaf children is critical for deaf children's access to education. Parents and siblings, as well as other extended family members, need to have contact with Deaf role models. It is essential to train Deaf role models to enable families to access LSM immediately on identification of hearing loss and provide them with a fully accessible language in their homes that will bridge the path to the languages used by the larger community.

In Malta, Deaf campaigners recognise the need for Deaf LSM users to also become literate in Maltese and English. However, the problem so far is that parents usually request LSM interpreting in school only when their child fails in a fully oral-aural environment. Providing Deaf sign language tutors to children and families would avoid a delay in the acquisition of a first language and strengthen educational quality. With the implementa-tion of Article 4, which mentions the use of LSM in education, this could become a reality, provided the Council can justify it. A similar rec-ommendation was made in 1998 but remains unimplemented (Commission on the Education of the Hearing-Impaired, 1998). The Council can, per-haps, start the ball rolling to consider the recommendations made.

Conclusion

Looking back at the process, the road to LSM recognition was not always smooth. The main barriers along the way were exclusion of Deaf representatives early on in the drafting of the bill, and the change in government and changes in ministers and parliamentary secretaries. This often meant that the campaigners, including the authors of this chapter, had to work at re-building relationships with those newly-appointed policymakers and their staff. This was a time-intensive process but the energy invested into requesting amendments to the draft bills paid off.

The size and location of Malta presents both advantages and disadvantages. Malta is much smaller than most other European countries, and has a small Deaf community. This allows for rapid organisation of meetings and preparation of campaigns, and facilitates collaboration. Deaf activists are able to develop working relationships with policy makers that would be more difficult to develop in larger countries (Council of Europe, 2015: section 3.6.1). It also enables Deaf activists to participate in both national and European events much more frequently than their European neighbours. On the other hand, they may not always benefit from the events since they do not have the resources other countries may have to prepare for such participation.

There is a great deal of goodwill among politicians and it is the Deaf Association's understanding that those in office always want to make things work. However, implementation of the Act depends on the Council and how they take on their responsibility. The initial two-year term leading to the first report to be tabled in Parliament will be crucial to measure how effective the law is. The Council has the responsibility to deliver. Fortunately, they have a great deal of support if they ask for it.

Notes

(1) Times of Malta (February 12th, 2018) Malta's Population Soars to 460,300, accessed 24 January 2019. https://www.timesofmalta.com/articles/view/20180212/local/resident-population-in-malta-at-end-2016-460300.670492.

(2) Chapter 556 Maltese Sign Language Recognition Act, 24th March 2016, ACT XVII of 2016, accessed 24 January 2019. http://www.justiceservices.gov.mt/DownloadDocument.aspx?app=lom&itemid=12478&l=1.

(3) In the context of this chapter, a Deaf person is a person who uses LSM as the preferred language and considers him/herself to belong to a community with others sharing the language and cultural norms. 'Deaf community' refers to the group of people using LSM as their preferred language.

References

Act XVII (2016) Chapter 556: Maltese Sign Language Recognition Act. See: http://www.justiceservices.gov.mt/DownloadDocument.aspx?app=lom&itemid=12478&l=1 (accessed 24 January 2019).

Azzopardi, M. (2001) The Maltese Sign Language (LSM) variety of two deaf Maltese children: An analysis. BA thesis, University of Malta.

Azzopardi-Alexander, M. (2003) *Maltese Sign Language Dictionary, Volume 1: Annimali – Animals*. Malta: Foundation for the Development of Maltese Sign Language with the Institute of Linguistics and Deaf People's Association.

Azzopardi-Alexander, M. (2004) *Maltese Sign Language Dictionary, Volume 2: Postijiet – Places*. Malta: Foundation for the Development of Maltese Sign Language with the Institute of Linguistics and Deaf People's Association.

Azzopardi-Alexander, M. (2009) Iconicity and the development of Maltese Sign Language. In Fabri, R. (ed.) *Maltese Linguistics: A Snapshot* (pp. 93–116). Bochum: Brockmeyer.

Azzopardi-Alexander, M. (2015) Accommodation of Maltese Sign Language – Forging of an identity. In P.P. Chruszczewski (ed.) *Languages in Contact 2014* (pp. 47–80). Wroclaw: The Philological School of Higher Education and Committee for Philology, Polish Academy of Sciences Wroclaw Branch, in cooperation with International Communicology Institute, Washington, DC.

Azzopardi-Alexander, M. (2018) Maltese Sign Language – Parallel interwoven journeys of the Deaf community and the researchers. In P. Paggio and A. Gatt (eds) *The Languages of Malta* (pp. 271–292). Berlin: Language Science Press.

Commission on the Education of the Hearing-Impaired (1998) Report on the Education of the Hearing-Impaired. University of Malta, Report to the Minister of Education.

Council of Europe (2015) *Language Education Policy Profile – Malta*. Strasbourg: Council of Europe Language Policy Unit.

CRPD Malta (2014) *Implementation of the Convention on the Rights of Persons with Disabilities*. Initial reports submitted by States parties under article 35 of the Convention, Malta.

D'Amato, T. (1988) Some aspects of the communicative competence of a Maltese deaf boy. Unpublished BEd thesis, University of Malta.

Equal Opportunities (Persons with Disability) Act (2000) Chapter 413. See http://www.justiceservices.gov.mt/downloaddocument.aspx?app=lom&itemid=8879 (accessed 24 January 2019).

Fenech, D. (2002) Narrative skills in Maltese sign-oriented deaf 13–14 year olds. BSc thesis, University of Malta.

Galea, A. (1991) An outline of the growth and the present state of education of the deaf in Malta. In National Commission for Persons with Disability. *Partnership Between Deaf People and Professionals: Proceedings of a Conference* (pp. 35–40). Malta: Ministry for Social Policy.

Galea, M. (2006) Classifier constructions in LSM: An analysis. Master's thesis, Institute of Linguistics. University of Malta, Malta.

Galea, M. (2008) *Rakkonti tal-Milied bil-kitba tal-Lingwa tas-Sinjali Maltija (LSM)* (Christmas stories in SignWriting of Maltese Sign Language (LSM]). Malta: University of Malta, Institute of Linguistics.

Galea, M. (2014) SignWriting (SW) of Maltese Sign Language (LSM) and its development into an orthography: Linguistic considerations. PhD thesis, University of Malta.

Independent (15 November 2014) Lack of sign-language interpreters a problem for the deaf community. http://www.independent.com.mt/articles/2014-11-15/local-news/Lack-of-sign-language-interpreters-a-problem-for-deaf-community-6736125673 (acessed 24 January 2019).

Insolera, H. (2015) Parliamentary secret: Maltese Sign Language will be recognised before end year. Looking forward! @EUD_Brussels @coe https://t.co/pxj25u0F4Z [Tweet]. See https://twitter.com/InsoleraH/status/662668985587130369 (accessed 24 January 2019).

KNPD (2013) *Working towards the Implementation of the United Nations Convention on the Rights of Persons with Disability (UNCRPD) – A Report by the National Commission of Persons with Disability (KNPD – Malta 2013*. Malta: KNPD.

Llewellyn-Jones, P. (1986) *Report on Phase III of the Project A Visit to Malta*. 30 November to 11 December 1986. Unpublished report to the Malta Department of Education.

Mifsud, M. (2010) A study of superordinates and hyponyms in Maltese Sign Language. Master's thesis, University of Malta.

Pace, T. and Borg, A. (2017) The status of Maltese in national language-related legislation and implications for its use. *Reviste de Llengua I Dret, Journal of Language and Law* 67, 70–85.

Portelli, R. (2017) Listening to silent stories: Maltese deaf people's participation in community life. Master's thesis, University of Malta.

Porter, D. (1995) Aspects of the communication system of two Maltese adults with a hearing impairment. BSc thesis, University of Malta.

Vella, A. (2013) Languages and language varieties in Malta. *International Journal of Bilingual Education and Bilingualism* 16 (5), 532–552.

Vere, A. (2014) Bimodal trilingual language acquisition – A case study looking at the linguistic development of a hearing child with deaf parents. Master's thesis, University of Malta.

Wheatley, M. and Pabsch, A. (2012) *Sign Language Legislation in the European Union. Edition II*. Brussels: European Union of the Deaf.

4 Recognising British Sign Language in Scotland

Lilian Lawson, Frankie McLean, Rachel O'Neill and Rob Wilks

Introduction

The role of English as a global language is clear, with a quarter of the world's population having a useful command of it (Seidlhofer, 2011). Borthwick (2018) confirms that the UK is becoming more and more linguistically diverse, though a majority remain monolingual. In addition to English, there are numerous other languages used in the UK, including sign languages (Nagy, 2013). Academics exploring language policy in the UK have tended to distinguish sign languages from autochthonous – that is indigenous languages – but De Meulder (2015) suggests otherwise. The UK's autochthonous languages thus include Scottish Gaelic, Welsh, Cornish, Irish and Manx, British Sign Language (BSL) and Irish Sign Language (ISL) (as used in Northern Ireland). Gaelic and Welsh are protected by the Gaelic Language (Scotland) Act 2005 and the Welsh Language Act 1993, respectively.

The BSL (Scotland) Act 2015 was passed on 17 September 2015, receiving Royal Assent on 22 October 2015, signifying a new era in the Deaf[1] community's campaign for the legal recognition of BSL across the UK. At present, the recognition of BSL in law is confined to Scotland by the Act, although there are efforts underfoot in Northern Ireland to recognise BSL and ISL (Department of Culture, Arts and Leisure, 2016). There is currently no UK-wide legal recognition of either sign language, and this position is unlikely to change in the near future. Many political parties, apart from the ruling Conservative Party, have included BSL recognition in their manifestos.

In order to fully understand the context in which the BSL (Scotland) Act 2015 was enacted in October 2015, we need to look briefly at the UK's legal system. The UK is made up of four distinct nations: England, Wales, Scotland and Northern Ireland. The UK's Houses of Parliament and Government – based in London – are the legislative and executive powers that govern the United Kingdom of Great Britain. Nonetheless, certain powers have been devolved to Scotland, Northern Ireland and Wales. In

Scotland, there is a Scottish Parliament, which is an elected body of Members of the Scottish Parliament (MSPs).

The devolved legislatures of Scotland, Northern Ireland and Wales have government departments headed by cabinet members and ministers responsible for priority areas of government such as education, health and the environment. Their remit is reserved for what is referred to as 'devolved matters', while matters that remain administrated by Westminster are referred to as 'reserved matters'. England has no such devolved executive or legislature and is administered and legislated for directly by the UK's Government and Parliament on all issues. Therefore, while Westminster governs the UK and England, there are certain matters delegated to the three devolved administrations.

Upon consideration of the devolved matters to the Scottish Parliament, it would appear that the recognition of a language is not within its law-making jurisdiction. Yet, the Act was passed without opposition from Westminster. The logical conclusion is that the Scottish Parliament may legislate on any matter as it sees fit and take the risk that Westminster may object to its passage before it is sent to the Queen for Royal Assent. This approach could now be extended to both the National Assembly for Wales and the Northern Ireland Assembly.

This chapter will undertake a review of the BSL campaign that led to the enactment of the BSL (Scotland) Act 2015, ascertain the main stumbling blocks and obstacles to progress, and explore what headway has been made since it entered the statute books.

Language in the UK

Despite the absence of a legal document or otherwise to suggest that English is the official language of the UK, it is nevertheless the de facto language of legislation, public administration and jurisdiction (Nagy, 2013). Since the enactment of the Welsh Language Act 1993 there has been a clear shift in language policy in the UK, generally attributed to the influence of European trends, and is manifested in the ratification of important European instruments and establishing the devolved governments in Northern Ireland, Wales and Scotland (Nagy, 2013).

In 2001, the UK also ratified the European Charter for Regional or Minority Languages (ECRML) (Council of Europe, 1992), making it clear that the UK owes special obligations to its autochthonous minority language communities and that it is obliged to take positive measures both to protect and promote such languages (Dunbar, 2005). Sign languages are specifically excluded from the ECRML, partly because, as Krausneker argues (2003), the Council of Europe had misinformation and false argumentation about the nature of sign languages. As Article 2.1 notes, signatories have agreed to apply it to 'all the regional or minority languages *spoken* within its territory' (Batterbury, 2012). Thus, with regard to the indigenous languages, all of the spoken languages such as Welsh and Gaelic have increasingly gained solid official support (Nagy, 2013), but the UK's sign languages have yet to receive similar support.

The House of Lords Select Committee (HLSC) on the Equality Act 2010 and Disability has to all intents and purposes dismissed the need for a BSL Act. When referring to the BSL (Scotland) Act 2015, the Committee opined that 'we wonder whether this very significant cost (the £6 million estimated for writing and reviewing plans under the Act) might not be better employed in directly training more BSL interpreters and increasing their availability where they are needed' (HLSC, 2016: para 177). The Committee stated that the Equality Act 2010 covers BSL users because it imposes on service providers a legal obligation to make reasonable adjustments in communicating with them; and where BSL is their first or only language, those adjustments will very often be the provision of BSL interpreters (HLSC, 2016). This, together with the then Minister for Disabled People, Justin Tomlinson MP's statement that the Government has no appetite to legally recognise BSL as a minority language (British Deaf Association, 2015a), suggests that a UK-wide BSL Act is some way off.

The Struggle for Recognition

Deaf people's struggle for recognition of BSL officially began in the 1970s with the National Union of the Deaf challenging the status quo (Ladd, 2003), and continued when in 1982, the British Deaf Association (BDA) published a manifesto asking for BSL to be recognised, followed by the publication of the report, 'BSL – Britain's Fourth Language: The case for the official recognition for British Sign Language' in 1987 (Bryan, 2013). Between 1987 and 1999, the BSL campaign was centred around the then European Economic Community's support for the recognition of sign languages (Stiles, 2013) and the ECRML, which did not include sign languages, culminating in a series of marches for BSL organised by an autonomous and radical Deaf grassroots organisation, the Federation of Deaf People (FDP) (BDA, 2015b). On 27 June 1999, 4000 people marched for BSL through London; a summary of the aim of the march was headed:

> We demand that the British Government fully and unconditionally accept BSL as a bona fide language, native to this land, with full access through it for all who wish to use it. (FDP, 1999: 3)

Further BSL marches followed in the summer of 2000 and 2001 (Stiles, 2013), and BSL was finally 'recognised' as an official language in Britain on 18 March 2003 by the Department of Work and Pensions (DWP) (Gulliver, 2003). It is surmised that the 'recognition' had little impact because the Government merely worked through existing channels and contacts with voluntary organisations for deaf people, handing out a relatively small amount of funding, rather than negotiating and listening to Deaf people's own organisations. The FDP thus responded with further marches in 2003 in London and Bradford to show dissatisfaction with the 'recognition' funding, which had gone to organisations which 'have had very little involvement in our campaign till now' (FDP, 2003).

According to the FDP, the Deaf community wanted a BSL Act which would recognise BSL as an official language of the United Kingdom, to promote and facilitate the use of BSL as a first and natural language, to recognise the right of Deaf people to have comprehensive access to education, information, and other services through the medium of BSL and to set up a BSL board (FDP, 1999). It appears that accepting BSL as a full language actually means changing the attitudes of hearing people towards Deaf people as well as 'achieving a recognition of the rights and dignity of the whole Deaf community' (Gulliver, 2003: 19–20). The role of the FDP as a pressure group operating outside of traditional Deaf organisations was crucial in mobilising widespread support from young Deaf people, and from a much wider range of ethnic backgrounds (see De Meulder & Haesenne, Chapter 18, this volume, for a similar scenario in Belgium). The FDP disbanded in 2004 with little progress having been made in England, where the activism was strongest. In Scotland, the FDP hardly existed, but nevertheless legislative progress was made there first.

Scotland

The situation in Scotland is in stark contrast to that of England and the other devolved nations, which can partly explain why Scotland was first to make legislative progress for BSL: there has been a very close relationship between MSPs and constituents in the newly established Parliament since 1999, and a careful balancing of interests of different deaf and Deaf organisations led by an umbrella organisation, the Scottish Council on Deafness (SCoD). For the purpose of this chapter, organisations will be distinguished as either 'deaf' or 'Deaf', with the former referring to organisations that represent deaf, Deaf, deafblind, Deafblind, deafened and hard of hearing people (e.g. Action on Hearing Loss), and the latter representing Deaf BSL users (mainly the BDA, but in Scotland also Deaf Action).

SCoD has described the BSL (Scotland) Act 2015 as an enabling piece of legislation; an 'empty wardrobe waiting to be filled' (McDonald, 2015). It requires Scottish Ministers to promote, and facilitate the promotion of, the use and understanding of the language known as BSL (BSL (Scotland) Act, 2015: section 1(1)). To date, Scotland is the only nation within the UK to have legally recognised BSL; that is, imposed a legal obligation on public bodies to promote BSL as a language. This is a considerable step further than the 'recognition' of BSL in 2003 by the DWP.

Early meetings and a parliamentary debate

In the early days of the new Parliament being set up, representatives of the BDA, Murray and McWhinney, met with MSPs to discuss recognition of BSL (*British Deaf News*, 1999). Members of the Scottish Deaf community were regularly contacting their MSPs about the same issue, and MSPs provided BSL/English interpreters at constituency surgeries (Lawson, 2018). MSP Winnie Ewing, a prominent Scottish Nationalist, secured a debate about 'sign language' on 16 February 2000. The language of motion S1M-529 resulting from the debate was a mixture of different language attitudes: sign language was described as a 'communication tool', but the language of rights was prominent from the BDA's contribution and 'the importance and necessity of BSL by integrating signing into the plenary sessions of the Parliament' was agreed (*Journal of the Scottish Parliament*, 2000: 143). From the start of the new Scottish Parliament, then, BSL was an issue the MSPs recognised as important – alongside a heightened awareness of other Scottish languages such as Gaelic, Scots and Doric, all discussed during the first session (Lo Bianco, 2017).

Tactical alliances

Deaf community activist and manager Lilian Lawson played a key role in managing the wide range of organisations of and for deaf people in Scotland as SCoD Director between 2000 and 2013. From 2011 onwards, SCoD chaired and administered the British Sign Language and Linguistic Access Working Group (BSLLAWG), which involved a tactical alliance of different Deaf organisations (SCoD, Scottish Association of Sign Language Interpreters, Deaf Action, BDA and others) and charities for deaf people (such as Action on Hearing Loss and the National Deaf Children's Society).

The tactical alliance with the charities for deaf people was crucial: they were still involved in discussions with the Government's Equality Unit. They had a chance to receive funding in relation to the groups they mainly focused on, deafened people or parents of deaf children, for example. The BSLLAWG allowed all the stakeholders to talk openly about their plans, so that there was a more orderly and transparent approach to dealings with Ministers and MSPs for funding particular projects.

Proposal for the first BSL Bill

A Labour MSP, Cathie Craigie, had supported language rights for BSL users since the 2000 debate and also chaired the Cross-Parliamentary Group on Deafness. This group was another forum where different deaf and Deaf organisations met regularly with MSPs. Lawson acted as the secretariat for this group. As De Meulder (2015) outlines, it was SCoD's briefing which encouraged Craigie to put forward a Private Member's Bill about the recognition of BSL. The consultation about the proposed legislation (Craigie, 2010) asked four questions, which were:

- Do you believe BSL should be granted legal recognition and protection by the Scottish Government?
- Do you think Deaf people in Scotland should be able to access information and services in BSL?
- How can the number of people able to use BSL be increased?
- Do you agree that the parents, grandparents, siblings and other family members of deaf babies and toddlers in Scotland should have the opportunity to access free BSL classes in order to be able to communicate effectively with the child?

Consultation

In order to share the power to influence policy, arrangements have been made to allow the Scottish Parliament and interested individuals and groups to be consulted about proposed legislation before it becomes a Bill. This pre-legislative consultation is designed to be open and participatory, allowing access to the decision-making process. This system also prevents the Scottish Government from being selective about which pressure groups have an opportunity to be consulted before policy is devised (Scottish Parliament, no date).

In 2010, the Government did not have a mechanism to consult with Deaf people, so it used the Cross-Party Group on Deafness to draw up consultation questions. Officially, Cathie Craigie received 427 responses, which were overwhelmingly in favour of the legislation. However, there were an additional 55 responses from Deaf people in BSL on video that were not translated, summarised or analysed. Nevertheless, the written submissions were heartfelt. This submission is typical, focusing on families' rights to learn a language to communicate with a deaf child:

> Why should you have to pay to communicate with your son? ... these classes should not be only for introduction to level 1 but they should go on right up to full interpretation level, as level 1 or 2 is only good enough up to a child of 7 years old, more detailed signing skills are required if we are to educate our kids as they grow older. I mean how can you educate a child on safe sex if you and them only have a basic level of BSL? Talking to them like babies? NO, the indigenous sign language should be taught to a very high level and stop short changing my son!. (Scottish Parliament Information Centre (SPICe), 2010: Respondent 208)

From this first consultation, Deaf community responses and hearing parents of deaf children put educational objectives as a very high priority for a BSL Bill. Cathie Craigie lost her seat in the 2011 Parliamentary elections, although Mark Griffin became Labour MSP in that same election and took up the mantle regarding the BSL Bill. As the youngest MSP in the Parliament, it was a huge task to take forward a Private Members' Bill.

Importantly, two of his great-grandparents had been deafblind (Freeman, 2015); this gave him a personal insight into a group who have so far been neglected in sign language legislation.

The second attempt at the BSL (Scotland) Bill was introduced in the Scottish Parliament on 29 October 2014, and thus a second consultation was launched in order to obtain stakeholders' views of the Bill itself. The Parliamentary Non-Government Bills Unit (NGBU) seems to have advised Cathie Craigie that the first draft Bill was straying onto reserved matters, that is, the Equality Act 2010. The NGBU advised Griffin not to include mention of education in his Private Members' Bill. So it was, that the draft Bill put forward was largely about plans, not content or detailed suggestions for change.

The second consultation ran between July and October 2012 and received 222 responses: 49 from organisations, 172 from individuals and a petition with 937 signatures (MacPherson, 2015). These submissions can be classified into three groups. First, public bodies who were against the Bill, but did not overtly state this; they regarded the Equality Act 2010 as sufficient and argued a BSL Act was not required; for example, the Scottish Qualification Authority. This group often commented on the very small number of BSL users. Secondly, deaf organisations that generally showed support for the Bill, and sometimes conveyed that they had consulted with their BSL 'service users', Action on Hearing Loss for example. Thirdly, individuals, both deaf and hearing, who had a personal interest in the Bill.

Amendments and Parliamentary engagement with BSL users

The most successful form of interaction during Stage 2 of the passage of the Bill was the 'British Sign Language (Scotland) Bill' Facebook group created by the Scottish Government in November 2014. The Government set up the group so that Deaf community members could submit evidence by uploading video clips, as Deaf people often had the technological skills to upload their views in BSL. Their assets – technological literacy – could be used to campaign, communicate and lobby. The Scottish Parliament embraced this idea and took notice of the messages. This approach was one of the highlights of the BSL recognition campaign in Scotland.

The Scottish Parliament also published various key documents in BSL, including their call for views and other briefing material. These introduced Deaf people to parliamentary processes and the details of the Bill in BSL videos, although viewing statistics remained low (Scottish Parliament, 2015e). Also, the parliamentary evidence sessions were broadcast with live BSL/English interpretation, as well as in Gaelic on one occasion. They received 95 written submissions and 39 BSL videos in response to the call for views on the Bill as it was going through Parliament. The evidence submitted in BSL via the Facebook group (332 video clips) was translated and summarised (BSL Bill Facebook Group, 2014). The Scottish Parliament also held two fact-finding visits in Falkirk and Edinburgh to understand the challenges experienced by Deaf people, discuss the importance and benefits of using BSL, and consider what impact the BSL Bill might have (Scottish Parliament Education and Culture Committee, 2015). All this showed an increasing commitment to listening to Deaf people, a marginalised group unfamiliar with parliamentary processes. Furthermore, the Scottish Parliament Information Centre (SPICe) briefing (MacPherson, 2015) summarised the widespread belief from the consultation that the Gaelic Language (Scotland) Act 2005 would be a useful model for a BSL Bill. Yet the communication channels between stakeholders and the Scottish Parliament tended to be unilateral. There were a few critical posts of the campaign for the Bill, particularly in relation to the organisations involved, on the Facebook group, and as it was moderated by the Scottish Parliament, some of these were removed. Debate on the Bill was therefore somewhat suppressed and not all views were openly discussed. This meant that a much-needed debate regarding the aim and content of the Bill among the various members of the Deaf community, as well as with the Scottish Parliament and the voluntary organisations, hardly happened in a public space (see also De Meulder, 2017).

An additional issue was the fact that most of the Deaf individuals who were ardent supporters of the BSL Bill were not aware of the intricacies of the legislative process for Scottish Parliament bills, particularly as they were not experienced lobbyists. In particular, it was not clear how amendments to the Bill could be put forward. Deaf individuals were at a disadvantage compared to deaf organisations in Scotland who had experienced lobbyists and policy officers working for them, and thus had access to MSPs to suggest amendments to the Bill. In particular, Deafblind Scotland and the National Deaf Children's Society (NDCS) suggested amendments that had a positive effect on the Bill, such as the inclusion of the tactile form of BSL used and understood by some deafblind people, and free sign language classes for the families of deaf children (BSL (Scotland) Bill, 2015b).

The development of the Bill

The purpose of the BSL (Scotland) Bill was to promote the use of BSL, including making provision for the preparation and publication of a BSL National Plan for Scotland and requiring certain public authorities to prepare and publish their own BSL plans in connection with the exercise of their functions. It also required these plans to be reviewed and updated at specified times in the political cycle (MacPherson, 2015).

From the beginning, the Bill did not have a board of fluent BSL users in the wording of any draft. This is in stark contrast to the respect shown to the Bòrd na Gàidhlig in the earlier Gaelic Language (Scotland) Act 2005. This was a disappointment to some commentators on the Facebook group, but the existence and operation of the Gaelic Board was not widely known about.

There was an indication as the Bill went through of who might be consulted about the language once the Act was passed:

> The persons consulted are to be those who, the Scottish Ministers consider, are likely to be directly affected by the National Plan or otherwise to have an interest in that plan and in particular are to include—
>
> (a)   persons who use British Sign Language, and
> (b)   persons who represent users of British Sign Language.

(BSL Bill, 2014: section 1(6))

The Government's continuing dependent view of Deaf people is illustrated by this statement; it would be inconceivable that the representatives of Gaelic speakers would be consulted alongside Gaelic speakers in a Gaelic Language National Plan. Even though the Government had supported Mark Griffin's Private Member's Bill, effectively making it into a Government Act, the pressure from the third sector organisations working for deaf groups is still evident. Some of the group in (b) above may be parents of deaf children; others were organisations which wanted to ensure they still had a say in all affairs concerning their client group. In May 2015, the Education and Culture Committee, overseen by the Scottish Government Equality Unit, shortened the list of public bodies that had to create individual BSL plans; public bodies that were omitted from the list were largely the ones which had complained at Stage 2 of the consultation and included national education bodies such as the Scottish Qualifications Authority, national health bodies such as NHS 24 and the Cochlear Implant Centre, criminal justice bodies such as Police Scotland, and emergency services such as Scottish Fire and Rescue (Scottish Parliament Education and Culture Committee, 2015).

The organisations remaining on the list by the time the Bill reached the end of Stage 2 included all 32 local authorities, 14 National Health Service health boards, all colleges and universities, and 11 other public bodies. This is a considerable achievement; these authorities are required to consult with BSL users and create BSL plans in the year after the publication of the first National Plan in October 2017 (Scottish Government, 2017).

A particular grey area was the National Plan; there were differences of opinion expressed in Education and Culture Committee meetings, the Scottish Government's responses and the final version of the Bill itself about the scope of the National Plan. The Education and Culture Committee discussed the National Plan and Minister Alasdair Allan explained that the content would be informed by the eight priorities set out by the BDA (Scottish Parliament, 2015a). This was heartening, but these priorities did not appear in the Act. The nearest the Act comes to discussion of actual content of the BSL plans is when it points to 'the use and understanding of British Sign Language within their areas of responsibility' (BSL (Scotland) Act, 2015: section 1(3)(b)).

Celebration, but concerns about implementation of the Act

The public galleries above the debating chamber were full of Deaf people and supporters on 17 September 2015, when the BSL (Scotland) Act was passed.

The BSL (Scotland) Act 2015 is a significant leap forward for the Deaf community in Scotland, but there are a number of areas of concern. The implementation of the Act fell to civil servants in the Government's Equality Unit, which outsourced it to a consortium of five organisations: SCoD, Deaf Action, the (NDCS), Deafblind Scotland and the BDA. Only the BDA is a Deaf organisation; most of the others are deaf organisations with a strong charity approach that exist to raise money for deaf children or people, not to directly represent them.

The Equality Unit also proposed a National Advisory Group (NAG), not mentioned in the BSL (Scotland) Act 2015, should be established under the Minister responsible for the implementation of the Act, the Minister for Childcare and Early Years. The NAG was designed to support the Government with establishing a starting point for the first National Plan, and was composed of 10 Deaf BSL users, a parent of a deaf child and 10 national bodies. Most of the hearing representatives did not know BSL, but many started to learn as they began to work on the NAG.

The decision was also made to exclude anyone from applying to join the NAG if they were employed by one of the consortium organisations, including part-time workers. The justification for this was that they may have a conflict of interest with their work. This was a blow to the BDA and Deaf Action because they employed many Deaf workers; the BDA's part-time outreach workers had been by and large the political leadership of the BSL campaign.

The result was that the Deaf BSL users nominated and then selected by the Scottish Civil Service for the NAG were mostly starting from a position of little political experience about language rights or campaigning. On the other hand, the representatives of national bodies on the NAG (such as the NHS and Police Scotland) have considerable political and leadership experience (Scottish Government, no date).

There are similarities, then, with other advisory boards on sign languages internationally such as New Zealand or Belgium, where up till now, most of the Deaf members generally had little political experience and the hearing members had considerably more social and political capital (De Meulder & Haesenne, this volume; McKee & Manning, this volume; Office for Disability Issues, 2014).

Also, in contrast to other sign language boards such as those in Belgium and New Zealand where members are usually appointed for three of four years, the Scottish NAG has a short life expectancy of only two years, so will not be in existence to review the first National Plan in six years' time (Public Appointments, 2016). As the NAG does not appear in the BSL (Scotland) Act 2015, we do not know if it is a group which will ever be seen again. The Act, therefore, allows a great deal of implementation to be determined by policy advisers.

What does the BSL Act say?

The BSL (Scotland) Act 2015 aims to promote the use and understanding of BSL (section 1(1)) and requires the Scottish executive to prepare and publish a national plan in relation to BSL (section 1(2)), which is expected to set out the Scottish Government's BSL strategy (section 1(3)(a)). It also requires public authorities, defined as 'any body or office-holder (other than the Scottish Ministers themselves) which is a Scottish public authority with mixed functions or no reserved functions' (section 7) to prepare and publish their own BSL plans (section 2(1)), setting out measures to be taken in relation to the use of BSL (section 2(2)(a)).

The first National Plan by the Scottish Ministers was published on 22 October 2017, pursuant to section 1(5) of the Act. The first draft of the consultation paper – published in March 2017 – proposed 10 long-term goals. These included making information and services across the Scottish public sector accessible to BSL users, giving families and carers with Deaf children information about BSL and Deaf culture, and offering support to learn to sign with their child. Children who use BSL will be encouraged to reach their full potential at school and be supported in their transition to post-school education. BSL users will be supported to develop the skills required to become valued members of the Scottish workforce and have equal access to employment opportunities. They will also be given access to information and services to live active, healthy lives, and access to public transport, Scotland's culture, leisure, sports and art facilities, and civil and criminal justice systems. Finally, BSL users will be afforded the opportunity to represent the people of Scotland as elected politicians at national and local level (Scottish Government, 2017).

The future of the Act

Local plans from local authorities have been drawn up in 2018 following the publication of the National Plan. As Walsh and McLeod (2008) have noted in relation to Gaelic Language Plans for Scotland and Ireland (2008), if language planning legislation is to make a real difference, then the capacity of more people to perform tasks confidently in the minority language must be an important target. If local authorities collaborate, then, it may be possible for them to set up a sign intensive environment for early years, so that parents and children can acquire BSL by being surrounded by the language (BDA, 2015c). This would be easier to implement in the central belt of Scotland with denser population concentrations, but would be much harder to set up in the Highlands and Islands and rural authorities. Currently, children attending Gaelic schools can receive taxi transport to the schools even across local authority boundaries. Deaf children are rarely allowed this, because the default position, enshrined in law for children with disabilities, is to attend the local mainstream school (Scottish Executive, 2002; Standards in Scotland's Schools etc. Act 2000). It is possible that we will see BSL schools in the future, attended by both deaf and hearing children, learning through the medium of BSL or bilingualism with BSL and English. More work, however, needs to be done to convince members of the public that bilingualism in BSL is as valuable cognitively and academically as bilingualism is in the higher status Gaelic or European languages (Phipps & Fassetta, 2015).

It is hoped that the Scottish Civil Service will change its advice to local authorities about the minimum level of BSL skill for teachers of deaf children. It is currently set at Level 1, which can be gained after 50 hours of study. A recent survey carried out by the Scottish Sensory Centre for the Scottish Government showed that 58% of teachers of deaf children were working with signing children, yet only 9% had Level 3 or above (Ravenscroft & Wazny, 2017). There is clearly a skills gap. However, civil servants within the Education and Culture Department of the Scottish Civil Service are not currently inclined to amend the Level 1 BSL minimum requirement for teachers (Scottish Government, 2007) and have shown no concern regarding the numbers of support staff acting as unqualified interpreters with deaf children. To do more would have significant financial implications, and the underlying consensus for the passing of the BSL (Scotland) Act 2015 within Parliament and the Scottish National Party Government was that it would incur little or no financial cost, except for the cost of producing the plans.

These plans may provide what we hope for from the BSL (Scotland) Act 2015, particularly if they emulate the model produced by the Gaelic Language (Scotland) Act 2005. However, since the BSL (Scotland) Act 2015 was passed there have been severe public sector cuts. As Mark Griffin MSP suggested when he proposed the Bill, the amount spent in future will depend on the Scottish Government of the day, and that the Bill was a starting point (Scottish Parliament, 2015). In the longer term, the Scottish Parliament could amend future Education Acts to make express provision for BSL in education, or establish a BSL Board, akin to the Bòrd na Gàidhlig (particularly as the NAG is not mentioned in the BSL (Scotland) Act 2015), following in the footsteps of the Gaelic language movement.

Conclusion: Where Next for BSL Recognition in the UK?

In Scotland, we have argued, the role of SCoD when led by a Deaf campaigner, Lilian Lawson, was instrumental in working with the Scottish Government, ensuring that they understood the linguistic and human rights issues put forward by the Deaf community. The other Deaf-led organisation in Scotland is the BDA, which the Government's Equality Unit acknowledged to be crucial for gathering views from the wider Deaf community. Other charities involved in the consortium (the NDCS,

Deafblind Scotland and Deaf Action) played different roles depending on how many Deaf leaders were within these organisations. Some of these organisations have made important gains by their involvement in the process: Deafblind Scotland highlighted the importance of hands-on signing, and the NDCS secured more funding for hearing parents to learn BSL. In general, the consortium has been an effective way for the Scottish Government to manage the implementation of the BSL (Scotland) Act 2015, although it has not given the respect to Deaf-led organisations which it offered to Gaelic speaking leaders on the Bòrd na Gàidhlig. It is clear from the Scottish example that the ambiguous influence of charities for deaf people is instrumental in the degree of progress that can be made towards legal recognition of sign languages.

Note

(1) According to Ladd (2003), the lowercase 'deaf' refers to those for whom deafness is primarily an audiological experience, whereas 'Deaf' refers to those born Deaf or deafened in early (sometimes late) childhood, for whom the sign languages, communities and cultures of the Deaf collective represents their primary experience and allegiance, many of whom perceive their experience as essentially akin to other language minorities. As the focus of this chapter is on the recognition of BSL as a language, it is appropriate to refer to the Deaf people involved in the process of recognition as such.

References

Batterbury, S.C.E. (2012) Language justice for sign language peoples: The UN Convention on the Rights of Persons with Disabilities. *Language Policy* 11, 253–272.

Borthwick K. (2018) Support unsung heroes: Community-based language learning and teaching. In M. Kelly (ed.) *Languages after Brexit* (pp. 185–194). Cham: Palgrave Macmillan.

British Deaf Association (2015a) Government reluctant to legally recognise BSL, says disability minister, 10 July. See https://www.bda.org.uk/news/government-reluctant-to-legally-recognise-bsl-says-disability-minister (accessed 4 May 2016).

British Deaf Association (2015b) Campaigning for a better life. See https://bda.org.uk/campaigning-for-a-better-life/ (accessed 30 September 2017).

British Deaf Association (2015c) Submission to the Scottish Parliament: Attainment of school pupils with a sensory impairment. See http://www.parliament.scot/S4_EducationandCultureCommittee/Attainment%20-%20sensory%20impairments/BritishDeafAssociationScotland.pdf (accessed 13 June 2017).

British Deaf News (1999) British Deaf Association calls on Scottish Parliament to recognise sign language, 7 December.

British Sign Language (Scotland) Bill Facebook group (2014) See https://www.facebook.com/groups/800527046656790/ (accessed 11 July 2018).

British Sign Language (Scotland) Bill (2014) See http://www.parliament.scot/largePDFfiles/SPPB220.pdf (accessed 29 January 2019).

British Sign Language (Scotland) Bill (2015) See http://www.parliament.scot/S4_Bills/British%20Sign%20Language%20(Scotland)%20Bill/b55s4-stage2-ml.pdf (accessed 1 August 2018).

British Sign Language (Scotland) Act (2015) See http://www.legislation.gov.uk/asp/2015/11/contents/enacted (accessed 11 July 2018).

Bryan, A. (2013) 'BSL recognition timeline: A work in progress', *Grumpy Old Deafies*, blog post, 18 March. See http://www.grumpyoldeafies.com/2013/03/bsl_recognition_timeline.html (accessed 7 September 2017).

Council of Europe (1992) European Charter for Regional and Minority Languages. Treaty No. 148. See http://conventions.coe.int/treaty/en/Treaties/Html/148.htm (accessed 24 January 2019).

Craigie, C. (2010) Consultation on BSL Bill. See http://www.parliament.scot/S3_MembersBills/Draft%20proposals/20100712ProofedconsultationBSLBill.pdf (accessed 11 July 2018).

De Meulder, M. (2015) A barking dog that never bites?: The British Sign Language (Scotland) Bill. *Sign Language Studies* 15 (4), 446–472.

De Meulder, M. (2017) The influence of deaf people's dual category status on sign language planning: The British Sign Language (Scotland) Act (2015). *Current Issues in Language Planning*, 1–18.

Department of Culture, Arts and Leisure (2016) *Sign Language Framework Northern Ireland*. See https://bit.ly/2IGVXDO (accessed 11 July 2018).

Dunbar, R. (2005) The Gaelic Language (Scotland) Act 2005, *Edinburgh Law Review* 9, 466–479.

Equality Act (2010) See https://www.legislation.gov.uk/ukpga/2010/15/contents (accessed 11 July 2018).

Federation of Deaf People (1999) Summary of the Rationale for the March on Sunday 27 June 1999: Demanding Recognition of Sign Language, *The Voice*, September.

Federation of Deaf People (2003) FDP Continues to press for BSL rights. See https://groups.yahoo.com/neo/groups/Bioethics/conversations/topics/7141 (accessed 24 September 2017).

Freeman, T. (2015) Sign language given formal status in Scotland. *Holyrood Magazine*, 18 September. See https://www.holyrood.com/articles/news/sign-language-given-formal-status-scotland (accessed 11 July 2018).

Gaelic Language (Scotland) Act (2005) See http://bit.ly/2sHSGQo (accessed 18 June 2017).

Gulliver, M. (2003) BSL OURS: Proposing a concept of ownership. Master's thesis, University of Bristol.

House of Lords Select Committee on the Equality Act 2010 and Disability (2016) *The Equality Act 2010: The Impact on Disabled* People. HL Paper 117. London: HMSO.

Journal of the Scottish Parliament (2000) 1 (1), p. 139, SIMD 529 Winnie Ewing. See http://www.parliament.scot/Journal/JSP1999to2000.pdf (accessed 11 July 2018).

Krausneker, V. (2003) Has something changed? Sign Languages in Europe: The case of minorised minority languages. *Deaf Worlds: International Journal of Deaf Studies* 19 (2). 33–48.

Ladd, P. (2003) *Understanding Deaf Culture*. Clevedon: Multilingual Matters.

Lawson, L. (2018) Discussion with chapter writing group, 25 June, Scottish Sensory Centre.

Lo Bianco, J. (2017) Policy activity for heritage languages: Connections with representation and citizenship. In D. Brinton, O. Kagan and S. Bauckus (eds) (2008) *Heritage Language: A New Field Emerging* (pp. 53–70). Abingdon: Routledge.

MacPherson, S. (2015) British Sign Language (Scotland) Bill: SPICe briefing. See http://www.parliament.scot/ResearchBriefingsAndFactsheets/S4/SB_15-05_British_Sign_Language_Scotland_Bill.pdf (accessed 11 July 2018).

McDonald, J. (2015) Verbal comment at BDA event in Glasgow, 12 January.

Nagy, N. (2013) Policies and legislation on autochthonous languages in the United Kingdom. *Studia Iuridica Auctoritate Universitatis Pecs* 151, 129–150.

Office for Disability Issues (2014) Promotion and maintenance of New Zealand Sign Language. See https://www.odi.govt.nz/assets/NZSL/documents-nzsl/pdf-word-cabinet-paper-nzsl-board-may-2014.pdf (accessed 29 January 2019).

Phipps, A. and Fassetta, G. (2015) A critical analysis of language policy in Scotland. *European Journal of Language Policy* 7 (1) 5–27.

Public Appointments (2016) Scottish Government announces plans to recruit Deaf BSL users to the British Sign Language National Advisory Group. See https://applications. appointed-for-scotland.org/pages/job_search_view.aspx?jobId=988 (accessed 17 June 2017).

Ravenscroft, J. and Wazny, K. (2017) The Qualification of Teachers of pupils with visual impairment, or pupils with hearing impairment or pupils with multi-sensory impairment (vision and hearing impairment). Scottish Sensory Centre. See http://www.ssc. education.ed.ac.uk/research/sg_teachers_sensory_impairment.pdf (accessed 11 July 2018).

Scottish Executive (2002) Guidance on presumption of mainstream education. See http:// www.gov.scot/Resource/Doc/46922/0024040.pdf (accessed 13 June 2016).

Scottish Government (2007) Competences for teachers of children and young persons who are hearing impaired, or visually impaired, or both hearing and visually impaired. See http://www.gov.scot/Publications/2007/01/29163203/3 (accessed 13 June 2016).

Scottish Government (2017) Consultation on the British Sign Language (BSL) National Plan. See https://consult.scotland.gov.uk/equality-unit/bsl-national-plan/ (accessed 13 June 2016).

Scottish Parliament (2015) SPICe Briefing: British Sign Language (Scotland) Bill. http:// www.parliament.scot/ResearchBriefingsAndFactsheets/S4/SB_15-05_British_Sign_ Language_Scotland_Bill.pdf (accessed 18 June 2017).

Scottish Parliament Education and Culture Committee (2015) Stage 1 Report on the BSL (Scotland) Bill 4 (4) SP Paper 711.

Seidlhofer, B. (2011) *Understanding English as a Lingua Franca*. Oxford: Oxford University Press.

SPICe (2010) BSL First round of consultations. Scottish Parliament.

Standards in Scotland's Schools etc. Act (2000) See http://www.legislation.gov.uk/ asp/2000/6/contents (accessed 13 June 2016).

Stiles, D. (2013) Official recognition of British Sign Language 1987–2003. *UCL and Action on Hearing Loss Libraries*, blog post, 13 November. See https://blogs.ucl.ac.uk/ library-rnid/2013/11/13/official-recognition-of-british-sign-language-1987-2003/ (accessed 24 September 2017).

Scottish Government (no date) British Sign Language. See https://www.gov.scot/policies/ languages/british-sign-language/ (accessed 29 January 2019).

Scottish Parliament (no date) The legislative process: Stages of a bill. http://www.parliament.scot/visitandlearn/Education/18641.aspx (accessed 28 September 2017).

Walsh, J. and McLeod, W. (2008) An overcoat wrapped around an invisible man? Language legislation and language revitalisation in Ireland and Scotland. *Language Policy* 7, 21–46.

Part 2

Implicit Legal Recognition

5 A Roof without Foundation: Shifts in the Legal and Practical Status of Turkish Sign Language (TİD) Since 2005

Deniz İlkbaşaran and Okan Kubus

Introduction

Academic interest in Turkish Sign Language (TİD) began in the early 2000s, decades after sign language research began in North America and Western Europe. Since then, there have been many publications on TİD and language practices of deaf people in Turkey, as seen in Engin Arık's online TİD bibliography[1] and edited volumes (Arık, 2013, 2016), but academic work directly analyzing TİD planning and policy are limited. Building on our previous work (Kubus, 2010; Kubus *et al.*, 2016), in this chapter we provide a critical overview of TİD language planning, situating key events in national academic and sociopolitical dynamics, and transnational discourse on disability, Deaf and sign language rights. The guiding questions that motivate this chapter are the following: (1) What are the key factors and events in the legal recognition of TİD? (2) How do key stakeholders involved in TİD planning and policy-making for the past decade evaluate their involvement, achievements and the challenges faced in this process? (3) To what extent were Turkish deaf people and the Deaf community included in these initiatives?

In order to address these questions, we have conducted interviews with key figures participating in the legal recognition process of TİD in late 2017, most of whom were heads of leading Deaf rights NGOs in Turkey. In our synthesis of key events leading to, during and after the legal recognition of TİD, we bring together their narratives. We also benefited from our collaboration as a Deaf and hearing scholar from Turkey; we each conducted interviews in our native languages (Kubus is a native signer of TİD and İlkbaşaran is a native speaker of Turkish). This multimodal, multilingual approach augmented the quality of our interviews and allowed us to tap into different levels of information, including the writing of this chapter. Although only a small section of our interviews have made it into this chapter, we are glad to have captured a critical Deaf cultural, institutional, political and historical period in Turkey. We have also acquired and analyzed original documents: copies of laws and legislations, reports of Turkish government agencies that are addressed to the UN regarding the Convention on the Rights of People with Disabilities (CRPD, 2006), surveys on people with disabilities in Turkey, and news reports of events concerning TİD planning. These documents helped us anchor the content of our interview narratives, and at times served as a tool for fact checking.

In our analyses, we use Reagan's (2010) framework on sign language planning to organize aspects of TİD planning in Turkey, while maintaining a critical political economy perspective in our review of implementations, particularly in line with the commodification of language framework elaborated by Heller (2010) and Heller and Duchêne (2012). The chapter begins with an overview of language laws and disability rights in Turkey. We then explain our theoretical framework regarding sign language planning and policy, outlining key areas of concern. The section on TİD planning is organized under three sections: work leading to the Disabilities Act of 2005; the content of law and legislation on TİD; and outcomes and challenges faced in the implementation phase. The chapter ends with a summary of lessons learned based on our research and analysis.

Turkey: Language Policies and TİD

Turkey as a nation-state and minority language rights

As in many other modern nation-states, language policies in Turkey historically have been shaped by nationalism. There are 39 living spoken languages currently used in Turkey: Turkish (87%) is the most widely spoken language with the highest percentage of daily users, followed by Kurdish (10%), Arabic (1%) and Zazaki (1%) (KONDA, 2006). As stated in the Constitution of the Republic of Turkey (1982), Turkish is the only official language of the Turkish Republic that is used in official correspondences and State services (Article 3). Furthermore, the Constitution limits the use of languages at educational institutions as follows:

> No language other than Turkish shall be taught as a mother tongue to Turkish citizens at any institution of education. Foreign languages to be taught in institutions of education and the rules to be followed by schools conducting education in a foreign language shall be determined by law. The provisions of international treaties are reserved. (Constitution of the Republic of Turkey (1982), Article 42)

Turkey became a candidate for the European Union (EU) in 1999, and was officially considered for full membership in 2005. The EU's emphasis on ethnic, linguistic and cultural diversity was key in the government's motivation to soften traditionally monolingual national policies (Sadoğlu, 2017: 62). The ban on the use of 'prohibited languages' in the dissemination of ideas and broadcasting was lifted in 2001 (Act No. 4709), by removing Articles 26 and 28 of the Constitution.

With regards to education, traditionally used minority languages in Turkey gained the right to be offered as foreign language courses in 2003 (Act No. 2923, amended by Act No. 4963). By 2009–2010, academic investigation of minority languages and their culture were made possible at institutes within university settings. Otherwise, Article 42 of the Constitution mentioned above holds, in that children born to minority language speakers do not receive education services in their home language.

Disability laws, organization and rights in Turkey

The most powerful disability rights organization with continued official relations with the Turkish State is the Disability Confederation of Turkey. Founded in 1986, the Confederation represents five member Federations for each disability group: deaf and blind people, and people with orthopedic disabilities, learning disabilities and cerebral palsy.

Based in Istanbul, the Turkish National Federation of the Deaf ('the Federation') was founded in 1960, is a member of the World Federation of the Deaf (WFD), and a participant in international assemblies among Balkan, Middle Eastern and North African countries. According to Ercüment Tanrıverdi (pers. comm., 2017), the President of the Federation since 2006, presidents have traditionally been either hard of hearing (YARIM in TİD, meaning HALF) or had become deaf later in life; however, there were two former hearing presidents with deaf relatives, like himself, who had deaf parents.

In July 2005, the Turkish government passed the Disabilities Act (the DA) (Act No. 5378). The DA includes the first mention of TİD in Turkish law and was the initial step in the status planning of TİD. Sign language is only mentioned in Articles 15 and 30 (see section 'Content of laws and legislations regarding TİD' below). In 2013, the term 'handicapped' (özürlü) was replaced by 'disabled' (engelli) in the DA and in 94 other laws concerning persons with disabilities. Similarly, in 2014, the Federation replaced the word 'hearing impaired' (işitme engelli) in its title with the word 'deaf' (sağır).

Turkey ratified the UN CRPD in 2009. In addition to agreeing to the terms of this Convention, there is also an indirect Constitutional guarantee in Turkey regarding its content, as 'International agreements duly put into effect have the force of law' (Article 90).

Theoretical and Analytical Frameworks

In our work, we use the comprehensive model of sign language planning and policy (SLPP) that Reagan (2001, 2010) arrived at building on earlier models (Hornberger, 2006), consisting of four interdependent categories: status, corpus, acquisition and attitude planning. Although this chapter is anchored in the status planning of TİD, these laws and legislations regulate how TİD is to be taught and circulated in Turkish daily life.

Language is at once a tool, a dynamic archive of cultural heritage, a form of capital and a governing device. In that sense, we believe that the political economy around language policies play a significant role in how legal commitments are shaped and actualized in social life. Since language policies regulate the distribution of services, resources and benefits across people, legitimizing some form of cultural and linguistic heritage over others, policies are closely tied to power and capital. The legal recognition of a minority language shifts linguistic value hierarchies, increasing its cultural capital by reframing it as a desired commodity in social life (Heller & Duchêne, 2012). This creates new economies around the newly commodified language, and opens up possibilities for it to be appropriated by anyone who sees this as an opportunity for profit. While policies capture intentions, their implementation materializes in complex sociopolitical landscapes, and may lead to unintended consequences for communities a policy appears to serve. All of these apply to sign language policies as well, although interactions between SLPP and political economy are relatively underexplored (Ricento, 2015). Thus we are also interested in exploring how the emergence of TİD as a new currency interacts with individual, institutional and national economies, and following avenues of profit – monetary, political or social.

Turkish Sign Language Planning and Policy

We divided this section into three chronological parts (see the timeline of key events presented in Figure 5.1). The first part outlines work leading to the first legal mention of TİD in the DA of 2005. The second part provides the content of TİD related Legislations and how they were modified over the years. Finally, we offer a description and analysis of how these policies were implemented, using Reagan's model and through a political economy lens.

Work leading to the Disabilities Act of 2005

Active negotiations between the Federation and the Turkish State date back to the late 1990s when the President of the Federation, Erol Efrand (1998–2001), joined forces with the Disability Confederation. Efrand had

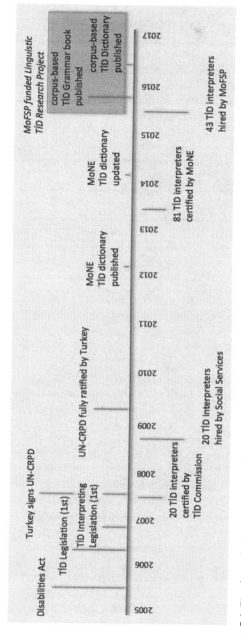

Figure 5.1 Timeline of official events in TİD language planning and policy

regular meetings in Ankara with other disability group leaders and government officials (Tanrıverdi, pers. comm., 2017). Between 2000 and 2004, there were a series of events that built on Efrand's efforts to raise awareness of TİD among government agencies and the public.

The first event was the involvement of linguists in TİD work. While Ulrike Zeshan (hearing) arrived in Turkey to study TİD (Zeshan, 2002, 2003), Aslı Özyürek (hearing) had a Turkish Academy of Sciences funded research project on the structure of TİD (2001–2004). Hasan Dikyuva and other Deaf signers were involved as research assistants and informants in both of these projects. Tanrıverdi states that the Federation benefited from Zeshan and Dikyuva's presence during their meetings with government agencies in raising awareness on TİD. In 2003, the first public assembly on TİD took place during the opening ceremony for the TİD unit located at İstanbul Metropolitan Municipality's Center for the Handicapped. Attending the assembly was Robert Mobley, a Deaf professor and director of the Center for Global Education at Gallaudet University, invited by the Federation President Yunus Bayraktar (2001–2004). During this assembly, Mobley, Zeshan and Özyürek gave talks on aspects of sign language and its acquisition by deaf people. Several administrators of this Center later took on significant roles in government positions concerned with disabilities.

Another important factor was the uptake of disability issues in Turkish political discourse. The Justice and Development Party foregrounded disability rights during their election campaigns, and these remained on their agenda after they came to power in 2002. In addition to compliance with accessibility standards of the EU and UN, people with disabilities and their network also represented a significant electoral body in Turkey. Moreover, Lokman Ayva, a blind rights activist, was elected as a deputy in the Turkish parliament. Ayva's presence in the parliament not only increased the visibility of people with disabilities in Turkish politics, but also created a more direct path for disability rights organizations to access the government, paving the way to the initial work for the Disabilities Act of 2005.

The Disability Confederation was the leading organization in the drafting of the DA, with input from different disability groups. Members of the Deaf rights working group for the DA consisted of board members of the Federation during the term of Bilal Cansu (2004–2006). Arif Hasbal, deafened later in life, led the drafting of the document submitted to the Confederation. While Hasbal drafted a long list of items on Deaf rights, only two of them made it to the DA. Compared to other disability groups, the Federation had limited agency during their coalition with the Confederation. Blind rights were significantly foregrounded during the drafting and finalization of articles, likely due to Ayva being in the parliament. Another reason why Deaf rights issues were not as prominent in the final version of the DA could be that other disability groups had problems that were easier for the public to understand, and their proposed accommodations were relatively simpler to provide (i.e. adding ramps, tactile pavements, braille) (Tanrıverdi, pers. comm., 2017).

Content of laws and legislations regarding TİD

The Disabilities Act of 2005

Article 15, paragraph 4 of the DA directly mentions TİD for the first time in Turkish law:[2]

> Turkish Sign Language system is to be created by the Turkish Language Association ['TLA'] in order to provide the education and communication of the hearing disabled. The methods and principles of the works towards creating and implementing this system are to be determined by the regulation to be issued jointly by the Ministry of National Education ['MoNE'], General Directorate for the Social Services and Children Protection ['Social Services'] and the Administration on Disabled People ['Administration'], coordinated by the Turkish Language Institution.

In addition, Article 30 of the DA amends the Law on Social Services (Act No. 2828), being the very first mention of sign language interpreting in Turkish law. Specifically, it designates government personnel who are fluent in sign language (TİD not specified) to interpret for the 'hearing and speaking handicapped' as needed, and that courses will be developed for the personnel to learn sign language.

TİD Legislation of 2006

'The legislation on the identification of procedures and principles concerning the constitution and implementation of the Turkish sign language system' (*Official Gazette*-o.g., No. 26139-14/4/2006) (the Legislation) was passed less than a year after the DA. One of the most important accomplishments of the Legislation was the constitution of a TİD Science and Approval Commission (the Commission), responsible for the research and development of TİD, the regulation of educational materials on TİD, and the appointment of three TİD signers with native-like skills and theoretical knowledge on the language to be responsible for the content development, administration and evaluation of TİD exams for the purpose of qualifying interpreters (Article 10). The Commission was to be constituted of eight delegates as following: two academics assigned by TLA, two delegates from the Federation, along with one delegate each from TLA, Social Services, MoNE and the Administration (Articles 4 & 7). Here, the Federation is defined as the 'the federation of the hearing disabled with the most number of members, who is actively engaged with all problems of the hearing handicapped' (Article 4c). To our knowledge, there is no Secretariat attached to this Board, and responsibilities were distributed among the agencies listed above.

The Legislation also included regulations concerning sign language interpreters and teachers (Article 2). MoNE was assigned permission to open a TİD instructor training and TİD interpreter training course, and the responsibility to conduct their proficiency exams (Articles 12a&b, 13a&b). Until the completion of research and analysis of TİD (no timeline or deadline indicated), TİD instructors were to be determined using a proficiency test conducted by MoNE, and certified (valid for two years) by the Commission (Article 8 & Temporary Article 1).

The Legislation has been amended twice since 2006. The first amendment included some changes in the make-up of the Commission and the definition of Federation in Article 4 (*Official Gazette*-o.g., No. 27819-01/18/2011); the clause 'having a status of public interest based on a Council of Ministers' decision, and being inspected by the Ministry of Internal Affairs' was added, in practice pointing to the Turkish National Federation of the Deaf. Months later, Social Services and the Administration merged under the Ministry of Family and Social Policy (the MoFSP). The second amendment reflects this institutional change and updates the Commission by going back to the original distribution of 2006, with MoNE getting an additional delegate (*Official Gazette*-o.g., No. 28330-06/21/2011 – Article 7).

With the amendment 'The legislation on the training and working procedures of personnel to provide sign language interpreting' (*Official Gazette*-o.g., No. 26264-08/19/2006), the Turkish government recognized sign language interpreting as a profession for its civil servants, initially within the MoFSP. Applicants who received sign language interpreter training would now be appointed as sign language interpreters for at least two years (Article 8b). Temporary Article 2 of the 2011 amendment to the Legislation also addressed the TİD interpreter certification process; individuals with certificates from various institutions would now take a proficiency exam administered by a commission (four from MoFSP and three appointed by the Commission) to get recertified by MoNE.

Outcomes and challenges in the implementation of TİD laws and legislation

The Commission: Lack of academic expertise and delays in implementation

According to the Legislation, the Commission meets every three months (Article 11b), but in practice they only met once every few years. There were two TİD workshops held by the Commission, to which national and international academics were invited, along with local Deaf people. The first workshop was held on 7–8 June 2007 in Ankara, where TİD's fingerspelling system was voted on and later approved by the Commission. The second workshop was held on 15–16 October 2010, where three working groups were identified for TİD: (1) grammar; (2) dictionary; and (3) instructional materials (Akalın, 2008, 2013; Kubus *et al.*, 2016). However, there was difficulty in putting these working groups into action. TLA led the Commission from 2005 to 2013, during which time there were conflicts on the source of funding for a nationwide study on TİD. There were also confusions and disagreements among institutions as to who should lead or be involved with the process (Tanrıverdi, pers. comm., 2017). After the Legislation, the few individuals familiar with sign language linguistics either no longer lived in Turkey or were going through graduate school. The academics initially selected for the Commission were familiar to TLA, yet unfamiliar with sign language research.

Corpus planning: Outcomes and challenges

The biggest obstacle in the implementation of the Legislation was in corpus planning. A nationwide corpus study of TİD did not materialize for nine years after the Legislation. For a long time, the closest to any accessible TİD dictionary were the two online video resources of limited capacity that were by-products of a university-based academic inquiry on TİD.

The first known resource on TİD is a photo dictionary printed in 1995 by the General Directorate of Guidance and Counseling Services under MoNE (MoNE, 1995). In 2012, the same institution collaborated with the MoFSP and TLA to publish an online TİD dictionary (MoNE, 2012). In 2015, this dictionary was updated with hard copies (MoNE, 2015). Regional variations were not included in any of these dictionaries; in their 2015 edition, MoNE openly states its goal as the standardization of TİD to aid instruction.

The MoFSP led a TİD project (2015–2017) aimed at creating a national database with regional differences and publishing a TİD grammar book. Led by Dikyuva (Deaf-linguist), Makaroğlu (hearing-linguist) and Arık (hearing-linguist), eight Deaf researchers were trained and conducted fieldwork in 26 cities with 113 native signers of TİD. This resulted in a corpus of naturalistic and elicitation data consisting of 800,000 signs. A TİD grammar book was published within six months, using a quarter of the data collected (Dikyuva *et al.*, 2015). The authors describe TİD as having some regional lexical variation, but as being grammatically consistent across the nation. In 2017, the first corpus-based dictionary of TİD was published by the same group, containing 2000 frequently used signs (Makaroğlu & Dikyuva, 2017). Unlike MoNE dictionaries, variants in TİD were presented when available, without indicating the region of origin. This is also the first bi-directional dictionary of TİD, allowing for searches using phonological parameters (handshape and location) of a sign.

Acquisition planning: Outcomes and challenges

Acquisition planning builds on corpus planning. For TİD, this includes the use of TİD in deaf education, the training and certification of TİD instructors as well as TİD interpreters, teaching TİD as a second language, and the production of educational materials and curriculum for these scenarios.

TİD instruction for deaf children

The biggest problem in Turkish deaf education has been teachers lacking TİD skills and resources to communicate with deaf students and the absence of Deaf teachers in deaf education (İlkbaşaran, 2015a, 2017). There are three four-year bachelor degree programs in Teaching for Deaf Education and TİD became a mandatory course in their curriculum as of the 2014–2015 school year (also an elective class in all higher education institutions) (Kubus et al., 2016). However one course is not sufficient to become fluent in a language, let alone using it in instruction. In 2015, MoNE's Board of Education approved an introductory TİD course (two hours/week) to be included in the 1st grade curriculum at deaf schools as of the 2015–2016 school year (MoNE-BoEd, 2015: Decision No. 2015/67). This was a monumental step, long-expected in Turkish deaf education, but it lacked resources and skilled TİD signers to be implemented as intended. Responding to these needs, MoNE released an activity book in 2017 for elementary school teachers to use while teaching TİD to 1st, 2nd and 3rd grade deaf students (MoNE-BoEd, 2016: Decision No. 2016/52).

Our informants think the Legislation did not have much direct positive impact on TİD use at deaf schools. Tanrıverdi points to contradictions within MoNE as one of the main reasons: while one of its branches, since the Legislation, is invested in spreading the use of TİD at deaf schools by producing materials, another branch providing counseling to the parents of deaf children recommends cochlear implants at an early age, discourages sign language use and promotes mainstream education. Almost 20 Turkish deaf schools were closed in the past decade due to low enrolment rates, a common trend in deaf education observed around the world (Humphries et al., 2016). For the 2014–2015 school year, the breakdown of deaf students at deaf schools and in mainstream education was 941 to 4365 in primary, 2080 to 4417 in secondary/middle school and 2065 to 704 in high school levels, respectively (TOHAD, 2015).

TİD as a second language

The majority of TİD learners are hearing adults learning TİD as a second language. Most courses are offered at Public Education Centers or Lifelong Learning Centers around the country. These are 120-hour beginner level (30 hours/week for four weeks) and in 210-hour (30 hours/week for seven weeks) intermediate level programs. A serious concern shared by all of our informants, is that hearing individuals completing the 210-hour TİD program at these institutions have been getting certified as both instructors and interpreters of TİD. Owing to the lack of research, documentation and teaching materials for advanced levels of TİD, coupled with the potential for a new career, TİD certification has turned into a domain for profit that threatens the healthy acquisition and attitude planning of TİD (see section 'Attitude planning' below). While commodification of TİD should benefit deaf people skilled in the language, it is mostly appropriated and capitalized on by hearing people. The popularization of sign language is a positive outcome, but it is highly problematic that certified TİD instructors and interpreters who are predominantly hearing lack the language skills that these professions require, and for dominant representations of TİD in instructional environments, television and social media to resemble signed Turkish at best.

To remedy this problem, one critical step is the training and certification of Deaf teachers of TİD. There were several attempts on this between 2002 and 2005, followed by almost a decade-long break. Finally, in 2014, around 20 Deaf people were certified as TİD teachers, following a course on TİD instruction and curriculum development at Boğaziçi University. Sixty-five certified Deaf TİD instructors are currently ready to be employed. Attempts in creating teaching modules for TİD, primarily to be used by Deaf teachers, go back more than a decade (Dikyuva & Zeshan, 2008), followed by Makaroğlu and Dikyuva's (2015) book *Turkish Sign Language as a Foreign Language (Basic Level, A1–A2)*. However, there is no particular regulation of who is qualified to teach TİD, or a push for replacing hearing TİD teachers with the newly certified Deaf ones.

TİD interpreting

Even certified TİD interpreters do not receive quality standardized professional training in Turkey and there are no BA programs on TİD interpreting. Prior to the Legislation, TİD interpreters were typically hearing children of deaf adults (CODAs) who worked for free. When anyone needed an interpreter, they would go to the Federation. After the Legislation, TİD interpreting became an occupation for hearing individuals, initially in the public sector. The first cohort of about 20 TİD interpreters were primarily CODAs certified in 2017. In 2014, another 87 became MoNE certified TİD interpreters from among 1000 applicants and MoFSP hired 43 of them in 2015. Deaf people can send a written request to hire interpreters employed as civil servants, as long as their local authority permits. It is uncommon for these interpreters to be sent to hospitals, and they tend to be used in educational or judicial settings.

In November 2011, the Association of Sign Language Interpreters (the Interpreter Association) was founded in collaboration with the Federation. Banu Şahin (hearing-CODA), the current president of the Association, states their goal as the improvement of working conditions and professionalization of TİD interpreters, collaborating with national and international interpreting organizations. The majority of TİD interpreters are not fluent in English, which limits their international correspondences and training opportunities. The Interpreter Association currently has 178 members and about 60 are State employed, receiving a fixed monthly salary. Deaf people often end up paying out of their own pockets for interpreting services.

Attitude planning: Outcomes and challenges

Most problems with the status, corpus and acquisition planning of TİD stem from attitudes to sign language, and misconceptions about what TİD is, who it belongs to, who is qualified to teach it and how lack of language access can disable a deaf person in a hearing world.

What is TİD and who does it belong to?

One big problem with the wording of the DA is the statement 'Turkish Sign Language system is to be created...' (Article 15), which was not a part of the draft that the working group at the Federation submitted to the Confederation. This overlooks TİD as an emerging language used among Deaf people in Turkey for generations. This poor word choice not only reflects legislators' lack of knowledge on how national sign languages emerge, evolve and are preserved, it also misguides implementing agencies and the Turkish public. None of the future amendments to the DA included a correction of this framing, clarifying that TİD does not need to be invented or tamed by a group of (hearing) professionals.

Prior to the documentation of TİD, a common misconception among government agencies was that regional variation across deaf signers in Turkey impeded communication, although Deaf community members disagreed. As seen on their public announcements and publications, the goal of MoNE and TLA has always been the standardization of TİD. This is not surprising given TLA's role as ensuring the 'correct' use of Turkish, and MoNE's need for efficiency in meeting educational needs of deaf children by providing a standardized set of tools and resources. Dominance of hearing people in sign language research and the push for standardization is a common problem around the world (Adam, 2015).

Primarily taught by hearing and unqualified instructors, signed Turkish and TİD are often falsely equated to one another. One way to provide proficient sign language models in deaf education and to accelerate deaf children's language acquisition is the inclusion of Deaf teachers in the system. However, Deaf teachers are not a part of deaf education in Turkey, even as teacher aides. This is mainly because it is nearly impossible for a deaf individual going through this system to become proficient enough in written Turkish to pass their college exams (Kemaloğlu, 2016). In addition, Deaf people in Turkey have typically struggled to see themselves as qualified for teaching positions owing to their limited negative educational experience, and despite their rich cultural and linguistic capital. According to Dikyuva (pers. comm., 2017), the employment of people with disabilities as teachers is legally restricted and regulated in Turkey, and conditional upon receiving health reports qualifying them for the requirements of a teaching position. This situation is in clear conflict with

CRPD Article 24.4, which promotes the use of teachers with disabilities. Ultimately, the lack of Deaf teachers in deaf education not only disregards their expertise in TİD, which would be of immense benefit to deaf students, it also creates a cultural and linguistic gap between young deaf children and the Turkish Deaf community at large.

Who should represent deaf people politically?

Initial political negotiations on TİD were largely led by the Federation and the Disability Confederation. This was not a grassroots effort where large masses of Deaf community members were politically engaged in the process. At the time, deaf people in Turkey were neither fully aware of the capacity of their language, nor what they could potentially demand from the government in order to freely practice their language and human rights. This has been changing, primarily due to the prevalent use of social media among Deaf people in Turkey, improving their national and transnational connectivity (İlkbaşaran, 2015b).

Collaboration with the Disability Confederation was beneficial, but also had its drawbacks. Members of other disability groups are typically more literate, better educated, have access to wider society and are more politically active in Turkey. Their relative political dominance at the community and NGO level was a factor in Deaf language rights issues being addressed only superficially.

Deaf people had minimal representation in the Commission, and thus in overseeing national research, documentation and certification of TİD, which have political, social and economic consequences. The Federation was the only Deaf rights organization representing deaf people in the Commission, and over the years even their seats were proportionally reduced, owing to structural changes in the breakdown of Commission members.

This monopoly in representation and agency is also one of the factors in the emergence of other Deaf rights NGOs. Several other Deaf federations have been founded in the past decade, some of which were led by Deaf or hard-of-hearing individuals who cannot reach elected positions of power within the Federation. These organizations compete for power by increasing their members, as well as partnerships in projects involving deaf people and TİD. In December 2015, Orkun Utsukarcı, a former Deaf board member of the Federation, founded the Deaf Confederation that encompasses several newer federations, with the plan to direct each federation to specialize in a key advocacy area. Meanwhile, there is ongoing tension between the Federation and the Deaf Confederation, as well as a divide among the Deaf community in Turkey, which weakens the community's political representation and legal legitimacy. Since 2016, the Deaf Confederation has been joining the Commission meetings, and has closer ties with government agencies and the Interpreters Association than the Federation. Moreover, the president of the Interpreter Association is currently employed as the Disability Advisee of the Turkish President's Principal Consultant, a key role in the Presidential administration. These growing close ties give both NGOs direct access to key government agencies, and could potentially improve their ability to make Deaf citizens' language rights more salient and legible to the Turkish State.

Conclusion

The initial legal recognition and planning of sign language in Turkey materialized in a climate of increased political interest on disability rights and academic interest on sign language at the turn of the 21st century, building on alliances between leading deaf and disability rights NGOs. The inclusion of disability as a topic of Turkish political discourse was a response to transnational human rights standards set by the EU and the UN, as well as an attempt to attract and politicize a large body of individuals with disabilities and their allies as a new group of voters. This political climate coincided with the onset of linguistic research in TİD, which helped raise public awareness on the language rights of deaf people, while also bringing this to the attention of key local and national agencies. The Disability Act of 2005 offered a critical paradigm shift and a roadmap for disability rights in Turkey, while the TİD Legislation of 2006 served as a blueprint for TİD status and corpus planning over the next decade. The ratification of the CRPD in 2009 added further obligations for the Turkish government. Overall, the initial decade of legal recognition and planning of TİD was a top-down, disability NGOs-driven process, before a significant group of deaf community members could reach a certain level of education and awareness. One of our informants likened this process to building a roof before the foundation or pillars, which would be structurally ill-conceived to begin with. We believe that the challenges and delays faced during implementation mainly resulted from this top-down approach, the lack of direct Deaf community involvement or skilled academics to support the research phase, as well as the lack of deadlines or penalties for delivery.

TİD has gained more direct legal recognition and status in the past decade than any other minority language in the country, including educational language rights. It is perhaps because Deaf rights organizations adopted an accessibility framework under disability rights instead of a minority linguistic rights framework that TİD-related policies could still be passed in Turkey. This appears to be a common avenue for sign language rights activism around the world (e.g. Murray, 2015). It could also be argued that TİD bypassed prevalent nationalistic protectionist instincts regarding minority languages, which is at the core of Turkey's nation-state identity, by identifying itself as the unifying sign language of the Turkish nation. With the Turkish Language Association (TLA) as the legally assigned coordinator of its research and constitution, TİD was also institutionally treated as the extension of a Turkish nationalist identity, in a new language modality. The protectionist and charity culture around disability in Turkish and Islamic traditions (Bezmez & Yardımcı, 2010) may have also augmented the extent to which government bodies took ownership of these new tasks.

The main drawback was that the leading role of the TLA and the Ministry of Education in the TİD Commission confirmed a dominant discourse of standardization. This approach not only had an impact on the status and attitude planning of TİD, but also how its corpus and acquisition planning were handled. Final drafts of the DA and the Legislation reflect common misconceptions about TİD, which informed how TİD-related activities were set to proceed. One obvious reason for this was the lack of an educated, professionally-trained and politically-active Deaf community with the skills and knowledge to navigate the legal system, who could ideally push for clarification and demand agency in the process. It is a vicious circle, however, that the education provided to deaf individuals in Turkey hardly allows for the rise of such an educated professional class. Instead, the few representatives of the Federation were the only Deaf presence in the TİD Commission. Ultimately, this problem of representational discontent in political agency was one of the main reasons behind fractures among Deaf community members.

The past decade has seen many gains, along with some new challenges: It is promising that in recent years, we see (1) Turkish government agencies and the public learning more about sign language; (2) the closer involvement and leadership of Deaf people and sign linguists in the research and documentation of TİD; (3) the training of more Deaf TİD teachers being on the agenda of Deaf community leaders; (4) being a teacher is becoming a more attractive occupation among Deaf people in Turkey; and finally that (5) there is more political connectivity and discourse among Turkish deaf people on social media. On the other hand, we observe that (1) TİD use is still limited to deaf schools that are closing due to low enrolment, making TİD-related investment less feasible for the MoNE; and (2) new avenues of opportunity and profit have emerged when TİD interpreting and teaching became occupational categories (along with the granting of certification) that mostly hearing people benefit from. It is clear that we need extensive studies on how deaf people in Turkey view these processes, their own language, the role and work of rights organizations, and their own political involvement.

Abbreviations of institutions

MoFSP

Turkish Ministry of Family and Social Policies (*Aile ve Sosyal Politikalar Bakanlığı*) (now Social Services and the Administration are merged under this ministry)

MoNE	The Ministry of National Education (*Milli Eğitim Bakanlığı – MEB*)
Social Services	The General Directorate of Social Services and Child Protection (Sosyal Hizmetler ve Çocuk Esirgeme Kurumu Genel Müdürlüğü – SHÇEK) (obsolete)
The Administration	Prime Ministry Department of the Administration of the Disabled – (Özürlüler İdaresi Başkanlığı – ÖZİDA) (obsolete)
The Commission	TİD Science and Approval Commission (*TİD Bilim ve Onay Kurulu – TİDBO*)
The Confederation	The Disability Confederation of Turkey (*Türkiye Sakatlar Konfederasyonu – TSK*)
The Deaf Confederation	Turkish Deaf Confederation (*Sağırlar Konfederasyonu*)
The Federation	The Turkish National Federation of the Deaf (*Türkiye Sağırlar Milli Federasyonu – TSMF*)
The Interpreter Association	The Association of Sign Language Interpreters (*İşaret Dili Tercümanları Derneği – İDTD*)
TLA	Turkish Language Association (*Türk Dil Kurumu – TDK*)

Notes

(1) See Arık's TİD bibliography: http://turkishsignlanguage.enginarik.com/bibliography (accessed 30 September 2017).
(2) With the exception of the Turkish Constitution, for which we identified an official English translation, the name and content of all laws and legislations were all translated from Turkish to English by the authors.

References

Act No. 2828 Law on Social Services (1983) See http://www.mevzuat.gov.tr/MevzuatMetin/1.5.2828.pdf (accessed 30 September 2017).
Act No. 2923 on Turkish Citizens' Learning Different Languages and Dialects via Foreign Language Education (amended by Act No. 4963 in 2001). (1983) See http://www.mevzuat.gov.tr/MevzuatMetin/1.5.2923.pdf (accessed 30 September 2017).
Act No. 4709 to Amend Several Articles of the Constitution of the Republic of Turkey. (2001) *The Official Gazette of the Republic of Turkey*, 24556, 17 October 2001. http://www.resmigazete.gov.tr/eskiler/2001/10/20011017M1.htm (accessed 30 September 2017).
Act No. 5378 on Disabled Persons and Amendments to Various Acts and Decrees (2005) See http://www.mevzuat.gov.tr/MevzuatMetin/1.5.5378.pdf (accessed 30 September 2017).

Adam, R. (2015) Standardization of sign languages. *Sign Language Studies* 15 (4), 432–445.

Akalın, Ş.H. (2008) Yetmiş Beşinci Yılında Türk Dil Kurumu: 2007 Yılı Çalışmaları [Turkish Language Association celebrates 75 years: Studies in 2007]. *Türk Dili Dil ve Edebiyat Dergisi* XCV (673), 1–31.

Akalın, Ş.H. (2013) Türk İşaret Dili [Turkish Sign Language]. *Yeni Türkiye* 55, 1496–1502.

Arık, E. (2013) (ed.) *Current Directions in Turkish Sign Language Research.* Newcastle upon Tyne: Cambridge Scholars Publishing.

Arık, E. (2016) (ed.) *Ellerle Konuşmak: Türk İşaret Dili Araştırmaları [Talking with Hands: Research on Turkish Sign Language].* Istanbul: Koç University Press.

Bezmez, D. and Yardımcı, S. (2010) In search of disability rights: Citizenship and Turkish disability organizations. *Disability & Society* 25 (5), 603–615. DOI: 10.1080/09687599.2010.489312.

Constitution of the Republic of Turkey (1982) See https://global.tbmm.gov.tr/docs/constitution_en.pdf (accessed 30 September 2017).

Dikyuva, H. and Zeshan, U. (2008) *Türk İşaret Dili – Birinci Düzey [Turkish Sign Language – First Level].* Nijmegen: Ishara Press.

Dikyuva, H., Makaroğlu, B. and Arık, E. (2015) *Türk İşaret Dili Dilbilgisi Kitabı [Turkish Sign Language Grammar].* Ankara: Aile ve Sosyal Politikalar Bakanlığı Yayınları.

Heller, M. (2010) The commodification of language. *Annual Review of Anthropology* 39, 101–114.

Heller, M. and Duchêne, A. (2012) Pride and profit: Changing discourses of language, capital and nation-state. In A. Duchêne and M. Heller (eds) *Language in Late Capitalism: Pride and Profit* (pp. 1–21). New York: Routledge.

Hornberger, N.H. (2006) Frameworks and models in language policy and planning. T. Ricento (ed.) *An Introduction to Language Policy: Theory and Method* (pp. 24–41). Malden, MA: Blackwell Publishing.

Humphries, T., Kushalnagar, P., Mathur, G., Napoli, D.J., Padden, C., Rathmann, C. and Smith, S. (2016) Avoiding linguistic neglect of deaf children. *Social Service Review* 90, 589–619.

İlkbaşaran, D. (2015a) Literacies, mobilities and agencies of deaf youth in Turkey: Constraints and opportunities in the 21st century. PhD thesis, University of California San Diego, San Diego, CA.

İlkbaşaran, D. (2015b) Social media practices of deaf youth in Turkey: Emerging mobilities and language choice. In M. Friedner and A. Kusters (eds) *It's a Small World: Inquiries into International Deaf Spaces* (pp. 112–124). Washington, DC: Gallaudet University Press.

İlkbaşaran, D. (2017) Tracing deaf youth geographies and mobilities in Turkey: Insights from a vocational high school. *The Journal of Cultural Geography (Special Issue: Deaf Geographies)* 34 (2), 194–221.

Kemaloğlu, Y.K. (2016) Türkiye'de Sağırların Görünürlüğü ve Toplumsal ve Eğitimsel Sorunları Üzerine Demografik Bir İnceleme [The visibility of Deaf in Turkey and a demographic investigation of their social and educational problems]. In E. Arık (ed.) *Ellerle Konuşmak Türk İşaret Dili Araştırmaları* (pp. 51–85). İstanbul: Koç Üniversitesi Yayınları.

KONDA (2006) *Toplumsal Yapı Araştırması 2006. Biz Kimiz? [Who are we? Social Structure Survey]* See http://konda.com.tr/en/rapor/who-are-we-social-structure-survey/ (accessed 25 September 2017).

Kubus, O. (2010) Der rechtliche Status der Türkischen Gebärdensprache und die gegenwärtige Sprachplanung [The legal status of Turkish Sign Language and current language planning]. *Das Zeichen* 24 (86), 382–389.

Kubus, O., İlkbaşaran, D. and Gilchrist, S. (2016) Türkiye'de işaret dili planlaması ve Türk İşaret Dili'nin yasal durumu [Sign language planning in Turkey and the current status of Turkish sign language]. In E. Arık (ed.) *Ellerle Konuşmak Türk İşaret Dili Araştırmaları* (pp. 23–50). İstanbul: Koç Üniversitesi Yayınları.

Legislation concerning the Identification of Procedures and Principles Concerning the Constitution and Application of the Turkish Sign Language System. (2006) *The Official Gazette of the Republic of Turkey*, No. 26139, 14 April 2006. See http://www.resmigazete.gov.tr/eskiler/2006/04/20060414-2.htm (accessed 30 September 2017).

Legislation concerning Regulation on the Training and Working Conditions of Personnel to Provide Sign Language Services. (2006) *The Official Gazette of the Republic of Turkey*, No. 26264, 19 August 2006. See http://www.resmigazete.gov.tr/eskiler/2006/08/20060819-1.htm (accessed 30 September 2017).

Legislation to Amend the Legislation concerning the Identification of Procedures and Principles Concerning the Constitution and Application of the Turkish Sign Language System. (2011) *The Official Gazette of the Republic of Turkey*, No. 27819, 18 January 2011. See http://www.resmigazete.gov.tr/eskiler/2011/01/20110118-3.htm (accessed 30 September 2017).

Legislation to Amend the Legislation concerning the Identification of Procedures and Principles Concerning the Constitution and Application of the Turkish Sign Language System. (2012) *The Official Gazette of the Republic of Turkey*, No. 28330, 21 June 2012. See http://www.resmigazete.gov.tr/eskiler/2006/04/20060414-2.htm (accessed 30 September 2017).

Makaroğlu, B. and Dikyuva, H. (2015) *Yabancı Dil Olarak Türk İşaret Dili (Temel düzey, A1–A2) Öğrenci Kitabı [Student Book – Turkish Sign Language as Foreign Language (Basic Level, A1–A2)]*. Ankara: Ankara Üniversitesi Yayınevi.

Makaroğlu, B. and Dikyuva, H. (eds) (2017) *Güncel Türk İşaret Dili Sözlüğü [Current Turkish Sign Language Dictionary]*. Ankara: Aile ve Sosyal Politikalar Bakanlığı. See http://tidsozluk.net (accessed 30 September 2017).

Ministry of National Education, Board of Education and Instruction (MoNE-BoEd) (2015) *Turkish Sign Language Course (1. Grade) Education Programme*. No. 2015/67, 29 July 2015. See http://orgm.meb.gov.tr/meb_iys_dosyalar/2015_08/17065456_tid1.snfprog1.pdf (accessed 30 September 2017).

Ministry of National Education, Board of Education and Instruction (MoNE-BoEd) (2016) *Turkish Sign Language Course Activity Book (1., 2. and 3. Grades)*. No. 2016/52, 26 July 2016. See http://orgm.meb.gov.tr/www/turk-isaret-dili-dersi-ogretim-programi-yururlukte/icerik/766 (accessed 30 September 2017).

Ministry of National Education, Directorate of Special Education (MoNE) (1995) *Yetişkinler İçin İşaret Dili Kılavuzu [Sign Language Guide for Adults]*. Ankara: MoNE.

Ministry of National Education, General Directorate of Special Education and Counseling Services (MoNE) (2012) *Türk İşaret Dili Sözlüğü [Turkish Sign Language Dictionary]*. Ankara: MoNE. See http://www.tdk.org.tr/index.php?option=com_content&view=article&id=264 (accessed 30 September 2017).

Ministry of National Education, General Directorate of Special Education and Counseling Services (MoNE) (2015) *Türk İşaret Dili Sözlüğü [Turkish Sign Language Dictionary]*. Ankara: MoNE. See http://orgm.meb.gov.tr/alt_sayfalar/duyurular/1.pdf (accessed 30 September 2017).

Murray, J. (2015) Linguistic human rights discourse in deaf community activism. *Sign Language Studies* 15 (4), 379–410.

Reagan, T. (2001) Language planning and policy. In C. Lucas (ed.) *The Sociolinguistics of Sign Languages* (pp. 145–180). Cambridge: Cambridge University Press.

Reagan, T. (2010) *Language Policy and Planning for Sign Languages*. Washington, DC: Gallaudet University Press.

Ricento, T. (ed.) (2015) *Language Policy and Political Economy: English in a Global Context*. New York: Oxford University Press.

Sadoğlu, H. (2017) Türkiye'nin yakın dönem dil politikaları [Turkey's recent language policies]. *PESA Uluslararası Sosyal Araştırmalar Dergisi* 3 (1), 57–66.

Turkish Social Rights and Research Association (TOHAD) (2015) *Mevzuattan uygulamaya engelli hakları izleme raporu 2014 [Disability rights monitoring report from legislation to practice 2014]*. Ankara: Hermes. See http://www.engellihaklariizleme. org/tr/files/belgeler/ozet_2014.pdf (accessed 30 September 2017).

UN Convention on the Rights of Persons with Disabilities (CRPD) (2006) New York: UN. See https://www.un.org/development/desa/disabilities/convention-on-the-rights-of-persons-with-disabilities.html (accessed 30 September 2017).

Zeshan, U. (2002) Sign Language in Turkey: The story of a hidden language. *Turkic Languages* 6 (2), 229–274.

Zeshan, U. (2003) Aspects of Türk İşaret Dili (Turkish Sign Language). *Sign Language and Linguistics* 6 (1), 43–75.

6 Progress and Problems in the Campaign for Sign Language Recognition in Japan

Soya Mori and Atsubumi Sugimoto

Introduction: The Legal Status of Languages in Japan

The Constitution of Japan does not specify an official language. Japanese is the de facto official language. Minority language policy is not well developed, and language curricula and public services are based on language instrumentalism. In this view, language is an instrument of communication that can be evaluated, altered, corrected, regulated and improved (Bull, 1993; Kubota, 2011; Wee, 2003). There have been some attempts at Japanese language planning in national laws and ordinances, but there has not been any unified language policy and principles among them (Sugimoto, 2016: 26).

Even though the most widely spoken language in Japan is Japanese, there are many other languages spoken. In addition to Japanese, Ryukyuan (Okinawa) languages are spoken in the Ryukyu Islands, and Bonin English in the Ogasawara Islands. The Ainu languages are spoken by the Ainu indigenous people of Hokkaido Island. Furthermore, there are old immigrant languages spoken such as Chinese and Korean, and new immigrant languages such as Spanish and Portuguese. In addition, there are the languages of foreign students from China, Korea, Thailand, Indonesia, the Philippines, Vietnam, Nepal, India, Taiwan, Russia, Mongolia and Arabic countries; and languages of tourists and business travelers from Asia, Middle East, Europe, Africa, North and South America, Oceania, etc. (Ministry of Justice, Japan, 2016). Altogether, there are about 30 languages spoken in Japan. To this list we must add *Nihon Shuwa* (NS, Japanese Sign Language), with some regional variations.

No laws or ordinances pertaining to NS and the rights of deaf people have been enacted or provided yet. 'Sign language' was legally recognized as a language for the first time in the Basic Act of Persons with Disabilities

(Government of Japan, 2013), which was amended in 2011 to ratify the UN Convention on the Rights of Persons with Disabilities (United Nations, 2006). Article 3 of this Law states:

> (3) All persons with disabilities are guaranteed the opportunity, insofar as possible, to choose their language (including sign language) and other means of communication for mutual understanding; and opportunities for them to choose the means of acquisition or use of information will be expanded.

Until now, this is the only article referring to sign language in Japanese domestic law. Japanese local governments, however, have been actively enacting ordinances about 'sign language' in recent years, which we describe later.

Since the 1990s, multilingualization in Japan has attracted the attention of Japanese sociolinguists, although Japanese remains the dominant language. Protection or conservation for linguistic minorities by the Japanese government does not exist or is still inadequate. Since 1997, the Ainu people have been recognized as an indigenous group, when the 'Act on the Promotion of Ainu Culture, and Dissemination and Enlightenment of Knowledge about Ainu Tradition, etc.' was adopted (Government of Japan, 1997). This act makes the national government responsible for the preservation and promotion of the Ainu languages and cultures. The Act lacks specific policies, however, on the education and official position of Ainu languages (Sugimoto, 2014). In contrast, residents of the Ryukyu Islands and the Ogasawara Islands are officially regarded as Japanese by the national government; thus their languages are also regarded as Japanese dialects, not independent languages. Descendants of earlier generations of immigrants from China and Korea are seen as foreigners, with no support from the Japanese government for their heritage language education. Due to the Japanese government's immigration policy, Japanese language education for overseas immigrants, necessary for their social integration, has been inadequate. Although legislation about Japanese language education for foreigners has steadily advanced in recent years, this legislation does not guarantee immigrants' language rights; its only purpose is to promote the economic interests of Japan by improving the language skills of foreign workers (Sugimoto, 2017). All these contextual factors affect the particular situation of NS, as we explain below.

The Constitution of Japan does not assume that minorities can expect linguistic rights. However, Japan is a state party to several international conventions of human rights that refer to linguistic rights, including the UN Convention on the Rights of Persons with Disabilities. Although these conventions should have efficacy in domestic law in Japan, the courts routinely avoid direct application of them at trial. In addition, the Japanese government has consistently suspended the procedure for individuals to appeal to the international community for the protection of their rights (Sugimoto, 2014, 2017).

In the next section, we first describe the Japanese Federation of the Deaf (JFD), which is the driving force behind the legislative campaign concerning 'sign language' in Japan. We problematize JFD's ideology that 'the sign languages are united' and discuss their stance on the status of NS. In the last section we explain specific legislative developments for recognition of 'sign language' and issues that are likely to arise in the future.

The Japanese Federation of the Deaf

The Japanese Federation of the Deaf (JFD) was established in 1947. It has affiliated organizations in all 47 prefectures (local governments covering a wide area) in Japan. The prefecture is the basic local entity of Japan, larger than cities and municipalities (which are smaller local governments, and of which there are 1741). In 2017, total membership of the JFD was 19,085, with membership including both signing and non-signing deaf people. There is no official number of NS signers. In addition, since hearing signed language learners are only allowed to be supporting members, the JFD is by design a closed organization. At the same time, hearing persons who are interested in the JFD's activities are encouraged to join *Zentsuken*, the national research association for Sign Language Interpretation, which is a member of the World Association of Sign Language Interpreters.

The combination of deaf NS signers and deaf people with spoken Japanese as their first language (L1) as members of the same organization creates conflicts within the Federation's affiliated organizations, because both groups have different expectations and demands for language policy. Deaf NS signers expect the recognition and dissemination of NS in Japanese society and improvement in the quality and quantity of NS interpreters. Deaf people with Japanese as their L1 are generally late learners of NS, and prefer that the standard for the Sign Language Interpreter Certificate is in most cases actually Signed Japanese (SJ). This group also advocates for more Japanese subtitles and notetaking, more than the deaf NS part of the membership.

When an affiliated organization taught technical NS terms in NS trainings, it faced opposition from deaf people with Japanese as their L1, because the terms did not follow spoken Japanese terminology. Shibuya (2012) writes that some deaf NS signers have expressed concerns that hearing learners could not distinguish SJ from NS. Indeed, in most signed language classes in Japan, instructors do not clearly explain the difference between NS and SJ. Oka (2012) states that the signed language used and selected for the JFD glossary book was SJ.

For the JFD, 'deaf people' means both deaf NS signers and SJ users. The JFD has primarily advocated for the development and institutionalization of sign language interpreting services, the elimination of discrimination against deaf people and promoting deaf people's social participation and independence.

The WFD (World Federation of the Deaf) World Congress held in Tokyo in 1991 triggered the establishment of new deaf organizations, including 'D-Pro', a cultural deaf organization established in 1993 by a group of young deaf people wanting to protect NS against spoken language influences (Nakamura, 2010). Subsequently, the JFD was no longer the only organization representing the interests of deaf community. The JFD's focus on social welfare and its perceived lack of acceptance of deaf people as a linguistic minority has been increasingly criticized within the deaf community (Kojima, 2006; Mori, 2010; Nakamura, 2010). Furthermore, from 2000 onwards, private sign language interpreting agencies and many private schools offering interpreter development courses began to operate without oversight of JFD-affiliated organizations.

The fact that deaf people with different linguistic backgrounds and informational needs had to work together for legislation on sign language had an impact on the content of 'the Draft Bill of the Nihon Shuwa Gengo (NSG)' proposed by the JFD. Indeed, the JFD argued that NS and SJ could be united in the NSG (see Nakamura, 2010 regarding language ideology in 2000's in Japan). We discuss this new term below in the next section.

The JFD's Argument: 'The Sign Languages Are United'

From the 1970s onward, the Japanese National government entrusted the JFD with two projects: 'Research Project on Standard Sign Language' and 'Promotion Project for Sign Language'. Following the signing by the Japanese government of the UN Convention on the Rights of Persons with Disabilities in 2007, the JFD began to consider a 'Draft Bill of the NSG'.[1] In Article 2 of the draft bill, the NSG was defined as a language having a unique linguistic system that Japanese deaf people use in their daily lives. However, what was called NSG in Article 2 is actually the language entity that includes Signed Japanese (SJ). Similarly, 'Japanese deaf people' in the draft bill meant the very diverse group of signing and non-signing deaf people. This situation reflects the language attitudes of the JFD, which are rooted in instrumentalism. To start the 'Promotion Project for Sign Language', the JFD first focused on SJ, which is more easily learned by hearing or deaf persons whose first language is Japanese. The JFD sees NS as 'a dialect of SJ', which is not standard and only used in the home domain. The JFD sees SJ as the first step for sign language learners, although it is linguistically very different from NS (Oka, 2012; Shibuya, 2012; Science and Japanese Subcommittee in the Language and Literature Committee of the Science Council of Japan, 2017; Yamauchi, 2017). The JFD's teaching of 'sign language' to hearing people and its curriculum for the training of sign language interpreters have long adhered to the of 'standard sign language' based on their NSG concept. Therefore, anecdotal evidence indicates that deaf people who are NS signers often do not understand the sign language used by interpreters, and that interpreters often do not understand or respect NS as used by deaf people.

This situation has changed considerably as a result of the 1995 'Declaration of Deaf Culture', which advocated the recognition of NS and was proposed by D-Pro (Nakamura, 2006: 8–9). Despite broad support for this declaration by deaf NS signers, and contrary to the findings of linguistics researchers and sign language interpreters (Kwak, 2017: 72), the JFD still neglected to distinguish between NS and SJ, considering such a distinction as a cause of the division among deaf people for more than 20 years after the Declaration.

In 2003, the National Association of Parents with Deaf Children, supported by an attorney, submitted a legal petition for human rights relief to the Japan Federation of Bar Associations (JFBA). In the petition, they claimed their children had been deprived of their educational linguistic rights, their right to receive education in NS as their first language and their right to learn written Japanese through NS, all of which were required and guaranteed by the Japanese Constitution. In particular, they invoked the right to education under Article 26 of the Constitution and equal protection before the law under Article 14 of the Constitution, in addition to Articles 29(1) (c), 30, 40 of the Convention on the Rights of the Child. All these articles refer to the language rights of children and parents. In October 2003, the JFD released its opinion on the petition, again questioning the distinction between NS and SJ, arguing that accusing the school of violating student's human rights would be inappropriate because it would give a false impression that the problem could be solved immediately. Ultimately, after accepting the petition, the JFBA did not request human rights relief of the Japanese government, and the educational circumstances have remained unchanged. Instead, the JFBA issued an opinion in April 2005 (Nihon bengoshi rengokai, 2005), which was in line with the JFD's opinion. They affirmed the necessity of guaranteeing the right of deaf children to receive education through 'sign language', but did not mention the distinction between NS and SJ as requested by the petitioners.

The Status of NS

Education

After the JFBA's opinion was released, education in the auditory/oral method was reviewed by the Ministry of Education, and the number of teachers fluent in 'sign language' have continually increased, even in primary schools for deaf children. However, most of the teachers' sign language is actually SJ, not NS, and deaf children cannot understand it because it does not follow NS's grammatical rules (Kwak, 2017; Saiki & Tachiiri, 2012; Nakajima, 2018). At the same time, teachers cannot understand NS conversations among deaf children. The single exception is Meisei Gakuen School for the Deaf, a private primary school established in 2008 as a charter school, which conducts bilingual education in NS and written Japanese. It was established by using the Special Districts for Structural Reform system, which involves local governments voluntarily setting revitalization standards, implementing specific projects according to the characteristics of their areas, as legislated by the Japanese government as a special measure in 2002. At Meisei Gakuen, a junior high school and a kindergarten have also recently opened, and establishing a secondary school has also been considered. In Japan, there are no secondary and higher educational institutions where all the education is provided fully in NS. There are two universities where parts of the courses are given in NS (Tsukuba University of Technology and Japan College of Social Work).[2] Services such as sign language interpreting service and notetaking are not institutionalized in many secondary and higher education institutions in Japan; it is left to the discretion of each educational institution whether to provide support measures for deaf students. In most institutions, students depend on the goodwill of volunteers.

In public primary schools for deaf children, there are a few classes taught in NS by hearing teachers who have learned NS voluntarily. However, in Japan there is no officially supported training course designed to teach NS and Deaf culture for teachers of deaf children. Whether teachers learn NS or not depends on individuals' motivation to do so. Very few higher education institutions offer NS as a language of study. The few universities where students can learn NS are mostly universities and faculties in medical, paramedical and welfare-related fields (The University of Tokyo and Keio University are exceptions).

Interpreting, access to information and public participation

In Japan, sign language interpreting is provided as a social welfare service, and the national government entrusts the training of interpreters to JFD-affiliated organization in each prefecture. If sign language interpreting was treated as a linguistic right, national or local governments or other social organizations (schools, hospitals, companies etc.) would understand themselves to be responsible for providing sign language interpreters. As it stands, when an interpreter is necessary, the deaf person has to place the request with the affiliated organization; the sponsoring organization of the activity is rarely asked to arrange the service. If an interpreter is necessary outside the prefecture or across plural prefectures, the deaf person may not be able to obtain sign language interpreters at all. As sign language interpreters receive basic training from JFD-affiliated organizations of each prefecture, there is disparity in interpreting standards, and in most cases the students have mastered only SJ. Although there is a national qualification system for sign language interpreters, many interpreters cannot earn a living from their interpreter service fee alone. Further, there is no public specified qualification system for medical, judicial or academic interpretation respectively, which require higher interpretation skills. Many deaf people have received unintended medical treatment as the result of not receiving sufficient information, have been subject to disadvantageous judgments and other case dispositions, or have been left without understanding academic information (Kimura, 2016: 99–100).

The provision of sign language interpretation or of subtitles during an election and the process of voting is not institutionalized as a human right in Japan. Candidates and political parties can introduce sign language interpreters or subtitles for their broadcast campaign speeches at their own expense, following standards set by statute, but sign language interpreters cannot be provided for live election speeches on the street. In addition, sign language interpreters in political broadcasts often use SJ. This is because translating a political opinion expressed in Japanese into other languages is regarded as a modification of the opinion's contents and is prohibited by the Public Offices Election Act. The only available option is literal transliteration, which means SJ, not following NS syntax and word usage.

Three deaf persons, one NS signer and two deaf people with Japanese as their first language, are now members of municipal assemblies in Japan. Nevertheless, the assemblies retain autonomy in deciding whether to guarantee their access to information. In recent years, the provision of sign language interpreters to observers is increasingly accepted, especially in local governments that have enacted ordinances about sign language. Sign language interpreters in court are increasingly allowed, although many judges do not yet fully understand the importance of interpretation or their role in court (Matsuo, 2011).

Research on NS

In Japan, linguistic description of NS began in the 1990s; however, the literature on NS remains relatively small. There is a lack of knowledge about the linguistic status of NS among linguists in Japan, and many introductory linguistics textbooks for university students have little or no mention of signed language. However, deaf researchers and their hearing colleagues continue to undertake research. In 1999, the parent council of the Meisei Gakuen founded the Bilingual Bicultural Education Center for Deaf Children, which is a private research institute on NS education for deaf children. The Japanese Sign Language Teachers Center, a specified nonprofit corporation, has trained deaf NS teachers in language classes at universities/colleges and other educational institutions. In addition, a sign language learning group at the center has been training deaf interpreters and the hearing interpreters who work with them since 2009. The center also has improved the skill of sign language interpreters and developed NS teaching methods. The Japanese Association for Sign Language Studies

(JASLS) is currently the only linguistic academic society in Japan where sign language interpreting and subtitling services are guaranteed in all research presentations and symposiums. This association collects not only findings of sign language linguistic research projects, but also those of Deaf Studies and sign language ethnography. Notably, JASLS encourages research activities by deaf people. The National Museum of Ethnology and the National Institute for Japanese Language and Linguistics have several researchers working on sign language. Founded in 2016, the Sign Language Research Center of Kwansei Gakuin University has recruited deaf people as researchers and is vigorously conducting research activities on NS. Finally, a JFD affiliated research institution named the Japan Institute for Sign Language Studies conducts research on the development and dissemination of glossaries of 'standard sign language' (SJ), research on deaf children's education at public schools, and research on foreign sign languages. However, the research by this institution is mainly about SJ and the majority of the researchers do not have academic backgrounds in linguistics.

Legislative Movement on NSG

History of the movement

Supported by a grant from the Nippon Foundation, in 2010, the JFD established the 'Committee to Promote the Enacting of a Law concerning Nihon Shuwa Gengo (Tentative Name)'. The committee was composed of seven directors of the JFD, four researchers in Deaf Education, three sign language interpreters, three lawyers, a sociolinguist, a psychologist, a researcher of disability legislation, a sociologist and an ex-teacher. There were only two deaf NS signers on the committee. The committee started research activities both in Japan and overseas for preparing the draft bill. Overseas research, beginning in 2011, included surveys of legislation concerning sign language in New Zealand (see McKee & Manning, Chapter 14 of this volume), Finland and Hungary. Finland and New Zealand were chosen because each had been introduced as the country that legally recognizes sign language in the Handbook for Parliamentarians on the Convention on the Rights of Persons with Disabilities and its Optional Protocol (Unitede Nations, 2007). Hungary was said to be a model country concerning sign language legislation among the member countries of the European Union (De Meulder, 2015; Japanese Federation of Deaf, 2012). Domestic research on discrimination cases, mainly concerning sign language, was conducted through surveys of the member organizations of JFD-affiliated organizations and sign language interpreters. On 11 March 2011, two committee members experienced the Great Earthquake in Northeast Japan, leading them to conduct a survey of difficulties faced by deaf people during the disaster. Based on these findings, the JFD held forums on sign language legislation targeting members of its affiliated organizations and cooperating organizations at seven locations in Japan from October 2011 to February 2012.

In April 2012, the JFD released a draft bill and two model ordinance draft bills about NSG. They are only private editions created by the JFD and it has been developing campaigns to encourage the Diet (the Japanese national parliament) to enact legislation based on this draft bill. Due to the lobbying efforts of JFD-affiliated organizations, local assemblies, one after another, adopted their own Opinion requesting the Diet to enact a law about NSG. Although Opinions are not legally binding, they can have a positive impact on local governments. By March 2016, all the local assemblies had adopted Opinions. At the end of April 2018, the local government ordinances based on the JFD model ordinance draft bills were enacted in 157 municipalities and 22 prefectures. In addition, existing organizations such as the Japan Association of City Mayors and the National Association of Chairpersons of Prefectural Assemblies, had already made resolutions as early as 2015 to encourage the Diet to enact the law on NSG.

There are two versions of the model ordinance draft bills for local governments: one for prefectures and one for municipalities, both drafted by the JFD at the same time as the draft bill.

The content of the two ordinance models drafted by the JFD is seemingly plausible at first glance. In particular, social welfare services and deaf education adequately correspond to the role shared by the national government and the local governments in the broader social welfare and educational systems in Japan. However, just as in the draft bill, the distinction between NS and SJ is not made clear. Additionally, some ordinances have been enacted with problematic provisions that are different from the roles expected by the JFD model ordinance. We will present examples of them in the next subsection.

Content of the draft bill by JFD

The draft bill on NSG by the JFD, published in April 2012, was modified slightly in March 2018. We will explain the contents of the 2018 version.[3] The draft bill is composed of six chapters and 21 articles, and in summary refers to the following:[4]

> The right of deaf children to acquire NSG and to receive bilingual education in NSG and Japanese in school education; the right of deaf children's families to be offered information about NSG and the opportunity to learn it; the responsibilities of national and local governments to provide awareness about NSG and provide opportunities to learn it in general school education curriculums; the right to receive information through NSG, the right to provide and receive information necessary for political participation through NSG; the right to receive NSG interpreters in

judicial proceedings and trial observation; the employer's duty to provide NSG interpreters or other measures that provide information for deaf employees; the duty of medical and health institutions to provide NSG interpreters; the responsibilities of national and local governments to encourage cultural, artistic and sports activities be made accessible through NSG; the right to NSG interpretation provided free of charge; the responsibilities of national and local governments concerning the training, qualification, placement and dispatch of NSG interpreters; the establishment of a NSG Council to evaluate and propose NSG policies implemented by national and local governments, and the establishment of a NSG Institute to conduct comprehensive research on NSG.

At first glance, the draft bill by the JFD seems to incorporate the advantages of New Zealand, Finland and Hungary's legislation. In particular, it refers to the right to have sign language interpretation service (cf. Finland and Hungary), and the right to bilingual education (cf. Hungary). Of course, there are variations in the content and implementation status of the acts of these countries (see McKee & Manning, Chapter 14 of this volume).

Looking more closely at the draft bill, it is possible to identify some challenges. The primary criticism of the draft bill by the deaf community is that the word 'NSG', despite not being clearly stated, is intended to obscure the linguistic distinction between NS and SJ. The JFD's draft adopted their newly invented term 'Nihon Shuwa Gengo', not the conventional term 'Nihon Shuwa' (NS). The term 'Nihon' means Japan, 'Shuwa' means sign language, and 'Gengo' means language, respectively. The general Secretary of the JFD argued that 'Shuwa' merely means 'Sign' and that therefore, 'Language' should be added to the name (Hisamatsu, 2016). To avoid confusion, we noted the name of 'Nihon Shuwa Gengo' as JSL, Japanese Sign Language, in the documents by the JFD.

Another problem with the draft bill is that in Article 6, the right of deaf children to acquire sign language is seen as equal to the right of late-deafened people to access SJ. Moreover, the proposed NSG Council would be made up of experts who conduct sign language research and representatives of JFD-affiliated organizations, which do not always include deaf NS signers as members. In addition, and especially after the Great Earthquake in Northeast Japan, the draft bill lacks: (1) the right to receive information through sign language interpretation and written Japanese about disaster or relief supplies; and (2) specification of the responsibilities of national and local governments concerning a disaster prevention system designed and implemented with consideration of deaf people.

At the time of writing, the JFD has gathered the mayors of local governments to urge the Diet to table the Act on NSG, and submitted petitions to several political parties. If the bill enters legislative procedures, an inter-party parliamentary group will prepare the bill for legislation because no party has sufficient knowledge of language rights. Moreover, the enacted law will present aspects of social welfare legislation on deaf people, rather than legislation on language rights of deaf people. There may be some improvement on the existing dispatch system of sign language interpreters, but it is doubtful whether the right of deaf children to bilingual education will be realized. In the course of study guidelines set by the Ministry of Education, Culture, Sports, Science and Technology, Japanese is the principal educational language and there is no course provided to train teachers to teach through NS.

Implementation of the sign language ordinances

Some ordinances differ from the JFD model ordinance. For example, some clearly outline the responsibility of the local government to provide access to information via services such as subtitles, interpreters and braille for deafblind people, none of which are included in the JFD model ordinance. Moreover, most of them refer to consideration of hearing-impaired persons, including hard-of-hearing people by age and late-deafened people during natural disasters. There are also municipal ordinances that refer to the introduction of sign language in general school education, and the arrangement of sign language interpreters in health agencies, which should be prescribed by an ordinance at the prefecture level. For example, in Ishikari city in Hokkaido, sign language courses have been established as optional subjects at the high school under the municipal ordinance. The ordinance of Asaka city in Saitama is the only ordinance that clearly declares the city guarantees the right to NS, not SJ.

Conversely, there are some prefectural ordinances that lack provisions concerning education which should be established at prefectural level. In the case of Kanagawa, not only were there inadequate provisions concerning education in the ordinance, there was also a problem in its enactment process. The local government of Kanagawa solicited public comments on the provisions of the ordinance, but initially accepted only comments via written Japanese and refused to receive video comments in sign language. This procedure was withdrawn after being criticized severely by deaf NS signer citizens. Furthermore, some ordinances do not have adequate budgetary provisions or procedures to consult with deaf NS signers.

Conclusion

Recently, there have been new developments that seek legislation for NS, distinct from SJ. In March 2017, a report titled 'Japanese and Japanese Sign Language' (Yamauchi, 2017)[5] was published in the bulletin issued by the Research Division on the Legislative Policy of the House of Councilors (upper house of the Diet). This report, among other things, explains the difference between NS and SJ, and points out the necessity of protecting the rights of NS signers. The main readers of this bulletin are members of the House of Councilors and their policy-making secretariats. In addition, the Science and Japanese Subcommittee in the Language and Culture Committee of the Science Council of Japan, which is the national academy established at the Cabinet Office in Japan, announced a proposal: 'Creating an Environment for the Preservation and Utilization of Diversity in Spoken Language and Sign Language' in August 2017. The proposal also clearly distinguishes NS from SJ and proposes the construction and utilization of archives related to spoken Japanese and NS. The proposal also asserts the establishment of a law guaranteeing the linguistic right to NS and providing for training of deaf NS signers as teachers of NS.

Still, the JFD maintains that the wider deaf community uses a form of contact sign language having elements of both NS and SJ, and that therefore they should not be separated.[6] Doing so, they claim, would not only have an impact on the solidarity within the 'hearing-impaired people community', but also lead to loss of identity for these 'contact sign language' signers. However, deaf people seeking distinction between NS and SJ are claiming their linguistic rights, and the right of deaf children to acquire NS as their first language. Furthermore, since they live in the linguistic environment of spoken Japanese, contact between NS and Japanese through SJ can develop for them naturally. Just as the borrowing of foreign language vocabulary or English expressions does not jeopardize the identity of Japanese speakers, the identities of SJ speakers/signers who use a contact form of sign language and of NS signers will not be jeopardized. Even if SJ users and NS signers are linguistically distinct, they can cooperate together to campaign for language rights that would benefit all of them.

Acknowledgements

We would like to express our great appreciation to the editors of this book for their valuable and constructive suggestions during the writing of this chapter. Advice given by Mr Aaron Brace and Prof. Susan Schweik at the University of California, Berkeley has also been of great help in writing this chapter.

Notes

(1) JFD is also aiming for legislation on information accessibility, but it has not yet reached the final draft bill such as the draft bill of NSG.
(2) One of this chapter's co-authors, Mori, teaches economics and Sign Linguistics in NS at the Japan College of Social Work.
(3) See https://www.jfd.or.jp/info/misc/sgh/20180511-sgh-shuseian.pdf. (accessed 24 January 2019).
(4) Translated from Japanese by the second author.
(5) Mr Kazuhiro Yamauchi was a researcher of the Research Division on the Legislative Policy of the House of Councillors at the time.
(6) See http://www.jfd.or.jp/yobo/2003/kenkai20031017.html; https://www.jfd.or.jp/2018/03/23/pid17437. (accessed 24 January 2019).

References

Bilingual Bicultural Education Center for Deaf Children, Japanese version only. See http://www.bbed.org/index.html (accessed 20 January 2018).

Bull, T. (1993) Conflicting ideologies in contemporary Norwegian language planning In E.H. Jahr (ed.) *Language Conflict and Language Planning Trends in Linguistics. Studies and Monographs (TiLSM)* 72, 21–38). Berlin, Germany: Walter de Gruyter.

De Meulder, M. (2015) The legal recognition of sign languages. *Sign Language Studies* 15 (4), 498–506.

D-Pro. See https://www.deaf-dpro.net/d-pro%E3%81%AB%E3%81%A4%E3%81%84%E3%81%A6/english/ (accessed 20 January 2018).

Government of Japan (1997) Act No. 52, *Act on the Promotion of Ainu Culture, and Dissemination and Enlightenment of Knowledge about Ainu Tradition, etc.*, outline translated into English. See http://www.japaneselawtranslation.go.jp/common/data/outline/h09Zzk00520101je2.0.htm (accessed 20 January 2018).

Government of Japan (2013) Revised Basic Act for Persons with Disabilities. See http://www.japaneselawtranslation.go.jp/law/detail_main?re=01&vm=04&id=2436 (accessed 24 January 2019).

Hisamatsu, M. (2016) Shuwa Gengo-Ho to Ro-Kyoiku (3): 'Shuwa' kara 'Shuwa-Gengo' no Jidai e [Japanese Sign Language and Deaf Education (3): From the time of 'Sign' to that of 'Sign Language']. *Rou-Kyoiku no Ashita [Tomorrow of Deaf Education]* 74, 12–26. http://www.normanet.ne.jp/~deafedu/syuwagenngohisamatsu.pdf. (accessed 24 January 2019).

Japanese Federation of Deaf. See http://www.jfd.or.jp/en/ (accessed 20 January 2018).

Japanese Federation of Deaf (2012) *Shuwagengoho (Kasho) Seiteisuishinjigyo Hokokusho [Report of Promotion Project about the Enacting of a Law concerning NSG (Tentative Name)]*, Tokyo. See https://www.jfd.or.jp/info/misc/sgh/20120728-sgh-report2012.pdf. (accessed 24 January 2019).

Japanese Association for Sign Language Studies, Japanese version only. See http://jasl.jp/modules/pico/index.php?content_id=4 (accessed 20 January 2018).

Japan Association of City Mayors. See http://www.mayors.or.jp/english.php (accessed 20 January 2018).

Japan College of Social Work, Japanese version only. See http://www.jcsw.ac.jp/ (accessed 20 January 2018).

Japan Institute for Sign Language Studies, Japanese version only. See http://www.com-sagano.com/jisls/index.html (accessed 20 January 2018).

Japanese Sign Language Teachers Center, Japanese version only. See https://www.jsltc.org/ (accessed 20 January 2018).

Kimura, H. (2016) Shuwa wo gengotoshite manabu, tsuyakusuru [Learning and interpreting sign language as a language]. In S. Mori and M. Sasaki (eds) *Shuwa wo Gengo to Iu no Nara [What Does it Mean to Say That NS is a Language?]*. Tokyo, Japan: Hitsuzi-shobo.

Kojima, I. (2006) *Rokyoiku-ga-Kawaru!- Nichibenren Ikensho to Bairingaru Kyoiku heno Teigen [Changing Deaf Education! – Statement of Position to Japanese Federation of Bar Associations and the Proposal for Bilingual Education for the Deaf]*. Tokyo, Japan: Akashi-Shoten.

Kubota, R. (2011) Questioning linguistic instrumentalism: English, neoliberalism, and language tests in Japan. *Linguistics and Education* 22 (3), 248–260.

Kwak, J. (2017) *Nihon Shuwa to Rokyoiku: Nihongonoryokushugi wo Koete [Nihon Shuwa and Deaf Education: Over the Japanese Language Proficiency Supremacism]*. Tokyo, Japan: Seikatsu-shoin.

Matsuo, Y. (2011) 6 Shuwatsuyaku wo meguru saibansho tono kyogi oyobi taio [Chapter 6, Discussion and correspondence with the court about sign language interpretation]. In Shogaisha jiritsushienho ikensosho bengodan [Lawyers of Litigation for

Unconstitutionality of the Services and Supports for Persons with Disabilities Act] (eds) *Shogaisha jiritsushienho ikensosho: Tachiagatta tojishatachi [Litigation for Unconstitutionality of the Services and Supports for Persons with Disabilities Act: Standing Interest Party]*. Tokyo, Japan: Seikatsu-shoin.

Meisei Gakuen School for the Deaf. See http://info.meiseigakuen.info/?lang=english (accessed 20 January 2018).

Ministry of Justice, Japan (2016) *Entry Status of Immigration Foreigners by Nationality/ Region (Table no. 16-00-06)*. See https://www.e-stat.go.jp/stat-search/files?page=1& layout=datalist&lid=000001183063 (accessed 20 January 2018).

Mori, S. (2010) Response pluralization – An alternative to the existing hegemony in JSL. In G. Mathur and D. Jo Napoli (eds) *Deaf around the World: The Impact of Language* (pp. 333–338). New York: Oxford University Press.

Nakajima, T. (2018) Rou-Kyoiku-to 'Kotoba'-no-Shakai-Gengo-gaku – Shuwa, Eigo and Nihongo-Literacy [Education for the Deaf and Socio-linguistics of the 'Language' for the Deaf–JSL, English and Literacy]. Seikatsu-shoin Co. Ltd.

National Association of Chairpersons of Prefectural Assemblies, Japanese version only. See http://www.gichokai.gr.jp/ (accessed 20 January 2018).

National Institute for Japanese Language and Linguistics. See http://www.ninjal.ac.jp/ english/ (accessed 20 January 2018).

National Museum of Ethnology. See http://www.minpaku.ac.jp/english (accessed 20 January 2018).

Nakamura, K. (2006) *Deaf in Japan: Signing and the Politics of Identity*. Ithaca, NY: Cornell University Press.

Nakamura, K. (2010) The language politics of Japanese Sign Language (Nihon Shuwa). In G. Mathur and D. Jo Napoli (eds) *Deaf around the World: The Impact of Language* (pp. 316–332). New York: Oxford University Press.

Nihon bengoshi rengokai (JFBA) (2005) *Suwakyoiku no jujitsu wo motomeru ikensho [Opinion seeking enhancement of sign language education]*: Tokyo. See https:// www.nichibenren.or.jp/library/ja/opinion/report/data/2005_26_1.pdf (accessed 20 January 2018).

Oka, N. (2012) Nihon Shuwa: Kakikotoba wo Motanai Shosugengo no Gendai [Nihon Shuwa: Present situation of Japanese Sign Language as minority language which does not have written language]. Unpublished PhD dissertation, Hitotsubashi University, Tokyo, Japan.

Saiki, A. and Tachiiri, H. (2012) Sign language used by hearing teachers at schools for students who are deaf: Sign with and without accompanying voice. *Japanese Journal of Special Education* 50 (3), 217–226.

Science and Japanese Subcommittee in the Language and Literature Committee of the Science Council of Japan (2017) *Onseigengo oyobi Shuwagengo no Tayosei no Hozon/Katsuyo to Sonotame no Kankyoseibi [Preservation and Utilization of Diversity of Spoken Language and Sign Language, and Improvement of Environment for That]*: Tokyo. See http://www.scj.go.jp/ja/info/kohyo/pdf/kohyo-23-t247-9.pdf (accessed 20 January 2018).

Shibuya, T. (2012) Bi-modal bilingualism (Bimodal and bilingual). *Kotoba to Shakai [Language and Society]* 14, 330–338.

Sign Language Research Center of Kwansei Gakuin University, Japanese version only. See https://www.kwansei.ac.jp/c_shuwa/ (accessed 20 January 2018).

Sugimoto, A. (2014) Saiko gengo to kenpogaku [An Essay on the constitutionality of the language planning in Japan 2014]. *The Journal of Tokyo International University* 20, 53–71.

Sugimoto, A. (2016) Shuwagengojorei to shuwagengoho: Hogaku/jinkenhoshoron no tachiba kara [Ordinances and draft bill of sign language of Japan: At the viewpoint from jurisprudence and human rights theory]. In S. Mori and M. Sasaki (eds) *Shuwa wo Gengo to Iu no Nara [What Does it Mean to Say that NS is a Language?]* (pp. 23–36). Tokyo, Japan: Hitsuzi-shobo.

Sugimoto, A. (2017) Gengoken kara mita 'Nihongokyoikusuishinhoan' no mondaiten [Problems of Japanese language education promotion bill from a viewpoint of linguistic rights]. *Shakai Gengogaku [Sociolinguistics]* XVII, 55–73.

The Ministry of Education, Culture, Sports, Science and Technology (2017) *Course of Study Guidelines.* See http://www.mext.go.jp/a_menu/shotou/new-cs/index.htm (accessed 25 January 2019).

Tsukuba University of Technology. See http://www.tsukuba-tech.ac.jp/english/index.html (accessed 20 January 2018).

United Nations (2006) Convention on the Rights of Persons with Disabilities. See https://www.un.org/development/desa/disabilities/convention-on-the-rights-of-persons-with-disabilities/convention-on-the-rights-of-persons-with-disabilities-2.html (accessed 24 January 2019).

United Nations (2007) Optional Protocol to the Convention on the Rights of Persons with Disabilities. See https://www.un.org/development/desa/disabilities/convention-on-the-rights-of-persons-with-disabilities/optional-protocol-to-the-convention-on-the-rights-of-persons-with-disabilities.html (accessed 24 January 2019).

Wee, L. (2003) Linguistic instrumentalism in Singapore. *Journal of Multilingual and Multicultural Development* 24 (3), 211–224. DOI: https://doi.org/10.1080/014346 30308666499 (accessed 20 January 2018).

Yamauchi, K. (2017) Nihongo to nihonshuwa: Sokoku no rekishi to kyosei ni mukete [Japanese and Japanese sign language: Their history of conflicts and toward the coexistence]. *Rippo to Chosa [Research and Legislative]* 386, 101–111.

7 American Sign Language Legislation in the USA

Joseph J. Murray

Popular conceptions of the USA present it as an English-speaking nation. But the world's third most-populated country has always been multilingual, with indigenous Native American languages joined by the languages brought over by immigrants from all areas of the world from before the country's founding to the present day. As of 2011, the US Census Bureau has identified over 300 languages other than English spoken in the USA (of which 161 are Native American languages), with 21% of the population speaking a language other than English at home (Ryan, 2013). According to data from the 2016 American Community Survey, 14 of these languages are spoken by more than 500,000 people. These data do not include American Sign Language (ASL) or other sign languages in the USA, since the US Census Bureau puts ASL users in the category of English speakers (US. Census Bureau, 2017).

ASL is one of several sign languages used in the USA. Estimates as to the number of ASL users vary widely and are often extrapolated from the number of deaf people in the USA. The US Census collected data on deaf people from 1830 to 1930, but stopped thereafter, except in 2000, with a question that asked about blindness and deafness together (Mitchell *et al.*, 2006). In a review of the literature, Mitchell *et al.* (2006) suggest the most reliable data point to the possibility of 500,000 users in 1972, which, if maintained at this level in 2016, would make ASL one of 15 languages in the USA to reach the half-million users threshold.

There is reason to believe the number of users may be higher than this. The teaching and study of ASL has expanded rapidly in the USA since the 1970s, to the point where ASL is the third most taught language in US higher education (Looney & Lusin, 2018), with slightly over 107,000 people learning ASL in postsecondary institutions in 2016. There are currently no reliable contemporary statistics on the total number of ASL users, include hearing ASL users, which include families with deaf members and hearing people who learn sign language in formal and informal educational settings. Other sign languages or varieties of ASL are used in the USA, including Black ASL (McCaskill *et al.*, 2011), Native American signed languages (Davis, 2017), and in Hawaii, an indigenous variety of Hawaii sign language has been discovered that has existed since at least the 1820s (Lambrecht *et al.*, 2013). Mexican Sign Language (LSM), is also used in the USA and there are anecdotal reports of deaf immigrant communities using other sign languages as well. Of these signed languages, ASL is currently the only sign language to have legislative recognition in the USA.

The USA has no *de jure* official language, nor an official national language. There have been attempts to enact legislation promoting English as an official language on the federal level, but these attempts have not yet succeeded. As a federal system, states are free to make their own laws on issues not otherwise regulated by the federal government. Language policies have been enacted on the state level, with 32 of 50 states having laws which confer some form of legislative recognition of English. Alaska and Hawaii also recognize indigenous languages as official languages (Language Legislation in the USA, 2012; Schwartz, 2014).

Legislative campaigns for the recognition of ASL in the USA have likewise taken place largely on the state level. In this chapter, I adopt De Meulder's (2015) distinction between explicit and implicit recognition of sign languages, using 'explicit' to refer legislation that accords status recognition and 'implicit' for legislation that enacts policies related to the provision of language-related services, often via a disability framework. There exists a broad range of state-level legislation regarding ASL, with 49 of 50 states having some form of explicit or implicit legislative recognition of ASL (the one exception is Mississippi). These laws range from status recognition laws to access legislation, to laws governing ASL acquisition, both among deaf and hearing people. Status recognition legislation can be seen as a form of status planning, in which a language is accorded certain areas of use, often via a government (Cooper, 1989; Reagan, 2010). In this case, ASL is accorded status as a language to be taught in specific educational settings. While there is no explicit legal recognition of ASL on the federal level, there exist several federal laws that confer implicit recognition. This combination of explicit recognition on the state level with implicit recognition on the national level has proven to be quite successful in ensuring the visibility of ASL in US society. Below, I begin by outlining the different types of state-level ASL recognition laws, move on to discuss federal laws and conclude with a discussion of the current status of ASL in the USA.

State-Level Recognition of ASL

The most common form of explicit ASL recognition on the state level is recognition for the purpose of accepting ASL as a language subject bearing credit in educational settings. As of this writing, 45 of 50 states have laws that confer this recognition. The first such law seems to have been a

1979 amendment of a 1971 law in Texas, which approved the teaching of 'dactylology' (the ASL manual alphabet) for elective course credit in Texas colleges and universities. The 1979 amendment's opening text: 'American Sign Language is recognized as a language' may be one of the first status recognitions of a *named* sign language in any legislation (as opposed to generic recognition of a 'sign language'.) (Elective Courses in Dactylology, 1979). While these laws seem to be largely about acquisition planning, there is almost always a form of status recognition in the law as a prelude to the clauses dealing with acquisition. These state recognition laws follow a similar template: they accord status recognition of ASL as a language, then go on to specify this language can be taught for college credit in higher education institutions in the state. The 1994 Massachusetts law states ASL is 'the equivalent of a spoken language for the purposes of foreign language study and course credit' (American Sign Language, 1994). Some state recognition laws vary in that they are aimed at elementary and secondary education. Three of the five states that do not have such laws have conferred recognition for the teaching of ASL in schools on an administrative level, with recognition by the State Board of Education in New Hampshire and Hawaii, and by the Department of Education in Missouri.

I classify these laws as explicit status recognition laws because they contain text directly recognizing ASL as a language and further accord ASL a status as a language to be taught in either or both postsecondary and K-12 educational settings. A significant subset of these laws go on to add a linguistic description of the language. One example is Louisiana, whose 1991 recognition law offers a detailed explanation of ASL's linguistic properties:

> As used in this Section 'American Sign Language' shall mean a visual language which has emerged from the deaf culture and is comprised of handshapes, movement, and body and facial expression, and possesses an identifiable syntax and grammar specific to visual languages which incorporates spatial relationships as a linguistic factor. (American Sign Language; secondary schools, 1991)

That a status recognition law needs a linguistic description is symptomatic of the unique status of sign languages, which need to be legitimized as languages in ways spoken languages do not (Reagan, 2011). This need for legitimacy is made explicit in the text of the Florida law: 'American Sign Language is a ... complete and complex language that has its own syntax, rhetoric, and grammar and that is used to convey information and meaning through signs made with the hands, arms, facial gestures, and other body movements.' (American Sign Language; findings; foreign-language credits authorized; teacher licensing, 2004). According to data collected by the author in 2015, 25 of 49 states with explicit and implicit ASL recognition laws have some sort of definition of ASL in the text of the law.

A curious result of this focus on college credit in most legislation is that in many states, status recognition is granted in a form that fits existing university disciplinary classifications: ASL is recognized as a 'foreign' language. This is an unusual formulation of what could be considered an indigenous language. Several scholars have attempted to justify the classification of ASL as a 'foreign language' in university settings (see Cooper, 1997; Reagan, 2011, for overviews). Reagan (2011: 624) suggests the term foreign means *'foreign to the student'* [emphasis in original]. Wilcox (1989), conceding the term is used to conform to university foreign language departments, notes American Indian Languages are also classified as foreign languages, despite their indigenous status. However, the classification of a language as foreign in a university setting is very different from the *legal codification* of a language as foreign. This discrepancy does not yet seem to have been a factor, since there have not been any legal proceedings to date in which these laws have been used to support the linguistic rights of ASL users. This may reflect the fact that the intent of these laws has been mainly symbolic and mostly aimed at a narrow result: granting instructional credit for students who study the language.

Campaigns for Explicit Recognition

The campaigns surrounding these laws have been minimally documented in research to date and the scope of archival collections on these efforts is currently unknown. The legislative recognition of ASL seems to have commonly taken place in coalitions of deaf people, sometimes via a state association of deaf people, working with hearing signers and/or university researchers and officials at state educational agencies (see Pfeiffer, 2003 for a brief overview of efforts in California, Virginia and Nevada). Selover (1988) describes the motivation behind California's successful campaign as being a desire to bring 'empowerment' to deaf people by making ASL more visible, thus leading to wider social acceptance and understanding of deaf people. An additional factor noted by Selover was the passage of PL 94-142, a law promoting the mainstreaming of deaf and disabled children. Selover considered the establishment of ASL instruction as promoting the potential for 'free flowing communication among deaf and hearing students' in light of the trend towards mainstreaming deaf children in local school districts (Selover, 1988: 206). More work is needed to uncover the disparate and possibly evolving motivations of different groups of campaigners and policymakers in 45 states over a span of several decades.

This combination of status legislation with the accordance of credit for instructional purposes is the most common form of ASL recognition. These laws could arguably be called a hybrid of status and acquisition laws, in that they not only recognize the status of ASL but prepare the way for hearing people to learn ASL. These campaigns can be seen in light of a push to promote the teaching of ASL as a means of legitimizing the use of ASL in wider US society (as outlined in Humphries, 2008 and Murray, 2017), a push that has been, measured in terms of public acceptance, extraordinarily successful.

The provision of ASL instruction in postsecondary education settings has grown exponentially since the 1980s. Between 1982 and 1986, the number of postsecondary education institutions offering 'manual communication' classes jumped sevenfold, from 101 to 772, demonstrating growing interest in ASL instruction across several institutions as far back as the 1980s (Cooper, 1997). Data from the Modern Language Association (MLA), the leading US academic body for language instruction, report the number of students taking ASL classes in postsecondary institutions: they list 1602 students taking courses in 23 institutions in 1990, a likely undercount considering the number of institutions reported to be offering sign language classes in 1986 (Cooper, 1997; Looney & Lusin, 2018). The number of students counted by the MLA survey has grown exponentially in each survey and since 2013, ASL has had over 100,000 students at the postsecondary level, surpassed only by French (175,667) and Spanish (712,240) (Goldberg et al., 2015). The most recent data show 107,060 students taking ASL classes at the postsecondary level in 2016. This does not include students at the elementary and secondary levels, nor does it include people who learn ASL in informal educational settings, such as at workshops offered by community organizations or at churches. Clearly, a large and growing number of people learn ASL, showing that the intent of state campaigners for ASL recognition laws has translated into concrete results.

Implicit Recognition at the State Level

State level implicit recognition can be largely found under laws governing the provision of interpreting services. In the USA, national sign language interpreting licensure has long been conducted by a professional organization, the Registry of Interpreters for the Deaf. This private licensing exam is supplemented in some states by state-level licensure requirements. According to data collected in 2015, 26 of 50 states have implicit recognition of ASL through the provision ASL/English interpreting services and regulation of standards. This includes both laws that accord the right to use interpreters in certain settings, such as in legal, medical, and elementary and secondary educational settings, and laws that regulate the licensure and certification of interpreters.

Another area of implicit recognition relates to acquisition planning for deaf children. A few states have passed legislation that recognize the right of deaf children to use sign language in educational settings. This is still infrequent, and a national advocacy coalition, titled *Lead-K* (Language Equality and Acquisition for Deaf Kids) works on the state level to promote the passage of laws mandating access to early language acquisition services for deaf children. Currently, seven states have legislation modeled after Lead-K's proposed legislation, with legislation pending in 20 other states (Bianco-Majeri & Holmes, 2018).

Federal Level Recognition of ASL

In 2012, deaf American Adrean Clark, along with a team of colleagues, utilized the petition function on the White House's website to call for 'official federal recognition of ASL' (Clark, 2012). The petition gathered over 27,000 signatures in a few weeks, exceeding the threshold for a response from the White House (Flock, 2012). The White House's response, the official response of the Obama Administration, elided the question of official recognition, stating instead 'We reinforce its importance in numerous federal laws, regulations, and policies.' (White House, 2013). The Administration's response pointed to the numerous federal laws that have accorded implicit recognition and instrumental rights to deaf people to use ASL.

While there is no explicit recognition of ASL on the federal level, the ability to use ASL to achieve access to public and private facilities and services is quite widespread in the USA. The first significant 20th century federal disability legislation used by deaf people for sign language rights was Section 504 of the Rehabilitation Act of 1973, which forbids discrimination on the basis of disability in institutions receiving federal funds. This affects a wide swathe of public life, with state and local governments, hospitals and educational institutions, among others, all receiving federal funds. One notable impact of this legislation was support for the training and provision of sign language interpreters in postsecondary education, with each institution now mandated to cover costs of interpreting access for deaf students.

Another important law with implicit recognition of ASL is the Americans with Disabilities Act (ADA) of 1990, which requires governments, nonprofit organizations and private businesses that serve the public to make their services accessible to persons with disabilities. The ADA also mandated equitable telecommunications access and set up a regulatory framework to ensure this access was commensurate with options available to hearing people. The advent of video relay services in 2000 (Brunson, 2012) in which ASL/English interpreting is conducted through video telephones has made ASL use an accepted part of the US telecommunications infrastructure. The ADA also mandates state and local governments to ensure their educational programs, services and facilities are open to all children with disabilities.

These access laws have had significant impact on the instrumental rights of ASL users in that they have given deaf ASL users the opportunity to use ASL in many areas of life. This access is not without its limits. Since interpreting costs are borne by the organization or institution providing services, the provision and payment of interpreting services is still contested by many public entities and private businesses, particularly smaller businesses. There is no central government interpreting fund for activities which fall into the sphere of private life activities. These activities, such as family events, need to be self-financed.

A key area of linguistic rights is acquisition rights, and deaf community members have often looked to educational settings to secure intergenerational transmission of their sign languages. Federal legislation related to the use of ASL in deaf children's educational settings does not reflect this priority. Rather, legislation on ASL access in education is enacted through disability education legislation and presents ASL as a means of providing access to educational settings, often via sign language interpreters. A key US federal law governing the education of children with disabilities, The 1975 Education for All Handicapped Children Act (later renamed the Individuals with Disabilities Education Act (IDEA)), or PL94-142, was reauthorized in 1999 with reference to 'sign language' as a native language of deaf children and required this language be taken into consideration when providing *support services* for deaf children. Rosen (2006) notes 23.4% of deaf children used interpreters in the 2003–2004 school year. Rosen (2006), echoing Selover (1988), has argued this increased use of sign language interpreters has led to an increased visibility for ASL in public school settings.

The current text of IDEA recognizes 'sign language' in *Section 300.29: Native Language*, stating 'For an individual with deafness or blindness… the mode of communication is that normally used by the individual (such as sign language, Braille, or oral communication).' (Individuals with Disabilities Education Act, 2004). The Statute specifies native language does not only mean paternal language, but can also mean the language used by the child 'at home or in the learning environment.' Another important federal disability law, the ADA, requires schools ensure deaf and hard of hearing children receive communications as 'effective as communications with others' and to provide 'auxiliary aids and services' to meet this requirement (Clerc Center, undated). This includes the use of sign language interpreters, both onsite and remote video relay interpreters. Federal legislative recognition of ASL in education springs from disability legislation and is largely focused on the use of ASL as a means of access to educational settings and services.

Conclusion

There exists today a large number of state and federal laws that explicitly and implicitly accord status recognition to ASL and instrumental rights to deaf people who use ASL. These instrumental rights are largely granted via federal disability legislation. State level status recognition laws are mostly designed with acquisition planning goals in mind, to enable hearing people to study ASL as an additional language in formal educational settings. Federal legislation exists which recognizes deaf children's right to use ASL in educational settings, but this has largely been read to mean the right to have access to sign language (and not necessarily ASL) interpreters in mainstreamed settings.

The predominant legislative treatment of ASL in the USA today can be said to be one in which ASL is seen as a tool for implementing legal mandates for access and to the inclusion of deaf people in wider society. Academic research and deaf community discourses regarding ASL may consider ASL the language of a US minority, but legislative recognition of ASL most commonly treats it either under disability classification, aimed at including deaf people in civil society, or as granting it linguistic recognition in mainstream educational settings, to be taught to hearing people, as well as to deaf people who learn ASL later in life. The cultural minority perspective is missing from legislation, with rights being accorded on an individual instead of a group basis (Kusters et al., 2015). The status of ASL in the US Census is illustrative of this point. As noted earlier, the US Census classifies users of ASL as English speakers, due to the US Census's interpretation of its mandate under the 1975 amendment to the Voting Rights Act as being to collect data 'on non-English languages that are spoken by members of racial minority groups' (US Census Bureau, 2017). The Census Bureau states they have no mandate to collect data on language use in 'the hearing disabled population' under that Act. Recognition of ASL as a language used by a linguistic minority within the USA would entail a very different formulation of the US Census Bureau's mandate.

The recognition of ASL on state and federal levels over the past four decades has enhanced the status of ASL in US society. The widespread teaching and learning of ASL has led to a boom in the number of people who know and can use ASL. ASL has also been prominent in television and film productions in this period. This subsequent widespread knowledge and increasing visibility of ASL in public spaces has led to greater acceptance of the language as a part of US society. In this, the US deaf community can be said to have conducted an extremely successful campaign over several decades – for the acquisition and acceptance of ASL among members of wider society.

Acknowledgements

The state-level data collected for this study was conducted as part of a graduate class project at Gallaudet University in Spring 2015. I thank the following for their participation in data collection efforts: Brenda Falgier, David Simmons, Guthrie Nutter, April Haggard, Ayisha Knight-Shaw, Kenny DeHaan, John Brand III, Jonathan McMillan, Justin Arrigo, Kristine Hall, Kurstin Chun, Marissa Polvere, Miranda Medugno, Sandon Larson, Tim Riker, Georgina Fitzpatrick, Geo Kartheiser, Serina

Arellano, Shannon Kapp, Sheena McFeely, Sherry Williams, Stephanie Gasco, Thuy Tien Nguyen, Jennifer Marfino, Jessica Brown, Wes Singleton, Brian Burns, Brittany Frank, Adam Stone, Andy Lim, Sandra Buchholz and Evelina Gaina.

References

American Sign Language (1994) Massachusetts General Laws, Chapter 15A, §9A.

American Sign Language; findings; foreign-language credits authorized; teacher licensing (2004) Florida Statute. Title XLVIII, 1007.2615.

American Sign Language; secondary schools (1991) Louisiana Statute. RS 17:284 Acts 1991, No. 512, §1.

Bianco-Majeri, K. and Holmes, T. (2018) NAD Updates on Language Deprivation. Paper presentation. *54th Convention of the National Association of the Deaf* July 3–7, 2018, Hartford, Connecticut.

Brunson, J.L. (2012) *Video Relay Service Interpreters: Intricacies of Sign Language Access*. Washington, DC: Gallaudet University Press.

Clark, A. (2012) Officially recognize American Sign Language as a community language and a language of instruction in schools. Archived screenshot of White House website in private possession.

Clerc Center (undated) Laws impacting students who are deaf or hard of hearing. Laurent Clerc National Deaf Education Center. See http://www3.gallaudet.edu/clerc-center/info-to-go/legislation-and-policies/laws-impacting-students.html (last accessed January 25, 2019).

Cooper, R.L. (1989) *Language Planning and Social Change*. Cambridge: Cambridge University Press.

Cooper, S.B. (1997) The academic status of sign language programs in institutions of higher education in the United States. PhD dissertation, Gallaudet University.

Davis, J. (2017) Native American Signed Languages. *Oxford Handbooks Online*. Oxford: Oxford University Press. DOI: 10.1093/oxfordhb/9780199935345.013.42.

De Meulder, M. (2015) The legal recognition of sign languages. *Sign Language Studies* 15 (4), 498–506.

Elective Courses in Dactylology (1979) Texas Education Code 3A.51 § 51.303 (1971, amended 1979).

Flock, E. (2012) Petition to officially recognize American Sign Language reaches threshold for White House response. *US News and World Report*, 11 December 2012. See https://www.usnews.com/news/blogs/washington-whispers/2012/12/11/petition-to-officially-recognize-american-sign-language-reaches-threshold-for-white-house-response (last accessed January 25, 2019.).

Goldberg, D., Looney, D. and Lusin, N. (2015) Enrollment in languages other than English in United States institutions of higher education, Fall 2013. Modern Language Association. See https://apps.mla.org/pdf/2013_enrollment_survey.pdf (last accessed January 25, 2019).

Humphries, T. (2008) Talking culture and culture talking. In H-D.L. Bauman (ed.) *Open your Eyes: Deaf Studies Talking* (pp. 35–41). Minneapolis: University of Minnesota Press.

Individuals with Disabilities Education Act (2004) 20 U.S.C. Section 1400–1487. Native Language. Sec. 300.29.

Kusters, A., De Meulder, M., Friedner, M. and Emery, S. (2015) On 'diversity' and 'inclusion': Exploring paradigms for achieving Sign Language Peoples' rights. MMG Working Paper 15–02. See http://www.mmg.mpg.de/publications/working-papers/2015/wp-15-02/ (last accessed January 25, 2019).

Lambrecht, L., Earth, B. and Woodward, J. (2013) History and documentation of Hawai'i Sign Language: First report. Third International Conference on Language Documentation and Conservation, University of Hawai'i, February 28–March 3, 2013.

Language Legislation in the USA (2012) See http://www.languagepolicy.net/archives/langleg.htm (last accessed January 25, 2019).

Looney, D. and Lusin, N. (2018) Enrollment in languages other than English in United States institutions of higher education, summer 2016 and fall 2016. Modern Language Association. See https://www.mla.org/content/download/83540/2197676/2016-Enrollments-Short-Report.pdf (last accessed January 25, 2019).

McCaskill, C., Lucas, C., Bayley, R. and Hill, J. (2011) *The Hidden Treasure of Black ASL: Its History and Structure* Washington, DC: Gallaudet University Press.

Mitchell, R.E., Young, T.A., Bachleda, B. and Karchmer, M.A. (2006) How many deaf people use ASL in the United States? Why estimates need updating. *Sign Language Studies* 6 (3), 306–335.

Murray, J.J. (2017) Deaf Studies: Scholarship and community interaction in the making of deaf identities. In A. Kusters, D. O'Brien and M. De Meulder (eds) *Innovations in Deaf Studies: The Role of Deaf Scholars* (pp. 77–100). Oxford: Oxford University Press.

Pfeffier, D.L. (2003) The implementation and administration of American Sign Language programs for foreign language credit in public secondary schools. Doctoral dissertation, George Washington University.

Reagan, T.G. (2010) *Language Policy and Planning for Sign Languages*. Washington, DC: Gallaudet University Press.

Reagan, T. (2011) Ideological barriers to American Sign Language: Unpacking linguistic resistance. *Sign Language Studies* 11 (4), 606–636.

Rosen, R.S. (2006) An unintended consequence of IDEA: American Sign Language, the Deaf community, and Deaf culture into mainstream education. *Disability Studies Quarterly* 26 (2). See http://dsq-sds.org/article/view/685/862 (last accessed January 25, 2019).

Ryan, C. (2013) Language use in the United States: American Community Survey Reports. US Census Bureau. See https://www.census.gov/library/publications/2013/acs/acs-22.html (last accessed January 25, 2019).

Schwartz, H. (2014) States where English is the official language. *Washington Post*, 12 August . See https://www.washingtonpost.com/blogs/govbeat/wp/2014/08/12/states-where-english-is-the-official-language/?utm_term=.0fd1f7b22d15 (last accessed January 25, 2019).

Selover, P. (1988) American Sign Language in the high school system. *Sign Language Studies* 59, 205–212.

US Census Bureau (2017) Language use: Frequently asked questions. Webpage last revised 10 October 2017. See https://www.census.gov/topics/population/language-use/about/faqs.html (last accessed January 25, 2019).

White House (2013) There shouldn't be any stigma about American Sign Language. See https://petitions.obamawhitehouse.archives.gov/petition/officially-recognize-american-sign-language-community-language-and-language-instruction (last accessed January 25, 2019).

Wilcox, S. (1989) Foreign language requirement? Why not American Sign Language? Washington, DC: Center for Applied Linguistics. (ERIC Document Reproduction Service No. ED 309 651).

8 Towards the Recognition of Chilean Sign Language

Maribel González, Andrea Pérez, Juan Luis Marín and Camila Villavicencio

Introduction

In the past few decades, Deaf communities around the world 'have begun to fight for the recognition of their sign languages and the right to have education and access to all spheres of society in their sign language' (Quer & Quadros, 2015: 122–123). Considering the dual category status of deaf people, as members of a disability group and at the same time as part of a culture-linguistic minority, there is a tendency on the part of policymakers to include sign languages in disability laws without corresponding linguistic and cultural recognition (De Meulder & Murray, 2017). The latter is the case in Chile, where sign language has been recognized by the 'Law setting the rules and standards on equal opportunities and social inclusion of people with disabilities' (hereafter, Law 20.422, 2010), which included sign language as 'a means of communication' used by the Deaf community.

In this chapter, we first present a general review of Chile's current language policies and history of the development of Chilean Sign Language (LSCh). We then focus on the background to the LSCh recognition process, as well as the policies and regulations that provided the context for the campaign for the recognition of the linguistic rights of the Chilean Deaf community. This is followed by a description of the main milestones of the campaign and, finally, we analyze some of the factors that have had an impact on LSCh recognition and dissemination. Considering the relatively few published sources available on this topic, we have referred to unpublished documents and conducted interviews with deaf activists campaigning for the recognition of LSCh. Two semi-structured interviews and one focus group were conducted, in which four persons participated. The interviews were done by the deaf authors of this chapter, who themselves were active participants in some of the campaigns we describe below.

Linguistic Policies and Status of Languages in Chile

Currently, Spanish is the de facto official language of Chile, since there is no legal recognition at either the constitutional or regulatory levels. Indigenous languages such as Mapuzungun, Aymara, or Rapa Nui were banned from schools in the mid-19th century (Vera, 2017). Despite Law 19.253 of 1993, which establishes norms regarding the protection, promotion and development of indigenous people and their languages, Chile is still predominantly monolingual (Vera, 2017). The National Corporation for Indigenous Development (CONADI), with the aim of preserving the language and culture of indigenous people, has focused exclusively on spoken languages. As a consequence, LSCh has never been considered in this legal and institutional framework. The first advances in LSCh recognition have been made solely within the context of the regulations for people with disabilities.

Background to the Struggle for Chilean Sign Language Recognition: Teaching, Learning and Interpreting

Deaf education and sign language acquisition

Deaf education in Chile goes back to 1852, the year in which the first Latin American residential school for deaf children, the 'Escuela de Sordo-Mudos' (School of Deaf Mutes) was established in Santiago. In 1889, the school turned to the oral method (Herrera *et al.*, 2009). Only at the beginning of the 1980s, did academics from the Department of Special Education at the Metropolitan University of Educational Sciences (UMCE), an institution that trains teachers of the deaf, begin to question this teaching approach due to its inefficiency in developing deaf students' communication skills. In 1984, after this group attended a seminar on Total Communication, they began to incorporate pedagogical strategies to include sign language in deaf students' education. In 1986, after liaison with Gallaudet University (Adamo & Cabrera, 1991), some deaf schools began to adopt the Total Communication approach and LSCh was incorporated into the curriculum of the bachelor's program in Special Education focusing on training future teachers of deaf students.

The 1992 International Conference on Bilingualism in Stockholm generated a shift in the prevailing educational models, supporting a bilingual education approach for deaf students (Herrera *et al.*, 2009). From 1994 onwards, students with disabilities began to go to regular primary schools and high schools, supported by a law on inclusive education (Law 19.284, 1994). In 1998, for the first time, sign language interpreting was mentioned as one of the support measures for deaf students (Supreme Decree No. 01, 1998), endorsing interpreters' presence in schools (González & Pérez, 2017; González, 2017). Today, the majority of deaf students in Chile attend a mainstream school, with only 21%

attending special education settings, and this trend is expected to increase (MINEDUC, 2016–2018).

Although the participation of deaf professionals and LSCh interpreters has increased, only 20% of mainstream schools employ professionals who promote LSCh in the school. Furthermore, given that around 67% of the mainstream schools have just one deaf student in the institution, there is a real risk of deaf students becoming isolated (MINEDUC, 2016–2018). One of the paradoxes of the inclusive education movement is that it seems to be more concerned with where children are educated than with the quality of their education (Lissi & Salinas, 2012; Lissi et al., 2012). Moreover, the increase of cochlear implants has led to 'curricular modifications dealing primarily with hearing loss rather than with the characteristics and needs of Deaf students' (De la Paz et al., 2016: 70).

Data gathered by the National Disability Service (SENADIS) demonstrate that almost 60% of Chilean deaf people have no educational qualifications beyond elementary school, while 6.4% do not have a formal education at all. Only about 23% of deaf people have completed secondary education and only 3.42% have had the chance to graduate from a high school institution (Lissi et al., 2019). The scarce educational opportunities for deaf people are an important barrier in terms of them being enabled to be involved in critical issues regarding their language, culture, and education.

Chilean Deaf organizations and Chilean Sign Language

Chile has one of the oldest national deaf associations in South America (Parks et al., 2011). Historical records show that around 1900, a group of deaf people gathered in the Santiago city center. In 1913, this group formed the 'The Chilean Society of Deaf and Dumb' (Demartini & Letelier, 2006). The same organization was refounded in October 1926, and is now called 'Asociación de Sordos de Chile' (Chilean Association of the Deaf), ASOCH (Oviedo, 2015). In the 1950s, due to differences emerging among ASOCH members, new groups began to be created mostly focused on sports. Although there are several deaf associations and organizations across the country, they are not well unified (Parks et al., 2011). Occasionally, specific campaigns have brought deaf organizations together in pursuing a common goal. In the 1990s, a group of young people founded the 'Club Real de Sordos' (CRESOR). Towards the beginning of 2000, CRESOR would take the lead, alongside ASOCH, to demand the provision of LSCh interpreters on television news broadcasts.

In the mid-1990s, Deaf organizations became involved with the teaching and dissemination of Chilean sign language. The first organization of this kind was the 'Center of Sign Language Studies' (CELENSE) in 1987, with the aim of teaching Chilean Sign Language to the community. These classes were taught by deaf people, and supported by hearing people in the creation of the study programs. Later, in 1991, the ASOCH created its own center, establishing a team of deaf instructors that has offered sign language classes at different learning levels.

Building on work from an earlier group, the 'Association of Sign Language Instructors and Interpreters' (ACHIELS) existed from 1996 to 2010. The aim of this deaf-led association was originally to standardize LSCh and to discuss its corpus (González & Pérez, 2017). However, this idea evolved as the Chilean Deaf community began to understand and accept the naturalness of the sociolinguistic variations of sign language. In 2012, the 'Foundation of Deaf Chileans' began offering LSCh courses and interpretation services, as well as participating in the process of sign language recognition and demands for the right to access information in LSCh.

Incorporating Chilean Sign Language in higher education

One of the milestones in relation to sign language teaching at the university level occurred with the incorporation of the first deaf instructor who taught LSCh in the Department of Special Education at the Metropolitan University of Educational Sciences (UMCE) in 1988. This was influenced by the experience of UMCE scholars who, after visiting Gallaudet University in the USA, decided to incorporate LSCh as part of the curriculum of the bachelor's program in Special Education with a focus on Hearing and Language Disorders (González & Pérez, 2017).

Since 2010, universities and institutes of higher education have begun to incorporate LSCh into their curriculum, especially in universities that offer a degree in pedagogy and special education. The growing need for LSCh instructors has meant that hearing people, such as children of deaf adults (CODAs) or interpreters, have started to teach LSCh. Although the Chilean Deaf community has questioned this practice, there is currently no regulatory framework providing orientation about who is responsible for teaching the language, nor the competencies that this person should have. Furthermore, there is no specific training required to become a sign language instructor.

Chilean Sign Language interpreting

Working interpreters in Chile are usually CODAs, special education teachers, members of religious communities and people who have attended sign language courses (Pérez, 2008). As in other countries, while interpretation services exist, there are no institutions in charge of the development of this profession (Muñoz et al., 2018). Although there is no undergraduate bachelor's degree in interpretation and translation, educational institutions have begun to offer training courses aimed at people who are already fluent in sign language (González & Pérez, 2017). Nevertheless, to date, there are no regulations that define the competencies of professionals who work as interpreters, nor the role and ethical code that they should fulfill in the different contexts in which they work. Despite this lack of professional training and accreditation, a group of interpreters in Chile have organized themselves through the Association of Chilean Sign Language Interpreters (AILES).

Chilean Sign Language research

In Chile, LSCh-related studies began to develop in the late 1980s. Up till now, research has mainly focused on stating the importance of teaching sign language in educational settings for deaf people and on describing grammatical and narrative aspects of LSCh (Acuña *et al.*, 2012; Adamo, 1993; Otárola & Crespo, 2015). There also have been some studies on the relation between LSCh development and deaf students' reading and writing skills (Herrera, 2007; Lissi *et al.*, 2010). In 2009, the first Chilean Sign Language–Spanish Bilingual Dictionary was developed by UMCE as part of an agreement with the Chilean Ministry of Education (MINEDUC). According to the authors, the dictionary was developed to meet the demands of the Chilean Deaf community and was later made available in an online format (Adamo *et al.*, 2013).

The Trajectory of Chilean Sign Language Recognition

In order to give an overview of the main milestones which have led to a progressive, but limited, recognition of the linguistic rights of the Chilean Deaf community, we have divided the campaign into three major periods.

During this first period (1994–2002), the Chilean Deaf community mobilized around filing lawsuits, focused on access to information to broadcast television, as well as public demonstrations by deaf people. A second period (2003–2012) started with Chile's ratification of the United Nations Convention on the Rights of Persons with Disabilities (CRPD) in 2008, which led to the incorporation of LSCh as a means of communication of Deaf people as part of the 'Law Setting the Rules and Standards on Equality of Opportunities and Social Inclusion of People with Disabilities' in 2010. The final period (2014 onwards) considers the impact of LSCh recognition granted by such law, including some of the current demands of the organizations and associations of the Chilean Deaf community. Figure 8.1 corresponds to a graphic representation of the milestones in this ongoing sign language recognition process.

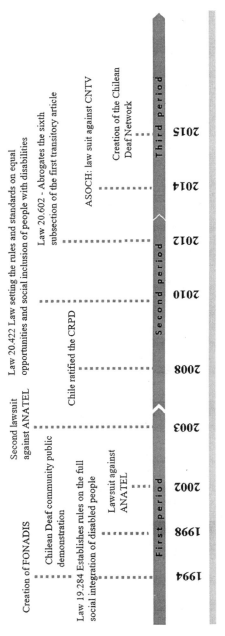

Figure 8.1 Timeline of the milestones related to the process of Chilean Sign Language recognition

First Period: Deaf Community's First Movements and Demands

The first precedents of the struggle for the rights of Chilean deaf people date from the 1990s. The main target in this period was demanding access to television through sign language interpretation and subtitles. The most common strategy to do this was filing complaints to the National Television Council (CNTV). To carry out these demands, the Deaf community received support from disability rights activists, government deputies and private lawyers.

Resources enabling people to access disability-related services and goods were allocated for the first time in 1994 with the enactment of the Law on Full Social Integration of People with Disabilities (Law 19.284). These resources were managed by FONADIS, which in 2010 becomes the National Disability Service (SENADIS) (Lissi *et al.*, 2019). A provision in this law stipulated the National Television Council was to make television broadcasting accessible to deaf and hard of hearing people (Article 19, Law 19.284). The Chilean Deaf community used this law to press for access to information in LSCh. Deaf associations, organized in a larger alliance called 'Confederación de no Oyentes de Chile' (Non-Hearing Confederation of Chile) (CONOYCH), made a formal complaint to the National Television Council (CNTV) demanding the incorporation of LSCh interpreters in broadcast television, a demand that was rejected.

At that time, the mobilization of the Chilean Deaf community was reflected in public demonstrations. In 1998, the first public celebration of the International Day of the Deaf was held in Temuco, La Araucanía region (Día Internacional de los Sordos, ¿Dónde están sus derechos? 1998). Under the slogan 'For the rights of the Deaf', the Deaf community wanted to increase the visibility of LSCh and to raise authorities' awareness about the barriers they were facing (González & Pérez, 2017). Since 2001, the International Day of the Deaf is commemorated annually with demonstrations in different regions of the country, advocating for the respect and recognition of Chilean Sign Language rights (González & Pérez, 2017).

While Deaf community mobilization was becoming stronger, a second opportunity to continue lobbying efforts for access to television content came about in 2002, led by CRESOR, the deaf youth organization. An important Chilean disability activist, María Soledad Cisternas, a blind lawyer, offered the chance to file a lawsuit against the national media to warrant access to information based on Law 19.284. This lawyer proposed that the Deaf community could choose between asking for LSCh interpreters or Spanish subtitles as a way to access the television news. After consulting several deaf organizations, it was decided to demand the incorporation of LSCh interpreters in the television news. CRESOR argued that this was the best option considering that on one hand, LSCh needed to become more visible and, on the other, that a high percentage of Chilean deaf people would not be able to read and understand subtitles.

CRESOR filed a lawsuit against the TV broadcasters grouped under the Chilean National Television Association, ANATEL, in the Appeals Court (CNTV, 2002). The Appeals Court rendered a positive judgment, but national TV broadcasters appealed to the Supreme Court, the highest court of appeal, which in turn favored them. CRESOR announced a second lawsuit, this time supported by a group of lawyers who proposed presenting the case to the Inter-American Court of Human Rights to sue the government of Chile for violating deaf people's human rights. This case generated a quick reaction from the government, which summoned a meeting to negotiate with ANATEL. Consequently, LSCh interpreters were provided on public television on a rotating basis[1] (P. Molina, pers. comm., 30 December 2017).

In order to reach this goal, deaf associations from all over the country needed to be aligned and sign the agreement with the television channels. Given the differing views on accessibility rights it was not easy to reach consensus, and many meetings across the country were necessary. In the end, all deaf associations of the country signed the agreement, and it was implemented in March 2003 (P. Molina, pers. comm., 30 December 2017).

Second Period: Incorporation of Sign Language into the Disability Law and First Formal Attempts towards its Recognition

The main milestone of this period was Chile's ratification of the CRPD in 2008 (Decree No. 201, 2008). One of the main articles supporting these actions has been Article 24 on education, particularly when referring to 'facilitating the learning of sign language and the promotion of the linguistic identity of the deaf community (…) in environments which maximize academic and social development' (UN General Assembly, 2007: 14), as well as the promotion of teachers with disabilities, including those who are qualified in sign language.

Countries are obligated to amend relevant laws to ensure the rights of people with disabilities. In Chile, this meant the revision of the disability law. Michael Stein, a deaf lawyer from the USA was visiting Chile to bring together deaf leaders from different organizations and discuss how to translate the CRPD into the current Chilean legal system. The deaf leaders decided to create a group called 'Movimiento Fuerza Sordo' (Deaf Force Movement), which reviewed the draft of the proposed amended legislation, identifying gaps and lack of clarity regarding the provision of services for deaf people (Stein, 2015).

Leaders of the deaf associations tried to negotiate with FONADIS, the National Disability Fund, before the enactment of the law which would regulate the inclusion of people with disabilities in the country. The aim was to modify clauses in the proposed law governing access to information and education for Deaf people in LSCh. However, it was not possible to negotiate, since at the time of the meeting the bill was already set to pass. This meant that the Deaf community was not invited to participate in writing or commenting on the appropriateness of articles related to their needs (Stein, 2015).

In February 2010, the 'Law setting the rules and standards on equality of opportunities and social inclusion of people with disabilities' (Law 20.422, 2010) was enacted. This law explicitly mentioned sign language for the first time in Article 26: 'Sign Language is recognized as the natural means of communication of the Deaf community'. This recognition as a means of communication and not a language is not aligned with Deaf community goals.

Article 25 of the law indicates that television broadcasters 'must apply audiovisual communication mechanisms that allow people with hearing disabilities access to their programming in appropriate cases, as determined by regulations'. This includes the inclusion of subtitles and sign language interpreting for specific programs.[2]

In order for Article 26 to enter into force, the law required the State and the Deaf community to define Chilean Sign Language within a period of three years (sixth paragraph, provisional Article 1, Law 20.422, 2010): 'The State, together with the community of people with hearing disabilities, will define, within three years, the Chilean Sign Language'. The inclusion of this provisional article may have originated in some erroneous interpretations generated during conversations between legislators and members of the Deaf community. During a meeting held in the National Congress, deaf people explained the concept of regional variation in LSCh. Lawmakers interpreted this as lack of a standard language, and considered that LSCh was not yet 'defined'. At that time, deaf activists did not yet have the required knowledge to explain that this variation is a natural part of LSCh (Olivarí, J. pers. comm., 29 March 2018).

A few days after the law came into force, a major earthquake affected the country. During this disaster, deaf people were not able to access media updates. One deaf organization, ACHIELS, took the lead in highlighting this lack of access and initiated new action against the television channels. First, the association filed a lawsuit and issued a remedy of protection to the Court of Appeal. Upon rejection, ACHIELS appealed to the Supreme Court, which also resulted in a negative decision (C. Muñoz, pers. comm., 22 January 2017). Both cases were rejected based on the aforementioned paragraph 6 of provisional Article 1. After these experiences, some deaf leaders sought support from policymakers. A federal Congressperson, Andrea Molina, encouraged the deaf community to campaign for the abrogation of paragraph 6 (C. Muñoz, pers. comm., 22 January 2017). Consequently, the Deaf community reunited under the group 'Deaf Force Movement', which was led by Deaf persons from different nationwide organizations and campaigned under the slogan 'Chilean Sign Language exists, there is nothing to define' (Stein, 2015).

On behalf of this movement, 14 representatives of deaf associations from different regions of the country signed a document to be presented to Andrea Molina who promoted the campaign, in order to start the legal process. Supported by multiple members of the Lower Chamber, and two years after the enactment of the Disability Law, this movement achieved its goal. In August 2012, paragraph 6 of provisional Article 1 was abrogated (Law 20.602, 2012). The whole Chilean Deaf community celebrated this victory as another step towards the recognition of Chilean Sign Language. This is the origin of the National Day of Deaf people and Sign Language, celebrated every 20 August (C. Muñoz, pers. comm., 22 January 2017). Soon after the August 2012 victory, the Deaf Force Movement dissolved (Stein, 2015).

Third Period: Initiatives by the Deaf Community and Consequences of Sign Language Recognition by the Disability Law

Since 2014, ASOCH, the oldest association in the country, has led a series of formal demands to State agencies for the guarantee the right of access to information, social participation and education of deaf people, as well as the provision and professionalization of services such as LSCh interpretation (ASOCH, 2014a). The current leaders of this organization have tried to develop a policy focused on human rights, generating conversations and agreements with public institutions. This is the case of the agreement established with the Supreme Court of Justice in order to incorporate interpreters in the justice system.

Furthermore, ASOCH has also been invited to be part of discussions related to public policies in the area of disability rights (ASOCH, 2014b). ASOCH also participated in the development of the civil society's parallel report to the CRPD Committee, a document analyzing the State of Chile's compliance with the CRPD, and stating those matters which have not been addressed by the State (ASOCH, 2016). In this way, the organization has positioned itself as the key deaf community organization for Chilean State agencies.

Governmental Initiatives to Address the Demands of the Chilean Deaf Community

The government, in turn, has sought to address part of the Deaf community's demands by strengthening financial benefits through agencies such as the National Disability Service (SENADIS). These benefits include the provision of technical support, such as hearing aids, voice recorders, remote interpretation through video calls and the financing of interpreters in educational contexts. The Chilean Ministry of Education continues to fund projects to support the engagement of Deaf people and the incorporation of LSCh into schools, such as an 'ICT and Diversity' project to provide schools with technological resources and technical-pedagogical advisory from a bilingual-intercultural approach since 2012 (MINEDUC, 2015). Furthermore, in 2018, thanks to a collaborative work with deaf educators across the country, the description of the profile of a Deaf teaching assistant of Chilean Sign Language and Deaf Culture was established. The aim of this profile is to start a process to validate the working skills of deaf educators that are currently working in deaf and mainstream schools.

Positive Consequences of Sign Language Recognition by the Chilean Legislation

The official recognition of Chilean Sign Language as means of communication of the Chilean Deaf community (Law 20.422, 2010) has had several positive impacts. There is a growing visibility of Chilean Sign Language, which has resulted in greater access for deaf people to spaces where they previously did not participate. One of the reasons has been the progressive incorporation of interpreters in different social spheres, such as television broadcasting, health, justice, and artistic and cultural events. The presence of LSCh interpreters has increased deaf people's access to information, and has given them the option of accessing services that were unavailable before.

With regard to education, the use of LSCh in schools has been promoted thanks to the increased use of interpreters and deaf people in the classroom. Additionally, higher education institutions have begun to include sign language into the curricula, especially in the field of education and health. This movement has opened up the possibility for more deaf people to teach sign language and to be involved in educational settings. Along with this, increased interest in learning LSCh among hearing people has led to increased demand for LSCh courses open to the public. Consequently, initiatives and work opportunities related to sign language teaching and interpretation have expanded, encouraging the creation of foundations dedicated to teaching and spreading LSCh, as well as the formation of groups of interpreters in different regions of the country (González & Pérez, 2017).

Unresolved Aspects

Although the enactment of the law and the implicit recognition (De Meulder, 2015) of Chilean Sign Language have had a positive consequences, there are still many issues to be resolved. In terms of sign language acquisition, although the MINEDUC has implemented actions to promote the use of sign language in schools with deaf students, there has not been a clear and consistent policy on the matter. Sign language is not part of the curriculum, and the teachers have not received training, nor sufficient tools to ensure deaf students acquire LSCh appropriately and learn the contents of the curriculum in their first language. This situation is due to insufficient knowledge of LSCh's linguistic principles. Research in this area is still incipient.

In terms of LSCh teaching, there is a lack of training and certification for LSCh instructors, limiting potential for professionalization in this area. A similar situation exists in sign language interpreting. Sign language interpreting is currently unregulated and there is a lack of minimum quality and performance standards. At the moment, the law does not require any institution to provide interpreters or any other means of communication and access to information for deaf people. Currently, there are no policies guaranteeing access to health services, education or employment through interpreters (Stein, 2015).

As for the features and dynamics of the Chilean Deaf community, Stein (2015) regards its low cultural capital as a barrier. In Chile, just a few Deaf people are sufficiently competent in reading and writing to understand complex texts dealing with the legal system. The multiplicity of deaf organizations may also present challenges. As this chapter shows, there have been situations that have encouraged the different deaf organizations to work together on specific objectives. Otherwise, the absence of planned collaborative work among deaf organizations has reduced the strength and scope of campaigns. Additionally, the lack of Deaf professionals or scholars in the legal field makes it difficult for the community to defend their rights, often relying on legal experts who are not familiar with the Deaf community and are not capable of understanding or interpreting their needs.

Regarding public agencies, the strategies implemented in the different government initiatives have failed to take into consideration the organization of the Chilean Deaf community as a cultural and linguistic minority. State agencies need to involve Deaf people in decision-making processes and legislative initiatives. Past attempts have only been partially successful due to the lack of full understanding of the community's organization, its needs and the best way to work with them.

Conclusion

The different periods reviewed in this chapter reveal the need to align local policy and practices with established international agreements. Chilean deaf organizations involved in the LSCh recognition process have adopted an accessibility framework in order to see their demands fulfilled. While some of these claims have been successful, mainly in the field of access to information, existing legislation does not sufficiently accord rights to the Deaf community. Existing legislation is weak, since it regards the use of sign language just as a means of communication (Law 20.422), and there is a lack of policy and planning in relation to language. At the moment, according to ASOCH, the absence of a government entity with oversight and sanctioning powers in the area of rights and interests of deaf people serves to deprive the Deaf community of their political, civil, economic, social and cultural rights (ASOCH, 2016). Thus, it is very difficult for deaf people to find legal support for their demands. This is exacerbated by poor participation of the Deaf community in discussions regarding their language, education and rights as Chilean citizens. Some of the state agencies dealing with social inclusion and promotion of the rights of people with disabilities have made attempts to contribute to the regulation of LSCh teaching and interpretation. Yet these proposals have not met the needs of the Chilean Deaf community, since the agencies have failed in offering a type of participation that could reflect the diversity of opinions and positions existing among its members.

The lack of both cultural and political capital of the members of the Chilean Deaf community has been another factor stymying the inclusion of deaf people's views in the political process. One key limitation has been the lack of autonomy for deaf people to generate their own language planning and policy projects related to the dissemination of LSCh. This has to do with the absence of deaf scholars capable of leading projects in those areas.

We consider the further empowerment of the Deaf community as a crucial step forward, specifically developing an increasingly active understanding of the Chilean legal system. Currently, many young deaf people are interested in obtaining legal degrees, and some deaf people have begun participating in LSCh research groups at universities. These two trends give us hope to envision a Deaf community developing the cultural capital and specific knowledge to take their struggle into their own hands.

Abbreviations

ACHIELS: Association of Sign Language Instructors and Interpreters
ASOCH: Asociación de Sordos de Chile (Chilean Association of the Deaf)
FONADIS: Fondo Nacional de Discapacidad (National Disability Fund)
LSCh: Lengua de Señas Chilena (Chilean Sign Language)
MINEDUC: Ministerio de Educación de Chile (Chilean Ministry of Education)
PIE: Programa de Integración Escolar (School Integration Programme)
SENADIS: Servicio Nacional de la Discapacidad (National Disability Service).

Notes

(1) There are four public channels that rotate during the year to incorporate a box with LSCh interpreter. The central news program is interpreted for three months per channel.

(2) 'Public service campaigns financed with public funds, electoral propaganda, presidential debates, nationwide broadcasting, news from the National Emergency Office of the Ministry of Interior and Public Security, and broadcast news segment transmitted due to emergency situations or public calamity' (Article 25, Law 20.422, 2010).

References

Acuña, X., Adamo, D., Cabrera I. and Lissi, M.R. (2012) Estudio descriptivo del desarrollo de la competencia narrativa en LS Chilena [Descriptive study on narrative competence development in Chilean Sign Language]. *Revista Onomazein [Onomazein Journal]* 26, 193–219.

Adamo, D. (1993) Estudio descriptivo de los parámetros básicos de la estructura sublexical de la langue de señas chilena [Descriptive study of the basic parameters of the sublexical structure of the Chilean sign language]. MA thesis, Universidad Católica de Chile.

Adamo, D. and Cabrera, I. (1991) Educación de las Personas Sordas y Lengua de Señas. [Education of Deaf People and Sign Language] *Revista Educación [Education Journal]* 186, 31–36.

Adamo, D., Acuña, X. and Cabrera, I. (2013) Diccionario bilingüe lengua de señas chilena/español: Un desafío lexicográfico [Bilingual dictionary Chilean sign language/Spanish: A lexicography challenge]. *Revista de Lingüística Teórica y Aplicada [Journal of Theoretical and Applied Linguistics]* 51 (2), 173–192.

ASOCH (2014a) *Carta al Consejo Nacional de Televisión [Letter to the National Television Council]*. See https://www.dropbox.com/s/a4xkizmej0vaebh/1.%20 ASOCH®%20-%20Denuncia%20CNTV%2031012014.pdf?dl=0 (accessed 8 January 2018).

ASOCH (2014b) *Conversatorio con la Sociedad Civil sobre Discapacidad, Desarrollo y Políticas Públicas [Discussion with Civil Society on Disability, Development and Public Policies]*. See https://www.dropbox.com/s/z8ariyigr0e81ap/4.%20 ASOCH®%20-%20CEPAL%20Ronda%201%2030052014.pdf?dl=0 (accessed 8 January 2018).

ASOCH (2016) *Informe sombra versión ampliada [Shadow report extended versión]*. See https://docs.google.com/document/d/1KF7cRkbC00b_mnCXptjdmCvUaf5Ph9lnl8nqqMwSKUI/pub (accessed 8 January 2018).

CNTV (2002) Acta de la sesión ordinaria del consejo Nacional de television del lunes 5 de Agosto del 2002 [Minutes of the ordinary session of the National Television Council on Monday, 5 August 2002]. See https://www.cntv.cl/cntv/site/artic/20150417/asocfile/20150417132541/agosto052002_acta.pdf (accessed 15 January 2018).

De la Paz, V., González, M. and Otárola, F. (2016) Deaf educators: Linguistic models in an intercultural-bilingual educational context. In B. Gerner and L. Karnopp (eds) *Change and Promise. Bilingual Deaf Education and Deaf Culture in Latin America* (pp. 82–102). Washington, DC: Gallaudet University Press.

De Meulder, M. (2015) The legal recognition of sign languages. *Sign Language Studies* 15 (4), 498–506.

De Meulder, M. and Murray, J. (2017) Buttering their bread on both sides? The recognition of sign languages and the aspirations of deaf communities. *Language Problems and Language Planning* 41 (2), 136–158.

Decree No. 201 (2008) Promulga la convención de las Naciones Unidas sobre los derechos de las personas con discapacidad y su protocolo facultativo [Decree No. 201

promulgates the United Nations Convention on the Rights of Persons with Disabilities and its Optional Protocol]. See https://www.leychile.cl/Navegar?idNorma=278018 (accessed 15 January 2018).

Demartini, G. and Letelier, K. (2006) Historia de la comunidad sorda: Elaboración de un texto escrito para niños y jóvenes Sordos en edad escolar [History of the deaf community: Elaboration of a written text for deaf children and deaf young people in school age]. Master thesis, Universidad Metropolitana de Ciencias de la Educación.

Día Internacional de los Sordos ¿Dónde están sus derechos? [International Day of the Deaf. Where are their rights?] 29 September 1998. El Diario Austral, IX región of La Araucanía.

González, M. (2017) Being and becoming a Deaf educator: The construction of Deaf educators' roles and pedagogies in Chilean Deaf schools. PhD thesis, University of Bristol.

González, M. and Pérez, A. (2017) La Lengua de Señas Chilena: un recorrido por su proceso de desarrollo desde una perspectiva multidimensional [Chilean Sign Language: A journey through its development process from a multidimensional perspective]. *Revista Espaço [Espaço Journal]* 47, 145–166.

Herrera, V. (2007) Códigos de lectura en sordos: La dactilología y otras estrategias visuales y kinestésicas [Deaf reading codes: The manual alphabet and other visual and kinesthetic strategies]. *Revista Latinoamericana de Psicología [Latin American Journal of Psychology]* 2 (39), 269–286.

Herrera, V., Puente, A. and Alvarado, J.M. (2009) The situation of the Deaf in Chile. In D. Moores and M. Miller (eds) *Deaf People around the World. Educational, Development and Social Perspectives* (pp. 315–316). Washington: Gallaudet University.

Law 19.253 (1993) Establece normas sobre protección, fomento y desarrollo de los indígenas, y crea la corporación nacional de desarrollo indígena [Establishes rules on protection, promotion and development of the indigenous, and creates the national corporation of indigenous development]. *Official Journal of the Republic of Chile,* 5 October 1993. See https://www.leychile.cl/Navegar?idNorma=30620 (accessed 20 January 2018).

Law 19.284 (1994) Establece normas para la plena integración social de personas con discapacidad [Establishes rules on the full social integration of people with disabilities]. *Official Journal of the Republic of Chile,* 5 January 1994. See https://www.leychile.cl/Navegar?idNorma=30651 (accessed 20 January 2018).

Law 20.422 (2010) Establece normas sobre igualdad de oportunidades e inclusión social de personas con discapacidad [Establishes rules and standards on equal opportunities and social inclusion of people with disabilities]. *Official Journal of the Republic of Chile,* 10 February 2010. See https://www.leychile.cl/Navegar?idLey=20422 (accessed 10 March 2018).

Law 20.602 (2012) Deroga el inciso sexto del artículo primero transitorio de la ley 20.422 [Abrogates the sixth subsection of the first transitory article of law 20.422]. *Official Journal of the Republic of Chile,* 25 September 2010. See http://www.leychile.cl/Navegar?idNorma=1044075 (accessed 10 March 2018).

Lissi, M.R. and Salinas, M. (2012). La educación de niños y jóvenes con discapacidad. Más allá de la inclusión [Education of children and youth with disabilities. Beyond inclusión]. In I. Mena, M.R. Lissi, L. Alcalay and N. Milicic (eds) *Educación y Diversidad: Aportes desde la Psicología Educacional [Education and Diversity: Contributions from Educational Psychology]* (pp. 199–237). Santiago, Chile: Ediciones UC.

Lissi, M.R., Salinas, M., Acuña, X., Adamo, D., Cabrera, I. and González, M. (2010) Using Sign Language to teach written language: An analysis of the strategies used by teachers of deaf children in a bilingual context. *L1 – Educational Studies in Language and Literature* 10 (1), 57–69.

Lissi, M.R., Svartholm, K. and González, M. (2012) El enfoque bilingüe en la educación de sordos: Sus implicancias para la enseñanza y aprendizaje de la lengua escrita [The bilingual approach to deaf education: Implications for teaching and learning written language]. *Revista Estudios Pedagógicos* 38 (2), 299–320.

Lissi, M.R., Sebastián, C., Vergara, M. and Iturriaga, C. (2019) When 'inclusion' jeopardizes the learning opportunities of deaf students: The case of Chile. In H. Knoors, M. Brons and M. Marschark (eds) *Deaf Education Beyond the Western World* (pp. 323–341). New York: Oxford University Press.

MINEDUC (2015) *Proyecto TIC y Diversidad [ICT and Diversity Project]*. See http://www.enlaces.cl/proyectos/ampliacion-proyecto-tic-y-diversidad-segunda-etapa-de-masificacion-implementacion-2015/ (accessed 15 January 2018).

MINEDUC (2016–2018) *Gestión de datos [Information management]*. Santiago: MINEDUC.

Muñoz, K., Sánchez, A. and Herreros, B. (2018) El intérprete de lengua de señas en el contexto universitario [Sign language interpreters in university contexts]. *Revista de Ciencias Sociales y Humanidades [Journal of Social Sciences and Humanities]* 3 (10), 159–173.

Otárola, F. and Crespo, N. (2015) Estructura y rasgos discursivos característicos de narraciones espontáneas en lengua de señas chilena: su valor para una educación bilingüe [Structure and discourse features of spontaneous narratives in Chilean sign language: their value for bilingual education]. *Foro Educacional [Educational Forum]* 24, 35–55.

Oviedo, A. (2015) *Chile, Atlas Sordo [Chile, Deaf Atlas]*. See http://www.cultura-sorda.org/chile-atlas-sordo/ (accessed 15 January 2018).

Parks, E., Parks, J. and Williams, H. (2011) A sociolinguistic profile of the deaf people of Chile. *SIL Electronic Survey Report 2011* 1–24. See http://www.sil.org/resources/publications entry/41625 (accessed 20 February 2018).

Pérez, A. (2008) Situación de intérpretes para estudiantes sordos. Reunión de instituciones que imparten cursos de Lengua de Señas Chilena [Situation of interpreters for deaf students. Meeting of institutions that teach courses in Chilean Sign Language] (unpublished document). Ministry of Education, Santiago, Chile.

Quer, J. and Quadros, R. (2015) Language policy and planning in deaf communities. In A. Schembri and C. Lucas (eds) *Sociolinguistics and Deaf Communities* (pp. 120–145). Cambridge: Cambridge University Press.

Stein, M. (2015) Implementing the Convention on the Rights of Persons with Disabilities: Supporting the deaf community in Chile trough legal expertise. In M. Friedner and A. Kusters (eds) *It's a Small World: International Deaf Spaces and Encounters* (pp. 173–184). Washington: Gallaudet University Press.

Supreme Decree No. 01 (1998) *Reglamenta capítulo II de la ley No. 19.284/94 de integración social de las personas con discapacidad.* [Supreme Decree No. 01. Regulates the chapter II of the Law 19.284/94 on the social integration of people with disabilities]. Ministry of Education. See http://www.fnd.cl/Ley_19.29...pdf (accessed 8 January 2018).

UN General Assembly (2007) *Convention on the Rights of Persons with Disabilities: Resolution/Adopted by the General Assembly, 24 January 2007, A/RES/61/106.* http://www.refworld.org/docid/45f973632.html (accessed 8 January 2018).

Vera, M.A. (2017) *Malestar social y desigualdades en Chile* [Social discomfort and inequalities in Chile]. Santiago: Ediciones Universidad Alberto Hurtado.

9 The Societal and Political Recognition of French Sign Language (LSF) in France: 1970–2018

Yann Cantin, Florence Encrevé and
Marie-Thérèse L'Huillier[1]

Introduction

In France, French Sign Language (*langue des signes française*, LSF) was recognised by Act No. 2005-102 of 11 February 2005, a general law on the rights of people with disabilities. It was the result of 40 years of mobilisation of the deaf community, assisted by hearing advocates of equal rights. In this chapter, we trace the emergence of this recognition, the conditions for its success and its consequences. To understand the recognition of LSF in 2005 in its historical context, we go back to the roots of the mobilisation of deaf people in the 19th century. In the first part of this chapter, we present the French deaf community from its foundation in the 1830s and its marginalisation from the 1880s, up to the 1970s. In the second part, which covers the 1970s to the 1990s, we present the deaf mobilisation movement that led to a cultural-linguistic renaissance, called the 'Deaf Revival'. In the third part, we discuss steps in societal recognition of LSF from the 1990s until today, including the 2005 law and its implementation.

Historical Roots (1830–1970)

Between 1760 and 1789, the teacher Abbé Charles-Michel de l'Épée had been a pioneer in the use of sign language in education, successfully educating many deaf students through signs, although, evidence of earlier use of sign language in France dates back to the 16th century (e.g. Cantin, 2016; Montaigne, 1979: 120). In the first half of the 19th century, the work of the Abbé de l'Épée endured, notably in the National Institution of Deaf-Mutes of Paris. In the 1830s, the Institution became the starting point for the first form of mobilisation of deaf people around Ferdinand Berthier, a deaf teacher of the Institution who taught in sign language. In 1834, he created annual banquets 'for the deaf and mutes', and in 1838, he founded the first association of deaf people in France: the Central Society of Deaf-Mutes of Paris (*Société centrale des sourds-muets de Paris*), which maintained the tradition of the banquets to make sign language and deaf people known to those who could afford to act on their behalf (Encrevé, 2012: 121–126). Through the publication of many books and the commission of statues and paintings of l'Épée – transformed into legend – this association and the community around it was the primary political vehicle for deaf people in France between 1838 and 1850.

Under the Second Empire (1852–1870), the influence of the 'family of deaf-mutes', as Berthier called it, became less important. This was not only because Berthier and the early activists were starting to age, but also because French society was changing. The effects of the industrial revolution had led to an increasing number of French people adopting the ideology of progress (Riot-Sarcey, 1998); that is, the belief that humans and nature are in a constant struggle against each other, that humans are the only ones to progress and to constantly improve themselves, and that they will therefore be victorious in this struggle. This idea emerged in the 18th century, and spread from the 19th century onwards, following societal changes caused by the industrial revolution (Encrevé, 2013). When applied to deaf people, the idea of progress led hearing people who did not know sign language to consider it a reflection of the past. They regarded learning to use spoken language as the progressive ideal as the means to integrate deaf people into society and to develop their intellectual capacities. Deaf people were not opposed to the idea of progress, but to the speech-based interpretation of it; for them, the use of sign language represented progress. Unfortunately, from the 1850s to the 1860s onwards, deaf people's interpretation of progress was no longer taken into account and the conception of oralism as progress became widespread.

This led the French government to reform radically deaf education by banning sign language from deaf schools and imposing the so-called 'pure oral method'. This method was widely supported by the participants at the Second International Congress 'on improving the lot of deaf-mute people' (also known as the Milan Congress) of 1880. The French government was not obliged to follow the resolutions adopted at the congress, since they were not binding. But it did so for several reasons, which we will summarise here (see also Encrevé, 2015). After the fall of Napoleon III in 1870, France once again became a Republic (the Third Republic) and by 1879, the Republicans occupied all positions of power. They were committed to the idea of progress and wanted to implement the 1789 principle of equality through the conception of equal means; that is, all French citizens should be able to benefit from the same means. This had the effect of preventing any special means adapted to a particular group, such as sign language for deaf students. Moreover, the Republican government launched an extensive campaign to unify the nation through linguistic unification: henceforth, they wanted all French people to learn and speak French, including deaf people (*L'oeil et la main*, 2016).

The implications for deaf people were significant: from 1880, deaf children in deaf schools no longer had access to sign language acquisition or learning through sign language. Deaf adults were no longer allowed to teach because they had to speak and hear to teach speech. Not all deaf children were enrolled in school and the most profoundly deaf, or those who were slightly deaf and myopic (therefore unable to read lips), were refused school places because of their 'inability to [use the] oral method'. (Compulsory education for deaf children was only established in 1975, see below, whereas it was mandated in 1882 for hearing people.) Deaf people who had been accepted into schools could only aspire to learn a manual trade and were not considered eligible for higher education. Nevertheless, the transmission of sign language survived, due to the creation of numerous associations, especially sporting associations, by the deaf community. These associations perpetuated the tradition of deaf peer-to-peer transmission and introduced young deaf people to the language, which had been banned from use in schools and denigrated. Deaf children from deaf families who had learned sign language at home transmitted it to their peers. Initially this was prohibited in schools; however, later on it was accepted as long as it happened outside the classroom (Cantin, 2014).

From 1880 to 1991, there was no re-introduction of sign language into deaf education. Although here and there educators tolerated students using sign language in the playground or dormitories, classes were still instructed in spoken and sometimes written French (Encrevé, 2015). This persistent ban on sign language throughout the 20th century can be explained by the continuing influence of the idea of progress in society, modernised after the Second World War. Progressivity applied to technical, scientific and technological advancement, which led to ways of improving hearing for deaf people and advances in speech therapy, reinforcing the ideal of rehabilitating deafness. The mobilisation of deaf people led by Berthier in the 19th century nevertheless endured, particularly in the sports movement and under the leadership of Ruben Eugène Alcais, founder of the Olympic Games for the Deaf, which were established in 1924 (Cantin & Cantin, 2017). The Deaf sports movement flourished during the 1920s and its spirit endured as the core of the Deaf Revival of the 1970s.

In the 1960s, after the disappearance of the Deaf Community's House in Paris (a project sustained for 40 years by Eugène Graff to bring together deaf people in Paris), other associations founded at the beginning of the 20th century started to disappear. These associations all served to animate deaf social and cultural life by encouraging cultural transmission and promoting intellectual development. In 1959, the disappearance of the Federation of Deaf-Mutes Societies (*Fédération des sociétés de sourds-muets*) left a great void, and the Republican Alliance of Silencers held its last banquet in 1963. With the disappearance of these associations, Berthier's legacy seemed to have been lost. In 1966, the National Confederation of the Deaf of France (*Confédération nationale des sourds de France*) was created by merging several associations. The National Confederation was more oriented towards remediating deafness, positioning itself in the field of disability and medicine. Because of the influence of the National Confederation, it became difficult for other organisations to defend and promote the use of sign language (Minguy, 2009). However, it should be pointed out that this again did not affect sports associations, which were not affiliated to the National Confederation.

In the 1970s, when deaf people decided to regain control of their societal position, they were viewed as socially inferior people who used a language that was denigrated and even considered a 'non-language'. As a result of a national French-only policy from 1879 to 1914, by the end of the 19th century, regional and minority languages had been banned from schools, and in the second part of the 20th century some of these language groups undertook revitalisation action. Thus, Law 51-46 of 11 January 1951 (an educational law), authorised optional and restrictive teaching of certain regional languages (Basque, Breton, Occitan and Catalan) at primary (one hour per week) and secondary levels. The aim of this law was both to help teachers to teach French through vernacular languages and to protect some regional languages, probably because their use was declining (Decree No. 74-33 of 16 January 1974 included the Corsican language in the law; in 1981, Decree No. 81-553 of 12 May 1981 added Tahitian; and Decree No. 92-1162 of 20 October 1992 added Ajië, Drehu, Nengone and Paicî – Melanesian languages of New Caledonia).

However, the situation of the deaf community in the early 1970s did not seem to be conducive to its emancipation through formal recognition of sign language.

The Deaf Revival (1970–1991)

The Deaf Revival can be described as a constellation of movements not necessarily coordinated or unified, but which together led to important changes for deaf people. This movement was part of a wider context, symbolised in particular by the civil rights movement in the USA and by the May 1968 uprising in France. This social context was reinforced by the slowdown of the French economy after several years of growth and by a changing demography with increasing numbers of younger (under age 25) people. At the same time, more people were beginning to question the idea of progress in its modern, technical, scientific and technological interpretation (Encrevé, 2015; Plessis *et al.*, 2013). In this period, several Western industrialised societies experienced a wave of social movements, such as those driven by oppressed minorities (cultural, linguistic or other).

Indeed, the Deaf Revival was possible because French society was more open to diversity claims.

Two distinct events marked the beginning of the Deaf Revival, instigated by two Americans. It is interesting to note that France exported sign language to America (via deaf teacher Laurent Clerc) in the 19th century, helping to form a national deaf community in the USA, which in time contributed to the 1970s LSF renaissance in France, through the influence of American individuals. In 1974, Harry Markowicz, an American hearing linguist, was invited by the linguist Shun-Chiu Yau to the *Centre d'étude des mouvements sociaux* at the *École des hautes études en sciences sociales (EHESS)* in Paris. There he met the sociologist Bernard Mottez and introduced him to deaf people and their language (Mottez, 2006: 18). In 1975, just after attending the World Federation of the Deaf Congress in Washington, DC, they began to set up regular seminars attended by deaf people and a French linguist, then a doctoral student, Christian Cuxac, whose research began to focus on demonstrating the linguistic value of the sign language of deaf people in France (Cuxac & L'Huillier, 1985; Cuxac, 2000). In 1977, continuing in the same vein as the seminars, Bernard Mottez and Harry Markowicz directed and edited a new journal, *Coup d'oeil*, the first one devoted to the deaf community in order to disseminate reflections from the *EHESS* seminars, academic research in progress and other information they felt was important.

The second key influence occurred in the world of theatre. In 1976, Jean Grémion (Grémion, 1990), a hearing actor with close ties to government ministries and the media, met Alfredo Corrado, an American deaf actor, at the world theatre festival of Nancy in France. Together they co-founded the current International Visual Theater (IVT). In 1977, the first IVT meeting took place, attended by many deaf people around Jean Grémion and Alfredo Corrado. The participants came from Deaf sports associations (deaf sports were the main domain where signing deaf adults still met) such as the Sports Club of Deaf-Mutes of Paris (*Club sportif des sourds-muets de Paris*), the Sports' 'Etoile' of the Deaf of Paris (*Étoile sportive des sourds de Paris*) and the Tennis Club for the Deaf of Paris (*Tennis club des sourds de Paris*), to name but a few. This first meeting triggered a strong awareness among deaf people of their cultural and linguistic distinctness. Of the 100 deaf people from all walks of life present at the beginning, about 20 people made up the core of the IVT, and created links with the deaf participants in Bernard Mottez's seminars at the *EHESS*. They then created a theatre workshop for deaf children and staged shows with deaf actors they had trained. Importantly, these activities involved deaf sign language users who had hitherto been marginalised because they did not use speech.

Bernard Mottez and Harry Markowicz also offered summer courses at Gallaudet University in the USA between 1978 and 1982 for groups of participants (French and Swiss Romanesque) consisting of one-third hearing parents of deaf children, one-third signing and speaking deaf people, and one-third professionals in deaf education. The impact of these trips was significant: signing deaf people felt valued and speaking deaf people realised the importance of sign language. As a consequence, hearing parents of deaf children made the decision not to follow oralist education methods for their children. Accompanying this movement, sign language/French interpreters (at that time all volunteers with other occupations) began to organise and in 1978 formed the National Association of Interpreters for the Hearing Impaired (*Association nationale des interprètes pour déficients auditifs*, now the French Association of Sign Language Interpreters and Translators – *Association française des interprètes et traducteurs en langue des signes*). In June 1979, introduced by Mottez and Markowicz (Abbou, 2017), the term '*langue des signes française (LSF)*' was adopted to designate what signing deaf people then called 'gestures'. Mottez and Markowicz's strategy was to encourage deaf people to take a leading linguistic and cultural role with deaf children and to raise awareness among hearing parents and professionals. After the establishment of IVT in 1977 (which also began teaching LSF to hearing people), in 1979, the association French Sign Language Academy (*Académie de la langue des signes française*) was created to teach LSF to hearing people. In 1980, the association Two Languages for One Education (*Deux langues pour une éducation* – 2LPE) set itself the goal of enabling deaf children to benefit from sign language instruction while retaining written French (Lamothe, 2017; Mottez & Markowicz, 1979). 2LPE was at the origin of the creation of some bilingual classes (written French and LSF), which was the first concrete challenge to the 1880 reform banning sign language from deaf education. This sequence of events, the creation of associations around deaf people, and the enhancement of deaf culture and sign language, was a strong reminder of the dynamic movement launched in 1834 by Ferdinand Berthier. It is for this reason that this period is called 'revival', marked by both individual emancipation and deaf community awakening after decades of submission.

But the Deaf Revival was also made up of other initiatives that gave full meaning to the expression 'constellation' that we used in the introduction to this section (*L'oeil et la main*, 2018). Unfortunately, we cannot detail here the totality of events and contributors all over France who took part in this movement; we can only give a few illustrative examples. From 1979 to 1988, public television ran a children's programme of stories told in sign language by a Deaf narrator, with French voiceover, which was regularly watched by many hearing and deaf children (and their parents) bringing sign language to a wider audience than before. In 1985, the association The Deaf Movement of France (*Le mouvement des sourds de France*) was created to promote LSF as the first language of deaf people. In 1986, this association organised the first demonstration of deaf people to make their linguistic and social demands visible. In 1989, an international festival celebrating deaf culture – 'Deaf Way' – was held at Gallaudet University in the USA, revealing the internationality of the deaf emancipation movement and empowering the French deaf people who participated. Subsequently in France, in December 1989, an exhibition was organised at the Sorbonne, entitled 'The Power of Signs' to commemorate the bicentenary of the French Revolution and the death of the Abbé de l'Épée. This exhibition, which was primarily historical, was coupled with a demonstration by deaf people who wanted to show that they were fully-fledged citizens, in the same way as other French citizens. Also in 1989, after resisting the Deaf Revival, the National Confederation of the Deaf of France (which became the National Federation of the Deaf of France – *Fédération nationale des sourds de France* – in 1987) began to open up to LSF by accepting membership of the new associations founded since 1975 and their presence helped counterbalance the influence of speaking deaf people. In French society in general, sign language began to be increasingly accepted and visible in public spaces.

By the early 1990s, the social renaissance of LSF was well underway and everything seemed possible, including recognition.

Recognition of LSF and its Consequences (1991–2018)

Legal recognition of LSF did not take place in the 1990s, but in the 2000s. Changing attitudes towards LSF parallelled society's movement away from the idea of progress from the 1990s, as French people's perspectives on technical, scientific and technological progress began to change; they were no longer convinced that the fight against nature inevitably leads to human victory, and ideologies focused on ecology and environmental protection have taken precedence over the idea of progress.

A first step towards the eventual legal recognition of LSF was the promulgation of Act No. 91-73 of 18 January 1991, 'to lay down provisions relating to public health and social insurance', which stated in Article 33: 'In the education of deaf young people, freedom of choice between bilingual communication – sign language and French – and oral communication is the law'. However, this article had no concrete results. First of all, it was included in a general social security law with no direct relationship to either languages or deaf people. Secondly, it did not recognise LSF as a distinct language, but only mentioned 'communication'. Therefore, this did not allow teachers to use sign language as a teaching language, but only as a means of communicating with students. This article was therefore not significant and cannot be considered to have officially abolished the ban on sign language. On the ground, however, it gave great hope to LSF campaigners. It also allowed young hearing teachers from deaf schools to add sign language to their teaching in French (which may have led some teachers to produce a contact variety of signed French). On the other hand, the legal vagueness behind the expression 'bilingual-sign language and French', without any further clarification on the written or spoken modality of French, resulted in several deaf schools declaring themselves 'bilingual' because they had merely set up a weekly LSF class for deaf children without modifying their teaching methods in other subjects. However, the *2LPE* were promoting 'true' bilingual education, which they defined as LSF as a 'first language (L1)' and written French as a 'second language (L2)' (L'Huillier, 1993). Unfortunately, this was not the majority view of bilingualism as a result of this section of the Act. As a consequence, some of the bilingual classes set up by *2LPE* had to close because of competition from the large, formerly oralist schools, which now declared themselves 'bilingual'.

In 1993, the National Federation of the Deaf of France became fully in favour of LSF. Many deaf people considered this change as a 'coup d'état' or even a 'revolution', because the National Federation of the Deaf of France was the top organisation representing the deaf community, and an official 'voice' to the public authorities. At the same time in 1993, a new association, *Sourds en colère* (Angry Deaf), was formed modelled on the Act Up AIDS activist association, to protest against the increasing medicalisation of deaf people, and especially against the invasion of cochlear implant surgery, in what was then called 'deafness treatment'. Until 1998, *Sourds en colère* was at the origin of major actions against the influence of cochlear implants in France (Dagron, 2008). In 1995, supported by proactive hearings doctors using sign language, the first unit of care for deaf patients was set up. In 1999, The National Federation reached an agreement with The Deaf Movement of France, despite their dissensions, to unite around two key moments: a major demonstration in Paris and several regional marches for the recognition of LSF, which culminated in the handing over of a file listing deaf people's linguistic and social demands to deputies in the National Assembly. The recognition of LSF was a cause that united the deaf community, as in the days of Ferdinand Berthier.

Around the same time in the academic world, the unprecedented recruitment of two professors of linguistics working on sign language took place: Richard Sabria in 1996 at the University of Rouen, and Christian Cuxac in 1998 at the University of Paris 8. Academic research on LSF has found recognition since then, particularly at the University of Paris 8 (e.g. Fusellier-Souza, 2012; Garcia & Sallandre, 2014; Sallandre & Garcia, 2013). This recruitment also made it possible to set up university training courses for deaf people and interpreters.

In 1998, an official report by the deputy Dominique Gillot entitled *The Rights of the Deaf: 115 Proposals* was submitted to the Prime Minister (Gillot, 1998). This report listed common barriers faced by deaf people and specifically recommended recognition of LSF. This was the first explicit recognition by the State of the difficulties encountered by the deaf community. In May 1999 at the last minute, LSF was added as a non-territorial language to the list of languages used in France, edited by the General Delegation for the French Language and the Languages of France, before the European Charter for Regional or Minority Languages entered into force (the Charter was signed by the French government, but has not yet been ratified). At this point, in 2002, deaf organisations also sought and received support for the recognition of their rights from disability organisations, in particular the French Association of People with Disabilities (*Groupement français des personnes handicapées*).

In 2004, united around the same objective, almost all national associations of deaf people (including the National Union for the Social Integration of the Hearing Impaired – *Union nationale pour l'insertion sociale du deficient auditif*) decided to exert their influence in the negotiations for the preparation of the law revising the 1975 law on persons with disabilities, to achieve LSF recognition. It is important to point out that deaf people were not concerned that this law pertained to disability measures. A language law would not have been possible because of the status of French as the sole official language of the Republic. The deaf organisations did not initiate change to the disability law: it was being revised at the initiative of the government, and deaf people took the opportunity to advocate for recognition of LSF within it (which was not initially envisaged by the government). While deaf advocates were not consulted directly in the formulation of the law, their arguments on the linguistic value of sign language were taken into account.

The result of this activism was that in February 2005, LSF was officially recognised and the banning of sign language in deaf education in 1880 was officially repealed. Act No. 2005-102 of 11 February 2005 'on equal rights and opportunities, participation and citizenship of persons with disabilities' was promulgated by the President of the Republic (Jacques Chirac). It contains 101 articles, all of which deal with persons with disabilities. It replaced Act No. 75-534 of 30 June 1975 'on guidance for persons with disabilities', which finally had made it compulsory for disabled children (including deaf children) to attend school free of charge. Apart from this major advance, Law No. 75-534 of 30 June 1975 contained no mention of sign language. It only spoke of 'the disabled', introduced quotas for hiring, social allowances and benefits, etc. In 2005, society had evolved and this law needed to be amended, which led to the 2005 Act. The spirit of this new law was to continue the efforts made by society to include people with disabilities, now called 'disabled persons'. It introduced new hiring obligations, the universal design of buildings, a new 'disability grant', among other things.

Most significantly for LSF, Article 75 of the 2005 Act states:

French Sign Language is recognised as a language in its own right. Any student concerned [i.e. deaf students enrolled in general schools, *author's note*] must be able to receive French Sign Language instruction. The Higher Council for Education shall endeavour to promote its teaching. It shall be kept regularly informed of the conditions of its evaluation. It may be chosen as an optional test for examinations and competitions, including vocational training. Its dissemination in the administration is facilitated. [2]

This article created Article L. 312-9-1 of the Education Code, to authorise LSF teaching. In line with this recognition, Articles 76, 77 and 78 of the 2005 Act specified that deaf persons have the right to use sign language in their communication with the State.

- Article 76: 'Before administrative, civil and criminal courts, every deaf person shall benefit from the communication system adapted to his or her choice [i.e. LSF/French interpreter or cued speech coder]. These costs are borne by the state.'
- Article 77: 'I. – In order to guarantee the exercise of freedom of movement and to adapt the new driving license tests for deaf and hard of hearing persons, an interpreter or sign language mediator will be present at the theoretical and practical tests of the driving license for light vehicles (permit B) during the special sessions for deaf persons, the minimum frequency of which will be fixed by decree. II – In order to enable candidates to follow the interpreter's or mediator's explanations in sign language, the necessary time will be given in the theoretical examinations, as defined by decree, for a good understanding of the translations between the candidates and the translator'.
- Article 78: 'In their relations with public services, whether they are managed by the State, local authorities or an institution representing them, as well as by private persons entrusted with a public service task, hearing impaired persons shall, at their request, receive simultaneous or visual written translation of any oral or sound information concerning them in accordance with the procedures and within a time limit laid down by regulation. The adapted communication device may, in particular, provide for the written transcription or the intervention of an interpreter in French sign language or a coder in cued speech [i.e. public bodies must pay for the cost of interpreter (or coder in cued speech), but the deaf person must first apply for it]. There is also an order-in-council for the access of hearing impaired persons to emergency telephone services.'

These four articles not only legally codified the linguistic status of LSF, but also provided more concrete measures for its use by deaf people in the public administrative sphere. However, there is no body with monitoring responsibility for the implementation of LSF provisions. The review process is devolved to the respective ministry departments connected with each Article.

The scope of Article 75 recognising French sign language as a language was not immediately understood by deaf activists. As this article modified the code of education, some activists imagined that LSF was only recognised in education. However, its scope was broader: recognition is absolute and not limited to a particular field. The 2005 Act was supplemented by various decrees. All four of these articles have been implemented. The teaching of LSF established by Article 75 has indeed been made possible. In 2008, LSF was added as an optional baccalaureate (the French A-level or high school diploma) language. In the same year, the Ministry of National Education set up a working group to implement LSF teaching. In August 2008, a circular (a text that allows the administrative authorities to inform their services) was signed, detailing the conditions for implementing the LSF programme in primary schools (for deaf children). This circular clarified the principle of bilingualism advocated by *2LPE* since its creation: LSF as the first language (L1) and written French as the second language (L2).

Moreover, in the first part of this circular, which retraces the regulatory context, LSF's constitutional status is clarified: '[...] the law recognises French sign language (L. S. F.) as a language of the Republic equally as French'. It should be noted that the French Republic recognizes the existence of regional and minority languages in the Constitution (Article 75-1: 'Regional languages belong to France's heritage.'), but not as languages of the Republic. So, this text de facto brings LSF into Article 2 of the Constitution of the Fifth French Republic: 'The language of the Republic is French'. By making it clear that LSF now has a status as a language of the Republic equal to French, the circular allows for an interpretation of constitutional 'French' as being composed of two distinct languages: French and LSF. The scope of this constitutional recognition is important: the Constitution authorises the use of only constitutional 'French' by the State. Thus, for example, the President of the Republic does not have the right to deliver speeches in a language other than constitutional 'French'. This now allows the President to deliver speeches in LSF without this being unconstitutional.

However, there are still many actions to be taken to implement the legal provisions. Not all deaf children have access to LSF or LSF education, because many hearing parents make the choice for an education without LSF, and because there are still not enough LSF teachers and teachers who can teach in LSF to meet all needs (especially in isolated schools with one or two deaf students). Public administrations and private companies may be reluctant to pay interpreting fees for deaf users or their employees (publics subsidies are not sufficient to cover all costs). Deaf teachers do not have the same status (or pay), depending on whether they work in private schools (or in national institutions) under the Ministry of Health, or in state schools under the Ministry of National Education (whether in primary or high schools). There are few completely bilingual classes: more and more deaf students attend school with hearing students where they communicate through interpreters instead of directly with deaf teachers. Video relay centres are active only since the end of 2018 (the government has been running trials since 2014 and the service is not yet open 24 hours a day). Deaf students in higher education find it difficult to get interpreters to attend all their courses (L'Huillier, 2014). Not all deaf people have access to medical care in LSF. Deaf people are discriminated against in employment, and so on. This list is not exhaustive (Abbou, 2017).

Today, 13 years after the enactment of the law, the deaf community continues to mobilise for full implementation of all its principles.

Conclusion

In the course of 40 years, the situation of deaf people in France has been significantly reversed. In 1975, deaf people were members of a marginalised, inferior and segregated community, and deaf children were deprived of the only language available to them. In 2018, deaf people live in a society that has recognised LSF as a language in its own right, and which offers deaf children the opportunity to learn it in school (even if this teaching has grown away from its original deaf cultural roots) and to follow a bilingual LSF-written French education (even though in practice, there are still few bilingual classes). From a historical point of view, this fairly rapid evolution can also be explained by changes in French society. In 1975, French people still largely subscribed to the ideology that technical, scientific and technological progress would one day enable deaf people to hear and speak. From our observation, this ideology is no longer so dominant in France and tolerance of sign language, the natural language of deaf people, is more aligned with the current ecological ideology. We believe that we are currently at a point of balance between these two ideologies. LSF has been recognised as a language in its own right; however, there are still proponents of the ideology of progress who favour the transformation of deaf children, particularly through cochlear implant surgery. This shows that there are still many issues for mobilisation, and that the deaf community's commitment to equality cannot wane.

Notes

(1) This text was translated into English with the help of Madeleine Papiernik.
(2) Translation of the Act's articles from French to English by the authors.

References

Abbou, V. (2017) *Une clé sur le monde [A Key to the World]*. Riom: Eyes éditions.
Cantin, Y. (2014) *Les Sourds-Muets de la Belle Époque, une communauté en mutations [Deaf-mutes of the Belle Epoque period, a changing community]*. PhD thesis, École des hautes études en sciences sociales.
Cantin, Y. (2016) Des origines du noétomalalien français, perspectives historiques [From the origins of the French Noetomalalian, historical perspectives]. *Glottopol, revue de sociolinguistique en ligne* (27), 8–19. See http://glottopol.univ-rouen.fr/telecharger/numero_27/auteurs_numero_27.htm#cantin.

Cantin, A. and Cantin Y. (2017) *Dictionnaire biographique des grands sourds en France, 1450–1920 [Biographical Dictionary of Great Deaf People in France, 1450–1920]*. Paris: Archives et Culture.

Cuxac, C. (2000) La langue des signes française (LSF): les voies de l'iconicité [French Sign Language (LSF): The paths to iconicity]. *Faits de langue* (15–16). Paris-Gap: Ophrys.

Cuxac, C. and Abbou-L'Huillier, M.-T. (1985) French Sign Language and Pantomime. In F. Loncke, P. Boyes-Braem and Y. Lebrum (eds) *Recent Research on European Sign Language* (pp. 141–148). Lisse: Swets & Zeitlinger B. V.

Dagron, J. (2008) *Les silencieux, chroniques de vingt ans de médecine avec les sourds [The Silencers, Chronicles of Twenty Years of Medicine with Deaf People]*. Paris: Presse pluriel.

Encrevé, F. (2012) *Les sourds dans la société française au XIXᵉ siècle: Idée de progrès et langue des signes [Deaf in French Society in the 19th Century: Idea of Progress and Sign Language]*. Grâne: Créaphis.

Encrevé, F. (2013) La 'famille' des sourds-muets face à l'idée de progrès au XIXᵉ siècle [The deaf-mutes 'family' facing the ideology of progress]. *Revue d'histoire du XIXᵉ siècle* (46), 145–161. See https://journals.openedition.org/rh19/4453.

Encrevé, F. (2015) Le corps des sourds dans la société française au XXᵉ siècle [The body of deaf people in French society of the 20th century]. *Revista inclusiones* (volumen especial), 132–150. See http://www.revistainclusiones.com/gallery/7%20oficial%20 paris%202015%20rev%20inc.pdf

Fusellier-Souza, I. (2012) Multiple perspectives on the emergence and development of human language: B. Comrie, C. Perdue and D. Slobin. In M. Watorek, S. Benazzo and M. Hickmann (eds) *Comparative Perspectives on Language Acquisition: A Tribute to Clive Perdue* (pp. 223–244). Bristol: Multilingual Matters.

Garcia, B. and Sallandre, M.-A. (2014) Reference resolution in French Sign Language. In P. Cabredo Hofherr and A. Zribi-Hertz (eds) *Crosslinguistic Studies on Noun Phrase Structure and Reference. Syntax and Semantic Series* (39), 316–324. Leiden: Brill.

Gillot, D. (1998) *Le droit des sourds: 115 propositions, rapport au Premier Ministre [The Rights of the Deaf: 115 Proposals, report to the Prime Minister]*. Paris: La documentation française. See https://www.ladocumentationfrancaise.fr/var/storage/rapports-publics/984001595.pdf.

Grémion, J. (1990) *La planète des sourds [The Planet of the Deaf]*. Paris: Messinger.

Lamothe, C. (2017) Association 2LPE CO: Bilingual enrolment for immersion and collective inclusion. In K. Reuter (ed.) *UNCRPD Implementation in Europe – A Deaf Perspective* (pp. 214–228). Brussels: European Union of the Deaf.

L'Huillier, M.-T. (1993) Rôle du professeur sourd dans la pratique bilingue et biculturelle [Role of the deaf teacher in bilingual and bicultural practice]. *Revue du Collège de psychanalyse* (46–47), 210–217.

L'Huillier, M.-T. (2014) Les représentations des sourds vis-à-vis des interprètes hier et aujourd'hui [Representations of the deaf vis-à-vis interpreters yesterday and today]. *Double Sens, revue de l'Association française des interprètes et traducteurs en langue des signes* (2), 61–72.

Minguy, A. (2009) *Le réveil Sourd en France: Pour une perspective bilingue [The Deaf Revival in France: For a Bilingual Perspective]*. Paris: L'Harmattan.

Mottez, B. (2006) *Les Sourds existent-ils? [Do the Deaf Exist?]*. Paris: L'Harmattan.

Mottez, B. and Markowicz H. (1979) *Les conséquences d'un choix politique sur la structuration et le mode d'existence d'un groupe minoritaire, les sourds [The Consequences of a Political Choice on the Structure and Mode of Existence of a Minority Group, the Deaf]*. Paris: Centre d'études des mouvements sociaux.

Montaigne de, M. (1979) *Essais [Essays]: Livre [Book] II*. Paris: Garnier-Flammarion (original work published 1580).

Plessis, C., Topçu, S. and Bonneuil, C. (2013) *Une autre histoire des 'Trente Glorieuses', modernisation, contestations et pollutions dans la France d'après-guerre [Another*

History of the 'Thirty Glorious', Modernisation, Protests and Pollution in Post-War France]. Paris: La découverte.

Riot-Sarcey, M. (1998) *Le reel de l'utopie [The Real of Utopia]*. Paris: Albin Michel.

Sallandre, M.-A. and Garcia, B. (2013) Epistemological issues in the semiotical model for the annotation of sign language. In L. Meurant, A. Sinte, M. Van Herreweghe and M. Vermeerbergen (eds) *Sign Language Research, Uses and Practices, Crossing Views on Theoretical and Applied Sign Language Linguistics* (pp. 159–177). Berlin/Boston: Mouton de Gruyter, and Nijmegen: Ishara Press.

Internet links

Act No. 75-534 du 30 juin 1975 'd'orientation en faveur des personnes handicapées [on guidance for persons with disabilities]'. See https://www.legifrance.gouv.fr/jo_pdf.do?id=JORFTEXT000000333976.

Act No. 2005-102 du 11 février 2005 'pour l'égalité des droits et des chances, la participation et la citoyenneté des personnes handicapées [on equal rights and opportunities, participation and citizenship of persons with disabilities]'. See https://www.legifrance.gouv.fr/affichTexte.do?cidTexte=JORFTEXT000000809647&categorieLien=id.

Broadcast 1980s' children's program on public television *Mes mains ont la parole*. See https://www.youtube.com/watch?v=AKfQL1y5sPs.

Circulaire no. 2008-109 du 21 août 2008 du ministère de l'Éducation nationale 'sur les conditions de mise en œuvre du programme de la langue des signes française à l'école primaire'. See http://www.education.gouv.fr/cid22246/mene0800665c.html.

Concerning the 19th century. See *L'oeil et la main* (2016) https://www.france.tv/france-5/l-oeil-et-la-main/51007-l-age-d-or-un-siecle-d-ascension-de-la-langue-des-signes.html.

Concerning the Deaf Revival. See *L'oeil et la main* (2018) https://www.france.tv/france-5/l-oeil-et-la-main/431671-des-femmes-en-mouvement.html.

French magazine in LSF for the deaf community *L'oeil et la main*.

Part 3

Ongoing Campaigns towards Explicit Legal Recognition

10 In Pursuit of Legal Recognition of the Sign Language of the Netherlands

Richard Cokart, Trude Schermer, Corrie Tijsseling and Eva Westerhoff

Introduction

The process of societal and legal recognition of the sign language of the Netherlands (*Nederlandse Gebarentaal*, henceforth NGT), started in the late 1970s and is still ongoing. Its beginning can be characterized as the pursuit of recognition of deaf people as a distinct cultural and linguistic minority,[1] and as a disadvantaged social group in Dutch society. The desire of deaf people to be recognized as a distinct minority was expressed in the theme of the first conference organized by the Dutch National Association of the Deaf (*Nederlandse Dovenraad*), in 1979: '*Plaatsmaken voor de Dove medeburger*' ('Making Room for the Deaf Citizen'). This conference can be viewed as the starting point of the emancipation of deaf people in the Netherlands. In 1981, deaf community leaders, the organization of parents of deaf children, the Dutch Foundation for the Deaf and Hard of Hearing Child (*Nederlandse Stichting voor het Dove en Slechthorende Kind*, NSDSK) and sign language researchers joined forces and published a book about the position of deaf people (Nederlandse Dovenraad, 1981). This book contained a strong plea for the use of signing in the education of deaf children, in the form of Total Communication (Tijsseling, 2014).

Fast-forward 37 years later to 2018, and the societal position of deaf people in the Netherlands has improved considerably: sign language interpreters are provided free of charge for personal affairs for 30 hours a year or more, if needed (e.g. to visit a doctor or to attend a church ceremony), to access education (for the full curriculum and for all levels of education) and the workplace (15% of working hours). A substantial number of television programs are captioned. Since 2000, NGT interpretation has been provided for television news broadcasts in the morning. In relation to interpreting services, the language needs of deaf people are thus largely met. On the other hand, in recent years in schools for deaf children, NGT is being increasingly substituted by Sign Supported Dutch (*Nederlands met Gebaren*, NmG) (Knoors & Marschark, 2012; Terpstra & Schermer, 2006). The use of signing as a communication method rather than a language is an element of the language policy of early intervention programs and schools for deaf children. In November 2017, *Siméa*, the organization for professionals educating deaf children, organized a working conference for educators, professionals and parents of deaf children about their desired form of education. The majority voted for bilingual education, but it remained unclear how 'bilingual' education should be defined.

However, even though NGT is accepted as the language of deaf people in Dutch society, it still is not formally recognized as a language by the Dutch government.

Part of the process of recognizing a language can be encompassed in language planning activities. Three aspects of language planning can be described for (sign) languages: status planning, corpus planning, and acquisition planning. The focus of this chapter will be on status planning in relation to NGT, the role of the Dutch deaf community, core campaigners, and other factors that have influenced the campaign for legal recognition of NGT and its current status. In this chapter, the term 'language planning' is used to refer to those political and educational measures that focus on the regulation or improvement of the use and/or status of a language. It is important to stress that for most languages and certainly for most sign languages, language planning is not formally and rationally conducted by some central authority. As Cooper (1989: 41) states: 'In reality, language planning rarely conforms to this ideal and more often than not language planning is a messy affair, ad hoc, haphazard, and emotionally driven'. Moreover, although language planning activities may be conducted by a wide range of institutions – apart from language academies, governments and departments of education – lobby groups and individuals play a crucial role in the process of sign language planning activities in various countries (De Meulder, 2016).

Status planning and corpus planning are very closely related. If the status of a language needs to be raised, a form of corpus planning is required. For example, the lexicon needs to be expanded in order to meet the needs of different functions of the language. Since 2004, the Dutch Sign Centre (*Nederlands Gebarencentrum*) has been systematically developing the lexicon of NGT in different domains to meet the expanding needs of deaf NGT users. Corpus planning in the Netherlands is relevant in relation to the legal recognition of NGT because the Dutch government presented standardization of the basic and educational lexicon in several discussions and meetings as a precondition for the legal recognition of NGT. A similar precondition has never been put forward for the legal recognition of spoken regional minority languages in the Netherlands, such as Frisian or Lower Saxon (for more on the process of standardization of NGT see Schermer 2003a, 2003b, 2012).

The four authors of this chapter are all involved in the process of the legal recognition of NGT. Trude Schermer is a linguist and CEO of the Dutch Sign Centre and has been involved in research on NGT and in the process of the recognition of NGT since the 1980s. Richard Cokart is a native signer and a linguist and works as a researcher at the Dutch Sign Centre. Corrie Tijsseling is a native signer and a researcher in history and the philosophy of education. Eva Westerhoff is a native signer and was trained as a teacher of NGT. She was the founder and president of the professional association of teachers of NGT. From 2013 to 2017, Westerhoff and Tijsseling have both been board member and president, respectively of the Dutch National Association of deaf people (*Dovenschap*), which is the successor of the aforementioned *Dovenraad*. Schermer, Tijsseling and Westerhoff are still involved in the political process of the recognition of NGT.

In this chapter, we will focus mainly on the explicit legal recognition of NGT and the steps that have been made in this process. In order to understand the arguments pro and contra of all parties involved in the legal recognition of NGT, we will firstly discuss the legal position of the national spoken language of the Netherlands, Dutch and the official regional language Frisian. Subsequently we will focus on the status of NGT in the period 1977 to 2018, the role of the deaf Community, and the main actors and factors in the process towards legal recognition of NGT. To conclude, we will describe its current status.

The Status of Dutch and Frisian in the Netherlands: A Brief History

The history of Dutch, the national language of the Netherlands, and Frisian, the language of the Dutch province of *Fryslân* (Friesland) in the north of the Netherlands, is relevant to understand arguments that have been put forward by the Dutch Government in the discussion around the legal recognition of NGT between 1980 and 2018.

Dutch

Dutch was proclaimed the official language in public and administrative law in the Netherlands in 1807, despite the fact that French was accepted as the only language in the south of the Netherlands (which is currently Belgium). After the disassociation of the south in 1830, Dutch became the official language of the Netherlands. The use of Dutch in the administrative domain was regulated in 1995 by a General Administrative

Law (Van der Sijs, 2004). Furthermore, Dutch is also mentioned in educational laws (see next paragraph regarding Frisian).

It is illustrative for the Dutch perspective on language policy that in the Netherlands, the Dutch language and culture is considered self-evident (Hemminga, 2000). This implicit policy was challenged in 1997 when the Dutch parliament discussed a motion of the political parties Reformed Political Union (*Gereformeerd Politiek Verbond, GPV*) and the Christian Democratic Party (*Christen-Democratisch Appèl*, CDA) to anchor Dutch as the official language in the constitution. With this motion the GPV and the CDA aimed to protect Dutch in light of globalization, European integration and ongoing Anglicization. Even though all other parties considered Dutch to be important and in need of protection, the outcome of this debate was that the very thought of Dutch being a threatened language was considered an overstatement (Ministerie van Binnenlandse Zaken, 1997, File 24431). Indeed, the status of Dutch in the European Union is confirmed by implicit policy and in documents where the European Union recognizes national languages as official languages and actively promotes multilingualism (Caviedes, 2003). Therefore, the status of Dutch in the European Union is protected and creating legislation for it was considered unnecessary (Ministerie van Binnenlandse Zaken, 1997, File 24431).

Thirteen years later, in 2010, the Minister of Internal Affairs, the Minister of Education, Culture and Science, the Minister of Justice and the Prime Minister brought forward a legislative proposal to constitutionally recognize Dutch as the official language of the Netherlands, similar to the one in 1997. They also proposed to add a constitutional article about Frisian. The main argument for the need for this legislative proposal was, again, the necessity to affirm Dutch as an essential part of Dutch culture due to globalization and increasing diversity of Dutch society (Van den Eijnden, 2011).

The States Council advised on the matter in September 2010. In the Netherlands there is a parliamentary system: the States Council advises the Minister of Internal Affairs on legal matters. Its first conclusion was that Dutch is indisputably the language of the Netherlands and therefore there was no need for it to be anchored as such in the constitution. The States Council did not consider language as a constitutional right and instead preferred to recognize a language in a specific language law. In case the government would want to maintain Dutch as a constitutional right, other languages used in the Dutch territory would consequently have to be recognized as well: Frisian, Papiamento and English (the languages of the Dutch Caribbean Isles Bonaire, Saint Eustatius and Saba). All of this would affect the minimalist character of the Dutch constitution (Raad van State, 2010; Van den Eijnden, 2011). NGT and other minority languages spoken in the Netherlands, such as Limburgish, Lower Saxon, Romani and Yiddish, were not mentioned in the advice of the States Council.

In 2017, a new government was installed, which decided to withdraw the aforementioned legislative proposal. They claimed it had no added value since Dutch is protected by a number of legal provisions. Moreover, recognition of Dutch as an official language would call into question the legal position of Frisian and the languages of the Dutch Caribbean Isles. In addition, the States Council consistently adhered to the view that such amendments to the Dutch constitution should only be accepted based on objective factors and if the need for change was widely recognized (Van den Eijnden, 2011). In February 2018, the legislative proposal was completely withdrawn (Parlement & Politiek, 2018).

Apart from the above, the Dutch government has put forward very few laws and initiatives with respect to Dutch language planning. One important initiative in relation to Dutch language policy has been the foundation of the *Taalunie* (Language Union) in 1980 by the Netherlands and Flanders (Belgium). Its mission is to promote the use of Dutch and Flemish in the most effective and efficient way possible. Therefore, the *Taalunie* proactively develops language policies, products and services for Dutch-speaking people in and outside of Europe, thus enabling the Dutch language to remain an attractive and vital language.

Frisian

Frisian has a special status in the Netherlands: in the province of Friesland, it has been recognized as the official language in addition to Dutch in primary education since 1955 and in 1956, oral use of Frisian in Frisian courts became accepted (Van der Velden, 2004).

Two decades before, in 1938, the Frisian Academy (*Fryske Akademy*) was founded to promote and implement scientific and applied research into the Frisian language (Hemminga, 2000). Frisian became the official language of public and administrative law in Friesland by a change in the General Administrative Law in 1997. The position of Frisian in education in *Fryslân* has become stronger over the years: since 1970 it has been an optional exam subject, in 1980 it became mandatory in primary schools in *Fryslân* and in 1993 also in the first years of secondary education (Hemminga, 2000).

Frisian has been recognized as a minority language both by Germany and the Netherlands, and since 1992 has been protected by the European Charter for Regional or Minority Languages Part II, Article 7, and Part III, Articles 8–14 (Ministerie van Binnenlandse Zaken, 2003). In the Netherlands, the Law for the Use of the Frisian language (*Wet gebruik Friese taal*) came into effect on 1 January 2014 (Staatsblad, 2013). The law states that both Frisian and Dutch are the official languages in the province of *Fryslân*. Frisian citizens have the right to use Frisian or Dutch in court and in communication with public offices in *Fryslân*. A new Institute for the Frisian Language has been installed with legal tasks to protect and promote the Frisian language. This language law has been a model for the proposed legislation in 2016 for NGT.

The Status of NGT in the Netherlands: 1977–2018

The status of NGT is very much linked to the education of deaf children and the methods used. With the first deaf school founded in 1790, the Netherlands has a long tradition of educating deaf people. During the early years of deaf education in the Netherlands, the language method differed depending on the institution and the time period, that is, from sign systems to oral methods. From 1864 onwards, the majority of the schools for deaf children used the oral method. Signing was forbidden in the schools, albeit a particular sign system remained in use at the Institute for the Deaf in Sint-Michielsgestel until 1918 (Cokart, 2016; Tijsseling, 2014).

The period of oralism as the only educational method for deaf children in the Netherlands came to an end around 1977 (Tijsseling, 2014; Van der Lem, 1987). Hearing parents of deaf children began exerting pressure to initiate a change in the Family-Centered Early Intervention (FCEI) program: they demanded the use of signing with their children. Around 1988, this experimental program became the national FCEI program, which focused on Total Communication and later bilingual education until the beginning of the 21st century (Van den Bogaerde & Schermer, 2008). The introduction of signing, as described above, had consequences for the policy with respect to NGT.

From 1981 onwards, interest in sign language became increasingly manifest among linguists inspired by the pioneering work of Bernard Tervoort, who studied the signing of deaf children in the Netherlands (Tervoort, 1953) and who initiated the first dictionary project on NGT (Schermer *et al.*, 1983) in which 15.000 signs from 100 deaf native signers from five regions were collected. This corpus formed the basis for the first dictionary in NGT containing all five regional varieties in the Netherlands (Schermer *et al.*, 1988). The linguistic department of the University of Amsterdam has studied NGT since 1981 and in 1998 the first chair in NGT was installed. In October 2018, the second chair in NGT was appointed at Radboud University.

In 1997, following the recommendations from the report *Meer dan een Gebaar* (More than a sign, literally meaning: more than a gesture of good will) into the consequences and implications of NGT recognition (Commissie NGT, 1997, see section 4), all schools for deaf children agreed in a covenant with the government to implement bilingual NGT/Dutch education, to develop an NGT curriculum for primary special education and to standardize the basic lexicon of NGT for educational purposes. As mentioned in the introduction to this chapter, standardization was a requirement from the government in order to legally recognize NGT as a language. However, a covenant is a moral agreement without legal power. By 2011, most schools changed their educational policy from bilingual back to monolingual/bimodal teaching (Knoors & Marschark, 2012) and NGT did not receive legal recognition.

In 1983, the Dutch National Association of the Deaf started to lobby for sign language interpreting services for deaf people, which led to the foundation of a two-year sign language interpreter-training program at vocational level in 1985. In 1997, a new sign language interpreter-training program started at the University of Applied Sciences in Utrecht. This four-year program offers a bachelor's degree in NGT interpreting and NGT teaching for deaf and hearing students (Van den Bogaerde & Schermer, 2008).

In 1996, the Dutch Sign Centre was founded by the schools for deaf children and the Dutch Foundation for the Deaf and Hard of Hearing Child in order to develop national teaching materials in NGT for various target groups. Since 2004, the Dutch Sign Centre has been funded by the Department of Education, Culture and Science as the National Institute for Lexicography of NGT tasked with maintaining and developing the NGT lexicon and the online NGT dictionary (Schermer, 2012).

NGT is increasingly visible in Dutch society. For example, there is the national storytelling competition where deaf pupils from primary schools compete with each other in signing a story from a book; the translation in NGT on television of significant events in Dutch society, such as the King's Speech, Kings Day, the Royal Christmas Speech and the national broadcasted arrival of Saint-Nicholas; an increasing number of Dutch museums are providing tours in NGT; and the national railroad company and the Dutch Sign Centre cooperated for the development of NGT signs related to public transport by train. Lastly, information on various websites of the Dutch government and programs of political parties is translated into NGT.

NGT has thus evolved from a form of communication that hearing educators saw as unacceptable in deaf education to its contemporary position as an accepted language in Dutch society. However, there is still no official legal recognition and deaf children are decreasingly exposed to the NGT of native signers, which makes the position of NGT in Dutch society vulnerable.

The Dutch Deaf Community: The Discovery of their Own Language

In 1985, the Dutch Foundation for the Deaf and Hard of Hearing Child, the Dutch National Association of the Deaf and the University of Amsterdam succeeded in bringing the Second European Congress on Sign Language Research to the Netherlands. This conference introduced Dutch deaf people to linguistics and to insights from sign language research

(Tervoort, 1986). As a result, a major shift occurred in the attitude of deaf people towards their own language and their position in relation to hearing society. As the oral method had been the prevailing method in Dutch deaf education since 1864, the very idea of signing being a true language provoked many discussions in the deaf community. Slowly but surely, Dutch deaf people became increasingly proud of their sign language (Tijsseling, 2014). A few years later, during the summer of 1989, several Dutch deaf teachers and research assistants visited the first Deaf Way International Conference in Washington DC, which inspired some of them to create poems in NGT (Emmerik, 1995).

As the deaf community became more empowered, their growing desire for NGT to be officially recognized as one of the languages in the Netherlands led to the publication of the aforementioned report, *Meer dan een Gebaar*, in 1997 (Commissie NGT, 1997). This report provided the necessary insights into the prerequisites for recognition and was drawn up by a committee, Platform Recognition NGT, that was installed by the Ministry of Education, Culture and Science and the Ministry of Public Health, Welfare and Sport. The report provided 64 recommendations as to how NGT could be officially recognized, and what the implications would be both for the private lives of deaf people, and for social, judicial, educational and (mental) health legislation and regulations.

In the 2000s, the Dutch deaf community organized marches to gain public attention for recognition of NGT. The first march was held in 2001, as a protest to the breaking news that the Platform Recognition NGT stopped its activities because there had been no further progress since 1997 (Commissie NGT, 2001; De Ronde, 2001).

In 2003, the then chairman of the Dutch National Association of the Deaf (*Dovenschap*) and the CEO of the Dutch Sign Centre initiated a new committee: the Committee on Sign Language Recognition, consisting of a smaller group of people[2] to focus solely on legal recognition of NGT. This committee initiated various meetings between stakeholders and the Ministers of the Department of Public Health, Welfare and Sport and the Department of Education, Culture and Science in order to convince the political establishment of the necessity to legally recognize NGT.

In January 2004, a meeting took place between the CEO of the Dutch Sign Centre, the chairman of the Committee on Sign Language Recognition, the chairman of *Dovenschap* and the Secretary of State of the Department of Public Health, Welfare and Sports. In preparation for this meeting, a document was presented to the Secretary of State and civil servants (Schermer *et al.*, 2004). It argued that even though NGT had become more visible, the integration of deaf people in Dutch society was still not self-evident: the biggest obstacle remained the communication itself between hearing and deaf people. This document once more emphasized the need for recognition of NGT, to protect the natural language of Deaf people in order to be equal to hearing people and to prevent NGT being oppressed ever again by hearing educators in Deaf education.

In the summer of 2004, the Dutch deaf community rallied once more for recognition of NGT (Schoevaart, 2004). Soon after this march, the Secretary of State wrote to the Parliament (Ministerie van Binnenlandse Zaken, 2004), in reaction to a report on the status of sign languages in Europe (Timmermans, 2003). The ministers involved stated that activities of the Council of Europe should be aimed at the instrumental rights of sign language users and not at the mere legal status of the language. Furthermore, the needs of sign language users should be studied before a choice for a legal instrument was made. The Secretary of State informed the parliament of her views: legal recognition of NGT would be of no added value. She preferred to solve the problems that might be experienced by the deaf community 'in a practical way' (Ministerie van Binnenlandse Zaken, 2004). It seems that the Secretary of State suggested an ad hoc solution in cases where a deaf individual might encounter a problem as a result of being deaf. As a consequence, the Committee on Sign Language Recognition ceased all its activities in 2010. Its members had to work their way through many different layers at many different departments and their efforts became diffuse and ineffective because no government department assumed responsibility for any action.

The First Legislative Proposal for the Recognition of NGT

In 2013, *Dovenschap* installed a new board and one of its goals was to pursue the legal recognition of NGT. In 2014, when the politician Roelof van Laar became a Member of Parliament for the Labour Party (PVDA), he announced that he was willing to submit a proposal for the legal recognition of NGT. The board of *Dovenschap* started negotiations with van Laar about the content of the proposal. The initial draft mostly awarded instrumental value to NGT, with deaf people seen as 'relying on' NGT and NGT being fundamental to deaf children's language development. In addition, the draft included a variety of topics related to the participation of deaf people in society such as telecommunication and emergency services. The draft legislative proposal intended to solve all the problems of deaf people. *Dovenschap*, however, wanted to move away from the old and inappropriate 'deficit' framework, which labels deaf people as having defective ears and being deprived from 'language' (defined as spoken language). Instead, *Dovenschap* wanted to profile deaf people as a linguistic and cultural minority, who are only disabled when they have no access to communication and information: being deaf is both a disability and a linguistic identity (De Meulder, 2016).

The small number of signers in any country is often used as an argument for withholding or limiting linguistic rights (Wilcox *et al.*, 2012). Even though this was never the case in the Netherlands, *Dovenschap* decided to determine the number of sign language users, and to compare this with the numbers of users of other minority languages and regional languages. Based on a recent study, there are approximately 11,900 to 20,400 deaf people in the Netherlands who were born deaf or became deaf in the first three years of life (Prawiro-Atmodjo *et al.*, 2016). Taking into account hearing parents and siblings of deaf people, who mostly learn NGT up to a certain level, along with hearing children of deaf parents who are often native signers and interpreters of NGT, there are an esti-mated number of 60.000 people who use NGT, at different skill levels.

In addition to recognition of NGT as a language in the Netherlands by means of a national law, *Dovenschap* wanted to protect NGT as a minority language under the European Charter for Regional or Minority Languages. In the Second Periodical Report regarding this Charter, pre-sented to the European Council (Ministerie van Binnenlandse Zaken, 2003), the Dutch government recognizes Frisian, which is used by 630,539 people, as an official language (in addition to Dutch, the other official language of the Netherlands). The Dutch government also protects other regional languages under the Charter (Ministerie van Binnenlandse Zaken, 2003). These are Limburgish (*Limburgs* – approximately 750,000 users) and Lower Saxon (*Nedersaksisch* – approximately 180,000 users). As for other minority languages, the Dutch government also recognizes Yiddish, which is used by some hundreds of people; Sinti, used by 4500 people and all variants of Roma, used by 750 people (Ministerie van Binnenlandse Zaken, 2003). Furthermore, on the Dutch Caribbean Isles (Bonaire, Saint-Eustatius and Saba) Papiamento and English are used in education, communication with public offices and court (Oostindie & Klinkers, 2003).

On 3 October 2016, the Labour Party and the Christian Union (hence-forth CU), sent the final legislative proposal for the recognition of NGT to the Dutch Parliament. The CU was involved because this political party had been advocating for the recognition of NGT for a number of years (Christen Unie, 2010). Van Laar had given in to *Dovenschap* on most points. The final legislative proposal – and the attached Explanatory Memorandum – focused on the legal recognition of NGT and the promo-tion of NGT. The proposal entails that for all public governmental com-munication such as public speeches of members of parliament and in administrative communication, NGT translations (either in the form of movie clips on a website or providing interpretation) must be available. In addition, it asks for the instalment of a governmental body for the protec-tion and promotion of NGT, and mentions the Dutch Sign Centre as the designated institute (Ministerie van Binnenlandse Zaken, 2016).

As mentioned before, *Dovenschap* used the law on Frisian language as a model for the legislative proposal for NGT. There are two similarities between the NGT proposal and the law on Frisian: the use of the minority language in communications with the government (either directly or through interpreters) and the installation of a governmental body for the protection and promotion of that language. However, the proposal for the legal recognition of NGT only mentions communication from the government to signing citizens – a one-way communication – and is limited to official public communication such as websites and speeches of government officials, whereas the law on Frisian mentions all governmental communication and the right of the Frisian citizen to use Frisian when communicating with governmental bodies. Also, the law on Frisian allows for the use of Frisian in legal communication, such as law courts, which is not mentioned in the legislative proposal for the legal recognition of NGT.

After the legislative proposal was sent to the Parliament it was subsequently sent to the States Council, which advises the Minister of Internal Affairs. Following this, the advice is put forward to the King for a possible additional reaction. The next step is to send the legislative proposal to the House of Representatives (*Tweede Kamer*). At this point in time, the advice of the States Council and the reaction of the Minister of Internal Affairs are made public; however, the government can still decide not to discuss the legislative proposal and to solve matters in a different way. If the House accepts the legislative proposal, it will be sent to the Senate (*Eerste Kamer*). If the Senate also accepts the legislative proposal, it will be sent to the King, and after signing it will come into effect.

In March 2017, elections took place for a new Parliament and the above-mentioned process came to a standstill. Van Laar's party suffered a devastating loss and he is no longer a member of parliament. The new government, which was installed on 26 October 2017, consists of four parties: the aforementioned CU, CDA, Democrats of '66 and the People's Party for Freedom and Democracy, VVD. *Dovenschap* contacted the CU to ask them to revive the process regarding the recognition of NGT. *Dovenschap* also started a petition, signed by 15,737 people and launched a campaign #*ngtnu* ('NGT now') to increase awareness about the importance of the legal recognition of NGT, which soon was joined by the Dutch National Youth Association of the Deaf. The CU responded positively to these actions and stated that significant steps needed to be made. In April 2018, CU and *Dovenschap* held a meeting to discuss the process and it was agreed that CU and the Labour Party would soon bring the legislative proposal up for discussion in the House of Representatives. On 29 September 2018, at the celebration of World Deaf Day, Carla Dik Faber of the CU, one of the initiators of the law proposal, informed the audience that the process was delayed due to lack of staff and time, but that she was still strongly determined to have NGT recognised.

An important instrument that is expected to enhance the willingness of Dutch politicians to accept the legislative proposal for the recognition of NGT is the UN Convention on the Rights of Persons with Disabilities (UNCRPD), which has been in force in the Netherlands since 14 July 2016. During the ratification process, *Dovenschap* often pointed out that the UNCRPD contains a number of clauses and directions regarding the recognition of national sign languages. During the 19th session of the UN Committee on the Rights of Persons with Disabilities in Geneva (CRPD, pers. comm., 2018) committee members confirmed to *Dovenschap* that the recognition of a sign language is considered fundamental to the implementation of the CRPD, in which the right to sign language is mentioned many times.

Conclusion

After more than 30 years of advocacy, Dutch signers almost do not dare to envision that at some point, NGT will be recognized by the Dutch government. At the same time, it is clear that there is an implicit recognition of NGT as society both accepts and appreciates NGT. It is accepted in education and NGT interpreters are available for all life domains. People enjoy museum tours in NGT by deaf guides and other artistic expressions of NGT are applauded. Recently, the documentary 'Deaf Child' (De Ronde, 2017), about de Ronde's deaf son Tobias, was highly awarded at the International Documentary Film Festival Amsterdam (IDFA). It portrays the upbringing of a deaf child in a hearing family using NGT and is a beautiful illustration of the efforts that were made in the 1980s and 1990s to enable deaf children to make their own choices with respect to language and culture.

Another conclusion is that in the Netherlands, over the years arguments shifted in focus from the instrumental value of NGT (deaf people need signing because they cannot hear) to the human right to language. Indeed, discussions have increasingly moved away from 'the problems of deaf people'. The legal recognition of NGT is considered a symbolic recognition because provisions granting the legal right to use NGT are already in place. Why, then, continue this struggle for recognition that has been going on since the late 1970s? Because even a symbolic recognition would have an emotional and psychological impact. It has an emotional impact on elderly deaf persons, whose hands were literally bound to prevent them from signing in an era when signing was forbidden. And thus, generations of deaf people were deprived of being themselves, being part of their community and their culture.

It would also have an impact on young deaf children. Taking into account that 90–95% of deaf children are born to hearing parents, sign language and the culture of sign language users, as well as taking pride in both, is thus rarely passed on from parents to children. Each generation of deaf children has to reinvent themselves. Their language being recognized as an official language would contribute to their citizenship and thus to confidence to claim their rights. And last but not least, legal recognition of NGT clearly distinguishes NGT as a language from a method of communication such as Signed Dutch, granting it the status and protection it deserves. Finally, it could lead to NGT becoming an official curriculum subject taught in mainstream schools.

Notes

(1) The distinction deaf/Deaf is currently being discussed (Kusters *et al.*, 2017). The authors hold the opinion that this distinction does not express the diversity of the deaf community. Also, it is an anachronism to write 'Deaf' in a historical context (Tijsseling, 2014). We therefore only write 'deaf'.

(2) Members of the *Commissie Erkenning Gebarentaal* between 2003 and 2005: Prof. Anne Baker (University of Amsterdam), Henk Bakker (former Chairman of the Board of Effatha-Guyot Group), Prof. Hans Bennis (former Director, Meertens Institute), Benny Elferink (former chairman, *Dovenschap*) and Trude Schermer (Director, Dutch Sign Centre).

References

Caviedes, A. (2003) The role of language in nation-building within the European Union. *Dialectical Anthropology* 27 (3–4), 249–268.

Christen Unie (2010) *Positie Doven Versterken, Nederlandse Gebarentaal Erkennen! [To Strengthen the Position of Deaf People, Recognition of NGT is Needed!]*. Den Haag: Christen Unie.

Cokart, R. (2016) De geheimen van Sint-Michielsgestel: Lexicale verschillen op basis van een corpus [The secrets of Sint-Michielsgestel: Lexical differences, based upon a corpus]. *Verslag OCW Activiteiten 2016 [Report OCW Activities 2016]*. Amersfoort: Nederlands Gebarencentrum.

Commissie NGT (1997) *Meer dan een Gebaar. Rapport van de Commissie Nederlandse Gebarentaal [More than a Sign. Report of the Commission on NGT]*. Den Haag: SDU Uitgevers.

Commissie NGT (2001) *Actualisatie 1997–2001 van Meer dan een Gebaar (1997) [Actualization 1997–2001 of More than a Sign]*. Utrecht: Dovenschap.

Cooper, R.L. (1989) *Language Planning and Social Change*. Bloomington, IN: Indiana University Press.

De Meulder, M. (2016) The power of language policy. The legal recognition of sign languages and the aspirations of deaf communities. PhD thesis, University of Jyvaskyla.

De Ronde, A. (2001) Nederlandse gebarentaal vóór 2002 erkend [Recognition of NGT before 2002]. *Woord & Gebaar* 21 (1), 8–9.

De Ronde, A. (2017) *Doof kind [Deaf Child]*. Amsterdam: Cinemien.

Emmerik, W. (1995) *Gedichten in Gebarentaal [Poems in Sign Language]*. Amsterdam: Het Komplex.

Hemminga, P. (2000) *Het Beleid inzake Unieke Regionale Talen [The Policy Regarding Unique Regional Languages]*. Ljouwert/Leeuwarden: Fryske Akademy.

Knoors, H. and Marschark, M. (2012) Language planning for the 21st century: Revisiting bilingual language policy for deaf children. *Journal of Deaf Studies and Deaf Education* 18 (4), 291–305. Please note the erratum: https://academic.oup.com/jdsde/article/17/4/535/393672?searchresult=1.

Kusters, A., De Meulder, M. and O'Brien, D. (2017) *Innovations in Deaf Studies: The Role of Deaf Scholars*. Oxford: Oxford University Press.

Ministerie van Binnenlandse Zaken (1997) Officiële bekendmakingen [Official publications], File 24431. See https://zoek.officielebekendmakingen.nl/behandeldossier/24431 (accessed 3 April 2018).

Ministerie van Binnenlandse Zaken (2003) *Second Periodical Report European Charter for Regional or Minority Languages, The Netherlands, 2003.* See https://rm.coe.int/CoERMPublicCommonSearchServices/DisplayDCTMContent?documentId=09000 016806c8e24 (accessed 3 April 2018).

Ministerie van Binnenlandse Zaken (2004) Officiële bekendmakingen [Official publications], File kst-29200-XVI-249. https://zoek.officielebekendmakingen.nl/kst-29200-XVI-249 (accessed 6 April 2018).

Ministerie van Binnenlandse Zaken (2016) Officiële bekendmakingen [Official publications], File 34562. See https://zoek.officielebekendmakingen.nl/dossier/34562 (accessed 3 April 2018).

Nederlandse Dovenraad (1981) *Wie niet Horen kan Moet maar Zien [Those Who Cannot Hear, Are Left to See].* Bussum: Uitgeverij Coutinho.

Oostindie, G. and Klinkers, I. (2003) *Decolonising the Caribbean: Dutch Policies in Comparative Perspective.* Amsterdam: University of Amsterdam Press.

Parlement & Politiek (2018) Wetsvoorstel verankering Nederlandse taal in grondwet ingetrokken [Legislative proposal for anchoring Dutch language in the constitution withdrawn]. See https://www.parlement.com/id/vkm0gkos9s5t/nieuws/wetsvoor stel_verankering_nederlandse (accessed 3 April 2018).

Prawiro-Atmodjo P., Langendoen M. and Tijsseling C. (2016) *Literatuurstudie naar de Leefsituatie van Vroegdove Volwassenen [Literature Review on the Living Conditions of Early Deaf Adults].* Sint-Michielsgestel: Koninklijke Kentalis.

Raad van State (2010) Advies over Nederlandse taal in de grondwet [Advice on Dutch language in the constitution]. See https://www.raadvanstate.nl/adviezen/samenvat tingen/tekst-samenvatting.html?id=44 (accessed 3 April 2018).

Schermer, G.M. (2003a) From variant to standard: An overview of the standardization process of the lexicon of sign language of the Netherlands over two decades. *Sign Language Studies* 3 (4), 469–486.

Schermer, G.M. (2003b) Standaardisatie, en nu? [Standardization, and now?]. *Van Horen Zeggen* 44 (1), 15–19.

Schermer, G.M. (2012) Sign language planning in the Netherlands between 1980 and 2010. *Sign Language Studies* 12 (4), 467–493.

Schermer, G.M., Stroombergen, M. and Tervoort, B. (1983) Het Nederlandse gebaren-woordenboekproject [The NGT dictionary project]. In B. Tervoort (ed.) *Hand over Hand, Nieuwe Inzichten in de Communicatie van Doven [Hand over Hand, New Insights in the Communication of Deaf]* (pp. 41–55). Bussum: Uitgeverij Coutinho.

Schermer, G.M., Harder, R. and Bos, H. (1988) *Handen uit de Mouwen: Gebaren uit de Nederlandse Gebarentaal in Kaart gebracht [Role One's Sleeves Up: Signs of NGT Charted].* Amsterdam: KOMVA/NSDSK.

Schermer, G.M., Wesemann, J. and Elferink, B. (2004) Notitie Nederlandse Gebarentaal [Memorandum NGT]. Unpublished manuscript, Nederlands Gebarencentrum.

Schoevaart, D. (2004) De mars [The march]. *Woord & Gebaar* 24 (6), 6–9.

Staatsblad (2013) Wet op Friese Taal [Law on Frisian Language]. *Inwerkingtredingsbesluit [Incorporation Decision.]* 12 December, p. 515. Deventer: Wolters Kluwer B.V.

Terpstra, A. and Schermer, T. (2006) Waarom gebruik je NmG? [Why do you use NmG?]. *Van Horen Zeggen,* 2006 (1), 10–17.

Tervoort, B. (1953) Structurele analyse van visueel taalgebruik binnen een groep dove kinderen [Structural analysis of visual language use in a group of deaf children]. PhD thesis, University of Amsterdam.

Tervoort, B. (1986) *Signs of Life. Proceedings of the Second European Congress on Sign Language Research.* Amsterdam: NSDSK/UvA.

Tijsseling, C. (2014) School, waar? Een Onderzoek naar de Betekenis van het Nederlandse Dovenonderwijs voor de Nederlandse Dovengemeenschap, 1790–1990 [School, where? A Study into the Meaning of Deaf Education in the Netherlands for the Dutch Deaf Community, 1790–1990]. PhD thesis, Utrecht University.

Timmermans, N. (2003) *A Comparative Analysis of the Status of Sign Languages in Europe*. Strasbourg: Council of Europe.

Van den Bogaerde, B. and Schermer, G.M. (2008) Deaf studies in the Netherlands. *Deaf Worlds* 23, 1–14.

Van den Eijnden P.M. (2011) De Nederlandse taal in de grondwet [The Dutch language in the constitution]. *Tijdschrift voor Constitutioneel Recht*, July 2011, 315–324.

Van der Lem, T. (1987) An early intervention program. In J. Kyle (ed.) *Sign and School: Using Signs in Deaf Children's Development* (pp. 155–161). Clevedon: Multilingual Matters.

Van der Sijs, N. (2004) *Taal als Mensenwerk, het Ontstaan van het ABN [Language as the Work of Humans, the Creation of ABN]*. Den Haag: SDU uitgevers.

Van der Velden, B.D. (2004) Waar gaan we heen met het Fries? Het gebruik van de Friese taal in het juridische en in het bestuurlijke verkeer in de laatste twee eeuwen [Where do we go with Frisian? The use of Frisian language in legal and administrative communication in the last two centuries]. PhD thesis, University of Amsterdam.

Wilcox, S., Krausneker, V. and Armstrong, D. (2012) Language policies and the Deaf community. In B. Spolsky (ed.) *Cambridge Handbook of Language Policy* (pp. 374–395). Cambridge: Cambridge University Press.

11 The 'Language Issue': The Struggle and Path to the Recognition of LIS

Carlo Geraci and Humberto Insolera

Introduction

The struggle for the legal recognition of Italian Sign Language (LIS, *Lingua dei Segni Italiana*)[1] officially started in the mid-1990s as a dispute between medical and linguistic perspectives on LIS and quickly developed into an issue of social inclusion after Italy ratified the UN Convention on the Rights of Persons with Disabilities in 2009 (hereafter 'the UN Convention'). Currently, the Netherlands (see Cokart *et al.*, this volume, Chapter 10) and Italy are the last two European Member States without a law recognizing the national sign language. The 'sign language issue', namely the struggle to have official recognition of sign language in Italy, is rooted in the past many decades earlier, and in certain respects interacts with the pursuit of a standard for spoken Italian, known among historians of Italian as 'the language issue'.

'We made Italy, now we have to make the Italians'. This motto is attributed to Massimo D'Azeglio, one of the most prominent Italian statesmen and pro-unification supporters of the mid-19th century (Gigante, 2011). The motto aimed at saying that despite territorial unification there was no identification with the Italian nation yet and that this would be the primary challenge for the newly established nation-state. The 'language issue', namely the issue of what would be the language of the new nation, was at the centre of the political debate. There were two positions: one aiming at a diglossia solution, with local dialects used as a proxy to target Italian, identified with the language of famous writers of 13th and 14th centuries; and a top-down solution aiming at imposing Italian as the only language of the nation, removing local dialects from the scene. Needless to say, the top-down solution was the one that prevailed and was strongly enforced in Italian language policy and planning. This was the climate around language diversity in the years before 1880, when in Milan, the International Congress on the Education of the Deaf established oralism as the only way to educate deaf[2] children, banishing the use of sign language. This brief overview of the language issue sheds some light on why Italy was one of the countries where oralism became so widespread.

In 2010, the International Congress on the Education of the Deaf (ICED) expressed regret for the resolutions adopted in 1880; however, studies on sign linguistics (Sandler & Lillo-Martin, 2006), language acquisition (Meier, 2016), psycholinguistics (Emmorey, 2007) and neuro-linguistics (Malaia & Wilbur, 2010) were already proving that sign languages are natural languages. Deaf communities around the world became aware of the status of sign languages as languages, and started fighting for the right to use their language, have it taught to Deaf children and have access to public life through it. This was also the case in Italy, where, parallel to the international scientific discoveries and the pioneering work of Virginia Volterra and her group at the CNR (National Research Council) of Rome, Deaf associations started claiming their right to use LIS (see Geraci, 2012 for LIS language and policy).

Despite the efforts of the Italian Deaf community, the scientific community and efforts on the part of some in the world of politics, LIS has not yet been legally recognized. In this chapter, we focus on the issues at stake, and the arguments used for and against recognition. Strong positions are taken against the recognition of LIS as a language, not just claimed by associations defending oralism, but also by medical associations such as the Italian Association of Audiologists. These positions became apparent during the debate about the most recent bill for LIS recognition proposed during the 2013 to 2018 legislative session (XVII Legislature). As with previous attempts during the XVI Legislature (2008 to 2012), this bill was not approved before the end of the legislative session. Nonetheless, several local governments (Italian regions) approved and supported LIS and its use in many ways and domains, which brought about the paradoxical situation of LIS being recognized by the majority of local governments but not by the national government.

In the remainder of the chapter, we offer a detailed analysis of the Italian situation. In the next section, we discuss the major approaches to sign language and how they are mirrored in the Italian debate on LIS recognition. This is followed by a presentation of the main points of the Bill discussed in the Italian parliament during the XVII Legislature. Next, we present the main arguments of the campaigners in favour and against the recognition of LIS. We then summarize the recent debate in the Italian Senate (3 October 2017). Finally, we discuss the factors that led to the current situation, and the possibilities for a successful recognition of LIS.

Main Views on Sign Language

When it comes to defining the status of sign languages, three main perspectives are usually offered in the political debate; that is, the linguistic, the medical and the sociocultural view (Reagan, 1995). In this section, we provide an overview of how these three approaches are represented in the Italian debate around the recognition of LIS.

The linguistic view considers sign languages as natural languages on a par with spoken languages, as stated in a document on language policy by the Italian linguist and former Minister of Education, Tullio De Mauro (De Mauro, 2016). The supporters of this view provide evidence ranging from purely technical (Sandler & Lillo-Martin, 2006) and linguistic (Geraci *et al.*, 2011) to cognitive (Geraci *et al.*, 2008; Goldin-Meadow & Brentari, 2017) and biological (Malaia & Wilbur, 2010). Deaf people are the main users of sign language, but hearing people may also have access to it; for example, in the case of children born into signing families or they may have learned it as a second language. According to this view, sign languages should be treated on a par with other languages and should be granted status as languages, and supported as language minorities.

The medical view subordinates sign language as a by-product of a sensory deprivation. Deafness is seen as a reversible condition that modern technologies paired with substantial speech therapy may reduce up to the point of being an irrelevant or a minor situation. The status of sign language is irrelevant to the real problem: deafness. Sign languages are considered tools to medically treat deafness and as such should be evaluated against other rehabilitation techniques. The medical view splits into two slightly different approaches. Under the most utilitarian view, sign languages constitute a more or less essential positive, which should be given to deaf children in addition to the most advanced technological aids. The other approach sees sign languages as an obstacle towards the process of full rehabilitation from a 'medical' condition, associated with a 'language deficit' view. The (unsupported) claim is that deaf children exposed to sign language would find the 'tool' so effective that they give up achieving the highest levels of proficiency in spoken language. As a direct consequence, deaf people's quality of life would be suboptimal because signing would make the disability plain and clear, and deaf people therefore would be easily stigmatized as handicapped. Finally, in this approach, sign languages should not be given any priority because (1) genetically transmitted deafness is such a rare situation that only a very small minority of deaf children would benefit from them; (2) congenital but not genetically transmitted deafness should be better treated by removing the hearing impairment rather than using a tool (communication mode) that would amplify the disability; and (3) sign languages are ineffective for late-acquired deafness. According to this view, the status of sign language is irrelevant. Policymakers should either give it a complementary role in the treatment of deafness or should favour other tools (including universal new-born hearing screening), which, at least in Italy, aim at removing deafness as a condition that undermines the independence of deaf people in everyday life, and do not consider sign language to be a part of the intervention.

The sociocultural view treats sign language as part of deaf people's broader situation. It is the fundamental ingredient of a group identity based on positively valued features (Lane, 1999). Language awareness is thus one ingredient in a richer recipe, which includes a shared history, stories, cultural traditions and a deaf social network. The sociocultural view supports all the arguments of the linguistic view and aims at giving sign language the status of a natural language. It differs from the linguistic view in that it goes beyond the formal recognition of a language per se, but aims at recognizing Deaf communities as minority groups. In the long-term perspective of inclusion, medical interventions are not seen as being a priori incompatible with sign language and the existence of Deaf communities. They are part of the free choices made by families of deaf children. Policymakers should strive to recognize and support Deaf communities and sign languages and to include Deaf communities with the dominant community by removing barriers and stigmatization of deafness as a disability in all environments.

The Path to Recognition

Italy ratified the UN Convention in 2009. Still, there is no specific law recognizing LIS as the language of the Italian Deaf and Deafblind community. Timmermans (2005) briefly summarizes the various attempts to recognize LIS in the 1990s, while Geraci (2012) discusses the debate around LIS in the early 2000s. Beside the various international resolutions and conventions that the Italian governments approved but never implemented, the situation is even more complex because in 1999, the government approved a law to support language minorities. This is Law 482/1999, which defines as minority languages those languages that are relatively far from Italian historically and typologically and, crucially, whose communities of speakers are concentrated in specific regions of the country. In other words, this law anchors language minorities to specific geographical areas, excluding a priori LIS, which is used throughout the country (see Geraci, 2012 for a more detailed discussion). The latest attempt to recognize LIS before the one described in this chapter goes back to 2011–2012, when the Senate approved a bill which recognized LIS as the language of the Italian Deaf community (Bill 831/2008). The Bill did not pass through Parliament before the end of the legislative session, in part because of lobbying by LIS opponents (Geraci, 2012).

Still, LIS has implicit recognition, especially in schools and universities, by the framework law on assistance, social integration and rights of people with disabilities (Law 104/1992, further modified in 2000 and

Table 11.1 Timeline of laws and proposals

	Law 104/1992 Disability	Law 482/1999 Minority languages	2009 UN Convention ratified by Italy	2008–2012 Bill 831/2008	2013–2018 Bill302/2013
Description	'Specialized languages' can be used in the education of disabled people.	Minority languages are recognized, but not LIS.	Sign language must be recognized.	Recognition of LIS, as the language of the Deaf community (linguistic view).	Recognition of LIS, and LISt (tactile LIS) as part of a general intervention on deaf people (social view).
Status	Active	Active	Active	Aborted	Aborted

2001). Among other things, Law 104/1992 recognizes the right to have access to education by using 'specialized languages' (Article 8, Section 1c). This is the crucial provision that allows LIS to be used in official and institutional situations even without explicit recognition as a language. Several regional governments, to whom social and health policies are delegated, took advantage of this possibility and recognized LIS at the local level. The timeline of the most relevant laws and proposals is given in Table 11.1.

It is against this background that a proposal to recognize LIS reached the parliament of the XVII Legislature. The legislative process started in March 2013, with a prospective duration of five years. On 26 March 2013, Senator Antonio De Poli of the centrist party, Scelta Civica, filed a bill on the 'rights of deaf people, people with hearing loss and deafblind people'. The Bill was then assigned to Senator Francesco Russo of the Democrat Party as rapporteur. The first draft only contained three articles: one defining the general frame of the proposal within the policies to implement human rights and the recognition of LIS; one about general dispositions of the situations in which the use of LIS should be supported; and a technical article on budgetary neutrality (see below). The draft was then assigned to the committee on constitutional affairs and discussed in the Senate. It took four years for the Bill to be approved by one of the two chambers (the Senate voted in favour on 3 October 2017). Unfortunately, the legislative session ended before the second chamber (the Parliament) could approve the Bill. All information about this proposal (debate in the Senate, expert interviews and discussions) is available on the website of the Italian Senate.[3] The reason why it took so long for the bill to go from presentation to first approval is the discussion in the Senate, in which several experts and representatives of Deaf associations were asked to present their arguments in favour (or against) recognition of LIS (see Section 4). In the remainder of this section, we introduce the main provisions of the Bill.

The proposal debated at the national level during the XVII Legislature

The Bill discussed during the XVII Legislature aimed at recognizing the citizenship rights of deaf people, people with hearing loss and deafblind people, and contains 14 articles. We first present the main points of the Bill and then comment on them.[4]

The very first article of the Bill recognized 'the rights of deaf people, hard of hearing and deafblind people' and LIS and tactile LIS as languages 'within a bilingual environment (Italian/LIS)' in which deaf people should be given access both to Italian and LIS. Article 2 ('free choice and non-discrimination') introduced 'the right for deaf people, hard of hearing, deafblind people and their families to freely choose any communication modality, education and tools to implement full social inclusion' in addition and in parallel to LIS. Note that the text of the Bill implicitly distinguished between 'tools that can be used to prevent and cure deafness and deafblindness' such as neonatal screening and other technological innovations, and LIS and tactile LIS which are given the status of language. Article 3 concerned 'prevention and early identification of deafness and deafblindness' and 'the tools to be used to reduce or fix the hearing deficit and the visual deficit'. Article 4 was about 'accessibility to communication, information public spaces and public administration', while Article 5 established the right for deaf and deafblind students to have a teaching assistant, a communication assistant or a (tactile) LIS interpreter at all levels of education, within a general view that also guarantees access to spoken Italian (at least in the written form). It also encouraged the creation of mixed classes with hearing and deaf students and delegated to the university system the task of training qualified communication assistants and interpreters. Articles 6 to 11 described the various environments in which (tactile) LIS can be used to guarantee social inclusion. Article 13 was specifically devoted to regulating the profession of (tactile) sign language interpreting. Finally, Article 14 of the Bill included a budgetary neutrality clause that no additional costs must be generated by the implementation of the law.

The spirit of this Bill was influenced by the sociocultural view on deafness, as per the UN Convention. This is clear by the fact that its main target is the right to citizenship rather than access to (sign) language. LIS and tactile LIS are given official status as means to achieve social inclusion. Nonetheless, (tactile) LIS plays a central role in achieving this goal, while technological supports are only marginally mentioned in the relevant articles. Another clear indication of a socio-cultural perspective comes by comparing the first draft of the Bill with the current one. In the article recognizing LIS and tactile LIS, and in the article regulating social inclusion in schools, the use of (tactile) LIS was mentioned together with an identical right to have access to monolingual education in spoken language (e.g. oralist education), the choice being left to the individual or their family. In the later draft of the proposal, any reference to oralism has been removed and article 5 pairs bilingual education with total communication (which is left undefined).

A few further comments are in order. Overall, the Bill incorporates the main aspects of the UN Convention and makes explicit reference to Deaf and Deafblind people as target of LIS and tactile LIS. The explicit provisions on Deafblind people and tactile sign language are an innovation compared to previous bills; however, the decision on which approach is more able to achieve social inclusion is left to the individual or their family. Finally, the budgetary neutrality clause may undermine any implementation of the proposal. Implementing bilingual programmes in schools, creating sign language interpreting tracks at the university level, providing accessible environment at work, museums, and so on involves additional costs. Thus, there is a serious risk that social inclusion is guaranteed only on paper.

The Struggle for Recognition

In this section, we review the major arguments in favour and against the recognition of LIS. Compared to the discussion around Bill 831/2008, where campaigners supporting LIS organized protests and marches (Geraci, 2012), this time the discussion has been less emotional and was publicly held in the Senate, with written documents issued as part of the proceedings. Despite the Bill targeting the social inclusion of Deaf and Deafblind people, the core of the discussion was about whether and why LIS should be recognized. In addition to campaigners, experts from various fields were heard in the Senate in the months preceding the discussion. The original documents can be downloaded from the Senate website.[5]

The view of the campaigners in favour of LIS

There are several Deaf associations in Italy that support LIS. The oldest and most prominent one is the National Association of Deaf People, Ente Nazionale Sordi (ENS), which first and before any other association campaigned for a law recognizing LIS. On the same side, and with very similar arguments, stand other Deaf associations and movements (e.g. LIS Subito), the associations of LIS interpreters, the State School for Deaf People, associations supporting Italian-LIS bilingualism and the National Association of Deafblind People.

All these associations recognize LIS as a language, providing scientific references, in particular work done by the group headed by Virginia Volterra at the CNR in Rome. In the use of sign language they see (1) an opportunity that should be offered possibly with other strategies in the education of deaf children (e.g. speech therapy); and (2) an option to overcome communication barriers and guarantee equal access and equal rights in all aspects of a person's life. They also claim the need to establish a controlled protocol to provide unbiased information about the various options available to families with deaf children. They see deafness not just as a sensory deprivation, but also as a social condition directly related to the individual's identity.

The view of the campaigners against LIS

The opponents to the recognition of LIS are mainly oralist associations and associations of families with deaf children. These associations see deafness as a disability, do not conceive of Deaf communities as cultural minorities and consider the recognition of LIS to be an overt stigmatization of deaf people. In what follows, we summarize their main arguments against the recognition of LIS and offer counter arguments.

The first argument tries to undermine the status of LIS as a language. It comes in two versions: one is based on the assumption that it is inconceivable to base the identity of a community on a disability. Without formal recognition of a community, there is no need to recognize its language. The problem with this argument is that it is based on the false assumption that deafness rather than the language itself is the real factor that brings Deaf people together. Deaf communities are such, not just because deaf people share social affiliation, but because they share a language. The other version of the argument is based on the fact that even if LIS is given the status of a language, it does not have the same expressive power as spoken languages and even if it did, it would still be missing a written form. This argument is based on two false assumptions; the first one that sign languages are inferior to spoken languages and the second one that the use of LIS automatically excludes access to the spoken language (via lipreading or in the written form). Both assumptions have been countered by scientific research on LIS (see, for instance, Terrugi, 2003; Volterra, 2004;).

A second argument is a *reductio ad absurdum* and tries to disprove the utility of LIS as a 'tool' for deaf people. The argument comes in two different facets: (1) the number of native signers is too small to justify implementing a system guaranteeing universal access for signers; and (2) medical interventions (including genetic ones) and modern technologies bypass the need for having an alternative communication system. While it is true that the proportion of native signers is small with respect to that of early and late learners, there is no precise information on the total number of Deaf LIS signers in Italy (the ENS reports 40,000 users) (Pabsch & Wheatley, 2012). Furthermore, it is unclear why the two options (sign language plus medical/technological interventions) should be mutually exclusive.

A third argument rejects the utility of the Bill a priori. Indeed, rather than benefiting deaf people, a bill recognizing LIS would favour the interests of interpreters (probably over the interests of hearing aids and cochlear implant manufacturers).

A final argument is based on costs. The cost of implementing a LIS-friendly environment for Deaf people would (1) exceed the limits of the Bill itself and (2) subtract resources from/going to other (medical) interventions. The first point is true in general of any budgetary neutrality clause, and can be countered: as a matter of principle, economic concerns are not superior to human rights. As for the second point, one may argue that beside cases of special language impairment (which are independent from deafness), the acquisition of sign language is an inevitable consequence of exposure for children and provides deaf people benefits both at the individual and the social level (many thanks to Natasha Abner for pointing out these aspects). This in turn may provide long-term economic benefits which could be superior to the initial investment to support sign language and a Deaf-friendly environment.

It is worth mentioning that all the arguments provided by these associations are explicitly against the use and recognition of LIS, but none is made against tactile LIS. Notice that very few of the arguments against LIS a fortiori extend to tactile LIS because Deaf and Deafblind signers are two completely different populations.

The opinion of the experts

In addition to associations campaigning in favour or against the recognition of LIS, the Senate also heard evidence from a number of (all hearing) experts. Below, we summarize the main arguments proposed by each speaker.

As part of the annex documentation, the Associazione Sordi Antonio Provolo included a commentary on the Bill by the Italian Society of Otolaryngologists and the Italian Society of Audiologists, who opposed the Bill. Fifty university professors from all over the country undersigned the document. Although none of the representatives of the two societies provided scientific evidence (at least to our knowledge), we include the main points of the commentary for the sake of completeness.[6]

The societies of Otolaryngologists and Audiologists acknowledge the necessity of social integration for (elderly) LIS signers, but opposes a view of a future society in which LIS could play a role in the education of deaf children, the main point being that hearing aids and cochlear implants reduce the communication disability for all deaf people, with the exception of extremely rare cases. The document includes three arguments against the recognition of LIS: (1) recognizing LIS would bring it to the same level as Italian with the risk of further increasing discrimination of deaf people. The implicit inference here is that sign language use prevents proper acquisition of spoken language (contra Terrugi, 2003 for the specific case of LIS); (2) the number of deaf children that currently choose a 'gestural language' is small, hence this would constitute inefficient expenditure of public money; and (3) implementing a sign language-friendly environment would have economic drawbacks. No scientific references have been provided to support the first argument, no quantitative measures were offered for the second one, and no cost comparison or cost/benefit analysis for implementing a sign language-friendly environment has been offered for the third one.

Dr Orzan, director of the audiology department of the IRCCS Hospital in Trieste, stated Deaf people are part of a group 'exclusively because they share a medical condition', although she recognizes sign languages including LIS as natural languages. She proposed two new (acquisition) arguments against the use of LIS in the education of deaf children: one against the use of LIS in situations of a deaf child with hearing parents; one in favour of early exposure to spoken language. It is easy to agree with the second point (see Guasti, 2007 for studies on spoken Italian). Early acquisition is essential for every individual. However, the argument per se supports the acquisition of the spoken language for deaf children; it is not against the acquisition of sign language. The first argument is trickier. It was used to deny the possibility of having genuine bilingualism in the case of deaf children born into hearing families. It denies the possibility that deaf children will be able to acquire sign language from a poor linguistic environment, because deaf children in hearing families will not be exposed to a qualitatively adequate linguistic input. There is no evidence to support this claim coming from LIS, but there is evidence of the contrary coming from ASL showing that impoverished input is still enough to develop a fully-fledged sign language (Singleton & Newport, 2004). Finally, if Orzan's argument carries any weight, it could apply to deaf children born in deaf families as well, with the clearly unwanted consequence that deaf children in deaf families should not be exposed to any spoken language because their parents would provide broken input to them.

Dr Caselli, a cognitive scientist at the CNR in Rome, presented the advantages of having a sign-spoken bilingual education, citing scientific evidence that learning a sign language does not interfere with proficiency in a spoken language (Mayberry et al., 2002) and highlighting that choosing a sign language does not exclude other kinds of approaches that could and should work in parallel.

Prof. Cardinaletti, professor of linguistics at Ca' Foscari University, pointed out that the sign modality is the only one that allows deaf people to acquire a human language by exposure without explicit training. Cardinaletti also offered another new argument in favour of using sign language: the special populations which may benefit from sign language use. Although no scientific reference was provided, she mentioned autism, Down syndrome, dyspraxia and Landau-Kleffner syndrome.

Prof. Pavani, a cognitive scientist at the CIMeC (Trento), provided a rich overview of scientific studies from a variety of disciplines showing that sign languages are natural languages and that sign-spoken bilingualism is not just an opportunity but the safest way to go when planning the education of deaf children. The rationale of the argument is that hearing aids and cochlear implants, even in ideal conditions, are not a guarantee for a complete success in mastering spoken language. It is also a fact that the acquisition of a sign language does not undermine the acquisition of a spoken language (if anything, scientific evidence points to the opposite conclusion). Since it is not possible to foresee in which cases there will be a failure in mastering the dominant language, it is safer for the good of each deaf individual's cognitive (and social) life to give them early access to sign language.

Prof. Sara Trovato, from the University of Milano-Bicocca, is a specialist in Deaf education and discussed whether the right to sign language is similar to the right of language minorities or whether it is a somehow stronger, inalienable individual right (Trovato, 2013). She showed that Deaf communities have the right to claim the recognition of sign language both as a language minority and as a right to have psychophysical integrity and that it is up to Deaf communities to make the call (and ultimately to politicians to implement the choice).

The Discussion in the Senate

The Senate approved the Bill on 3 October 2017 after an hour of debate during which members of the Senate expressed their informed opinions about whether to support the Bill or not, based on the information provided by the experts and stakeholder organizations. The Bill was then passed to Parliament for further discussion if no modifications were added for final approval. Unfortunately, no time was left in the legislative session to cover these final steps. The session ended on 22 March 2018 and the Bill was never passed (see also note 4). Below, we summarize the main points discussed during the debate in the Senate.

Reasons to vote against the Bill

These are some of the reasons put forward to support a vote against the Bill:

(1) Although LIS has an independent grammar, it is still less expressive than spoken Italian (i.e. it has lower communicative power) and it has no written form.

(2) LIS is not a language because there are too many varieties and it is not standardized.
(3) International sign language should be used rather than LIS, because it would allow deaf people to communicate with deaf people all over the world rather than with the small community of Italian signers.
(4) Other kinds of intervention should be given priority, such as hearing aids and cochlear implants.
(5) There is no consensus among the various deaf associations on the use of LIS in the education of deaf children; hence it is not worth recognizing LIS.
(6) The Bill does not support deaf people but the interests of LIS interpreters.
(7) The budgetary neutrality clause is fake, and the costs to support a LIS-friendly environment are too high.
(8) There is no financial coverage to concretely support the Bill, so recognition of LIS will not improve the everyday life of deaf people.

Reasons to vote in favour of the Bill

(1) The systematic presence of LIS in public environments will overcome communication barriers and provide full access to society, improving the quality of life of Deaf people.
(2) Bilingualism in mixed classes will help create a more inclusive society, because over the years there will be more signers, even among hearing people.
(3) The use of LIS is an option within a variety of possibilities for Deaf education and it is not in conflict with other approaches.

General Discussion

The debate around the Bill on the rights of deaf people has almost exclusively focused on whether it is appropriate to (1) recognize LIS as a natural language; and (2) use LIS in the education of deaf children. Unlike previous debates, there has been no attempt to undermine the status of LIS as a language, for instance by proposing different names such as the 'mimical-gestural language' (see Geraci, 2012). There has been an attempt to undermine its utility, though, by pointing out the lack of standardization and the lack of written from. Still, the core arguments against recognition of LIS were that (1) the use of signs would undermine full mastery of the spoken language; and (2) new technologies will eradicate deafness and hence the need for a sign language. Part of the Senate rejected the evidence given by linguists and cognitive scientists in favour of LIS. This shows that there is still a strong biased ideological climate, also illustrated by the fact that no comments were made over tactile LIS and its use by deafblind people.

Coming to what kind of right Deaf people should claim in relation to LIS, the right to be recognized as a language minority only or as a social group with other traits in addition to sharing the language, the current Bill has clearly taken the latter perspective. On the one hand, this was done in part because the UN Convention suggests such a view on sign language and Deaf communities and the Bill aimed at implementing this via the Italian legal system. On the other hand, recognizing LIS as a minority language would mean changing the law on language minorities (Law 482/1999). Indeed, the major obstacle for a straightforward implementation of the linguistic view of LIS is that it is at odds with the current law on language minorities. Geraci (2012) already pointed out how the legislation on linguistic minorities aimed at excluding Romani languages as minority languages based on the absence of a specified area in which the linguistic community is concentrated. LIS is an involuntary casualty of this. The only alternative left then, is to base the argument on the right to sign language as a fundamental right for humans to receive a language in the most natural way possible, because only in this way is the individual guaranteed healthy cognitive and social development.

Conclusion

Every time a new government is formed in the Italian parliament, the Italian Deaf community, ENS and all other supporters of LIS recognition wish that this time it will be the 'good one'; that LIS is officially recognized as a language, the language of Deaf people. Each time, a bill is filed and the slow process for recognition starts. Each time, LIS campaigners know that this will be a race against the clock; that if the discussion ever starts, it will come to an end in the very last days of the legislative session. Every time, they have seen the proposal not going through the final step for one reason or another.

We were facing the same situation in 2011 as well. An important result has been achieved, namely one chamber has approved the Bill. After that, the situation was very similar to that of 2011, when, the Bill arrived at the second chamber for final approval at the very end of the legislative session (Geraci, 2012). This time as well, the legislative session ended before the Bill could be discussed in Parliament. The struggle of Italian deaf people to have their language recognized is not over yet.

Acknowledgements

The research leading to these results has been possible thanks to the Fyssen Grant on Historical Relations across Sign Languages, Language Families, Typological Similarities or Language Contact? (PI Carlo Geraci) and the SIGN-HUB project, which has received funding from the European Union's Horizon 2020 research and innovation programme under grant agreement No. 693349 (Co-Proponent Carlo Geraci). The research was conducted in part at the Institut d'Etudes Cognitives (ENS), which is supported by grants ANR-10-IDEX-0001-02 PSL* and ANR-10-LABX-0087 IEC.

Notes

(1) The original name of the language was Lingua Italiana dei Segni, hence the acronym LIS. The name can be traced back to the 1980s when the first publication in Italian appeared (Volterra (ed.), *La Lingua Italiani dei Segni*, 1987). However, the Italian phrase can be misinterpreted as meaning a kind of signed Italian, rather than the sign language used in Italy. Nowadays, people refer to LIS as lingua dei segni italiana (Italian sign language). Indeed the most recent edition (Volterra, 2004) of the same pioneering book changed the title to *Lingua dei Segni Italiana*.

(2) In this chapter we will adopt the convention of referring to deaf signers and their communities by using capital 'D'. We use lower case to refer to the physical condition.

(3) There are different ways in which a law can be proposed in Italy. Independently from the procedure, the text of each Italian law has to be approved by both chambers, the Parliament and the Senate. In this particular case, the Bill was first approved by the Senate and then sent to Parliament. The link to the webpage of the bill is: http://www.senato.it/leg/17/BGT/Schede/Ddliter/42737.htm, while the video of the discussion and first approval in the Senate can be found here: http://webtv.senato.it/video/showVideo.html?seduta=888&leg=17&xmid=1017 (accessed on November 2018).

(4) The original text of the Bill is written in Italian. Unless otherwise specified, the quotations reported in the chapter are English translations made by Carlo Geraci.

(5) See http://www.senato.it/leg/17/BGT/Schede/Ddliter/42737.htm (accessed on November 2018).

(6) The original documents can be found on the Senate website, see note 5.

References

De Mauro, T. (2016) Democrazia linguistica: Sette tesi e un obiettivo. In F. Gobbo (ed.) *Lingua Politica Cultura. Serata Gratulatoria in honorem Renato Corsetti* (pp. 3–14). New York: Mondial. [Language and democracy: Seven arguments and an objective. In F. Gobbo (ed.) Language, Politics, Culture. In honour of Renato Corsetti.]

Emmorey, K. (2007) The psycholinguistics of signed and spoken languages: How biology affects processing. In G.M. Gaskell (ed.) *The Oxford Handbook of Psycholinguistics* (pp. 703–722). Oxford: Oxford University Press.

Geraci, C. (2012) Language policy and planning: The case of Italian Sign Language. *Sign Language Studies* 12 (4), 494–518.

Geraci, C, Gozzi, M., Papagno, C. and Cecchetto, C. (2008) How grammar can cope with limited short-term memory: Simultaneity and seriality in sign languages. *Cognition* 106, 780–804.

Geraci, C., Battaglia, K., Cardinaletti, A., Cecchetto, C., Donati, C., Giudice S. and Mereghetti, E. (2011) The LIS Corpus Project: A discussion of sociolinguistic variation in the lexicon. *Sign Language Studies* 11 (4), 528–574.

Gigante, C. (2011) Fatta l'Italia, facciamo gli Italiani. Appunti su una massima da restituire a d'Azeglio, *Rivista europea di studi italiani* 26 (2), 5–15.

Goldin-Meadow S. and Brentari D.K. (2017) Gesture, sign and language: The coming of age of sign language and gesture studies. *Behavioral and Brain Sciences* 1–82.

Guast, M.T. (2007) *L'acquisitione del linguaggio*. Milano: Raffello Cortina Editore. [Language acquisition].

Lane, H. (1999) *The Mask of Benevolence*. San Diego CA: DawnSignPress.

Lucas, C., Bayley, R. and Valli, C. (2001) *Sociolinguistic Variation in American Sign Language*. Washington DC: Gallaudet University Press.

Malaia, E. and Wilbur, R. (2010) Sign languages: Contribution to neurolinguistics from cross-modal research. *Lingua* 120 (12), 2704–2706.

Mayberry, R.I., Lock E. and Kazmi, H. (2002) Linguistic ability and early language exposure. *Nature* 417, 38.

Meier, R.P. (2016) Sign language acquisition. In *Oxford Handbooks Online*. Oxford: Oxford University Press.

Pabsch, A. and Wheatly, M. (eds) (2012) *Sign Language Legislation in the European Union*. Brussels: European Union of the Deaf.

Reagan, T. (1995) A sociocultural understanding of deafness: American sign language and the culture of deaf people. *International Journal of Intercultural Relations* 19 (2), 239–251.

Sandler, W. and Lillo-Martin, D. (2006) *Sign Language and Linguistic Universals*. Cambridge: Cambridge University Press.

Singleton, J.L. and Newport, E.L. (2004) When learners surpass their models: The acquisition of American Sign Language from inconsistent input. *Cognitive Psychology* 49 (4), 370–407.

Terrugi, L.A. (2003) *Una scuola, due lingue. L'esperienza di bilinguismo della scuola dell'Infanzia ed Elementare di Cossato*. Milano: Franco Angeli.

Timmermans, N. (2005) *The Status of Sign Languages*. Strasbourg: Council of Europe Publishing.

Trovato, S. (2013) Stronger reasons for the right to sign languages. *Sign Language Studies* 13 (3), 401–422.

Volterra, V. (2004) *La lingua dei segni italiana: La comunicazione visivo-gestuale dei sordi*. Bologna: Il Mulino. [Italian sign language: the visuo-gestural communication of Deaf people] First edition Volterra, V. (ed.) (1987) *La lingua italiana dei segni: La comunicazione visivo-gestuale dei sordi*. Bologna: Il Mulino.

12 Sign Language Legislation in Norway

Arnfinn Muruvik Vonen and Paal Richard Peterson

Introduction

In recent years, there has been a tremendous strengthening of the status of Norwegian Sign Language (NTS). First described through linguistic research in 1981, NTS was recognized as a language in a Norwegian white paper in 1985, with the remark that this recognition should have educational consequences for deaf children. In 2018, deaf children and youth have the legal right to instruction in NTS and NTS is a designated subject in the standard national curriculum. There is approximately one NTS interpreter to 10 deaf people in the country. Meanwhile, paradoxically, arenas for sign language socialization are dwindling, and there is concern about teachers' NTS competence.

In this chapter, we will present and discuss aspects of the political history of NTS, with an emphasis on the past three to four decades. First, we will explore the dynamics of sign language policy in the Norwegian context. We will then focus on the policy area in which NTS policy has been most clear, the education area. Next, we will trace the emergence of a more general recognition of NTS in Norwegian society. We will also present and discuss trends that contribute to the simultaneous marginalization of NTS even in the context of its strengthening in the policy arena, and finally we will propose possibilities for the further development of sign language policies in Norway.

Sign Language Policy History in the Norwegian Context

Sign language policies do not develop in a vacuum, but in a complex social and political context. In order to understand the history of sign language policies in Norway, let us look to international histories of sign language policies as well as to national characteristics of general language policies.

Regarding the historical sequence of sign language policies, Norway patterns with many other countries. In the early decades of deaf education in the 19th century, classroom communication was based on children's

visual communication skills. Subsequently, professional teachers convinced schools and the government that deaf children could, through rig-
orous speech and listening training and abstaining from sign language (a
philosophy known as oralism), become fully competent participants in
speaking-hearing society (see Anderson, 1960; Skjølberg, 1989). The
schools and the government patiently waited for many decades for this
goal to be reached, their hope for success being renewed with each new
generation of auditory technology. In the second half of the 20th century,
however, inspired by the international trend towards Total Communication
(see, e.g. Hansen, 2005: 17–18), schools and educators took a renewed
interest in visual communication. First, they turned to communication by
means of sign supported speech, and then, inspired by the revolutionary
scientific discovery of signed languages as linguistic objects, in the mid-
1980s, they turned to communication in sign language itself. Even after
this breakthrough of knowledge-based bilingual educational policy, however, the continuing progress in auditory technology, in particular the
proliferation of cochlear implants, has brought into question the role of
sign language in education and provided new temptations to take recourse
in old ideas of oralism (see, e.g. Kermit, 2007).

   We may question how far the implementation of the pure oral method
went in Norway, with regard to communication practices inside the classroom versus outside of it – that is, during leisure time and in activities in
the rest of society. In the classroom, the goal was to educate children
through speech only, but NTS was commonly used among pupils outside
of the classroom.

   Nevertheless, the sequence of phases or periods looks internationally
familiar, involving periods that have been referred to, in the US context,
as the 'Golden Age' of deaf education (early manualism) and the 'Dark
Age' of sign language history (oralism) (Bauman et al., 2006). Although
outside the scope of the present chapter, the specifics with regard to timing
and other details of the sequence seem to depend on national characteristics of language policy in general. For example, the only country among
the Nordic countries whose constitution mentions sign language, Finland,
is also the only country in the region whose constitution mentions two
national languages (Finnish and Swedish).

   Norway is a country in northern Europe that has about 5 million
inhabitants. No official statistics exist that might give us the number of
NTS signers, but a Norges Døveforbund (NDF, Norwegian Association
of the Deaf) estimate establishes the number at 16,500, of which 5000 are
deaf, 10,000 have deaf family members or friends and 1500 use NTS for
professional purposes. In Norway, the long period of oralist oppression of
NTS (described by Schröder, 1993) overlapped significantly with the
country's period of linguistic 'Norwegianization', during which spoken
minority languages such as the Sami languages, Kven and Scando-Romani
were actively oppressed as part of the promotion of a national language

for a new nation. Having gained independence from Denmark in 1814, Norwegian authorities put considerable effort throughout the century into the development of a national written language that was distinct both from that of the former colonial rulers, the Danes, and from the language of the Swedes, whose king would also remain Norway's king until 1905. Norwegian, Danish and Swedish are mutually comprehensible spoken languages, but function as strong markers of national identity. In fact, two paths were taken simultaneously in this effort in Norway, resulting in the two written standards of Norwegian that still exist today and are formally equal in status. Bokmål, the more widely used standard, is the result of gradual 'Norwegianization' of written Danish, while Nynorsk, the less used standard, is the result of a systematic and historically informed search for a standard for the relatively diverse spoken dialects of Norwegian. In fact, even within the limits of each of these two written standards, there is quite broad variation in the sets of officially approved spellings and inflection patterns. No spoken variety of Norwegian has been elevated to the status of a 'standard', and today, dialect diversity is considered one of the valuable characteristics of the Norwegian language (see, e.g. Vonen, 2012).

General features of Norwegian language policies for a long time, thus, were the oppression of languages other than Norwegian on one hand, and the tolerance of variation within Norwegian on the other. Even though the oppression of NTS before its linguistic discovery was not quite parallel with the oppression of Sami (which was at least known to be a language, or even several distinct languages), there are at least two other features of NTS policy that clearly mirror spoken language policies.

First, the recognition of NTS was at least temporally linked with the recognition of the Sami languages in Norway. When the pioneering NTS researcher submitted her master's thesis in special education, the first linguistic study of the language, in 1981 (Vogt-Svendsen, 1981), only two years had passed since the highly visible climax of a long-standing conflict over pasture land and hydropower energy between the indigenous Sami people and the central Norwegian government. In hindsight, the Sami-related events of 1979 may be seen as having contributed to a significant awareness raising among majority Norwegians concerning the rights of the Sami minority and of minorities more generally (see also below). According to Marit Vogt-Svendsen (pers. comm., 2018), it was the increased awareness of society's responsibility for minority groups and their language in general, rather than Sami policy specifically, that served as a source of inspiration for her in 1981.

Secondly, after NTS became recognized as a language in 1985 (see below), there has never been much pressure for standardization of the language. In certain other countries, official recognition of a sign language is granted on the condition that the language should be standardized (cf. the situation of the Sign Language of the Netherlands (Schermer,

2016)). The tolerance for diversity in NTS on the part of language authorities may be understood in the light of the tolerance for diversity in spoken Norwegian. Any official attempt to standardize NTS would probably have met with strong opposition from signers themselves, who, in the decade previous to NTS recognition, had been through an ambitious – and some might say brutal – community-led project for standardizing NTS signs vis-à-vis Norwegian words (Holten & Lønning, 2010).

The 'Norwegianization' effort from the mid-19th to the mid-20th century weakened the established spoken minority languages of the country, and several of them are severely endangered today. Norway recognizes the Sami languages spoken in its territory (basically, North Sami, Lule Sami and South Sami) as indigenous languages and the Kven, Romani and Scando-Romani languages as national minority languages. For these languages, Norway has committed itself to the Framework Convention for the Protection of National Minorities (Council of Europe, 1992) and the European Charter for Regional or Minority Languages (Council of Europe, 1995), both of the Council of Europe, and, for the Sami languages, to the Indigenous and Tribal Peoples Convention of the International Labour Organization (1989). As far as national legislation is concerned, the Constitution (Article 108) states that the government should facilitate the Sami people's opportunity to secure and develop their language, their culture and their community life. Chapter 3 of the Sami Act is devoted to language policy. Today, the Sami languages are officially equal with the Norwegian language in those local communities that have chosen to become 'administrative areas for the Sami language' ('forvaltningsområde for samisk språk'). According to the Act of Education, Sami pupils have specific rights to education in and about the three Sami languages, as regulated in Chapter 6 of the Act (Articles 6-1 through 6-4). Also, according to Article 2-7 in the Act of Education, pupils with Kven-Finnish background have certain rights in compulsory education to be taught Finnish as a subject in the two northernmost Norwegian counties.

Recognition of NTS in Education

The linguistic recognition of NTS as a language started with a hearing teacher of the deaf, Marit Vogt-Svendsen's master's thesis in special needs education at the State Special Teacher University College (Statens spesiallærerhøgskole) in 1981 (Vogt-Svendsen, 1981). In contrast with what is often seen in countries where sign language research is emerging, the work almost immediately had consequences for the government's attitude towards NTS. The thesis was revised into a book published two years later (Vogt-Svendsen, 1983), and already in 1985, the Ministry of Church and Educational Affairs recognized NTS as a language in a report to the Parliament on special education (KUD, 1985):

The sign language which is today mostly used in the instruction of deaf children, is based on spoken/written language principles. The sign language that deaf people use among themselves, differs from this both in its selection of signs (corresponding to vocabulary) and in its grammar. Earlier, little has been known about deaf people's language, and neither has it been considered an independent language. It is only for the last 15–20 years that research has taken an interest in this sign language. This research has shown that deaf people's sign language must be equalled with other languages. As this sign language is now accepted as a language, this must have certain consequences for the education of deaf children. Among other things, it should be considered how to involve deaf people more in the education of deaf people. (KUD, 1985: 28, our translation)

These promised consequences did not appear immediately, and many signers were disappointed when, two years later, NTS was not mentioned in a new national advisory curriculum for primary and lower secondary school (KUD, 1987). In the following years, however, a pilot bilingual curriculum for deaf pupils was tested, and in 1997, pupils 'with sign language as their first language' were given the right to sign language education at preschool, and to 'education on and in sign language' in a new Article 2-4 in the regulatory law on primary and lower secondary education (KUF, 1997). In the same year, a new national curriculum for primary and secondary school in Norway was introduced, and among the new school subjects were 'Sign language as a first language' as well as 'Norwegian for the deaf', 'English for the deaf' and 'Drama and rhythm for the deaf', which replaced the sound-dependent subjects of Norwegian, English and music, respectively. The rest of the school subjects would be the same as for hearing pupils, but taught with NTS as the medium of instruction. Extra resources were allotted in order to make it possible to add the subject 'Sign language as a first language' to the school subjects without having to reduce the number of lessons in any of the other subjects. This basic structure of the curriculum still exists in 2018, although the names of the subjects have changed several times with 'hearing impaired' replacing 'deaf' in the course names.

In 1998, a new Act of Education (covering primary and secondary education and aspects of preschool education) was passed by Parliament, and the right from Article 2-4 of the regulatory law was established in the new law as Article 2-6. In 2000, a similar right for pupils in upper secondary school was granted in a new Article 3-9 in the same law. In 2016, with the introduction of a new Preschool Act, the right for preschool-age children to education in NTS, also introduced in 1997, was transferred to that law as Article 19h.

The legal right to 'education on and in sign language' is an individual right and independent of the choice of school. That is, not only special schools for the deaf, but also local schools have to offer this kind of bilingual education to their deaf pupils. This particularity has entailed that the closing down of all state special schools for the hearing-impaired (four primary and lower secondary and two upper secondary schools) during the 2000s and the 2010s has not violated any pupil's formal right to bilingual education, since the law does not say anything about special schools. (However, the implications are discussed in the section, 'Implicit Marginalization of NTS' below.) Some of the larger cities such as Oslo, Bergen, Trondheim and Stavanger offer bilingual education in municipal special schools or special departments of general municipal schools.

Explicit Recognition of NTS

Soon after the research-based recognition of NTS in 1985 (KUD, 1985), the Norwegian Association of the Deaf (NDF) started advocating for general recognition of NTS as a minority language of Norway, not limited to the education sector. The idea was, and still is, that a fundamental recognition of the language as a language, and as part of the national heritage of Norway, would promote awareness of NTS in society, which would in turn not only make everyday life easier for signers, but would also prepare the road to achieving political goals in particular sectors of society.

The NDF suggested to the government in 1991 that a Sign Language Act should be provided, inspired by politicians in parliament who had supported deaf schools when they were at risk of being closed down (Herland, 2018: 385), and attached a suggested wording for the act (rendered in Bergh, 2004: 62–63). The text was inspired by the then recently passed Sami Act (see section, 'Sign Language Policy History in the Norwegian Context', above). In the 1990s, much progress was made in the educational field (see above), but no Sign Language Act appeared. In 2001, the NDF presented the Ministry of Culture with a position paper, 'Right to Sign Language' ('Rett til tegnspråk', rendered in Bergh, 2004: 10), to demand a Sign Language Act that would provide this fundamental recognition. The ministry, which was now the ministry responsible for language policy in Norway, agreed to develop a report on the subject, in which the issues would be examined in detail. The Norwegian Archive, Library and Museum Authority, which was affiliated to the Ministry of Culture, was charged with the task and presented the report later in the same year (Bergh, 2004). The 'Bergh Report' recommended that the Ministry of Culture should prepare a Norwegian Sign Language Bill.

The recommendations in Bergh (2004) did not immediately result in any new steps from the government. However, the Ministry of Culture and Church Affairs and its affiliated expert organ for language issues, the Language Council of Norway, had for several years been working on designing a comprehensive language policy for Norway, based on a recognition that the Norwegian language was becoming threatened by English in several important areas of society, such as higher education and in internationally oriented companies. In a report by the Language Council in 2005 (Language Council of Norway, 2005), the NTS and other minority languages were mentioned, but the report was focused on the status of the Norwegian language. After this report was published, other languages, among them NTS, were included in the ministry's efforts to formulate a comprehensive language policy. This meant, however, that NTS policy became part of a larger and more time-consuming process.

In 2007, expressing impatience and frustration over the lack of follow-up from the government, the NDF organized a rally that ended up in front of Parliament, to demand passage of a Sign Language Bill. Nearly 2000 protesters participated, a remarkable number given the size of the Norwegian Deaf community. The heavy turnout clearly showed that the campaign for increased official recognition of NTS, which had been managed mostly through the central administration of the NDF, had broad support in the Deaf community.

A few months later, in June 2008, the government finally took action and presented a white paper with recommendations for a comprehensive language policy for Norway, the 'Language Report' (KKD, 2008). The Language Report, prepared by the Ministry of Culture and Church Affairs (now the Ministry of Culture), deals with all languages of Norway and all aspects of national language policy, and expresses a comprehensive language policy for the country. The primary motivation and the main objective of the Language Report is to protect and strengthen the Norwegian language as Norway's main language and the main expression of Norwegian national identity. It does so with what we interpret as a recognition of the complexity of human identity and a willingness to protect this complexity. Thus, the Language Report simultaneously promotes linguistic community and linguistic diversity: on the one hand, the uniting function of the Norwegian language, and on the other, linguistic variation both within the Norwegian language and among minority languages. This complex political goal is nicely phrased trough the definition of a 'society-supporting' (samfunnsberande) language:

> By the concept of a society-supporting language, what is meant is a super-ordinate common language which is, in a modern, multicultural society, used for administration and public debate, which keeps large-scale society together and gives it identity, while at the same time giving good conditions for life and development to all the linguistic subcultures that exist in society. (KUD, 2008, Chapter 1.1.3.1. Our translation)

In the Language Report, and for the first time ever in an official document, NTS was fully recognized not only as a language, but as a part of the country's shared cultural heritage. The chapter on NTS in the Language Report also included a section on the vague notion of 'official language' and an argument against a separate Sign Language Bill. The document announced that the ministry intended to produce a general Language Bill, which should state the respective statuses of all languages in the country, including NTS. The report stated also that the government intended to extend the responsibilities of the Language Council of Norway, the government's professional agency for language, affiliated with the Ministry of Culture. In addition to continuing its activities in the policy and planning of the Norwegian language, the Language Council would also take an interest in the broader linguistic situation of the country and, specifically, start work on policy and planning for NTS. The report was discussed in Parliament in 2009, and Parliament's own report on it was quite positive (Stortinget, 2009). In particular, the inclusion of NTS in the comprehensive language policy of the country was well received by the parliamentarians. Since then, the Language Report has been seen as the official language policy document of Norway.

The Language Council's work to strengthen NTS in accordance with the Language Report started in 2011 and has become an important motivating and coordinating force for the efforts carried out in various parts of the NTS community. As far as the Language Bill is concerned, it still has not been announced at the time of writing. Parliamentarians have enquired about it formally several times to the Minister of Culture (Norway had five Ministers of Culture from two different political parties in the period from 2009 to 2017), and each time the essence of the response was that the preparation of the Bill was complex and demanding, but that it was on its way. In 2018, a new Minister of Culture, Ms Trine Skei Grande, from a third political party, entered the cabinet. Earlier, as a Member of Parliament, Ms Grande had served as spokesperson for the Parliament's handling of the Language Report in 2009. Ms Grande has been an important politician for the campaign for NTS for the last 10 to 15 years and she knows the deaf association well. In a personal e-mail to one of the authors (Paal Richard Peterson (PRP), 3 July 2018), she stated that an important reason for her advocacy for sign language and inclusion is that a deaf politician at the local level once had to leave a meeting because there were no interpreters. She also says she has deaf colleagues and friends that have taught her about the language and the culture. She says that we must never forget that sign language is a vehicle of culture ('kulturbærer'). The authors of this chapter expect that the issue of the long-awaited Language Bill will soon reappear on the political agenda. Given the unanimous support from the Parliament concerning the broad recognition of NTS in the Language Report, it is likely not the NTS policy that is the reason for the delay of the Bill.

Which arguments were used by the deaf organization in the campaign? In 2007, the NDF initiated a working group to prepare a report (Erlenkamp et al., 2007) to argue for a sign language act, based on different perspectives on language, and inspired by Bergh (2004). Erlenkamp et al. (2007) pointed out three main categories of arguments: (1) All languages are tools for communication. These tools must be protected. (2) All people have the right to express their views in the language they themselves feel most comfortable with. For most deaf people, this language is a sign language. (3) A living language has value in itself, allowing knowledge and wisdom to be transmitted across generations. When a language dies, we lose these values. The report concluded that, for many reasons, the sign language community in Norway already had what we could expect regarding school policy (see section, 'Recognition of NTS in Education', above), interpreting services (free use of interpreters for deaf people in Norway) and other services. What was wanted was an act that could symbolically support and recognize the language and its users and, through this, strengthen and develop the already existing rights for deaf people. We believe this line of argument helped to allay politicians' concerns about high costs connected with increasing the legal status of NTS.

The recognition and rights connected with NTS did not have any binding international anchoring until the United Nations Convention on the Rights of Persons with Disabilities, which contains numerous passages on promoting sign languages and responsibilities towards Deaf communities. The Convention was signed in 2006 and ratified by Norway in 2013. Thus, there is now in place an international regime for monitoring Norway's actions in the sign language area. In Norway's first official report to the United Nations on the Convention (CRPD, 2015), an account is given of sign language users' legal rights in many areas. In an additional report by the Equality and Anti-Discrimination Ombud (The Norwegian Equality and Anti-Discrimination Ombud, 2015), examples are given of problems arising because public meetings are organized without sign language interpreting services. In an alternative (shadow) report representing the perspectives of the civil (i.e. deaf) sector (FFO, 2015), strong statements were made about the government's responsibility to ensure the vitality of NTS in broadcast media, interpreting services and in educational settings, including the development of more and larger learning environments in NTS for deaf and hard-of-hearing pupils on the municipal level.

Strengthening of NTS in Society

Outside of the primary and secondary education sector, important progress has been made on the status of NTS in several areas.

Since 1996, hearing parents of deaf children have been offered a 40-week programme in NTS, Deaf culture and Deaf history called 'Se mitt språk' (See my language), distributed over the child's first 16 years. The number of participating parents has been stable for years. The programme is offered by Statped, the government agency for supporting services for special educational needs affiliated with the Directorate of Education (which is affiliated to the Ministry of Education). In offering the programme, Statped collaborates with Ål Folk High School and

Workshop Centre for the Deaf (see below) and an educational centre within the Signo Foundation (see below). All expenses for the parents – tuition, travel, food and accommodation as well as salary expenses at their workplace during their 40 weeks of full-time absence – are covered in a collaboration between the Norwegian Labour and Welfare Administration (affiliated to the Ministry of Labour and Social Affairs) and the family's municipality of residence.

There are a number of institutions and businesses that serve in the role of 'bearers of culture', including the Deaf Church, the Signo Foundation (a nationwide social services provider), and media and entertainment companies. The state broadcaster, NRK, offers sign language interpreting on a sign language channel, dedicated to interpreting programmes into NTS as well as programmes originally in NTS. It offers live interpreting approximately 23 hours a week, mostly children's programmes, news programmes, debates and documentaries. Døves Media (Deaf Media) was founded in 1985 to ensure videos and TV programmes in NTS, but the making of videos in NTS can be traced back to 1972. Teater Manu, a professional sign language theatre, was established in 2001. Both Deaf Media and Teater Manu are supported through annual grants from the Ministry of Culture. Recently, several small organizations such as FONTS – Forening for norsk tegnspråk (Association for Norwegian Sign Language) and Hørselshemmede Barns Organisasjon (HHBO, Organization of Hearing-Impaired Children) have joined the NDF and other organizations in their work of strengthening NTS in Norwegian society.

NTS is offered as a subject at the university and adult education levels, as well as by some local deaf associations. Three higher education institutions offer bachelor's programmes in Sign Language and Interpreting: OsloMet – Oslo Metropolitan University (Oslo), Western Norway University College of Applied Sciences (HVL, Bergen) and the Norwegian University of Science and Technology (NTNU, Trondheim). In 2015, the three institutions established the National Academic Council for Sign Language and Interpreting (Nasjonalt fagråd for tegnspråk og tolking) within the framework of Universities Norway (UHR). They also offer part-time programmes in NTS for primary and secondary school teachers who teach, or are preparing to teach, deaf pupils. Ål folkehøyskole og kurssenter for døve (Ål Folk High School and Workshop Centre for the Deaf) in Ål offers year-long full-time study adult education programmes for hearing as well as deaf pupils, in addition to a broad array of week-length courses in an NTS environment for various target groups.

As we can see, NTS has had a notable impact on society and it is recognized as a language through public disbursements. How did these rather rapid and important achievements come about? We limit ourselves to suggesting a combination of fortunate timing, personal initiatives and effective organization, within the context of a society that has been enabling social equity through the commitment of public resources to support NTS initiatives.

Implicit Marginalization of NTS

The advent of cochlear implants has had a significant impact on the discourse on deafness in Norway, and thus also on NTS (Kermit, 2007, 2010). All costs of the equipment, surgery and fitting are covered by the government, and today almost all children who meet the medical criteria for implantation, receive two implants at an early age, often before their first birthday. Conventional hearing aids have also improved significantly and their costs are also largely covered by the public health insurance system. As is well-known, the effect of cochlear implants shows large individual variation, but most of these children develop a sense of hearing that makes it possible for them to spontaneously acquire spoken language skills and to function in spoken language communication in favourable settings (few interlocutors, good lighting, limited background noise, etc.). In more complex settings, such as a classroom or a class excursion, these children's hearing impairment often prevents them from full participation, and the result sometimes is a spoken-language vocabulary delay that goes undetected for years (Barli, 2003; Kermit et al., 2005, 2010; Ohna et al., 2004).

Many implanted children's speaking and listening skills appear to be so good that educational advisers (who are usually not sign language experts) consider it unnecessary for them to attend special schools or classes, at least if these provisions require travelling far away from home. Norway is a sparsely populated country with long distances between services, so these considerations led over the years to a decrease in the number of applications to attend state schools for deaf people. Arguing that the schools were expensive and were becoming so small that running them could no longer be defended financially, the Ministry of Education made a series of decisions to close down the state schools. In the 2000s, the two existing upper secondary schools were closed, and in the 2010s, the four primary and lower secondary schools. The last state school, A. C. Møller skole (school) in Trondheim, was established in 1825 as the first special school in Norway and was reorganized in 2017 as a department within a municipal school. These actions on the part of the government caused much concern in the Deaf community, even though some care was taken in most cases to ensure that the city where the schools had been located would be able to offer its local pupils education 'on and in NTS'. Several cities therefore still have 'deaf schools' or 'units'.

Since the state schools – traditionally boarding schools – had been meeting-places for pupils from many municipalities, the closing of the schools inevitably has led to reduced possibilities for signing children to grow up together in a rich language environment. The effect of this weakening of language socialization arenas remains to be seen. Compensatory measures are currently being taken, such as the further development of an already existing system of week-long gatherings for signing children in an NTS environment, the exploitation of current videoconferencing technology to organize virtual classrooms in NTS (cf. Hjulstad, 2017) and NTS training for local classroom teachers. Still, many signing children spend most of their school time in classrooms with only hearing peers who are not expected to learn NTS, and with hearing teachers whose NTS skills are far poorer than the corresponding Norwegian skills of teachers of hearing pupils. The Language Council of Norway is among those who warn that the educational right signing children have according to the Education Act, is often not fulfilled, because of the variable and, in part, low quality of the education received (Language Council of Norway, 2017: 141).

A major barrier to fulfilling the rights of signing children is a lack of knowledge and understanding in greater society, and also among medical and educational counsellors and local decision-makers, of the significance of having access to a fully developed sign language. Also, basic knowledge about sign language is lacking, such as understanding the difference between NTS and sign-supported Norwegian. Thus, the decentralization of deaf education, which is the result of the closing down of the state schools, means a risk of devolving more power to decision-makers who are not equipped to take informed decisions regarding deaf learners.

The phrasing of Article 2-6 of the Education Act states that those pupils who have the right to education 'on and in NTS' are 'pupils who have Sign Language as their first language, or who, according to an expert judgment, are in need of such education'. The passage 'or who, according to an expert judgment, are in need of such education' was added in 2008 in order to make the article available for pupils with cochlear implants, even if they (or their parents) do not consider NTS their first language.

However, hearing children from signing families (CODAs) with NTS as a first language are not considered to be covered by Article 2-6. On this point, therefore, not only the local decisions, but also the legislation itself (as it is interpreted by lawyers), still contributes to marginalizing the language. To put it simply, hearing children of signing parents have no legal right to learn how to tell their parents about what they learn at school.

Towards a Better Future?

In this chapter, we have traced considerable development in NTS policy over the past 30 to 40 years, from no recognition to considering it as an official part of Norwegian cultural heritage. Paradoxically, however, the same period has seen the closing of the state schools for the deaf and a situation where NTS–Norwegian bilingualism for some decision-makers does not seem to be the default recommendation, but more like a last resort. We think too much advice given to parents of deaf children does not draw upon a thorough understanding of bilingual development in children, and much teaching seems to be occurring that does not involve sufficiently NTS-competent teachers.

We take an optimistic stance and believe that more targeted initiatives towards educational advisers and decision-makers, and higher standards for educators and education in NTS, will lead to improvements in the educational sphere. The institutions who serve as 'culture bearers' should be enabled to develop and increase their relevant activities to ensure NTS's continued vitality.

References

Anderson, P. (1960) *Hovedlinjer i døveundervisningens historiske utvikling. Sammendrag av forelesninger ved utdanningskurs for døvelærere. Oslo 1954.* [*Main Lines in the History of Deaf Education. Summary of Lectures at Educational Courses for Teachers of the Deaf. Oslo 1954.*] Oslo: S. Hammerstads boktrykkeri.

Barli, K.S. (2003) *Døv i 'den inkluderende skole': 'I spenningsfeltet mellom einskap og mangfold' (St.meld. nr. 28 1999: 10,11).* [Deaf in 'the Inclusive School': *'In the Field of Tension between Unity and Diversity' (Report to the Storting No. 28, 1999, pp. 10, 11.)*] Oslo: Skådalen kompetansesenter [Skådalen Resource Centre].

Bauman, H-D.L., Nelson, J.L. and Rose, H.M. (2006) Appendix A. Time line of ASL literature development. In H-D.L. Bauman, J.L. Nelson and H.M. Rose (eds) *Signing the Body Poetic: Essays on American Sign Language literature.* Berkeley, CA: University of California Press.

Bergh, G. (2004) *Norsk tegnspråk som offisielt språk* (ABM-skrift #10). Oslo: ABM-utvikling. See https://www.kulturradet.no/vis-publikasjon/-/norsk-tegnsprak-som-offisielt-sprak (last accessed 29 January 2019).

Council of Europe (1992) *European Charter for Regional or Minority Languages.* See https://www.coe.int/en/web/european-charter-regional-or-minority-languages/text-of-the-charter (last accessed 29 January 2019).

Council of Europe (1995) *Framework Convention for the Protection of National Minorities.* See https://rm.coe.int/16800c10cf (last accessed 29 January 2019).

Erlenkamp, S., Gjøen, S., Haualand, H., Kvitvær, H.B., Peterson, P.R., Schrøder, O.-I. and Vonen, A.M. (2007) *Begrunnelser for å gjøre norsk tegnspråk til offisielt språk.* [*Reasons for Making Norwegian Sign Language an Official Language.*] Oslo: Norges Døveforbund [Norwegian Association of the Deaf]. See http://www.bgds.andata.no/bodyFrame/aktiviteter/2007/47/Hevetstatusfortegnsprak.doc (last accessed 29 January 2019).

Funksjonshemmedes fellesorganisasjon [Common Organisation of the Disabled] (2015) *Alternativ rapport til FN-komiteen for rettighetene til mennesker med nedsatt funksjonsevne.* [*Alternative Report to the UN Committee for the Rights of Persons with Disabilities.*] See http://ffo.no/globalassets/altrapptilfn_web.pdf (last accessed 29 January 2019).

Hansen, Aa.L. (2005) Kommunikative praksiser i visuelt orienterte klasserom. En studie av et tilrettelagt opplegg for døve lærerstudenter. [Communicative practices in visually oriented classrooms. A study of an adapted programme for Deaf teacher students.] Dr.art. dissertation, The Norwegian University of Science and Technology, Trondheim. See http://www.acm5.com/kompendier/kommunikative%20praksiser %20i%20visuelt.pdf (last accessed 29 January 2019).

Herland, H. (2018) *Norges Døveforbund 1918–2018. 100 år.* [*Norwegian Association of the Deaf 1918–2018. 100 Years.*] Oslo: Norges Døveforbund [Norwegian Association of the Deaf].

Hjulstad, J. (2017) Embodied participation in the semiotic ecology of a visually-oriented virtual classroom. Doctoral dissertation, Norwegian University of Science and Technology, Trondheim. See https://brage.bibsys.no/xmlui/bitstream/handle/11250/2434026/47_Hjulstad.pdf?sequence=5&isAllowed=y (last accessed 29 January 2019).

Holten, S.M. and Lønning, H.R. (2010): 'Hørende er våre sjefer.' Språkplanlegging og språkendringer i norsk tegnspråk. ['The hearing are our bosses.' Language planning and language changes in Norwegian Sign Language.] MA thesis in Sign Language, University of Oslo, Oslo. See file:///Users/arnvon/Downloads/HoltenLonning_Horendexerxvarexsjefer%20(2).pdf (last accessed 29 January 2019).

International Labour Organisation (1989) C169 – Indigenous and Tribal Peoples Convention (No. 169). See http://www.ilo.org/dyn/normlex/en/f?p=NORMLEXPU B:12100:0::NO::P12100_ILO_CODE:C169 (last accessed 29 January 2019).

Kermit, P.S. (2007) Bioethical discourses on deafness: Critical remarks and suggestions for a new approach. In M. Hyde and G. Høie (eds) Constructing Educational Discourses on Deafness (pp. 40–57). Oslo: Skådalen Resource Centre.

Kermit, P. (2010) Choosing for the child with cochlear implants: A note of precaution. Medicine, Health Care and Philosophy 13 (2), 157–167.

Kermit, P., Holm, A. and Mjøen, O.M. (2005) Cochleaimplantat i et tospråklig og etisk perspektiv. [Cochlear Implants in a Bilingual and Ethical Perspective.] HiST – ALTrapport 14. Trondheim: Høgskolen i Sør-Trøndelag, Avdeling for lærer- og tolkeutdanning.

Kermit, P., Mjøen, O.M. and Holm, A. (2010) Å vokse opp med cochleaimplantat: Barns språklige samhandling med hørende jevnaldrende og voksne. [Growing up with cochlear implants: Children's linguistic interaction with hearing peers and adults.] Sosiologisk tidsskrift [Sociological Journal] 18 (3), 249–272.

Kirke- og undervisningsdepartementet (KUD) [Ministry of Church Affairs and Education] (1985) St.meld. nr. 61 (1984–1985) 'Om visse sider ved spesialundervisninga og den pedagogisk-psykologiske tenesta'. [Report to the Storting No. 61 (1984–1985) 'About Certain Aspects of Special Education and the Educational-Psychological Service.'] Oslo: Kirke- og undervisningsdepartementet.

Kirke- og undervisningsdepartementet (KUD) [Ministry of Church Affairs and Education] (1987) Mønsterplan for grunnskolen: M87. [Pattern Plan for Primary and Lower Secondary Education: M87.] Oslo: Aschehoug.

Kultur- og kirkedepartementet (KKD) [Ministry of Culture and Church Affairs] (2008) St.meld. nr. 35 (2007–2008) 'Mål og meining – ein heilskapleg norsk språkpolitikk'. [Report to the Storting No. 35 (2007–2008) 'Goals and Meaning – A Comprehensive Norwegian Language Policy'.] Oslo: Kultur- og kirkedepartementet. See https://www. regjeringen.no/no/dokumenter/stmeld-nr-35-2007-2008-/id519923/ (last accessed 29 January 2019).

Kirke-, utdannings- og forskningsdepartementet (KUF) [Ministry of Church Affairs, Education and Research] (1997) Læreplanverket for den 10-årige grunnskolen. [The Curriculum for the 10-Year Primary and Lower Secondary School.] Oslo: Nasjonalt læremiddelsenter.

Language Council of Norway [Språkrådet] (2005) Norsk i hundre! [Norwegian in One Hundred!] Oslo: Språkrådet. See http://www.sprakradet.no/localfiles/9832/norsk_i_ hundre.pdf (last accessed 29 January 2019).

Language Council of Norway [Språkrådet] (2017): Språkstatus 2017. Språkpolitisk tilstandsrapport frå Språkrådet. [Language Status 2017. Language Policy State Report from the Language Council of Norway.] [Oslo:] Språkrådet. See https://www.sprakradet.no/globalassets/vi-og-vart/publikasjoner/sprakstatus/sprakstatus-2017.pdf (last accessed 29 January 2019).

Schermer, T. (2016) Language variation and standardization. In A. Baker, B.v.d. Bogaerde, R. Pfau and T. Schermer (eds) *The Linguistics of Sign Languages* (pp. 279–298). Amsterdam: John Benjamins Publishing Company.

Schröder, O.-I. (1993) Introduction to the history of Norwegian Sign Language. In R. Fischer (ed.) *Looking Back: A Reader on the History of the Deaf Communities and their Sign Languages* (pp. 231–248). Hamburg: Signum.

Skjølberg, T. (1989): *Andreas Christian Møller. Døvstummeinstituttet i Trondhjem og pionértiden i norsk døveundervisning.* [*Andreas Christian Møller. The Deaf-Mute Institute in Trondhjem and the Pioneer Era in Norwegian Deaf Education.*] Bergen, Norway: Døves Forlag A.S.

Stortinget (2009) *Innstilling frå familie- og kulturkomiteen om Mål og meining. Ein heilskapleg norsk kulturpolitikk.* [Recommendation from the Standing Committee on Family and Cultural Affairs on Goals and Meaning: A Comprehensive Norwegian Language Policy.] Oslo: Stortinget. See https://www.stortinget.no/no/Saker-og-publikasjoner/Publikasjoner/Innstillinger/Stortinget/2008-2009/inns-200809-184/ (last accessed 29 January 2019).

United Nations Convention on the Rights of Persons with Disabilities (CRPD) (2015) *Committee on the Rights of Persons with Disabilities. Consideration of reports submitted by States parties under article 35 of the Convention. Initial reports of States parties due in 2015. Norway.* [Geneva:] United Nations Human Rights Office of the High Commissioner. See https://tbinternet.ohchr.org/_layouts/treatybodyexternal/Download.aspx?symbolno=CRPD%2fC%2fNOR%2f1&Lang=en (last accessed 29 January 2019).

Vogt-Svendsen, M. (1981) Undersøkelse av tegnspråk. [Investigation of sign language.] Hovedoppgave (candidate thesis) in special education. Statens spesiallærerhøgskole [State Special Teacher University College], Hosle.

Vogt-Svendsen, M. (1983): *Norske døves tegnspråk – noen språkvitenskapelige og pedagogiske aspekter.* [*The Sign Language of the Norwegian Deaf – Some Linguistic and Educational Aspects.*] Trondheim: Tapir.

Vonen, A.M. (2012) Diversity and democracy: Written varieties of Norwegian. In R.V. Fjeld and J.M. Torjusen (eds) *Proceedings of the 15th EURALEX International Congress*, 7–11 August 2012. Oslo: Department of Linguistics and Scandinavian Studies, University of Oslo.

Part 4

Implementation of Sign Language Laws

13 Austrian Sign Language: Recognition Achieved but Discrimination Continues

Franz Dotter, Verena Krausneker, Helene Jarmer and Lukas Huber

Background: Multilingual Austria

Austria is a federal republic with 8.8 million inhabitants.[1] Article 8 clause 1 of the constitution declares that German is the official language of the state, without prejudice to the 'rights given to linguistic minorities'.[2] The rest of the constitution does not mention linguistic minorities but in 8 (2) it defines autochthonous ethnic groups (*Volksgruppen*) who were awarded specific rights in the 1955 Austrian independence treaty and the 1976 *Volksgruppengesetz* (Baumgartner, 1995; de Cillia *et al.*, 1998).

As of 2018, six autochthonous ethnic groups are legally recognized with their minority languages spoken in certain more or less clearly defined geographical areas of Austria: Czech (approximately 17,000 speakers), Burgenland-Croatian (19,000), Romani (6000), Slovak (10,000), Slovenian (25,000) and Hungarian (40,000) (all numbers from the national census of 2001[3]).

Austria has rather sophisticated and formally well-established linguistic minority regulations (de Cillia & Vetter, 2011), but two remarks are in order: (1) explicit language policy only focuses on the 'autochthonous' minorities and basically neglects the half a million speakers of Turkish, Kurdish, Bosnian, Croatian and Serbian, who constitute the biggest groups of immigrants, and speakers of many other immigrant languages. Furthermore, laws define linguistic minorities ethnically and territorially – which posed a huge barrier to the legal recognition of Austrian Sign Language (*Österreichische Gebärdensprache*, ÖGS), as we will see.

(2) There is a 'big gap between rhetoric and reality'[4]: many laws and regulations regarding the autochthonous minorities took decades to be finally implemented and the path was paved with very serious, even

violent, public conflict and tough opposition by majority members (de Cillia, 2003).

Implicit language policies differ from these tardily legally prescribed ones, especially in the area of education: the Ministry of Education as well as regional school authorities have reacted to the fact that 24% of pupils in Austrian schools do not have German as their first language and are multilingual (in Vienna it is 50%). Schools can and do offer many more languages to pupils than are officially recognized, especially immigrant languages. It must be pointed out that many of these activities and policies originate with individual civil servants and school authorities, who see the given multilingual realities instead of applying monolingual wishful thinking. The most important resource in this respect has been created by the Ministry of Education: the website, www.schule-mehrsprachig.at, offers background information on multilingual school practices, on curricula and on 30 different languages used by pupils in Austrian schools, including ÖGS.

Due to a lack of statistical data, the number of deaf[5] sign language users living in Austria can only be estimated by employing the estimate of 1:1000, which equates to between 8000 and 10,000. The Austrian Deaf Association (ÖGLB, founded in 1913) documented an incident during the 2011 national census where citizens could tick-box several languages they used as 'everyday languages'. When a deaf man wrote ÖGS in an empty field in which people could fill in other than the prescribed 10 languages this was crossed out by a civil servant (ÖGLB, 2004: 42). The reliability of Austrian data on language users has been criticized also regarding spoken languages (see, e.g. the Language Education Policy Profile (BMUKK & BMWF, 2008: 14)).

In addition to the six recognized autochthonous ethnic groups and their languages, ÖGS is legally recognized by the constitution as a language. We will now report on how this came about, will describe what exactly the constitutional recognition entails and offer an analysis of the actual linguistic rights of deaf sign language users in Austria.

1991–2001: Deaf Leaders and Linguists Unite to Campaign

The following description of 14 years of activities and campaigning that finally led to the recognition of ÖGS is based on Jarmer and Krausneker (2014) and will highlight the who, the what and the how, that is: specific strategies employed.

Attempts to achieve legal recognition of ÖGS started in 1991, at the time when research on ÖGS first began at the universities of Klagenfurt and Graz – three years after the European Parliament passed its first 'Resolution on Sign Languages of the Deaf' (see Krausneker, 2000).

In November 1991, the attendants of the 19th Austrian Linguistics Conference passed a resolution with the central demand to recognize 'the sign language of the deaf in Austria'. The resolution was turned into a petition and formally handed over to the president of the National Assembly by four government spokespeople (who represented people with disabilities). It was then assigned to the committee on petitions and citizen's initiatives, discussed there in March 1992 and again in July 1992, when an expert hearing was called for. The said hearing ('parliamentary enquete') on the topic 'Living situation of Deaf People' was held in October 1992 (Nationalrat, 1993: 10). All deaf clubs and associations were invited, as well as a handful of academics. It was probably the first time that Austrian Sign Language was used in Austrian Parliament and that interpreters were present.

In January 1993, the parliamentary committee's report was ready. It included a statement issued by the office of the chancellor that curtly declared deaf people and their language are not a minority in the sense of being a *Volksgruppe*, an ethnic group living in a clearly defined 'habitat' as defined by abovementioned *Volksgruppengesetz* (Nationalrat, 1993: 2). Finally, the National Assembly passed a resolution that asked the federal government to 'take any action needed in order to improve the living conditions of deaf and hard-of-hearing people in Austria' (Nationalrat, 1993: 10). While individual points from the original linguists' petition were granted, the demand to legally recognize ÖGS was ignored. A working group, uniting members of different federal ministries, was created for the 'Improvement of the living conditions of deaf and hard-of-hearing people in Austria.'

Three years later, the Austrian Deaf Association made a second attempt: the ÖGLB collected about 10,000 signatures for a petition including essential demands such as bilingual early education, school and vocational training, sufficient interpreting and subtitles on television, as well as a sign language programme on public television. This petition was submitted to parliament in 1997 and initiated a similarly complicated and slow process as its predecessor in 1991. But one change was achieved: in 1998, the 145th session of the National Assembly (XX.GP) brought about a relevant amendment of the code of criminal procedure and the civil procedure rules. Since then, deaf people have the right to use ÖGS in Austrian courts, while the state of Austria bears the expenses. Thus, in 1998, ÖGS became a legal language in Austrian courts. Although by now there were a number of well-informed and highly engaged members of parliament who argued for more substantial changes, the crucial demand that ÖGS was legally and formally recognized was again not taken care of. The Ministry of Education and the Arts made it very clear in its statement that the right to sign language in schools would only be granted after 'official recognition as a minority language' (BMUKK, 1997: 2). The office of the chancellor again declared that deaf people and their language are not a minority in the sense of being a *Volksgruppe* (Bundeskanzleramt, 1997: 4).

In response to the failed attempts, in 1999 the Austrian Association for Applied Linguistics (*Verband für Angewandte Linguistik*) published a resolution for the recognition of ÖGS initiated by the second author of this chapter, thus supporting the attempts by the sign language community. In October 2001, the Association composed the 'Klagenfurt Declaration on Austria's Language Policy' (Verbal, 2001) in which several paragraphs were inserted on ÖGS, and which was accepted by the annual Austrian Linguistics Conference on October 27, 2001 in Klagenfurt. The comprehensive document demanded an improvement of the relevant Austrian policy on multilingualism and general language rights for all people living in Austria, and in point 1 of the recommendations it included the demand for legal recognition of ÖGS. Leading minority language linguists also published a collected volume on language policies in Austria and ensured that a chapter on ÖGS was included (Krausneker, 2003).

We now leave the first decade of joint efforts by linguists and sign language community representatives to achieve legal recognition (and thus safe and stable everyday linguistic rights) for ÖGS and move to the next phase of activism, led predominantly by the ÖGLB.

2001–2005: The Sign Language Community, their Allies and Recognition

In 2001, the ÖGLB installed a new board, with all board members being under the age of 30. This was the start of a new era of deaf political activism and a new culture of lobbying. Starting in 2001, board members of the ÖGLB frequently contacted politicians and representatives of the state both in writing and in person to explain their needs, to get their demands across and to build personal relationships. The president of the ÖGLB arranged for interpreters for her meetings, but then confronted her hosts at the Austrian parliament or in ministries with the question: 'And where can the interpreters kindly send their bill to?' – thus literally educating everyone involved about the responsibility of interpreter services.

Only a year later, the ÖGLB had yet another petition ready. This 'Petition for Equal Opportunities of Deaf People in the Austrian Educational System' was a 'citizens' initiative' and was officially submitted to the president of the Austrian parliament in June 2002. Due to the premature termination of a political coalition and early general elections in Austria, this petition had to be redrafted and all supporting signatures collected again. It was resubmitted in 2003. In the meantime, the ÖGLB continued direct lobbying of politicians. For example, in May 2003 it sent a letter to all the members of the National Assembly to inform them of the newest developments regarding sign language rights: the recommendations by the Council of Europe (CoE, 2003). In July 2004, the relevant committee in parliament organized a hearing where deaf representatives, linguists and parents of deaf children were invited, thus repeating a procedure that it had already applied 10 years before. The hearing, which Krausneker and Jarmer both attended, went well; there was great open-mindedness and basically, the discussion was not *if* but *how* and where exactly the recognition should be put into law. But in the end, the ÖGLB's petition was never fully discussed because other events took place.

In July 2003, the Austrian parliament decided to develop a federal disability law. A forum of organizations representing disabled persons had initiated and drafted a list of core demands for such a law. This list and all following drafts and proposals by the forum included the needs of deaf people as voiced by the ÖGLB. In January 2004, the Ministry of Social Affairs finally presented a first draft of the law that included several clauses on the legal situation of Sign Language users. The draft law, dated January 19 2004, stated 'Deaf, hearing disabled and language disabled people have the right to use Austrian Sign Language.'. This paragraph was misleading and legally absurd because the mere *use* of ÖGS was not forbidden or illegal – the granting of 'the right to use' was rhetoric. The actual recognition of ÖGS, however, was seen as a constitutional matter by politicians and concrete language rights were not mentioned in the draft. In March 2004, the member organizations of the abovementioned forum of representatives of all disability groups issued a joint statement on the law. One of the changes that was demanded was that concrete effects of the theoretical 'right to use ÖGS' should be explained – and granted – in detail. In August 2004, the Austrian Deaf Association was one of the groups that decided to entirely reject the second draft of the law (made available for comment by the Ministry of Social Affairs on 28 July 2004) because it included no specific rights for deaf people and made a legally weak suggestion about recognising ÖGS.

Again, all the while the ÖGLB continued letter writing and lobbying members of parliament. It introduced the 'turquoise ribbon', a positive image campaign for 'Deaf Power and Sign Language' (see www.oeglb.at/ueber-uns/tuerkiser-ribbon) and in May 2005 published the 'First Discrimination Report of the Deaf in Austria' (ÖGLB, 2005), accompanied by a press conference. Additionally, each member of the Austrian parliament received a paper edition of the report with an explanatory letter. For many months, the ÖGLB was actively involved in consultations on the formulation of the new Federal Disability Equality Act.

On July 6, 2005, the members of the Austrian parliament voted in favour of the Federal Disability Equality Act[6] and, following an informal agreement between activists and politicians, simultaneously in favour of a constitutional amendment to legally recognize Austrian Sign Language (Krausneker, 2006: 134–145; Wheatley & Pabsch, 2012: 38–41). Since 1

September 2005, Article 8 of the Austrian constitution includes a third paragraph that reads:

> Austrian Sign Language is recognized as a fully-fledged language. Full particulars shall be determined by further laws. (Austrian Constitutional Law, Article 8 (3))[7]

When both the Disability Equality Act and the constitutional amendment were passed, many activists and disabled people were disappointed with the disability law while the sign language community held a public celebration in the park next to the parliament. At that point, nobody yet anticipated that the second sentence of the new constitutional article was going to impede the further development of linguistic rights for deaf people in Austria for many years.

To conclude, the second phase of campaigning for legal recognition of ÖGS was characterized by both deaf civic activism (lead by the ÖGLB) and by close cooperation with allies from other disability groups. In practice, this alliance was delicate because the discourse of deaf emancipation included rejecting the 'disabled' status for deaf sign language users and asserting a linguistic minority identity; accordingly, representatives from the disability sector had to be reassured that they were not being 'looked down upon' by deaf activists premising their claims based on language use rather than disability.

Legal Status of ÖGS and Effects

Constitution: The legal reservation

The original text for the legal recognition of ÖGS proposed by the Social Democrats in 2003 read: 'ÖGS is an autonomous language, part of deaf culture and deaf persons' instrument to access education and equal opportunities. Therefore, it has to be respected and protected.' (our translation).

As we saw above, the way ÖGS was eventually recognized at first glance looks much more concrete and reliable than this, but there is the ominous second sentence of Article 8 (3): 'Full particulars shall be determined by further laws'. This second sentence is a so-called 'legal reservation', a constitutional instrument that allows a state to restrict or limit fundamental rights in national laws. A legal reservation can be used in two ways. The first one is by reference to existing laws ('intervened reserve'): a basic right can be restricted if its realization/enjoyment by a person would violate the interests of other persons. For example, the freedom of expression can be restricted in order to avoid insulting other persons. The second form (a 'control reserve') means that the legal reservation formulates the necessity to concretize by means of additional laws to be decided on in the future. These new laws should describe how the fundamental right is to be implemented.

The reservation added to Article 8 (3) of the Austrian constitution is the only one concerning a national constitutional act in general.[8] However, since 2005 the Austrian parliament has not adopted any new laws concerning the use of ÖGS. The lack of practical consequences of the Austrian recognition of ÖGS has been criticized by Wilcox *et al.* (2012) and termed 'purely symbolic' by De Meulder (2016: 84). In 2014, the parties of the parliamentary majority (constituting the government) voted against the introduction of ÖGS as a language of instruction as proposed by the opposition (see Jarmer *et al.*, 2014), thus showing that they had no intentions to actually put into practice Article 8 (3) of the Austrian constitution.

Austria has nine counties, some of which have paid attention to ÖGS in their county laws. The most prestigious in terms of legal hierarchies – but still only symbolic – formal recognition of ÖGS can be found in Article 9 (4) of the county constitution of *Oberösterreich*. As far as we know, regionally, no concrete rights are awarded to sign language users based on this recognition, either.

Signed language interpreting

As for most other deaf communities in countries where high quality professional signed language interpreting services are established, in Austria access to those services is key to full participation, the fulfilment of the right to education and to accessibility etc. (see e.g. European Parliament, 2016). Interestingly, this area has apparently developed independent from, if not to say, well ahead of, the formal recognition of ÖGS. In Austria, there are several paths to becoming a signed language interpreter, one of them a BA and MA degree at the University of Graz, while others are outside the formal education system and organized by the interpreter association itself.

In the late 1990s, Austrian Sign Language interpreters founded a professional representative organization, the *Österreichischer Gebärdensprach-DolmetscherInnen- und ÜbersetzerInnen-Verband* (ÖGSDV). It is very active in organizing training opportunities, in quality control and in negotiations with federal and regional institutions that need to finance interpreter services. Today, there are slightly over 100 members of the ÖGSDV, which is still not enough to meet the demand for interpreters by deaf sign language users.

Payment of interpreter services is organized individually in each of the nine Austrian counties – with the exception of legal interpreting, as described above – and thus cannot be described in detail here. Generally, interpreting in employment settings is covered, but there is no right to interpreter services for social, medical or other events that can be termed 'community interpreting' and individuals have to re-apply for funded services on each occasion. Specifically, children and retired sign language users have no right to interpreters (since funding is employment related), which is unsatisfactory.

In order to obtain facts on the interpreter situation, three federal ministries commissioned a study on the 'demand for ÖGS-interpreters in secondary and tertiary education as well as everyday life'. In their study, Hartl and Unger (2014) calculated that for 'social rehabilitation' and tertiary education the demand for interpreters amounts to approximately 300,000 hours per year, while services provided amount to approximately 100,000 hours. The authors concluded that there is a huge unmet demand for sign language interpreters (Hartl & Unger, 2014: 49–50).

Education

Starting in 1779, the Austro-Hungarian Monarchy (the predecessor of today's Austria) established more than a dozen schools for the deaf all over the monarchy. These schools presumably applied a more or less bilingual 'Austrian method', a variant of de l'Epée's approach, putting special emphasis on fingerspelling and spoken/written language (Czech, 1836). Charitable foundations then ensured that most deaf children could attend these (mostly boarding) schools. Although this method was given up in favour of the monolingual approach in 1867, as promoted by Heinicke, a legacy of sign language use in deaf education created a rather self-confident deaf community, which in 1865 founded its first local self-representative organization in Vienna, the *Wiener Taubstummen-Unterstützungsverein* (Viennese Support Club of the Deaf and Dumb).

In the 19th and 20th century, Austrian deaf education experienced the same dynamics and developments as many other central European countries (for an overview of current statuses, please consult www.univie. ac.at/map-designbilingual).

A nationwide study on the status of ÖGS in schools and universities (Krausneker & Schalber, 2007) gathered data in 38 different classroom settings in special and mainstream schools, and found that reforms were needed. In 2006/7, the use of ÖGS for bilingual education was the exception nationwide, especially in mainstream schools. Most pupils in mainstream education had access to only a few hours per week of extra teacher support. Krausneker and Schalber (2007) noted that pupils as well as teachers suffered from lack of access to ÖGS resources and competencies, and that actual conditions for implementing 'co-enrolment' of deaf and hard of hearing pupils were less than ideal. Today, there is one fully bimodal bilingual inclusive[9] kindergarten and a dozen bimodal-bilingual classrooms all over the country. (For an up to date overview of all previous and present bimodal-bilingual co-enrolment models and practices in Austria, see Krausneker & Kramreiter, 2019). However, the state does not provide the legal basis for bimodal-bilingual education. As of today, ÖGS is not an official language of instruction and not an official school subject. The first generation of teachers to properly learn ÖGS in their basic teacher training only started in 2017 at the University of Vienna. All schools for the deaf are currently managed by hearing principals who are not competent in ÖGS.

The Federal Austrian Education Act (*Schulunterrichtsgesetz*[10]) states:

§ 16 (1) German is the language of instruction, unless law or international conventions allow different provisions for schools specified for linguistic minorities.

§ 16 (3) Moreover, school authorities can prescribe the use of a modern foreign language as the language of instruction (working language) if this is appropriate due to the number of persons living in Austria, using a foreign language [as their mother tongue] or in the interest of a better education in foreign languages. (our translation)

Both the *Schulunterrichtsgesetz* and regulations concerning the languages of instruction for autochthonous minorities allow for the use of other languages than German in schools. So far, ÖGS has not been granted this privilege. In effect, ÖGS-using pupils are discriminated against when compared to the other autochthonous ethnic minorities (*Volksgruppen*) and to immigrant children. Deaf pupils are discriminated in terms of their right to use their mother tongue because they are deprived of experiencing their mother tongue as a language of instruction and because they cannot study it as an obligatory school subject in class and they cannot have it listed and graded in their school reports. ÖGS is currently – even 13 years after constitutional recognition – not included in the respective paragraphs of the *Schulunterrichtsgesetz* listing possible languages of instruction.

In 2017, the Ministry of Education contracted the development of curricula for ÖGS (grade 1 to grade 12), both as a mother tongue and as a foreign language. Once the ministry implements them, these curricula will not only make it possible to offer ÖGS as an obligatory school subject for any pupil (hearing or deaf, grade 1 to 12), but will also automatically pave the way for ÖGS as a language of instruction.

While pupils have no right to learn, use or develop ÖGS in schools as yet, they have the option to use interpreters in school. However, this interpreter service is not a right, and where it is provided, it depends on annual requests (by teachers, pupils and their parents) and agreements with school authorities to finance it.

Once we move to tertiary education, sign language using university students face challenges, with the notable exception of Vienna: the Ministry of Education, Science and Research has invested in a long-term project that offers support to deaf students at any university or college in Vienna: *Gehörlos Erfolgreich Studieren* (GESTU, Deaf Success at

University, https://teachingsupport.tuwien.ac.at/gestu). Thus, most deaf sign language users decide to study in Vienna. The team of GESTU has – again, with the financial support of the ministry – created an online database for newly created, necessary technical signs that students and their interpreters need in their everyday life at university. This very important resource (https://fachgebaerden.tsc.tuwien.ac.at/startseite) is also highly interesting and relevant because it was deaf-led and actually broadened ÖGS in a most creative and unique way (Krausneker *et al.*, 2017a).

Both deaf civil activists and hearing and deaf academics in Austria would probably agree that the most crucial changes for ÖGS rights concern education. And when pressed about details, they would describe the necessary changes and hoped for resources very similarly or even exactly as experts in all other European countries (see Krausneker *et al.*, 2017b, in review).

Broadcasting and access to information

The Austrian National Television, ORF, has been offering interpreted news once a day since 2004. Note that ORF was ahead of politics and implemented this long-requested service a year before ÖGS was legally recognized. However, the interpreted news reports are hidden on a satellite channel, so the majority of the Austrian population never see it nor for the most part do they even know that it exists. There is still no programme that is led and presented by deaf people. The directorate-general of ORF countered this with the argument that it would be a 'ghetto programme' (see Krausneker, 2006).

Many other fields relevant for access to information have achieved great improvements (subtitles, digital information services, visual announcements in public transport etc.) that mean better accessibility, but not necessarily the use of ÖGS.

The political domain, foremost parliamentary practice, first saw the use of sign language interpreters when a (hearing, non-signing) disability spokesperson, Franz-Josef Huainigg, became a Member of Parliament. In 2003 he established that his own parliamentary speeches must be interpreted into ÖGS. Not only did he point that out at the beginning of his speeches so that it may not go unnoticed, but he made a point of mentioning that the parliamentary budget was paying for it. Parliamentary practice and accessibility underwent a big change after 2009, when the Green Party positioned Helene Jarmer – a deaf sign language user – as a Member of Parliament. Unfortunately, the Green Party lost all their seats in 2017, but parliament has since (so far) kept up the practice of having the sessions professionally interpreted into ÖGS.

In her eight years as a spokesperson for disabled people, Jarmer advanced some goals especially relevant for deaf people: deafblindness is now recognized as a disability, which in turn means more support from the state for deafblind individuals. Another of Jarmer achievements included the fact that Austrian National Television (ORF) is now legally committed to make binding plans to reach 100% accessibility in its programmes. She set several initiatives to improve teacher training in ÖGS, including that in the future, language competencies of teachers who learn ÖGS will have to be classified by using the Common European Framework of Reference for Languages (CEFR) and be confirmed on their attendance certificates (see Nationalrat, 2017: 1).

Anti-discrimination legislation

Deaf sign language users could argue that they are directly and indirectly discriminated against – especially by Austrian educational laws: directly, because they are not provided with a barrier-free education; indirectly, because they are subject to rules, criteria and procedures defined for non-disabled, especially hearing people, without respecting their human rights and needs. Actually, three annual Austrian shadow reports on racism included examples of discrimination based on language as reported by deaf clubs (ZARA, 2002, 2003, 2004).[11]

But identifying discrimination against sign language users differs from suing. The Federal Disability Equality Act is an ordinary law and cannot serve to invalidate any part of another ordinary law by appealing to a court. This means that contradictions between ordinary laws (namely the Disability Equality Act and the Education Act etc.) remain unresolved to the disadvantage of deaf people.

The main field requiring changes is education, especially schools, and the right to be taught in ÖGS. In July 2017, a deaf person, joined by the ÖGLB, delivered a 'communication' (i.e. a complaint) on this issue against the Republic of Austria regarding violations of Articles 7, 21, 24 and 30 of the UN Convention on the Rights of Persons with Disabilities, to the Office of the United Nations High Commissioner for Human Rights. According to the rules of OHCHR such a communication can only be delivered if all national official legal channels have been exhausted. This was the case in April 2017.

While all of this looks rather sombre, solidarity among self-representing NGOs remains alive. The Austrian Disability Council (*Behindertenrat*) as the umbrella organization of Austria's self-representative NGOs for people with disabilities, supports the demands of the sign language community, but it does not have any legal influence. The same is true for the Independent Monitoring Committee for the Implementation of the UN Convention on the Rights of Persons with Disabilities (*Monitoringausschuss*).

The Disabled Persons Advocacy (*Behindertenanwaltschaft*) on the other hand, is strongly influenced by the Ministry of Social Affairs and appoints only representatives directly from or close to the government.

They have been effective concerning individual complaints, but have never dedicated themselves to pursuing changes to achieve what was defined as a goal in the 1990s: to sustainably improve the 'living conditions of the deaf'.

What is Missing (Outlook)

ÖGS was constitutionally recognized in 2005. Judicially, it seems to remain open whether the constitutional article recognizing ÖGS 'as a fully-fledged language' means that ÖGS is recognized as a minority language, especially as there is no such thing in Austrian law – only the languages of ethnic minorities.

The negative consequence of a legal reservation as described in the previous section is not explicitly mentioned in Article 8 (3): the laws which 'determine the particulars' (cf. the second sentence of Article 8 (3)) 'overrule' the fundamental right. This means that when applying to an administrative body or claiming rights at a court it is not possible to directly refer to the fundamental right under reservation. It is only possible to refer to the laws 'determining the particulars', not to the 'abstract' constitutional right itself. Ironically, this rule is also valid if there is no law 'determining the particulars'. The judicial consequence is that the legislator can obstruct any implementation of an enacted fundamental right under legal reservation by simply not deciding on any respective law 'determining the particulars'. This is presently the case for ÖGS: its recognition was put in place in Article 8 of the constitution, but since the parliament has never decided on any laws implementing it, it remains for civil activists to demand that civil servants and politicians breathe life into it.

Acknowledgements

This chapter was initiated and primarily written by our colleague Franz Dotter, who tragically died in an accident on 26 March 2018, a few days after his 70th birthday. Franz was not only the pioneer of Austrian sign language linguistics and a respected academic, but as such also an engaged, humble, passionate and true ally to the Austrian deaf community. Less than two weeks before his passing, Franz consulted Verena Krausneker and discussed this paper with her, thus she took on the task of completing the chapter.

Notes

(1) See https://www.statistik.at/web_de/statistiken/menschen_und_gesellschaft/ bevoelkerung/bevoelkerungsstand_und_veraenderung/bevoelkerung_zu_jahres-_ quartalsanfang/index.html (accessed 28 January 2019).

(2) www.ris.bka.gv.at/GeltendeFassung.wxe?Abfrage=Bundesnormen&Gesetzesnum mer=10000138 (accessed 28 January 2019).
(3) See http://www.statistik.at/web_de/statistiken/menschen_und_gesellschaft/ bevoelkerung/volkszaehlungen_registerzaehlungen_abgestimmte_erwerbsstatistik/ bevoelkerung_nach_demographischen_merkmalen/022896.html (accessed 28 January 2019).
(4) Rudolf de Cillia, personal communication, 19 April 2018.
(5) In this chapter, we use 'deaf' and do not try to differentiate between deaf/Deaf, as was convention for a while, thus following Kusters et al. (2017).
(6) Bundes-Behindertengleichstellungsgesetz. All laws quoted in this chapter can be accessed in the official Austrian law information system: www.ris.bka.gv.at.
(7) Another translation reads: 'Austrian Sign Language is a language in its own right, recognized in law. For details, see the relevant legal provisions.' (BMUKK & BMWF, 2008: 22). And yet another translation reads 'The Austrian sign language is recognized as independent language. Details are regulated by the laws.' See www.ris.bka. gv.at/Dokumente/Erv/ERV_1930_1/ERV_1930_1.pdf (accessed 28 January 2019).
(8) The legal reservation in Article 5 (2) of the Constitutional Act on the Rights of Children relates (a) to the international treaty on children's rights, which was the basis for this constitutional act and (b) is restricted to a small part of the act. The other uses of reservations in paragraphs 23b (1), 50 (1) and 81b (3) of the Austrian Constitutional Law concern also very special limited cases.
(9) The term 'bimodal bilingual' in this chapter describes education with a spoken/written language and a signed language. In this case the whole kindergarten, all groups and staff act/are bimodal bilingual (not just one group 'for' the deaf kids) This also means that the entire kindergarten is officially bimodal bilingual (it is not somebody's 'project').
   Inclusive means that there are hearing and deaf kids who learn together in an environment that is accessible for everyone and that is in this case not in the context of a special school.
(10) See https://www.ris.bka.gv.at/GeltendeFassung.wxe?Abfrage=Bundesnormen&Ges etzesnummer=10009600 (accessed 28 January 2019).
(11) ZARA defines racist discrimination as follows: 'Racism applies if a person and/or a group of people is subject to any form of discrimination on the grounds of their colour of skin, language, appearance, religious belief, citizenship or origin.'

References

Baumgartner, G. (1995) 6 x Österreich. Geschichte und aktuelle Situation der Volksgruppen. Klagenfurt/Celovec: Drava Verlag.
BMUKK (1997) Betrifft Petition Nr. 23, Annerkennung der Gebärdensprache. GZ 26.150/7-I/8/97. Statement of the Federal Ministry of Education and the Arts to the Office of the National Assembly.
BMUKK and BMWF (2008) Language and Language Education Policies in Austria. Language Education Policy Profile. See www.coe.int/t/dg4/linguistic/Profils_EN.asp (accessed 19 April 2018).
Bundeskanzleramt (1997) Betrifft Petition Nr. 23 Forderungsprogramm des Österreichischen Gehörlosenbundes, GZ 600.127/20-V/2/97. Statement of the Office of the Chancellor to the Office of the National Assembly.
Council of Europe (CoE) (2003) Recommendation 1598 on the Protection of Sign Languages in Member States of the Council of Europe. See http://assembly.coe.int/nw/xml/XRef/ Xref-XML2HTML-EN.asp?fileid=17093&lang=en (accessed 13 April 2018).
Czech, F.H. (1836) Versinnlichte Denk – und Sprachlehre, mit Anwendung auf die Religions – und Sittenlehre und auf das Leben. Wien: MechitaristenCongregations-Buchhandlung.

de Cillia, R. (2003) Braucht Österreich eine Sprachenpolitik? In B. Busch, and R. de Cillia (eds) *Sprachenpolitik in Österreich. Bestandsaufnahme 2011* (pp. 9–42). Frankfurt am Main: Peter Lang.

de Cillia, R. and Vetter, E. (eds) (2011) Sprachenpolitik in Österreich. Bestandsaufnahme 2011. In R. Wodak and M. Stegu (eds) *Reihe: Sprache im Kontext*, Vol. 17. Frankfurt am Main: Peter Lang.

de Cillia, R., Menz, F., Dressler, W.U. and Cech, P. (1998) Linguistic minorities in Austria. In C. Bratt Paulston and D. Peckham (eds) *Linguistic Minorities in Central & Eastern Europe* (pp. 18–36). Bristol: Multilingual Matters.

De Meulder, M. (2016) The power of language policy. PhD dissertation, University of Jyväskylä. See https://jyx.jyu.fi/dspace/handle/123456789/52219 (accessed 17 April 2018).

European Parliament (2016) *European Parliament Resolution on Sign Languages and Professional Sign Language Interpreters.* B8-1241/2016. See www.europarl.europa.eu/sides/getDoc.do?pubRef=-//EP//TEXT+MOTION+B8-2016-1241+0+DOC+XML+V0//EN (accessed 18 April 2018).

Hartl, J. and Unger, M. (2014) *Abschätzung der Bedarfslage an ÖGS-DolmetscherInnen in Primär-, Sekundär- und Tertiärbildung sowie in Bereichen des täglichen Lebens.* See https://bildung.bmbwf.gv.at/schulen/sb/oegs_bedarfslage_dolmetsch.pdf?61edk0 (accessed 18 April 2018).

Jarmer, H. and Krausneker, V. (2014) Steps. National Recognition of Austrian Sign Language (ÖGS) – Brief Description of our Activities. Manuscript. Distributed to EUD and other NADs on 8 January 2014.

Jarmer, H. *et al.* (2014) *Entschließungsantrag betreffend Einführung der Gebärdensprache als Unterrichtssprache. Stenografische Protokolle, 831/A(E) XXV. GP am 10.12.2014.* See www.parlament.gv.at/PAKT/VHG/XXV/A/A_00831/index.shtml (accessed 17 April 2018).

Krausneker, V. (2000) Sign languages and the minority language policy of the European Union. In M. Metzger (ed.) *Bilingualism & Identity in Deaf Communities* (pp. 142–158). Washington DC: Gallaudet University Press.

Krausneker, V. (2003) Ungehört. Zum Status der Österreichischen Gebärdensprache und ihrer VerwenderInnen. In B. Busch and R. de Cillia (eds) *Sprachenpolitik in Österreich. Bestandsaufnahme 2011* (pp. 102–113). Frankfurt am Main: Peter Lang.

Krausneker, V. (2006) Darf ein Ghetto sichtbar sein? In der frei Raum (ed.) *Der Auftrag. Öffentlich-rechtlicher Rundfunk. Positionen – Perspektiven – Plädoyers* (pp. 123–125). Wien: Sonderzahl Verlag.

Krausneker, V. and Schalber, K. (2007) *Sprache Macht Wissen.* See www.univie.ac.at/sprachemachtwissen (accessed 17 April 2018).

Krausneker, V. and Kramreiter S. (2019) Bilingual, inclusive, mixed-age schooling in Vienna. In M. Marschark, S. Antia and H. Knoors (eds) *Co-Enrollment for Deaf Learners* (pp. 133–147). Oxford: Oxford University Press.

Krausneker, V, Dürr X., Fenkart, L., Hager B. and Moser, K. (2017a) Sprachplanung: Die ÖGS erweitern – Das Fachgebärdenprojekt von GESTU in Wien. *Das Zeichen* 106, 178–190. Hamburg: Signum Verlag.

Krausneker V., Becker C., Audeoud M. and Tarcsiová D. (2017b) Bimodal bilingual school practice in Europe. In K. Reuter (ed.) *UNCRPD Implementation in Europe – A Deaf Perspective. Article 24: Education* (pp. 154–171). Brussels: EUD.

Krausneker V., Becker C., Audeoud M. and Tarcsiová D. (in review) Bimodal bilingual school education in Europe. In K. Snoddon and J. Weber (eds) *Critical Perspectives on Plurilingualism in Deaf Education.* New York: Springer.

Kusters, A., O'Brien, D. and De Meulder, M. (2017) Innovations in deaf studies: Critically mapping the field. In A. Kusters, M. De Meulder and D. O'Brien D. (eds) *Innovations in Deaf Studies: The Role of Deaf Scholars.* (pp. 1–53). Oxford University Press.

Nationalrat (1993) *Einzelbericht des Ausschusses für Petitionen und Bürgerinitiativen. Beilagen zu den Stenographischen Protokollen des Nationalrats XVIII.* GP, 12. 01.1993.

Nationalrat (2017) *Entschließung des Nationalrates vom 28 Juni 2017 betreffend Qualität der Ausbildung von Lehrkräften in der Österreichischen Gebärdensprache.* 211/E XXV. GP

ÖGLB, Austrian Deaf Association (ed.) (2004) *1. Diskriminierungsbericht der Österreichischen Gebärdensprachgemeinschaft.* See https://www.academia.edu/36398625/1._Diskriminierungsbericht_der_%C3%96sterreichischen_Geb%C3%A4rdensprachgemeinschaft (accessed 13 April 2018).

ÖGLB, Austrian Deaf Association (ed.) (2005) *Diskriminierungsbericht 2005.* See https://www.yumpu.com/de/document/view/4940589/diskriminierungsbericht-2005-oster reichischer-gehorlosenbund (accessed 13 April 2018).

Verbal, Verband für Angewandte Linguistik (2001) *Klagenfurter Erklärung zur österreichischen Sprachenpolitik.* See http://www.verbal.at/index.php?id=59 (accessed 13 April 2018).

Wheatley, M. and Pabsch, A. (2012) *Sign Language Legislation in the European Union* (2nd edn). Brussels: EUD.

Wilcox, S., Krausneker, V. and Armstrong D. (2012) Language policies and the deaf community. In C.B. Spolsky (ed.) *Cambridge Handbook of Language Policy* (pp. 374–395). Cambridge, New York: Cambridge University Press.

ZARA (2002) *Racism Report.* See https://assets.zara.or.at/download/pdf/racism-report-2002.pdf (accessed 17 April 2018).

ZARA (2003) *Racism Report.* See https://assets.zara.or.at/download/pdf/racism-report-2003.pdf (accessed 17 April 2018).

ZARA (2004) *Racism Report.* See https://assets.zara.or.at/download/pdf/racism-report-2004.pdf (accessed 17 April 2018).

14 Implementing Recognition of New Zealand Sign Language: 2006–2018

Rachel L. McKee and Victoria Manning

Progress towards sign language recognition in each country is shaped by local events, individuals and political opportunities, and by wider paradigm shifts and points of international contact. The trajectory of New Zealand Sign Language (NZSL) towards official language status was propelled by local developments in indigenous (Māori) language rights, human rights and disability rights, and was also influenced by ideologies about sign language inherited first from Europe (19th century oralism) and later from the USA (sign language pride in the latter 20th century). In this chapter we describe the strands of activity that led to the NZSL Act (2006), explain the scope and constraints of that law and critically reflect on progress following recognition.

New Zealand is a nation of 4.8 million with a democratic electoral system that typically results in coalition governments, in a single tier parliament. New Zealand is historically socially progressive, being a pioneer of universal suffrage, public education and health systems. Fifteen percent of the population identify as Māori, of whom only 21% can speak Māori to varying levels; after 40 years of revitalisation effort, the language remains vulnerable (Benton, 2015). English is the de facto official language, and the Māori Language Act (1987) and the NZSL Act (2006) officialised these two minority languages. Although there is state support to strengthen Māori language in New Zealand society, and certain rights for speakers of other languages are protected through translation and interpreting provision in public services, overt planning and policy for languages is generally underdeveloped (The Royal Society of New Zealand, 2013).

We write this chapter as involved participants and observers. Manning (Deaf) has been a campaigner, a policy adviser in the public service and currently manages strategy for the national Deaf association (Deaf Aotearoa NZ/DANZ). McKee (hearing) has been an interpreter since 1985 and an applied linguist since 1992, producing NZSL research and training interpreters and Deaf[1] NZSL teachers. Manning is the first chair-person of the NZSL Board and McKee is a board member. These roles inform our perspective on events.

Early Steps towards Legal Recognition of NZSL

An aspiration for government recognition of NZSL was first formally articulated by the Deaf Association in its 1993 'five-year plan', and reiterated in their updated plan for 1995–2000 (Dugdale, 2001). In 1996, the Deaf Association commissioned a survey of 'Attitudes to the Deaf', to explore tension between medical and cultural understandings of deafness that was hampering advocacy. The report noted that 'while there was strong agreement among hearing people that Deaf people have their own language and that Deaf culture should be respected and valued, there was also strong agreement that being Deaf is a disability' (Dugdale, 2001: 275). Commenting on this in 2001, Dugdale predicted that, 'the need for the community to be recognized as a cultural and linguistic minority is likely to influence the plans and achievements of the Deaf Association for some time to come'. Indeed, the 2001 revision of the Deaf Association's constitution articulated a vision for 'the promotion of Deaf culture with official recognition of NZSL' (Dugdale, 2001: 276).

From the 1990s, access to education in NZSL was a major focus of Deaf community engagement with policymakers. In 1995, a forum of community, professional and institutional representatives (Deaf Education Access Forum) was established with the initial objective of employing trained interpreters in mainstream schools. This has not yet materialised, but an outcome of the Forum was a policy produced in cooperation with the Ministry of Education, which stated that 'all Deaf and hearing impaired children will be able to access NZSL and Deaf culture from a young age', and 'will have access to a nationally developed Deaf Studies Curriculum' (Deaf Education Aotearoa NZ, 2005). The aspirations of this policy have yet to be fully realised in practice, but the forum opened a 'dialogic space' (Wegerif, 2016)[2] in which Deaf NZSL users engaged with educators, parents and policymakers. Their participation confronted the establishment with lived evidence of oralist education, and steered educational discourse towards a linguistic-cultural model of deafness.

Developing the NZSL Act

The route to legal recognition of NZSL piggybacked on the development of disability policy. In 2000, the newly elected Labour Government passed the NZ Public Health and Disability Act, which resulted in development of the NZ Disability Strategy (Dalziel, 2001), a policy directive requiring the government sector to equalise participation for people with disabilities. Sign language recognition was understood to be central to this objective for Deaf people, as existing anti-discrimination legislation did not protect a right to use sign language (Wolf, 2005). In 2002, the government established a new Office for Disability Issues (ODI) and a Minister for Disability Issues, which provided an administrative home to work on fulfilling the government's promise to the Deaf community for recognition of NZSL (Wolf, 2005). In 2002, Manning (second author) was appointed as a policy analyst in the ODI. In 2003, the Minister directed the ODI to begin work on drafting an NZSL Bill[3] and Manning was one of the government advisers to the NZSL Bill from initial policy proposals throughout government and parliamentary stages leading to its passage in 2006.

Consultation with NZSL stakeholders about a law identified their dual desire for status recognition and for instrumental access rights. Following drafting of the Bill, government departments were consulted about their capacity to implement the proposed law. Feedback revealed that they 'could not implement a Bill that moved very far from the status quo, because of resource limitations', and highlighted 'difficulties in specifying enforceable rights or obligations with enough clarity to apply these in the myriad of circumstances in which they operated' (Wolf, 2005: 3). Following this step, a select committee received 195 public submissions on the Bill, including 104 from Deaf people who submitted comments in NZSL. Submissions overwhelmingly supported its intent (Office for Disability Issues, undated (a)), but in order to be administratively and politically acceptable, the final New Zealand Sign Language Bill (2004) specified only one enforceable right: to use NZSL in courts (already common practice), and declared official status without defining how this status might take effect, nor committing any resources.

The absence of budget allocation and enforceable measures in the Bill (especially regarding education and access) was criticised in public submissions and by some politicians, who argued that that this would render the law merely symbolic, raising status but without practical gains for NZSL users. For example, remarks by a conservative minority party MP, Heather Roy, echo those of some other speakers at the third (final) reading of the Bill:

> Good intentions alone do not automatically translate into good lawmaking. Making New Zealand Sign Language an official language will not in itself achieve very much without proper support and definite funding allocations'. (New Zealand House of Representatives, 2006: 2595)

The Select Committee's response was to contend that departments could implement the principles of the Act through policy and practice, and that the law would be reviewed after three years (McKee, 2007).

Another issue raised in submissions was the need for a monitoring body, parallel to the Māori Language Commission established by the Māori Language Act (Section 6), which has administrative powers to promote and regulate official and community uses of the language, Instead, the NZSL Act (Section 9) encourages government agencies to observe the principles of the Act 'so far as reasonably practicable', and to consult with the Deaf community in doing so. The Select Committee rationalised the lack of an implementing mechanism by stating:

> We consider this matter is better left to the Government to progress separately from this bill, but would recommend its serious consideration' (Justice and Electoral Select Committee, 2005)

It was another decade before the government addressed the need for an implementing body.

With these identified weaknesses, the NZSL Bill was shepherded through parliament between 2004 to 2006 by the Minister for Disability Issues, and passed on 6 April 2006 with 119 votes in favour and two against.

Provisions of the NZSL Act

The three main provisions of the NZSL Act[4] are set out in Sections 6 7, and 9 of the law, as summarised below.

- § 6 *Recognition*: New Zealand Sign Language is declared to be an official language of New Zealand.

- § 7 *Right to use New Zealand Sign Language in legal proceedings:* any party (court, witness, counsel) may use NZSL, and a competent interpreter must be provided. Part 2 (§ 13) enables administrative regulations to be made for standards of competence for interpreters. Subsequently, a minimum standard was set, but has not been reviewed.

- § 8 *Effect of recognition*: Subject to § 7, § 6 does not create any legally enforceable rights.

- § 9 *Principles to guide Government departments*
  (1) A Government department should, when exercising its functions and powers, be guided, so far as reasonably practicable, by the following principles:
      (a) the Deaf community should be consulted on matters relating to NZSL
      (b) NZSL should be used in the promotion to the public of Government services and in the provision of information to the public:
      (c) Government services and information should be made accessible to the Deaf community through the use of appropriate means (including the use of NZSL).

The Act also states that 'nothing in subsection (1) is to be read as conferring on the Deaf community advantages not enjoyed by other persons', and allows for a review of the law after three years.

Pursuing Implementation

Since Section 8 of the NZSL Act states that recognition 'does not create any legally enforceable rights', no implementation measures ensued. The legislation described indirect monitoring of the effects of the Act, via annual reports from government departments to the Minister of Disability Issues on their progress implementing the Disability Strategy. The Act (Section 11) stated that the law should be reviewed 'as soon as practicable after three years', to determine how it had operated and 'whether any amendments to the scope and contents of this Act are necessary or desirable'. In 2010–2011, the ODI undertook a review but its scope was narrow. Submissions reiterated the issues and suggestions that were identified during the original development of the Bill, most of which were excluded from the provisions of the Act. The review nevertheless concluded that no change to the law was needed, but that government agencies could improve implementation through policy and practice (Office for Disability Issues, undated (b)). The Deaf Association expressed frustration with the tokenistic review:

> The review suggests that Government Ministers could model best practice by including a NZSL greeting at all official events, as is done in Māori, whether or not the content of the Minister's portfolio is relevant to Deaf people. We Deaf are not interested in symbolic use of NZSL at the beginning of ministerial presentations, we are more interested in the content of the Minister's portfolios and their plans to engage with the Deaf community to find effective solutions to our issues. (Deaf Aotearoa New Zealand, 2011)

In response to evidence of persisting discrimination experienced by NZSL users, the New Zealand Human Rights Commission (HRC) conducted a formal inquiry into NZSL issues in 2012, led by Manning, who was then employed there as an Advisor on Disability Rights. The Human Rights Commission is independent of the government, and has the authority to inquire generally into any matter that involves the infringement of human rights, in accordance with the Human Rights Act (1993).

The HRC Inquiry considered barriers for NZSL users from a human rights perspective, and focused on priority areas previously identified by the Deaf community and by the UN Convention on the Rights of Persons with Disabilities (CRPD), which New Zealand ratified in 2008. Focus areas were the right to education, to freedom of expression, to access services and information, and the promotion and maintenance of NZSL. The Inquiry took place over one year and entailed consultation with Deaf NZSL users and critical analysis of government agencies' actions in relation to the status of NZSL. Informed by findings from a concurrent research project on the vitality of NZSL (McKee, 2017), the report drew overt parallels between NZSL and Te Reo Māori as official, but threatened, languages:

> The cornerstone for protecting both Te Reo and NZSL is ensuring that each language can be accessed, transmitted and learnt within families

and through education … There are concerns about the maintenance of NZSL, as there are about te reo Māori … For indigenous peoples across the world, the protection and maintenance of language is vital to identity and wellbeing … Similarly, access to NZSL is pivotal to Deaf people's ability to learn, communicate and participate in society. (New Zealand Human Rights Commission, 2013: 75–76)

The Inquiry report highlighted a need to support early acquisition of NZSL by Deaf children and their families, and called on the Ministry of Education to implement its own policy on NZSL in schools.[5] It recommended further state support for interpreting and translating services to improve communication access, and the final key recommendation was to create a body to guide promotion and maintenance of NZSL and to monitor effects of the Act. In doing so, the Inquiry again made a comparison with the Māori Language Act, noting that international approaches to recognising minority languages usually entail a custodial entity to implement language planning. By articulating NZSL issues in terms of international human rights obligations and indigenous language claims, the HRC Inquiry effectively pressured the government to act on the intent of the NZSL Act. The government responded quickly and positively to two of its three main recommendations. First, the Ministry of Education funded a new service to support family-based NZSL learning for Deaf children aged 0–5 years, 'First Signs', delivered by Deaf Aotearoa NZ (rather than the education system) from 2014.[6] Secondly, additional funding was committed for approximately 100 Deaf children using NZSL in mainstream schools, in a policy known as 'NZSL@School', which entails visiting Deaf personnel working with individual deaf children, their teachers and classmates to support acquisition and use of NZSL in their school contexts (Kelston Deaf Education Centre, 2015). This is an improvement, but not an adequate model for delivery of bilingual education.

Also as a result of the HRC Inquiry, late in 2013, an NZSL Expert Advisory Group was established by the Ministry of Social Development (which hosts the ODI), to scope options for a language management entity for NZSL. The Expert Advisory Group comprised six Deaf and two hearing members with expertise on NZSL and officials from four government departments. The group considered overseas models of sign language planning bodies (e.g. those of Flanders, Finland and Turkey), although there were few established at the time. The most relevant to the New Zealand context was felt to be the Advisory Committee on VGT (Flemish Sign Language) in Flanders, Belgium, which was established by the 2006 decree on VGT (see De Meulder & Haesenne, Chapter 18, this volume). Without a mandate for a statutory body in the law, the government opted for an NZSL Advisory Board, established by Cabinet mandate. A commitment of NZD$6 million over four years was announced in May 2014, for a Board to provide the government with an expert voice on NZSL. The annual budget (committed for six years) includes a

NZD$1.25 million contestable NZSL Fund to be allocated by the Board to initiatives that promote and maintain NZSL. A further NZD$250,000 per year was committed for Secretariat support (Office for Disability Issues, undated (c)).

The NZSL Board: An 'Implementing' Body

In this section, we describe the work of the NZSL Board as a language management mechanism (Spolsky, 2009), and reflect on progress and constraints in its operation.

The terms of reference for the NZSL Board state its purpose as being to:

'promote and maintain the use of NZSL by ensuring the development and preservation and acquisition of the language; ensure the rights of Deaf people and NZSL users to use NZSL as outlined in the NZSL Act 2006 and United Nations Convention on the Rights of Persons with Disabilities and other national and relevant international legislation; provide expert advice to Government and the community on NZSL'. (Office for Disability Issues, undated (d))

Given the limited provisions in the Act to 'implement', the Board aims to progress the *intent* of the Act to improve the status of NZSL and government sector responsiveness to NZSL users. It has a wide brief to provide advice, monitoring, strategy and coordination around NZSL issues (principally for the government sector), and to monitor promotion and maintenance, although its practical capacity to do this is limited.

The government approved establishment of a board in May 2014, but members were not appointed until May 2015, with the first meeting convened in June 2015. This delay was apparently bureaucratic inertia. The Board comprises 10 members, all fluent NZSL users, the majority of whom must be Deaf (at least 6 out of 10). Appointments are made to individuals in their own right, not to representatives of stakeholder groups. Determining membership composition was contentious within the NZSL Expert Advisory Group: government officials wanted representation of non-Deaf NZSL user groups such as parents, interpreters and non-deaf speech impaired users, whereas NZSL community experts felt strongly that strategic direction for NZSL should be driven by the primary (i.e. Deaf) NZSL community, not by secondary user groups. This principle was eventually agreed. The exception to non-representative membership status is that the Board must include 'two members (NZSL users) who identify as Māori and one member representing Deaf Aotearoa New Zealand Incorporated, the officially recognized Disabled People's Organisation for the Deaf community' (Office for Disability Issues, undated (d)). The terms of reference outline the desirable skills and attributes of Board members and suitable applicants are encouraged to apply.

A panel that includes Deaf community representation advises on appointments, and the Minister for Disability Issues recommends appointments to the Cabinet committee responsible for appointments to government boards and committees. Members are appointed for either three or four years, to ensure transition of membership. The ODI hosts the Secretariat, for which one full-time policy adviser position was created, and filled by a Deaf person.

The year-long delay in appointing a board after budget approval meant that at the inaugural meeting, members were briefed on the terms of reference and their advisory role, received a short presentation on fundamentals of language planning (by a board member) and were then immediately tasked with allocation of almost NZD$1 million by assessing project applications to the NZSL Fund, to be disbursed within weeks of the meeting. Early meetings of the Board thereafter focused on grant allocation and determining criteria for the second round of the NZSL Fund. The Board were also tasked with developing an Action Plan (Office for Disability Issues, 2016). Time pressure to allocate grants and determine action plans before developing an informed strategic plan, meant that early decisions were not necessarily aligned with long-term Language Policy and Planning (LPP) priorities.

Since this headlong start, the Board has had to learn the parameters of a governance role and government protocols that interact with their advisory function. Initial Board meetings provided briefings on these topics; however, this was identified as insufficient and the Board requested more comprehensive governance training sessions that occurred half way through their term in late 2016. Ongoing training has clarified that the Board's primary relationship is with the government sector to advise on policy at a high level, rather than to directly respond to specific Deaf community interests. With regard to the capacity of Board members to engage effectively with government policy processes, the pool of Deaf NZSL users is estimated to be between 2500 to 4000 (McKee, 2017), who have had significant barriers to education and very few of whom hold a university qualification. This creates a challenge for the Board to reflect community diversity in its membership, yet also have the skills to operate at a strategic level by engaging critically with a government policy framework.

Internal and external expectations of the Board to address a raft of NZSL issues are high, and containing the workload for members and the Secretariat is challenging. The number of meeting days per year has exceeded the terms of reference and increased each year. While meetings are conducted in NZSL, there is a large volume of written documents that need to be understood prior to each meeting and some of these are translated into NZSL for the Board, which creates pressure on Secretariat workload, timelines and budget that were not fully anticipated. Much of this work, in addition to formulating policy advice for the government sector, is done by the Policy Advisor. Additional administrative and policy advice capacity in the Secretariat has been provided for particular pieces of work (e.g. writing a strategic plan, administration of grants).

As mentioned, the Board was required to assess applications to the NZSL Fund before determining a long-term strategic focus. This generated a perception, inside and outside the Board, that its main role was to address gaps by funding community initiatives, perhaps at the expense of developing strategic advice to the government, as per the terms of reference.

After further learning about principles of language planning and the determinants of language vitality, it became clearer to the Board that some core language activities require stable funding, others require policy advocacy, while others can be supported through contestable project funding. Assessing applications to the first and second NZSL Fund rounds also revealed that there was a need to support activities such as research and documentation, that do not have immediate impacts, but underpin other LPP activities such as acquisition. A newly developed NZSL Strategy 2018–2023 (NZSL Board 2018) is framed by the language planning components of status, corpus, acquisition, attitude and access/use, to provide a long-term framework for the Board's work. 'Access/use' is an addition to the usual areas of language planning, due to Deaf sign language users need for access, and 'use' reflects the aim to maintain and expand domains in which sign language is used in society.

The contestable NZSL Fund stimulated creative bottom-up responses to addressing gaps for NZSL users. On the flip-side, soon after the establishment of the Board, it was observed that some government agencies began to expect the NZSL Fund to support NZSL-related initiatives that should arguably be covered by their internal budgets. For example, previous government funding to Deaf Aotearoa to run the national awareness campaign, NZSL Week,[7] was significantly reduced in 2016, and the Board was asked to allocate major funding to this from 2016 onwards. Public health accessibility projects have also been supported by the NZSL Fund. Ongoing concern about the status of NZSL in education was noted earlier in relation to the Human Rights Commission Inquiry (2013). Accordingly, the NZSL Board's strategic plan seeks to ensure NZSL users in schools have sufficient access to NZSL to enable their academic and social development. Primarily, this should be progressed by policy advice to the Ministry of Education; however, in the second round of the NZSL Fund, almost a third of the funding was allocated to education and acquisition-related initiatives such as developing NZSL assessment instruments for Deaf children and for staff. While such projects would appropriately be funded by the state education budget, an independent fund can provide a more agile response to enable innovative work than waiting on the internal work programme of a large government department that has many competing priorities; this is taken into consideration in making exceptions to the general principle of not funding work in areas of core government responsibility.

An inherent challenge for the Board is managing real and perceived conflicts of interest. As in all minority communities, capable individuals tend to have multiple roles and organisational allegiances. Board members and secretariat staff are professionally and voluntarily involved in activities that contribute to NZSL maintenance and promotion, including work that may receive support from the NZSL Fund. This raises the risk of actual and perceived conflict of interest in relation to allocating resources to a community in which material capital, and the power to distribute it, are scarce commodities. Over the Board's first three years of operation it has been necessary to continuously re-visit protocols to mitigate conflict of interest, and to increase participants' reflexivity about how conflicts can manifest and be perceived, within the Board itself, and by the community and government.

The range of project applications to the NZSL Fund illustrates the breadth of perceived opportunities to strengthen the status and vitality of NZSL. Examples include: youth camps and youth mentoring, training and resources for NZSL teachers, NZSL acquisition by families, expanding NZSL language arts and media resources and research. The availability and criteria of the Fund have raised awareness that NZSL can be framed as a central element in addressing diverse community needs and goals. This is positive, but prompts ongoing discussion for the Board over the balance of support for community development activities (such as youth connectedness or Deaf sports), which contribute to language vitality, and more overtly language-focused activities. Examples of 'grey areas' include projects supporting intersecting (deaf) identity groups (e.g. Māori, LGBT, disability); fostering Deaf leadership capacity; and addressing barriers for NZSL users in mental health and employment contexts. Language vitality is so contingent upon individual and collective wellbeing in the Deaf community, that demarcating the scope of what a language fund should rightly be supporting is difficult. Analysis of NZSL Fund project grants between 2015 and 2017 shows that the breakdown into strategic LPP categories is as follows: status, 1%; corpus (documentation, research), 19%; acquisition (L1 and L2), 30%; attitude (critical awareness, promotion), 30%; and access/use, 20%. Work on status and access is mainly progressed by policy advice to government departments, while acquisition is chiefly supported by the education sector.

Reflecting on Effects of Recognition

We have previously observed that outcomes of legal recognition of NZSL fell short of Deaf community hopes (McKee & Manning, 2015), and that the vitality of NZSL is threatened by declining user numbers and weakening conditions for intergenerational language transmission (see

McKee, 2017). Before and after legal recognition, key concerns for the community remain deaf children's access to acquiring and using NZSL in education; both require stronger policy measures, as neither is guaranteed in language or disability law.

Although work on NZSL recognition was enabled by disability policy and is still viewed in that frame by most non-Deaf observers, subsequent analysis shows that Deaf stakeholders perceive the NZSL Act as aligning with claims for indigeneity, cultural identity and legal status (De Bres, 2015; McKee, 2007). Since 2015, state support for NZSL has increased – motivated less by the NZSL Act, and more by the 2013 HRC NZSL Inquiry, which reminded government of the reasons for the NZSL Act and of its obligations under the UN CRPD.

Opening a dialogic space in which community members, government and language experts jointly engage in conversations about language problems was mentioned earlier as a critical step. The formation of an NZSL Board has authorised NZSL users as participants and language managers, rather than lobbyists, in a formal dialogue where differing knowledge of the issues contributes to a joint strategic purpose. For instance, government officials can attend the NZSL Board to brief the Board on the progress of their department, and to seek advice on policy affecting NZSL users. The Board can make representations to core departments such as health and education, which raises administrative awareness of Deaf perspectives and priorities in relation to social policy. Conversely, these exchanges inform Board representatives about the extent and rate of change that can realistically be achieved through government processes. But a conduit such as an appointed Board raises the risk of community members perceiving that another layer of elite decision-makers could further exclude them, and/or it may create unrealistic expectations for resolving many historical issues. The Māori Language Commission, for instance, was envisaged as a conduit between government agencies and the people to advance the language, but a recent review questioned its capacity to achieve this, commenting that 'the lack of coordination of a strategy [across Government sectors] has marginalised their [Commission's] role over time' (Higgins, 2014: 8). The creation of an NZSL Board has brought some additional state investment in the NZSL community, and while it is not a comprehensive solution to implementing recognition, it does open a door directly to policymakers that was previously closed to NZSL users.

Conclusion

It is only in hindsight that it is possible to see how disparate strands of action have woven a path towards NZSL recognition; these include advocacy led by the national Deaf Association, growth of critical language awareness, serendipitous points of international advice and inspiration, strategic collaboration with disability activists and language experts, and the agency of individual leaders who have been in opportune positions to progress change. Of course, this account only highlights prominent events and actors, and leaves out underlying spheres of activity and that have also contributed.

Making NZSL an official language signalled societal recognition of NZSL users, but this status-raising action did not progress practical rights that resolve language-based inequities. The establishment of the NZSL Board as an implementing body, while not perfect, and introducing new challenges, authorises the participation of NZSL advocates in the government policy arena and presents strategic opportunities to use the law as a lever to push for instrumental rights. Current strategy in the new dialogic space around NZSL is guided by a language planning framework that signals the need to maintain the future vitality of the NZSL community, as well as to empower the everyday lives of current users through effective policy measures.

Notes

(1) We use the capitalised form of Deaf in this chapter, in keeping with the NZSL Board's 2017 decision to use capitalised 'D' to refer to adult members of the NZSL community and 'd/Deaf' to refer to children in its documentation.

(2) In the domain of education, Wegerif defines the notion of dialogic space as, 'a space defined by openness and a multiplicity of voices. It is the opening of a shared space of possibilities in which the dialogue is more important than ownership of ideas. Even the identities of the participants enter into the dialogue. This is why people can learn from dialogue.' (Wegerif, 2016). LPP scholar, Joseph Lo Bianco applies this term to contentious language planning contexts in which officials, minority language community members and academic experts cooperate to develop an understanding of each other's perspective on critical language issues and plan how to address them.

(3) A Bill is the draft form of a proposed law introduced to parliament as the first step towards being passed as an Act of Parliament.

(4) See http://www.legislation.govt.nz/act/public/2006/0018/latest/whole.html – DLM372786. (accessed 24 January 2019).

(5) For example, the recommendations of Fitzgerald & Associate's 2010 report on NZSL users in schools.

(6) See http://www.firstsigns.co.nz. (accessed 24 January 2019).

(7) See http://deaf.org.nz/nzslw. (accessed 24 January 2019).

References

Benton, R.A. (2015) Perfecting the partnership: Revitalising the Māori language in New Zealand education and society 1987–2014. *Language, Culture and Curriculum* 28 (2), 99–112. DOI: 10.1080/07908318.2015.1025001.

Dalziel, L. (2001) *The New Zealand Disability Strategy*. Wellington: Ministry of Health.

Deaf Aotearoa New Zealand (2011) Symbolic gestures do not support Deaf. Deaf Aotearoa New Zealand press release. 6 October 2011. See http://www.scoop.co.nz/stories/GE1110/S00027/symbolic-gestures-do-not-support-Deaf.htm. (accessed 24 January 2019).

Deaf Education Aotearoa New Zealand (2005) *National Plan for the Education of Deaf and Hearing Impaired Children and Young People in Aotearoa/New Zealand* (2nd revised version). Unpublished policy paper. See https://2ears2hear.files.wordpress.com/2012/09/national-plan-05-doc-1.pdf (accessed 24 January 2019).

De Bres, J. (2015) The hierarchy of minority languages in New Zealand. *Journal of Multilingual and Multicultural Development* 36 (7), 677–693.

Dugdale, P.O. (2001) *Talking Hands, Listening Eyes: The History of the Deaf Association of New Zealand*. Auckland: Deaf Association of New Zealand.

Fitzgerald & Associates (2010) *Scoping Support for New Zealand Sign Language Users Accessing the Curriculum Part II: A New Zealand Overview*. Report prepared for the Ministry of Education. See http://www.educationcounts.govt.nz/publications/special_education/scoping-support-for-new-zealand-sign-language-users-accessing-the-curriculum-part-ii-a-new-zealand-overview/5.-numbers-of-Deaf-students-who-use-sign-language-in-new-zealand. (accessed 24 January 2019).

Higgins, R. (2014) *Review of Te Reo Mauri Ora*. Prepared for Te Māngai Pāho (Māori Broadcasting Agency). http://www.parliament.nz/resource/0000182099 (accessed 24 January 2019).

Human Rights Commission (2013) *A New Era in the Right to Sign. He Houhanga Rongo te Tika ki te ReoTuri. Report of the New Zealand Sign Language Enquiry*. Wellington: New Zealand Human Rights Commission.

Justice and Electoral Select Committee (2005) *New Zealand Sign Language Bill, as Reported from the Justice and Electoral Committee, 1–19*. Wellington: House of Representatives.

Kelston Deaf Education Centre (2015) NZSL@School: Frequently asked questions for schools. http://www.kdec.school.nz/Media/pdf/NZSLSchoolFAQInformationforSchoolsSept2015.pdf. (accessed 24 January 2019).

Levitt, D. (1986) *Introduction to New Zealand Sign Language*. Auckland: Deaf Association and National Foundation for the Deaf.

McKee, R.M. (2007) The eyes have it! Our third official language – New Zealand Sign Language. *Journal of New Zealand Studies* NS 4–5, 129–148.

McKee, R.M. (2017) Assessing the vitality of New Zealand Sign Language. *Sign Language Studies* 17 (3), 322–362.

McKee, R. and Manning, V. (2015) Effects of language planning and policy on language rights and the vitality of New Zealand Sign Language. *Sign Language Studies* 15 (4), 473–497.

New Zealand House of Representatives (2006) *Parliamentary Debates (Hansard)*, vol. 630, 21 March–4 May 2006. Wellington: New Zealand House of Representatives. https://drive.google.com/file/d/0B1Iwfzv-Mt3CZWRXV3ZZMUxfMGM/view (accessed 24 January 2019).

New Zealand Human Rights Commission (2013) *A New Era in the Right to Sign. Report of the New Zealand Sign Language Enquiry*. Wellington, NZ: Human Rights Commission.

New Zealand Sign Language Bill (2004) See https://www.parliament.nz/en/pb/bills-and-laws/bills-proposed-laws/document/00DBHOH_BILL6011_1/new-zealand-sign-language-bill. (accessed 24 January 2019).

NZSL Board (2018). *NZSL Strategy 2018–2023*. Wellington: Office for Disability Issues. https://www.odi.govt.nz/nzsl/nzsl-strategy-2018-2023/ (accessed 24 January 2019).

Office for Disability Issues (undated (a)) *NZSL Act 2006 History*. See http://www.odi.govt.nz/nzsl/act-2006/history-of-the-new-zealand-sign-language-act/. (accessed 24 January 2019).

Office for Disability Issues (undated (b)) *NZSL Act Review 2011 Report*. See http://www.odi.govt.nz/nzsl/act-2006/nzsl-act-review-2011/. (accessed 24 January 2019).

Office for Disability Issues (undated (c)) *About the NZSL Board*. See http://www.odi.govt. nz/nzsl/about-Board/. (accessed 24 January 2019).

Office for Disability Issues (undated (d)) *Terms of Reference: Purpose*. http://www.odi. govt.nz/nzsl/about-Board/nzsl-tor/.(accessed 24 January 2019).

Office for Disability Issues (2016) *NZSL Board Action Plan 2016–2018*. https://www.odi. govt.nz/nzsl/about-board/action-plan-2016-2018/. (accessed 24 January 2019).

Spolsky, B. (2009) *Language Management*. Cambridge: Cambridge University Press.

The Royal Society of New Zealand (2013) *Languages in Aotearoa New Zealand*. Wellington: The Royal Society of New Zealand.

Wegerif, R. (2016) What is dialogic space? See http://www.rupertwegerif.name/blog/ what-is-dialogic-space.(accessed 24 January 2019).

Wolf, A. (2005) *The New Zealand Sign Language Bill (Case Program)*. Parkville, Victoria: The Australia and New Zealand School of Government.

15 The Legal Recognition of Icelandic Sign Language: Meeting Deaf People's Expectations?

Valgerður Stefánsdóttir, Ari Páll Kristinsson and Júlía G. Hreinsdóttir

Introduction

The campaign for the legal recognition of Icelandic Sign Language (*Íslenskt táknmál*, ITM) had been ongoing for more than 20 years when Act No. 61/2011 'Respecting the Status of the Icelandic Language and Icelandic Sign Language' (hereafter, the Act) entered into force on 7 June 2011. Members of the Althing, the Icelandic parliament, noted that it constituted a significant reformulation of rights and a crucial victory in a decade-long campaign by speakers[1] of sign language (Althingi, 2011a). The Icelandic Association of the Deaf (hereafter, the Association) equated the recognition of their language with recognition of themselves as people and members of Icelandic society (Visir, 2011). The members of the Association were confident they had obtained instrumental rights and social mobility and, most importantly for them, that the legal recognition granted deaf children educational linguistic and language acquisition rights.

This chapter chronicles the campaign for the legal recognition of ITM, the progression through the Icelandic Parliament, and discusses expectations of the recognition expressed by key people in the ITM community, and whether the legal recognition satisfied their expectations. It is the first published account of the campaign for the legislation on ITM, the aspirations of the ITM community and the outcomes of the legislation. Our data consist of interviews with one former deaf member of Parliament, as well as six chairs of the Association who served from 1983 to the present day.[2] Apart from the interviews, data consist of documentation from the Association, the Communication Centre for the Deaf and Hard of Hearing, the Icelandic Ministry of Education, Althing, the Icelandic Sign Language Council and other official bodies in Iceland.

Our findings suggest that for interpersonal communication, the Act is a significant step towards ensuring the status of ITM as a language with the same status as Icelandic. However, the findings also suggest the Act is not sufficient to meet the expectations of the deaf community. This chapter demonstrates that in legislation, judgments, education and administrative practices, ITM is still associated with disability and impairment. Although it aims to ensure the status of ITM as equal to Icelandic for interpersonal communication, in practice this status is not guaranteed, and people face linguistic discrimination.

ITM, Icelandic and Other Languages in Iceland

With its 340,000 citizens, Iceland is a small, sovereign island state in the North Atlantic. Icelandic is the only national and official language of Iceland (de facto and *de jure*).

Icelandic is a Nordic language most closely related to Faroese, and to some Western Norwegian varieties. It is a relatively homogeneous language with little geographical and only minimal social variation. Icelanders are thus, by and large, accustomed to only minimal variation in language use.

Icelandic is the first/native language of about 90% of the population of Iceland. The traditional homogeneity of the Icelandic language and the relatively straightforward correspondence between the population and the national language has changed rapidly in recent years, as the cultural and ethnic profile of Icelanders has become more multifaceted. About 10% of the present inhabitants of Iceland are speakers of recent immigrant languages such as Polish, Lithuanian, Thai and English.

While there is greater language diversity in Iceland than ever before in the history of the nation, ITM is the only indigenous minority language in Iceland. Thus, language minorities in Iceland fall into two main types of language communities: (1) ITM speakers; and (2) speakers of immigrant languages, among them several foreign sign languages. Their official status, or lack thereof, determines the position of these two categories of minority language communities. It is not unusual in Northern Europe for governments to treat indigenous minority languages differently from native languages of 'more recent' groups in a polity, such as the languages of immigrants (Kristinsson, 2017: 26–28). Thus, while ITM is a recognized language in Iceland, Polish, for example is not, even though it has 50 times more speakers than ITM.

ITM is the first language of about 250 deaf people in Iceland (Thorvaldsdóttir & Stefánsdóttir, 2015). In addition, about 50 deaf immigrants speak ITM and a variety of different sign languages. Many more hearing people have acquired communication skills in ITM, for example, relatives of deaf people, teachers, researchers and so on. While recent estimates of the number of these L2 signers vary, we are inclined to follow

Thorvaldsdóttir and Stefánsdóttir (2015) who refer to 1000 to 1500 hearing signers in Iceland. For communication within the public sphere, deaf people have the legal right to sign language interpreting services, for example in education, in the healthcare system and for communication with public institutions. The authorities offer ITM speakers 3000 interpreter hours per year or 10 hours per year per person, free of charge, for communication in the private sphere, such as for employment and for attending various meetings or gatherings.

Knowledge of and proficiency in English is widespread in Iceland, with minority languages only serving a limited function. Icelandic is the principal language of the more intimate domains in Iceland (Fishman, 1972), and also by far still the most common language for communication, publishing, administration and culture (Hilmarsson-Dunn & Kristinsson, 2013). As the national language, it is also the language of instruction in Icelandic schools at all levels (Kristinsson & Bernhardsson, 2014).

The International Standardization Organization (ISO) assigned the three-letter code 'icl' to Icelandic Sign Language, but the Icelandic deaf community and ITM researchers in Iceland prefer another abbreviation: ITM. This is an abbreviation of the Icelandic name of the language: '*Íslenskt táknmál*'. The vitality of both Icelandic and ITM has been estimated using the Expanded Graded Intergenerational Disruption Scale (EGIDS) – the 13-level framework for assessing language vitality (Fishman, 1991; Lewis & Simons, 2010). The Ethnologue, which applies the EGIDS scale, lists Icelandic as a grade 1 language (National), while it grades ITM as 6b (Threatened) (Ethnologue, 2017) (for another sign language graded at level 6b, New Zealand Sign Language, see McKee, 2017).

Implicit Recognition of ITM in Education

In 1999, the Icelandic National Curriculum Guide for Compulsory Schools mentioned ITM as the first language of deaf pupils. The curriculum guide from 2013 states that a solid knowledge of Icelandic and ITM is one of the mainstays of a solid education and the teaching of both languages enhances the role of language as the medium of thinking. The curriculum goes further than that, stating ITM is no less critical than Icelandic as a key to societal participation. It also provides to organize the bilingual school subject of ITM and Icelandic as an integral subject similar to Icelandic as a mother tongue, with education in language and literature and, not least, in usage. In addition, all compulsory school subjects should integrate practice in ITM, written and spoken Icelandic (if children use it for communication). The curriculum guide states that sign language pupils should have an opportunity to use ITM in their studies in all subjects, as far as possible, and receive proper sign language interpretation. It recognizes ITM as a daily communication language and language of instruction, in addition to Icelandic, or at least written Icelandic. At the completion of compulsory school, pupils should be able to recognize their status and responsibility as language users. In grades 1–7, the curriculum prescribes a total of 1800 minutes per week in the reference timetable for Icelandic, Icelandic as a second language or ITM (The Icelandic national curriculum guide for compulsory schools -with Subjects Areas, 2013). This has to be seen in the context of the Compulsory School Act (2008), which has the goal for deaf and hard-of-hearing pupils to be bilingual.

The only Deaf school in Iceland closed in 2002. Currently, *Hlíðaskóli*, a mainstream elementary school in the capital Reykjavik, is the only school which specializes in education for deaf children. The school has 450–480 hearing pupils and 12–17 deaf pupils. A recent evaluation report on *Hlíðaskóli* (Evaluation – Ytra mat, 2016) defines the school as 'a bilingual school where Icelandic and the sign language of the deaf should be equal'. However, in practice, Icelandic and ITM are not equal within the school since it does not offer an ITM environment and the children are far from enjoying active bilingualism (Stefánsdóttir *et al.*, 2014). According to the same evaluation report, a Sign Language Department in the school 'provides hearing impaired and deaf pupils with specialized teaching and services where they are included in general classes'. The ideologies projected in this text and the stance towards ITM positions ITM pupils as disabled, needing specialized services. The pupils receive services to be able to follow 'general classes', and are not approached as a group speaking a legitimate language. The Icelandic Sign Language Council has expressed concerns about the viability of ITM if a school that specializes in education for deaf children cannot offer an ITM environment fundamental for language development (The Icelandic Sign Language Council, 2013). The hearing children in grades 1–7 can take one lesson (20–40 minutes) in ITM per week. In grades 8–10, ITM is an optional subject. For comparison, the subject 'foreign languages' (i.e. English and Danish) is assigned 800–900 minutes per week in grades 8–10. Five deaf pupils from grades 1–5 attend joint Icelandic reading classes in ITM for 360 minutes and ITM classes for 80–160 minutes a week. ITM students in grades 6–10 study ITM for 80 minutes a week. Deaf history and culture form a part of ITM instruction. Every other school subject is taught in Icelandic with the aid of an interpreter or a deaf teacher. The vast majority of teaching materials is in Icelandic. No teaching materials exist on ITM and Icelandic for ITM pupils. Teachers cannot obtain the necessary education to teach bilingual pupils in accordance with the national curriculum.

The Campaign for the Legal Recognition of ITM

This section is based on interviews with one former deaf Member of Parliament as well as six presidents of the Association who served from 1983 to the present day. The interviews were filmed, conducted in ITM and translated into Icelandic.

1983–1987: From the Deaf Club to early interpreter training

When Vilhjálmur Vilhjálmsson served as president of the Association between 1983 and 1987, no interpreting services were in place. The Association was a club where people played cards and chatted with only cursory discussions about the recognition of ITM. In 1974, the Association joined the Nordic Council of the Deaf (DNR). DNR's goal was to advocate for the equality of deaf people and promote collaboration between the Nordic countries. In 1985, the DNR decided to hold the 1986 Nordic Culture Festival in Iceland to empower deaf people in the country. The DNR requested seven Icelandic sign language interpreters for the festival, who had to be trained in ITM at a short notice. From September 1985 to June 1986, three deaf students of the Deaf school (including Hreinsdóttir, the third author) instructed a group of 10 people.

At the time, neither the students in interpreting nor the sign language instructors were aware of the difference between the grammar of ITM and Icelandic and could not understand why interpreted sentences became unintelligible even when all the signs were correct. They started to become aware of the distinct grammar of sign language and the different structures of ITM and Icelandic. Eventually, in June 1986, four sign language interpreters graduated (including V. Stefánsdóttir, the first author).

From this point on, nascent interpreting services began to evolve. Vilhjálmsson believes the Nordic Culture Festival, and the instructions provided by the Association, were a watershed moment in the history of ITM, both for the advancement and promotion of the language.

1989: The teaching of sign language begins to evolve

From 1986 to 1989, Hreinsdóttir studied at the School of Social Education and V. Stefánsdóttir, then a secondary teacher at the Deaf school, was her interpreter. The principal decided to offer sign language interpreting as an optional subject at the school and hired Hreinsdóttir and V. Stefánsdóttir to teach ITM and interpreting. For the planning and teaching of sign language and the assessment of learning outcomes, she also sought assistance from Brita Hansen and Asger Bergmann at the Communication Center for the Deaf in Denmark (KC). At this time, people started discussing the recognition of ITM, and an idea began to form to set up a communication centre similar to KC.

In 1987, the year after the Nordic Culture Festival, Haukur Vilhjálmsson, V. Vilhjálmsson's brother, became the president of the Association. He had studied at Gallaudet University in Washington, DC and there had become accustomed to using sign language interpreters to access services. Under his leadership, the Association began to strengthen their advocacy, emphasizing equality of opportunities, ITM and interpreting services in ITM. When Bergmann came to Iceland, H. Vilhjálmsson used the opportunity to ask him whether he thought it more sensible for the Association to begin advocating for the recognition of ITM or first establish a new communication centre. Bergmann advised the Association to focus on a communication centre, because this could be used to develop the required knowledge and arguments for the recognition of ITM.

The idea of establishing a communication centre found broad support by politicians and stakeholders. The centre was to conduct research in ITM, teach ITM and provide interpreting services. H. Vilhjálmsson emphasized that the preparation for the communication centre, and its establishment, were a prerequisite for the work undertaken for the legal recognition of ITM.

In the late 1980s, the recognition of ITM and the right to participate in society through interpreting services became the Association's leading cause. In 1989, the government made its first proposal on services for deaf people with a regulation under the Act on the Affairs of Disabled People. According to the proposal, the institution tasked with providing these services should be under the Ministry of Social Affairs. Subsequently, the Association requested a meeting with the Minister of Education, because they thought the issues the proposal addressed all involved language rather than disability and thus should not fall under the Ministry of Social Affairs. Deaf representatives emphasized the exclusion of signers from Icelandic society as well as educational and other barriers. They further emphasized that to improve the status of deaf people, it was imperative to bolster sign language interpreting services, research into ITM, teaching in ITM and counselling for parents.

1990s: The Communication Center for the Deaf and Hard-of Hearing

Ultimately, it was the Minister of Education, Gestsson, who submitted the bill on the communication centre. It is clear from the 1990 Communication Center Act that the centre was considered by the government to be a language institute. The notes attached to the bill state that the centre was intended to conduct sign language research in collaboration with linguists because research was seen as a precondition for teaching sign language and preparing for and teaching sign language interpreters (Althing, 1990b). In a speech proposing the Bill to Althing, Gestsson stated 'It can be said that this bill on the Communication Center is actually the first step in recognizing the sign language as a language for expression in Iceland next to Icelandic, the native language. This is, of course, a significant step, a step towards equality, for deaf people in Iceland' (Althing, 1990a).[3] The Deaf and Hard of Hearing Communication Centre Act thus implicitly accorded ITM legal status and considered the speakers of ITM a linguistic and cultural minority and not (only) a group of persons with disabilities.

The minister appointed V. Stefánsdóttir as manager and B. Stefánsdóttir as the centre's first chair, which she remained until 1996. B. Stefánsdóttir's appointment was instrumental in the process towards recognizing ITM. She studied sign language linguistics at Stockholm University, taught sign language at the centre and later became president of the Association of the Deaf. She thus took a direct and active part in the fight for the recognition of ITM.

Lárusdóttir served as the Association's president from 1991 to 1996. According to her, during that time, the Association advocated for instrumental language rights rather than for status recognition of ITM. For example, ITM speakers still only had limited access to interpreters. Lárusdóttir noted she learned about the concept of recognition of sign languages at DNR meetings, as well as about the perspective that recognition and the resulting instrumental rights were key to participating in society at large.

From 1992 to 1994, the centre engaged in discussions with the University of Iceland on teaching sign language and interpreting at the university's linguistics department. It was granted a special appropriation from the Ministry of Education to fund a trial ITM interpreter instruction project from 1994 to 1998, and provided the university with a teaching manager, Svavarsdóttir, and teachers for the courses. A total of 14 interpreters matriculated.

In 2001, the university established a teaching programme in sign language linguistics and interpreter training at the Faculty of Humanities along with other languages, and in January 2002 appointed a lecturer in Icelandic Sign Language. For the Deaf Association, this was yet another victory towards the explicit recognition of ITM.

1996–2003: Campaign for language legislation

During B. Stefánsdóttir's time as president (1996–2006), linguistic human rights were still violated in many areas. She describes ITM speakers during that time as living in a glass cage: seeing everything that was offered, but having no access to it. B. Stefánsdóttir observed that the Nordic countries, except for Finland, focused on gaining the right to full access to services, but did not advocate for specific language legislation. In Finland, however, the deaf association successfully advocated for the recognition of their sign languages and in 1995 'sign language' was recognized in the Finnish constitution (De Meulder, 2016). This recognition inspired the campaigners in Iceland to seek to gain recognition of ITM in the constitution or in special language laws.

In 1997, the Association hired a lawyer to work with them on legal issues and to file lawsuits when ITM speakers did not have access to services. This attorney stressed the importance of having ITM legally recognized because it was impossible to appeal in a court of law without legislation protecting language rights. Moreover, he argued that legal recognition would be a prerequisite for other rights. The CEO of the Association between 1997 and 2005 described the campaign methods as consisting of four main strategies:

(1) Marketing and advertisement. ITM and the manual alphabet were advertised on bus stops. The media published news, articles and interviews concerning ITM.
(2) Outreach. Members of Althing were provided with information and offered courses in ITM.
(3) Community work. The Association consulted club members, listened to the complaints of people, informed individuals of their rights, and encouraged the community to request an interpreter to communicate with any public entity, and to lodge complaints with the CEO when not provided with an interpreter.
(4) Follow-up on the administration procedures when the Association found the members' linguistic rights not respected.

The Association searched for good cases, sued and appealed whenever the decision of an authority gave cause for complaint. For example, it sued the National Broadcasting Service for not providing interpreters for an election debate; and the City of Reykjavík for not providing a deaf parent with an interpreter in an interview with a teacher. When authorities rejected paying for interpretation services it lodged appeals with ministries and directorates. In one year there were almost 30 Administrative Procedure Appeals based on non-discrimination and the equality clause of the constitution. When funding for interpreter services was exhausted, an appeal was handed over to parliamentarians. During a demonstration in October 2004 in front of the Althing, B. Stefánsdóttir addressed protesters while they blew whistles non-stop (Figure 15.1). The sound was heard in the live broadcast and got a lot of media attention.

Gestsson, the former Minister of Education, now sitting in opposition, continued supporting the campaign for the recognition of ITM in Althing. He drafted several proposals in three legislative sessions (1996–1999), asking Althing to task the Minister of Education with preparing a bill recognizing ITM as the first language of deaf people in Iceland. When the Education Committee finally discussed the proposal, it noted the absence of the recognition of Icelandic, in a national law or in the constitution, as the first language of the Icelandic speakers. The Committee opined that the preparation for the recognition of ITM required due diligence as its effect would be broad. This is probably a key problem for any legislation of this type. To address the issue the Education Committee recommended tasking the Minister of Education with examining the legal status of deaf people in Iceland compared to that of deaf people in the neighbouring countries (Althing, 1999). In March 2000, the Minister of Education presented the results of the report. It stated that the legal foundation of ITM in the school

Figure 15.1 October 2004 demonstration in front of the Althing. The placard reads: 'Specific language legislation on the Icelandic Sign Language Immediately!!!'

system was strong, but deaf people's right to sign language interpreting services needed to be strengthened. Subsequently, a committee was established consisting of lawyers from three different ministries to work on recommendations. The committee concluded its activities at the end of September 2001. It prepared a bill on sign language services addressing the role and organization of the Communication Centre as a sign language centre, tasked with research, teaching, preparation of learning content and providing interpreting services in all areas. However, the minister believed there remained unsolved concerns related to the proposed legislation. Most notably, it remained unclear who would cover the expenses arising from such services (Althing, 2002). In the end, the bill was not proposed.

2003–2007: Campaign for equality and against discrimination

On 1 October 2003, Sigurlín Margrét Sigurðardóttir (Liberal Party) became the first deaf member of Althing. On 28 November already, Sigurðardóttir proposed a bill on ITM with 16 other members from the Liberal Party, the Left-Green Movement and the Social Democratic Alliance, all of which were in the opposition. Sigurðardóttir used the British Equality Act as a model for the bill on ITM. According to the bill, ITM should be recognized as the first language of deaf, hard-of-hearing and deafblind Icelanders. It ascribed equal status to ITM and Icelandic as a medium of expression for interpersonal communication and prohibited discrimination based on language. The bill also addressed the rights of deaf people to learn ITM and retain the services of sign language interpreters, the training of sign language interpreters, research on ITM, the promotion of the language and the subtitling of television content. At the same time another bill was proposed to amend 11 acts regarding the right to use ITM in communication with the government, municipalities and their institutions. The Education Committee considered the bills and requested comments from 97 different parties. A total of 16 comments from ministries, municipalities, universities, institutions and non-governmental organizations were received. All were in favour of recognizing ITM, although again, questions were raised about the financial implications of the proposed legislation. Althing did not find time to discuss the bills and they were both proposed again in 2004 and 2007.

Hjördís Anna Haraldsdóttir became president of the Association in April 2007. One of her first tasks in office was presenting a petition to the Speaker of Althing signed by 2859 people pressing the government to recognize ITM and adopt Sigurðardóttir's bill. The petition noted that deaf people had limited access to society and that this was impeding their opportunities to become active citizens. The proposed legislation was said to recognize deaf people's right to exist and open their access to society (Althing, 2007). However, Althing rejected the bill owing to excessive expenses resulting from it.

2004: Cooperation with the Icelandic Language Institute

In October 2004, representatives from the Association, the Communication Centre and the Icelandic Language Institute, which at that point housed the Icelandic Language Council, set up a new collaboration. The Icelandic Language Council advises the government on issues relating to the Icelandic language in an academic context and makes recommendations to the minister regarding language policy. As a result of this collaboration, in January 2005 the Ministry of Education appointed a committee to address the promotion of ITM. The group was tasked with making proposals on how to strengthen the status of ITM and to decide whether it could be possible to establish a Council on Icelandic Sign Language. A representative of the ministry served as chair, the Association appointed two members, and the Communication Centre and the university selected one representative each (Stefánsson & Kristjánsson, 2005). In May 2005, the committee delivered recommendations to the ministry on legislation concerning a Council on Icelandic Sign Language. Pursuant to the recommendations, the role of the Council on Icelandic Sign Language would be to promote and protect ITM as well as consult and collaborate with stakeholders. However, the ministry did not adopt the committee's recommendations.

The committee's work did have impact though, because when the Icelandic Language Council provided the ministry with recommendations on Icelandic language policy, it noted the importance of ensuring the legal status of ITM next to Icelandic. In November 2008, Gunnarsdóttir, the Minister of Education, proposed a resolution in Althing to adopt the recommendations of the Icelandic Language Council on language policy as public policy in matters regarding the Icelandic language (Althing, 2008). Althing passed the proposal in March 2009. Following the council's recommendations, a committee of lawyers was appointed to address the legal status of Icelandic and ITM. The committee concluded it was not opportune to add provisions on the languages to the constitution, but that it was imperative to develop general laws to promote them. One of the 10 articles in the committee's recommendations concerned ITM.

2009–2010: A new government and an Executive Committee on services to deaf and hard-of-hearing people

In 2009, a new left wing government was formed. The new minister of Education, Science and Culture, Jakobsdóttir, appointed an Executive Committee on services for deaf and hard-of-hearing people to survey the status of the group, analyse existing data and policies, make recommendations for future arrangements in coordinated services and propose the necessary legislative changes (Jakobsdóttir & Guðmundsson, 2010). The discussions in the committee increased the ministry's understanding about the status of ITM and the importance of legal recognition. Also not unimportant was that Svavarsdóttir, a former employee of the Communication Centre and a teaching manager in the sign language studies at the university, was now a minister in the government.

The Act

On 27 May 2011 Althing adopted the 'Act respecting the status of the Icelandic language and Icelandic sign language'. The Act consists of 13 articles, of which five address the promotion of ITM.[4] Article 3 confirms that:

> Icelandic sign language is the first language of those who must rely on it for expression and communication, and of their children. It must be fostered and supported by public authorities.

The article further states:

> All persons who have a need for sign language must be given the opportunity to learn Icelandic sign language and to use it from the beginning of their language acquisition, or as soon as deafness, hearing impairment or deaf-blindness has been diagnosed. Their immediate family members shall have the same right.

The wording 'those who must rely on' and 'who have a need for' and the context 'as soon as deafness, hearing impairment or deaf-blindness has been diagnosed' is a weakness of the law in ensuring linguistic rights for ITM speakers, especially children, because of the connotations with the need for medical diagnosis. It associates ITM with impairment instead of its status as a legitimate language. When ITM is paired with impairment in the legislation, an ideological context is created. The condition constricting ITM to people who must 'rely on it' entails that it is a matter of judgment, for example, of medical personnel, teachers or parents, whether children may be granted access to ITM (Stefánsdóttir *et al.*, 2014). De Meulder and Murray (2017) have argued that if Sign Language Peoples are regarded on medical considerations only, this confounds the interpretation of their language rights.

Article 5 addresses, among other things, the obligation of the Icelandic government and local authorities to 'facilitate the development, study, teaching and wider use of Icelandic sign language' and furthermore 'to provide other support for cultural activities and formal and informal education for deaf, hearing-impaired and deaf-blind people.' De Meulder (2015) has pointed out how unusual it is for existing recognition laws to mention cultural recognition as the focus is mainly on language recognition. The Ministry of Education, Culture and Science gave some support to cultural festivals on The Day of ITM in the early years, but so far, no other support to culture has been granted.

Article 7 addresses The Icelandic Sign Language Council:

> The Minister shall appoint five members, and an equal number of alternates, to the Icelandic Sign Language Council for a four-year term. The School of Humanities of the University of Iceland, the Communication Centre for the Deaf and Hard of Hearing, special interest groups for the deaf and hard of hearing in Iceland [in practice, the Association, note of the authors] and the Association of Local Authorities in Iceland shall be consulted on appointments to the Council. The Minister shall select the Chair and Vice-Chair of the Icelandic Sign Language Council.

There are no regulations about the number of deaf or hearing members on the council. The current council comprises three hearing and two deaf members. Because the hearing members are not all fluent in ITM, interpreters are present during all meetings. The chair (from May 2017), Guðmundsdóttir, is a hearing person with a deaf mother, and a speech-language pathologist. The vice chair is a professor of Icelandic linguistics. Other members include an assistant professor in sign language studies, the Icelandic Association of the Deaf President and a deaf teacher at Hlíðaskóli Primary School.

The role of the council 'shall be to advise public authorities on any matter concerning Icelandic sign language, and to facilitate the promotion of Icelandic sign language and its use in Icelandic society.' From 2011 to 2016, V. Stefánsdóttir was chair of the council. During those years, the emphasis was on acquisition planning, attitude planning (Reagan, 2010) and on cultural promotion. The council's tasks mainly consisted of writing letters and recommendations to public authorities on any matter concerning Icelandic Sign Language, publishing reports on the status of ITM and celebrating the Day of ITM on 11 February. From 2017, Guðmundsdóttir served as chair. The emphasis was now on collecting data on services and use of ITM, from institutions, educational boards and schools in Iceland.[5] The information gathered served as a basis for the council's recommendations to the Ministry of Education, Science and Culture. For the Day of ITM in 2018, the goal was to get media attention and visibility of ITM through the Icelandic National Broadcasting Service (RUV). Indeed, the current chair considers the translation of Icelandic programmes into ITM as one of the most significant challenges for the deaf community (Guðmundsdóttir, 2018). However, the language council receives insufficient financial support to achieve its goals: less than €23,000 a year at the time of writing.

Article 9 covers 'Interpreting and sign language interpreting before public authorities.' Article 13 states the duties of central and local authorities and the status of Icelandic sign language.

> Central and local authorities shall ensure that all those who need Icelandic sign-language services have access to them. Central and local authorities shall be responsible for preserving, developing and facilitating the use of Icelandic sign language. Emphasis shall be given to enabling Icelandic sign language to develop academic terminology in different fields and put it to use.
>
> Icelandic sign language has the same status as Icelandic as a medium of expression for interpersonal communication, and discrimination between persons on the basis of which of the two languages they use is prohibited.

Comments on the bill mention that the 2011 State Budget does not provide for an increase in expenditure. This inevitably influenced the unanimous adoption of the Act, but also means there was no earmarked budget for implementation of the law. It was further stated that subsequent provisions will be enacted regarding the obligations of the authorities to ensure access for all those who need Icelandic Sign Language (Althing, 2011b).

The Expectations and Experience Gained from the Enactment

Everyone interviewed for this chapter expected the Act to provide people whose language is ITM with the same language rights as of those whose language is Icelandic. Informants also expressed the hope that ITM would be become part of Iceland's cultural heritage and respected by the Icelandic community. The interviewees noted that while the Act had given them appreciation and recognition for who they are it had not conferred them the rights expected to follow from legal recognition.

Indeed, the law recognizing ITM seems to be insufficient. Since the adoption of the Act, no provisions have been enacted on the obligations of the authorities to ensure access for all those who need ITM as stated in the comments to the bill for Act No. 61/2011. ITM speakers do not feel they have equal civil rights. The interviewees noted that the position of children is the most severe and pointed out that they are not afforded the language rights that the Act was hoped to provide. They further commented that ITM is not equal to Icelandic in everyday communications and in employment. According to De Meulder (2016), the right to language acquisition and receiving services directly in a signed language (without an interpreter) is a conspicuous weakness of sign language legislation around the world. The Icelandic legislation is no exception.

Since the Act has entered into force, two lawsuits have been filed against the Communication Centre for refusing to grant interpreting services free of charge when its funds were exhausted. However, the Act was not used in the arguments to ensure the right to sign language services or in the judgment in the cases. On the contrary, interpreting services between ITM and Icelandic were considered to be a social service and ITM to be an aid for disabled and sick persons (Reykjavík District Court, 2015; The Supreme Court of Iceland, 2017). The right to designated services for people with a disability and the right to interpreter services for people speaking another language is still conflated.

All interviewees pointed out that language ideologies were a significant impediment to attaining recognition. According to Eiríksdóttir, the current president of the Association, the public and the administration do not understand what ITM is, the value it has for deaf people and the significant role it plays in the lives of its speakers for their identity and education, and do not understand how the language is learned or acquired. She also notes it is significant who the responsible authorities are, because with every new authority, priorities might change.

De Meulder and Murray (2017) note that when financial obligations do not follow recognition, when public practices do not change and when sign language is not visible in the public arena, the participation of Sign Language Peoples remains hindered. As for now, this seems to be the case in Iceland, despite legislation recognizing ITM.

Notes

(1) The general custom in Icelandic discourse, which we will be following throughout the chapter, is to use the expression *to speak* ITM (tala táknmál). We are aware that the use of this expression can be controversial. 'Speakers' in this case does not refer to spoken language or to the use of voice but to the use of a language (ITM or Icelandic) in the 'here and now' communication in juxtaposition to text. In the discourse we distinguish between signed languages and voiced languages (i.e. not spoken).

(2) The interviews were conducted in ITM by Júlía Guðný Hreinsdóttir, the third author.

(3) Translations of notes and speeches from the Althing website from Icelandic to English
     was done by the authors.
(4) The official English translation of the law is available at: https://www.government.
     is/media/menntamalaraduneyti-media/media/frettir2015/Thyding-log-um-stodu-islen
     skrar-tungu-og-islensks-taknmals-desember-2015.pdf (last accessed 28 January 2019).
(5) It is not clear whether the information gathered focuses only on the use of ITM in
     services designated for deaf people or if the services are aimed at hearing signers as
     well (i.e. children of deaf adults (CODAs)).

References

Act No. 61/2011 (2011) Respecting the Status of the Icelandic Language and Icelandic Sign
     Language. See https://www.government.is/media/menntamalaraduneyti-media/
     media/frettir2015/Thyding-log-um-stodu-islenskrar-tungu-og-islensks-taknmals-
     desember-2015.pdf (last accessed 28 January 2019).
Althing (1990a) See http://www.althingi.is/altext/113/r0/0318.html (last accessed 28
     January 2019).
Althing (1990b) See http://www.althingi.is/altext/113/s/0102.html (last accessed 28
     January 2019).
Althing (1999) See https://www.althingi.is/altext/123/s/1137.html (last accessed 28
     January 2019).
Althing (2002) See https://www.althingi.is/altext/128/12/r11152548.sgml (last accessed
     28 January 2019).
Althing (2007) See https://www.althingi.is/altext/erindi/133/133-1647.pdf (last accessed
     28 January 2019).
Althing (2008) See http://www.althingi.is/altext/136/s/0248.html (last accessed 28
     January 2019).
Althing (2011a) See http://www.althingi.is/altext/upptokur/hlusta/?lidur=lid20110527
     T145411&end=2011-05-27T15:01:53 (last accessed 28 January 2019).
Althing (2011b) See https://www.althingi.is/altext/139/s/0870.html (last accessed 28
     January 2019).
Codes for the representation of names of languages – Part 3: Alpha-3 code for comprehen-
     sive coverage of languages. See https://www.iso.org/standard/39534.html (last
     accessed 28 January 2019).
Compulsory School Act (2008) See https://www.government.is/media/menntamalara-
     duneyti-media/media/law-and-regulations/Compulsory-School-Act-No.-91-2008.pdf
     (last accessed 28 January 2019).
Deaf and Hard of Hearing Communication Centre Act (1990) See https://www.government.is
     /media/menntamalaraduneyti-media/media/frettatengt2016/Log-nr.-129_1990-um-
     Samskiptamidstod-heyrnarlausra-og-heyrnarskertra---ENSKA.pdf (last accessed 28
     January 2019).
De Meulder, M. (2015) The legal recognition of sign languages. *Sign Language Studies* 15
     (4), 498–506.
De Meulder, M. (2016) Promotion in times of endangerment: The Sign Language Act in
     Finland. *Language Policy* 16, 189–208.
De Meulder, M. and Murray, J.J. (2017) Buttering their bread on both sides?: The recogni-
     tion of sign languages and the aspirations of deaf communities. *Language Problems
     and Language Planning* 41 (2), 136–158.
Evaluation – Ytra mat (2016) See https://reykjavik.is/sites/default/files/ymis_skjol/skjol_
     utgefid_efni/107_1.1_skyrrsla_hlidaskoli.pdf (last accessed 28 January 2019).
Ethnologue (2017) *Languages of the World*. See https://www.ethnologue.com/language/
     isl (last accessed 28 January 2019).

Fishman, J.A. (1972) The relationship between micro- and macro-sociolinguistics in the study of who speaks what language to whom and when. In J.B. Pride and J. Holmes (eds) *Sociolinguistics. Selected Readings* (pp. 15–32). Harmondsworth: Penguin.

Fishman, J.A. (1991) *Reversing Language Shift: Theoretical and Empirical Foundations of Assistance to Threatened Languages.* Clevedon: Multilingual Matters.

Guðmundsdóttir, B. (2018) (V. Stefánsdóttir, personal communication).

Hilmarsson-Dunn, A. and Kristinsson, A.P. (2013) The language situation in Iceland. In R.B. Kaplan, R.B. Baldauf, Jr. and N.M. Kamwangamalu (eds) *Language Planning in Europe: Cyprus, Iceland and Luxembourg* (pp. 100–169 + Addendum 26–28). London/New York: Routledge.

Jakobsdóttir, K. and Guðmundsson, A. (2010) Skipun framkvæmdanenfndar í málefnum heyrnarlausra og heyrnarskertra [Letter to Valgerður Stefánsdóttir].Mennta- og menningarmálaráðuneyti, Reykjavík.

Kristinsson, A.P. (2016) English language as 'fatal gadget' in Iceland. In P. Bunce, R. Phillipson, V. Rapatahana and R. Tupas (eds) *Why English? Confronting the Hydra* (pp. 118–128). Bristol: Multilingual Matters.

Kristinsson, A.P. (2017) *Málheimar. Sitthvað um málstefnu og málnotkun. [Worlds of Language. On Language Policy and Language Use].* Reykjavik: Háskólaútgáfan [University of Iceland Press].

Kristinsson, A.P. and Bernharðsson, H. (2014) Landerapport Island: Islandsk eller engelsk i islandsk universitetsvirksomhed? [Country report Iceland: Icelandic or English in Icelandic universities and academia?] In F. Gregersen (ed.) *Hvor parallelt. Om parallellspråkighet på Nordens universitet.TemaNord* 2014: 535 (pp. 427–486). Copenhagen: Nordic Council of Ministers.

Lewis, M.P. and Simons, G.F. (2010) Assessing endangerment: Expanding Fishman's GIDS. *Revue Roumaine De Linguistique* (55), 103–120.

McKee, R. (2017) Assessing the vitality of New Zealand Sign Language. *Sign Language Studies* 17 (3), 322–362.

Reagan, T. (2010) *Language Policy and Planning for Sign Languages.* Washington, DC: Gallaudet University Press.

Reykjavík District Court (2015) See https://www.heradsdomstolar.is/default. aspx?pageid=347c3bb1-8926-11e5-80c6-005056bc6a40&id=f20c3c58-0227-4e8b-8b8b-c1e5f50a2a86.

Stefánsdóttir V., Kristinsson, A.P., Eiríksdóttir, H.D., Haraldsdóttir, H.A. and Sverrisdóttir, R. (2014) Skýrsla Málnefndar íslenska táknmálsins [Report from the Icelandic Sign Language Council]. See https://www.stjornarradid.is/media/menntamalaraduneyti-media/media/ritogskyrslur/skyrsl_malnef_isl_taknmal_2014.pdf (last accessed 28 January 2019).

Stefánsson, S. and Kristjánsson, K. (2005) Ref. MMR04030217/2.3.0/GO/--[Letter to Valgerður Stefansdóttir]. Mennta- og menningarmálaráðuneyti, Reykjavík.

The Icelandic National Curriculum Guide for Compulsory Schools: General Section 2011 and 2013. See https://www.stjornarradid.is/verkefni/menntamal/namskrar/.

The Icelandic Sign Language Council (2013) See https://www.stjornarradid.is/media/menntamalaraduneyti-media/media/ritogskyrslur/skyrsl_malnef_isl_taknmal_2013.pdf (last accessed 28 January 2019).

The Supreme Court of Iceland (2017) See https://www.haestirettur.is/default. aspx?pageid=347c3bb1-8926-11e5-80c6-005056bc6a40&id=ce2ad6f4-899f-4f84-ae6b-c3a25d63526f.

Thorvaldsdóttir, K.L. and Stefánsdóttir, V. (2015) Icelandic Sign Language. In J. Bakken Jepsen, G. De Clerck, S. Lutalo Kiingi and W.B. McGregor (eds) *Sign Languages of the World* (pp. 409–429). Preston, UK: De Gruyter Mouton.

Vísir (2011) See http://www.visir.is/g/2011110528954 (last accessed 28 January 2019).

16 Recognizing Brazilian Sign Language: Legislation and Outcomes

Ronice Müller de Quadros and
Marianne Rossi Stumpf

Introduction

Brazilian Sign Language (Libras) has considerable status in Brazil, as a result of Law 10.436/2002, which recognizes Libras as the national language of Brazilian deaf communities and has had ramifications for public policy. Law 7.387/2010 further establishes a language policy according status to all Brazilian languages. In this chapter, we will describe the process by which national deaf organizations and academic endeavours achieved the recognition of Libras and the ensuing effects. Many of the developments described relate to the educational domain, since deaf children's access to education was a key impetus for recognition, and the increased participation of Libras users in academic domains resulting from legislation has significantly raised the status of Libras.

Languages in Brazil

Brazil has the fifth largest population in the world, and a complex ethnic and political history. It is a plurilingual country in which more than 200 languages are spoken. Approximately 1 million Brazilians do not have Portuguese as their first language; an estimated 190 languages are autochthones (indigenous languages) and 20 are allochthones (from immigrants who share a national language other than Portuguese) (Oliveira, 2017). The Brazilian Constitution names Portuguese as the country's official language; however, Decree 7.387/2010 establishes language policies that recognize Brazilian language diversity. The decree recognizes all languages, spoken and signed, as part of Brazilian heritage and culture, and establishes a policy to protect, value and empower these languages, especially endangered languages. Additionally, there is a national sign language, Libras (Brazilian Sign Language), and several other village sign languages have been identified, such as Cena Sign Language, Urubu Kaapor Sign Language, Pataxós Sign Language, Caiçara Sign Language, etc. (Quadros, 2016a, 2016b, 2017; Quadros & Silva, 2017). According to Quadros and Silva (2017), knowledge about the different varieties of sign languages used in Brazil is scarce (as is the case in many countries), and urgent action is needed to establish policies to strengthen the protection of all varieties of sign languages in Brazil.

In the 1990s, discussion began regarding the linguistic situation of Brazilian deaf people who use Libras. This discussion started in the educational context, where international declarations about the educational inclusion of people with disabilities specifically mentioned the role of sign language. The Salamanca Statement (UNESCO, 1994) had a very important role, as it recognized the linguistic status of sign languages and proposed to guarantee deaf people's access to education through sign language. In parallel with this, Brazilian deaf organizations participated in the World Federation of the Deaf Congresses, which advocated the recognition of the country's sign language. Brazilian deaf people joined a political movement to promote the recognition of their own language (Brito, 2013; Quadros, 2006) and linguistic studies of Libras, from the late 1980s, began to document its linguistic status (Ferreira-Brito, 1995; Karnopp, 1999; Quadros, 1999). Research also analysed the impact of not having access to sign language in the early stages of language acquisition and during education.

The Brazilian deaf movement

In 1981, the National Federation for Education and Integration of Hearing Impaired People (FENEIDA) was founded. The initiative to establish a national federation came from parents of deaf children and, as such, was an organization led by hearing people with a disability perspective of deaf people. However, in 1987 a deaf person, Ana Regina Souza e Campello, was elected its president. This was a historic moment in the organization of the Brazilian deaf movement. For the first time in the country, a deaf person was leading a national organization to formally represent deaf people. After that, members of the deaf community reorganized it as a Deaf organization controlled by Deaf people. The organization changed its name from FENEIDA (National Federation of 'hearing impaired' people) to FENEIS (National Federation of 'Deaf' people).[1] After this revolution, in 1988, FENEIS affiliated to the World Federation of the Deaf (WFD), officially representing Brazilian deaf communities.

FENEIS works in partnership with Brazilian deaf associations, with around 120 affiliates from across Brazil. It began a national social and political movement of events, coordinated with its affiliates and in cooperation with educational institutions. The main theme of the talks offered by the FENEIS representatives was the recognition of sign language and of deaf people. In addition to this strategy, FENEIS started representing the Brazilian deaf community in meetings with government officials to discuss proposals to promote the recognition of Libras and the rights of deaf people to access education in their own language.

During the 1990s, some deaf people attended university, but with difficulty, as universities were unaware of the deaf students' need for classroom access, including interpreters. The deaf students allied with FENEIS to demand that the Federal Attorney General mandated the hiring of professional Libras interpreters. The Attorney General's office requested a meeting with the technical officer of the Ministry of Education (MEC) and a group of deaf university students, to understand their demands. This officer was surprised to learn that there were deaf students at university. She gathered further documentation about Libras, and further discussions between the Ministry of Education and FENEIS resulted in a requirement to provide sign language interpreters for deaf students at all educational levels, leading to an increase of deaf students in universities across Brazil.

FENEIS continued to advocate for the legal recognition of Libras. From the late 1980s to the late 1990s, government officials took an interest in issues related to Brazilian deaf communities. In 1996, the CORDE – National Coordination for Integration of People with Disabilities, an official national organization – promoted an important meeting to discuss legislation for Deaf people. FENEIS representatives as well as Deaf people from different organizations attended and participated in the drafting of a document which was the precursor of the Libras Law 10.436/2002.

In 2001, the Ministry of Education offered a course called 'Teaching Libras instructors through learning mentors: The language as we see it', to train Libras instructors to disseminate Libras in Brazil, focusing especially on Brazilian deaf leadership, in order to raise consciousness in this group about the importance of the teaching of Libras in Brazil (Felipe, 2001). The first step was to train Deaf leaders who were teaching Libras around the country. These leaders then offered courses for other Deaf instructors in their respective states. In this same period, MEC offered a course for interpreters of Libras, guaranteeing the certification of these professionals and contributing to the increasing status of Libras.

FENEIS also allied with researchers, linguists and educators,[2] who began studying Libras and Deaf education in Brazil, producing information to support their demands for the recognition of Libras. In 2002, Law 10.436, also known as the 'Libras Law', was signed by the President and entered into force. Deaf representatives were present at the court's decision in Brasília and celebrated this important step for Deaf peoples' lives in Brazil. FENEIS, as an organization with Deaf people, played a fundamental role in this process, making Libras visible through public marches, parades and publications across the country (Brito, 2013). These local movements resulted in local laws recognizing Libras. The strategy provoked a general mobilization in favour of Libras in which several national politicians, senators and deputies were engaged. Also, FENEIS had promoted talks about Libras around the country to deaf community members, which raised awareness of Deaf language, culture and identity. At the federal level, passage of the Libras Law took six years, from 1996 to 2002, starting with submission of the original bill. These social movements began by invoking civil rights as the theme of the campaign, but shifted towards the linguistic status of Libras as an emblem of Deaf culture and identity (Brito, 2013). In 2005, Decree 5626 regulated the Libras Law with an action plan to guarantee its implementation. All this came about due to the efforts of the Deaf social movements and networks around the country, coordinated through sign language by deaf people (Miranda, 2001; Quadros, 2006; Quadros *et al.*, 2014). After 2005, FENEIS created new regional offices in the Brazilian states to support the new Libras instructors as well as to educate new interpreters, while continuing to maintain a strong network among local Deaf associations, empowering the Deaf movement across the whole country.

The Libras Law

The Libras Law recognizes Libras as the language used by Brazilian deaf communities and guarantees access to public bodies and deaf education in Libras in its four articles:

Box 16.1: Law 10436/2002[3]

Art. 1º Brazilian Sign Language – Libras – is recognized legally as a means of communication and expression, as are other means of communication associated with this language.

Single paragraph. The term Brazilian Sign Language is understood to mean – Libras, the form of communication and expression in which the visual-kinetic linguistic system, with its own grammatical structure, constitutes a linguistic system for the transmission of ideas and facts, originating from communities of deaf persons in Brazil.

Art. 2º The government and private bodies appointed by the government to provide public services must guarantee institutional ways to support the usage and diffusion of Libras as an objective means of communication and currently used by deaf communities in Brazil.

Art. 3º All public institutions and companies with concessions to provide public healthcare services must guarantee proper attention and treatment to the hearing impaired, according to existing laws.

Art. 4º The federal educational system, and the state, municipal and federal district educational systems must guarantee the inclusion of the teaching of Brazilian Sign Language – Libras – in courses of

Special Education, Speech therapy and Pedagogy both at primary and secondary and university levels, as part of the National Curriculum Parameters – PCNs, according to current legislation.

Single paragraph. Libras will not substitute the written form of Portuguese.

So far, the Libras Law is the only law recognizing a language other than Portuguese, which is included in the constitution as the official language of Brazil. Despite this recognition of Libras as a national language of deaf communities, the law includes a final paragraph establishing that this language cannot replace the written form of Portuguese. This paragraph goes back to the monolingual policy established during Brazilian colonization, maintaining the supremacy of Portuguese, while recognizing the existence of another national language, Libras. However, the paragraph has had some negative consequences for Brazilian deaf people, such as the use of Portuguese as the language for job applications. Thus, Portuguese is still an excluding factor for Deaf professionals in some states where the law is applied, although in other states, Libras access is guaranteed. Apart from that, the most important benefit of the Libras Law has been the establishment of bilingual education, recognizing Libras as the language of instruction and teaching, and written Portuguese as a second language that must be taught to deaf children in schools, as explained further below.

Implementation of the Libras Law: Federal Decree 5.626

Federal Decree 5.626 from 2005 regulates the implementation of the Libras Law. The actions indicated by the decree are as follows:

Box 16.2: Summary of Decree 5626/2005

(1) Libras should be inserted as a compulsory curricular subject in teacher training courses.
(2) Libras will be an optional curricular subject in the other courses of higher education and professional education.
(3) Training for the teaching of Libras in the final years of elementary school, high school and higher education should be undertaken at university level.
(4) The training of Libras teachers in early childhood education and in the initial years of elementary education should be carried out in pedagogy courses or in regular university courses, in which Libras and written Portuguese are languages of instruction, enabling bilingual education.

(5) Deaf people will have priority in teacher training courses for the teaching of Libras and in bilingual training courses.

(6) Federal educational institutions must guarantee deaf people access to communication, information and education in the selection processes, activities and curricular contents developed at all levels, stages and modalities of education, from kindergarten to university.

(7) The training of translators and interpreters of Libras–Portuguese must be carried out by a higher education level course in translation and interpretation, with a qualification in Libras–Portuguese.

(8) Federal educational institutions responsible for school-age education must ensure the inclusion of deaf or hard-of-hearing students through the organization of:

   (i) bilingual schools and bilingual education classes, open to deaf and hearing students, with bilingual teachers, in early childhood and in the first years of elementary school; and

   (ii) bilingual schools or regular schools within the regular school network, open to deaf and hearing students, for the final years of elementary education, secondary education or professional education, with teachers from different areas of knowledge, aware of the particular linguistic situation of deaf students, as well as with the presence of translators and interpreters of Libras–Portuguese.

The effective implementation of the decree has a direct impact on the lives of deaf people in Brazil. All deaf students who graduate to become teachers in any subject area have at least one Libras course in their training. This inclusion of Libras in the curricula of teacher training in all Brazilian universities generated a new field of work for Libras teachers. Libras teacher training was also established to ensure qualified education for these teaching training courses. The 'Letras Libras' course started in 2006, through a project approved by the federal government for undergraduate distance learning. The Letras course corresponds to a Bachelor of Arts, an undergraduate course for language teachers and translators. In Brazil, Portuguese teachers graduate in Letras Portuguese, English teachers in Letras Inglês, Spanish teachers in Letras Espanhol and since 2006, Libras teachers graduate in Letras Libras. More than 1000 Libras teachers have gone through this training. The very creation of this course, which now exists in 27 Brazilian federal universities, is a manifestation of the recognition of the linguistic status of Libras.

The bilingual pedagogy undergraduate programme (Libras and Portuguese) is offered in some Brazilian states, to train elementary school teachers who will teach deaf children using a bilingual approach. This course is provided for in Decree 5626, but is still not widely offered. Its further establishment requires policy support, as happened with the undergraduate course of *Letras Libras*.

Another effect of the decree was the inclusion of an article in the National Education Plan (PNE), the federal Law 13005/2014, which refers to bilingual education for deaf children from 0 to 17 years old. This law establishes a broad and diversified Deaf education policy, legally formalizing public provision of bilingual schools for the deaf. FENEIS played an important role in getting this statement included in the law. The PNE sets priorities for education over the next 20 years. FENEIS and Deaf representatives took part in consultations to guarantee the inclusion of a statement about a model of bilingual education in which sign language is taught as a first language and used as the medium of instruction, with Portuguese as the second language. The plan also describes settings for bilingual education, including bilingual schools. Specific statements referring to bilingual schools were removed three times during the consultation process; however, sustained pressure from the Deaf community, with support from researchers, eventually led to the original text being preserved, which was an important victory. The bilingual school model reflects a longstanding priority of the Brazilian deaf community, as well as evidence from academic research over the last two decades. It is now a formalized part of the Brazilian education system, which is a historic achievement of the National Movement for Deaf Education and Culture, led by FENEIS.

While the PNE is in force, there are still no concrete actions to implement bilingual education. The PNE allows for the establishment of bilingual education in bilingual schools, in mainstream schools with specialist units (schools for hearing children that have special resource provision for Deaf students), and in mainstream schools; however, the government continues to promote a model of inclusive education in mainstream schools. Only a few bilingual schools remain. In São Paulo city, there are six bilingual schools for Deaf children and some other cities have established their own bilingual school.

Another important outcome of Decree 5626/2005 was to guarantee deaf people access to participation in higher education through Libras. Some universities began to conduct entrance examinations in Libras and to use sign language interpreters in classrooms. For example, the questions in the entrance examinations for postgraduate programmes in linguistics and translation studies at the Federal University of Santa Catarina are translated into Libras, and the candidates for master's and doctoral degrees sit the examinations using a video-test format and film their answers in Libras. Candidates can also submit their research proposals in Libras by recording their projects for evaluation by the committee. Upon entering this study programme, students can take classes directly in Libras with sign language professors or interpreters. They can also submit their work assessments in Libras. Dissertations and theses in this programme can also be presented exclusively in Libras, with the option of subtitles or audio in Portuguese. Even though the Libras Law states that Libras cannot replace written Portuguese, it is possible in this case, because the law can be interpreted as meaning that Libras is the language accessible to Deaf people and they have the right to produce work in their language. The principle is that Portuguese cannot be an exclusion factor for deaf students.

In Brazil, students must take a specific admissions examination to enter Brazilian universities. The exam is set by each Brazilian university and includes questions relating to high school knowledge of natural sciences, social sciences and language. The Brazilian government has also implemented a national exam (ENEM) used for admission by several universities in the country. The Federal University of Santa Catarina was the first university to offer the admission exam in Libras, in 2006, to selected candidates for the *Letras Libras* course. This event was an innovation in the forms of preparation and presentation of an exam in Libras. FENEIS filed an action against the State to ensure that the ENEM tests were translated into Libras in advance of the examination, following the model applied by the Federal University of Santa Catarina. The judge found in favour of FENEIS and ordered the translation of the exams into Libras. From 2017, the ENEM test has been available to deaf candidates in Libras, improving equal access to university study.

Another action deriving from Decree 5626/2005 was the establishment of public employment admission exams in Libras. In Brazil, public institutions are required to advertise vacancies to the public, who can apply through a public examination process. Among the various stages of this application process for teaching jobs, there is a selection test and a teaching method test. In addition, deaf teachers are frequently on the selection committees when vacancies are open for positions involving Libras, such as Libras instruction, and translation and interpretation of Libras and Portuguese. Reis (2015), a deaf researcher, notes 286 deaf professors were hired through public admission exams from 1997 to 2015 in public universities.

Despite all the achievements since 2002 when the Libras Law was published, deaf leaders have formally presented a document to public representatives, asking for concrete measures to guarantee the legitimacy of the actions foreseen by Decree 5626/2002 and the National Education Plan (PNE), which still need effective action to guarantee deaf people's rights. There are still specific points that have not been implemented, because of bureaucratic inertia and tension between the aims of special education and a bilingual education model.

Outstanding items on the deaf community's agenda encompass academic, educational, social and government issues. These include items such as giving priority to deaf teachers in the teaching of Libras; requiring hearing candidates to take tests in Libras for positions involving the teaching of Libras and bilingual education; the promotion of research on Libras with the deaf researchers; the establishment of bilingual education and hiring of deaf professionals in educational settings; ensuring the acquisition of Libras by deaf babies with deaf professionals; extending the use of Libras throughout the school community; priority of deaf educators in bilingual education for deaf people; the establishment of care centres for deaf people in municipalities; the establishment of a registration system for professional translators and interpreters of Libras and Portuguese; and the establishment of a permanent committee of deaf representatives and academics to define public policies involving deaf people.

Changing the Status of Libras in the Educational Domain

Brazilian deaf education followed an oralist philosophy until the 1980s, when some schools began to permit the use of some sign language, including the Total Communication approach. Bilingual education was introduced during the first half of the 1990s. In 1997, a well-known school for deaf children, Escola Especial Concórdia in Porto Alegre, introduced Libras as a subject from primary through to high school level. School administrators decided that this subject should only be taught by deaf teachers. The objective was to focus on themes pertaining to linguistic, social, cultural, historical and educational issues related to deafness, such as writing sign languages, deaf history, deaf cultures, sign language grammar and human rights. There was great resistance to this from hearing teachers and from other schools. It is interesting to note that this process began before the Libras Law was adopted. Introducing Libras into the curriculum in some Deaf schools contributed to the recognition of Libras, as most Deaf teachers working in these schools were also Deaf leaders, who were involved in campaigning for a Libras Law.

In 1999, the Federal University of Rio Grande do Sul organized the 5th Latin American Congress of Bilingual Education for the Deaf, gathering researchers from different continents, deaf activists, teachers and professors, Deaf academic leaders and community members, bringing together approximately 1500 participants, in Porto Alegre. This conference was an important meeting site for Deaf professionals to discuss issues related to linguistic rights and education. These discussions resulted in a document: *The Education We Deaf People Want* (FENEIS, 1999), which was presented to the Ministry of Education (MEC) by the president of FENEIS. The Ministry agreed to consider the demands in the document, including the implementation of courses for Libras teachers and interpreters at university level, as well as addressing bilingual education from a Deaf perspective.

The MEC invited the directors of FENEIS, Deaf academic leaders, and deaf education and sign language researchers to discuss the demands in the document. One request implemented immediately was the creation of national Centers for Deaf Support Services (CAS) across the whole country to support sign language instructors, sign language interpreters and train teachers working with Deaf children. The centres offered training by Deaf professionals and other specialists recommended by FENEIS, guaranteeing that this work came from a Deaf perspective. Unfortunately, over time, the influence of a Deaf perspective has diminished in CAS units with increased emphasis being put on 'education for all people' from the inclusion perspective. However, the document is still used as a benchmark for discussions of bilingual education. Through this initiative, deaf movements occupied a space for reflection about the transformation of bilingual education.

Also as a result of the petition, the MEC promoted courses to train and certify Libras instructors and Libras interpreters. Such courses were not at university level, but they were politically and linguistically important for the Brazilian deaf community at that historic moment. The courses mobilized deaf leadership all over the country and contributed to the political organization of Brazilian deaf people in their campaign to improve deaf education.

Around the same period, there was a movement to implement university level courses and the MEC prepared specific legislation involving Libras. The legislative proposal included clauses with the intent of implementing bilingual education throughout the country, in collaboration with the departments of education in each state. Federal laws and recommendations apply at the federal level of education, but they are also highly influential on the formation and implementation of local education policy in each state because they ensure funding. The policy process culminated in the Libras Law in 2002. The education of Libras instructors and Libras translators and interpreters began shortly afterwards (not yet at the graduate level); and school books with videos in Libras, Libras dictionaries and bilingual literature books (Portuguese and Libras) were produced and distributed.

From 1999 to 2002, several other noteworthy events took place in Brazil's deaf community. The employment of deaf university professors with master's and PhD degrees changed the status of Deaf agents involved in policy planning. The MEC started to include Deaf leaders and Deaf professors in each decision about Deaf education and sign language issues. There were persistent efforts to implement bilingual education with deaf instructors, teachers and researchers, as well as demands for equal conditions compared to hearing people in schools.

In 2004, the Universidade Federal de Santa Catarina (UFSC) ran a project for Deaf people to take master's and PhD degrees in the education programme; eight masters and three doctors graduated. Subsequently, Deaf candidates were selected every year to start their master's and/or PhD not only in education, but also in linguistics and translation studies. All are working in different universities around the country in Libras programmes and they are also the Deaf intellectual leaders who work with social movements, including FENEIS. Since 2004, Deaf academics have participated in meetings related to Deaf people at federal and state levels, having the appropriate credentials and status to propose policies related to the Deaf community. They also made possible the implementation of public laws in accordance with Deaf demands.

These courses rely on the presence of deaf professors and bilingual students, with appropriate academic training (most have PhDs). These professors have the important role of knowledge sharing and building the capacity of a deaf academic community. In the period from 2004 to 2018, there were 44 deaf masters and 12 deaf PhDs graduates from UFSC. Other universities also enrolled deaf students in graduate programmes. Today, there is a total of 128 deaf people with master's degrees and 27 with PhDs in Brazil (Reis, 2015, updated in 2018). Deaf presence in academia empowers deaf people themselves to adopt recognized leadership roles in decision and policy making within the field of deafness.

Tension and Negotiation

The achievements of the deaf movements and the advances of scientific research in the fields of education, linguistics and translation studies since the 1990s have contributed significantly to the advances in Libras, bilingual education and the citizenship of deaf people in Brazil. However, all these achievements have faced resistance stemming from the asymmetric power relations between languages in society.

A historical tension lies in the field of special education, which operates from a disability perspective on deafness. In the field of education, special education advocates promote 'inclusion'. In this view, deaf people need to integrate into society and sign language becomes a tool for this to happen. The vision of the linguistic identity of the deaf community is lost in favour of deaf children learning with hearing peers in Portuguese. Federal officials therefore advocate a model that they believe to be inclusive, but actually excludes deaf learners who use sign language, since bilingual education requires peer-to-peer relationships.

This resistance to deaf people's views is the greatest challenge faced by Brazilian deaf people. We believe that this difficulty arises because deaf people remain a linguistic-social minority. Depending on the attitude of the government, they are not always part of the decision-making and implementation process in education. Therefore, deaf people need to be constantly vigilant to the real threat posed by those who hold such power.

Future Challenges

A key challenge is the implementation of bilingual education as promised by the legislation. Ongoing dialogue between representatives of the deaf community and education officials is needed to convince officials that the legislation on bilingual education for the deaf means more than providing sign language interpreters in education. The implementation of PNE requires creation of bilingual environments in schools for deaf children as well as at local schools, with deaf educators fluent in Libras. This is the critical challenge for Brazilian public policies for the education of deaf people.

Beyond education, Brazilian deaf leaders have identified other challenges. Relations between deaf and hearing people present many conflicts involving asymmetric relations of power. Labour market spaces for Libras are disputed between deaf and hearing people, generating real relationship conflicts. Many deaf people feel threatened by hearing people who have learned Libras, as they begin to occupy positions that could (and should) be occupied by deaf people, for example, teaching Libras, thus raising the ethical issue of 'ownership' of Libras. Some deaf people talk about hearing people 'stealing Libras' from them. Members of the Deaf community consider sign language to be their language, but some hearing people may feel that they also have ownership of the language. A sign language that emerges from a Deaf community is part of that community's heritage and Deaf people feel it belongs to them. The ethical issue in this respect lies in who brings this language to the communities, deaf and hearing. In this sense, sign language is owned by Deaf community; however, we can see that, increasingly, the bilingual status of deaf and hearing people weakens claims of ownership. All who use a language, own the language. The ethical position is to recognize that sign language is part of the heritage of Deaf communities.

Decree 5626/2002 establishes that deaf people have priority in training for teaching Libras. As a result, many deaf people were trained as teachers, but when it was time for them to enter the labour market, they found hearing people already occupying positions teaching Libras. PNE 13.005/2014 has now established that deaf people have priority in teaching Libras. Now the challenge is to implement this priority.

Conclusion

The legal recognition of Libras in Brazil came about through the combined efforts of Deaf organizations and academic institutions. At every stage, Deaf people have been involved as true agents representing Deaf communities' interests. Over the last three decades, they have contributed to sign language research and teaching that supports their claims. Sign language recognition resulted from legal recognition in different sectors of society. Today, Deaf representatives are key players in the negotiation of language policies and Deaf rights. The negotiation process is ongoing and necessary to guarantee genuine inclusion of Deaf people in Brazilian society through their sign language, particularly in public education.

Acknowledgements

This research is supported in part by funding from CNPq (Brazilian National Council of Technological and Scientific Development) Grants # 303725/ 2013-3 and # 471355/ 2013-5. We thank Rachel Sutton-Spence and Ana Regina Souza e Campello for suggestions made to previous versions of this chapter, and Maartje De Meulder, Joseph J. Murray and Rachel L. McKee for relevant comments and suggestions during the review process.

Notes

(1) The Deaf leaders that had an important role in this moment must be cited: Ana Regina e Souza Campello, Antônio Campos de Abreu, Fernando Valverde, Nelson Pimenta, Antônio Cardoso, Neivaldo Zovico Sérgio Masmorra and André Reichert.
(2) Such as Lucinda Ferreira-Brito, Tanya Felipe, Ronice Müller de Quadros, Carlos Skliar, Gladis Perlin, Regina Maria de Souza, Sandra Patrícia Farias do Nascimento and Marianne Rossi Stumpf (in chronological order).
(3) Our translation from Portuguese to English.

References

Brito, F.B. de (2013) O movimento social surdo e campanha pela oficialização da língua brasileira de sinais. [The Deaf social movement and the campaign for the Brazilian Sign Language recognition]. Tese: Doutorado – Programa de Pós-Graduação em Educação, Área de Concentração: Educação Especial, Faculdade de Educação da Universidade de São Paulo, São Paulo.

Felipe, T.A. (2001) *Ano do Reconhecimento do Instrutor Surdos: CORDE e MEC juntos com a FENEIS em torno da LIBRAS* (No. 12, pp. 7–9). Rio de Janeiro: Revista FENEIS.

FENEIS. (1999) A educação que nós surdos queremos [The Education We Deaf People Want]. Documento elaborado pela comunidade surda a partir do pré-congresso ao V Congresso latino-americano de Educação Bilíngue para Surdos, realizado em Porto Alegre/RS, no salão de atos da reitoria da UFRGS, nos dias 20 a 24 de abril de 1999. Disponível em: <http://inclusao-jane.blogspot.com/2012/01/educacao-que-nos-surdos-queremos.html>. Acesso em: 10/12/2018.

Karnopp, L.B. (1999) Aquisição fonológica na Língua Brasileira de Sinais: Estudo longitudinal de uma criança surda. Tese de Doutorado, PUCRS, Porto Alegre.

Law 10.436/2002. Presidência da República. Casa Civil. Brazil. Língua Brasileira de Sinais. See http://www.planalto.gov.br/ccivil_03/LEIS/2002/L10436.htm (accessed Januanry 2019).

Law 7.387/2010. Presidência da República. Casa Civil. Brazil. Inventário Nacional da Diversidade Linguística. See http://www.planalto.gov.br/ccivil_03/_ato2007-2010/2010/decreto/d7387.htm (accessed January 2019).

Law 13005/2014. Plano Nacional de Educação. http://www.planalto.gov.br/ccivil_03/_Ato2011-2014/2014/Lei/L13005.htm (accessed January 2019).

Miranda, W. (2001) Comunidade dos Surdos olhares sobre os contatos culturais. Dissertação de Mestrado, Universidade Federal do Rio Grande do Sul.

Oliveira, G. (2017) *Línguas como Patrimônio Imaterial*. See www.ipol.org.br (accessed March 2017).

Quadros, R.M. de (1999) Phrase structure of Brazilian sign language. Tese de Doutorado, PUCRS, Porto Alegre.

Quadros, R.M. de (2006) Políticas linguísticas e educação de surdos em Santa Catarina: Espaço de negociações. *Cadernos CEDES*, Campinas, SP, vol. 26, no. 69, 141–161. See www.scielo.br/pdf/ccedes/v26n69/a03v2669.pdf (accessed 23 January 2018).

Quadros, R.M. de (2016a) Documentação da Libras. In *Seminário Ibero-Americano de Diversidade Linguística* (Vol. 1, pp. 157–174), 2014, Foz do Iguaçu. Brasília: IPHAN – Ministério da Cultura.

Quadros, R.M. de (2016b) A transcrição de textos do Corpus de Libras. *Revista Leitura* 1 (57), 8–34.

Quadros, R.M. de (2017) *Língua de Herança: Língua Brasileira de Sinais*. Porto Alegre: Editora Penso.

Quadros, R.M. and Silva, D.S. (2017) As comunidades surdas brasileiras. *Em Comunidades surdas na América Latina: Língua – Cultura – Educação – Identidade*. Romana Castro Zambrano e Cleide Emília Faye Pedrosa. Florianópolis: Editora Bookess.

Quadros, R.M. de, Strobel, K.L. and Masutti, M.L. (2014) Deaf gains in Brazil: Linguistic policies and network establishment In H-Dirksen L. Bauman and Joseph J. Murray (eds) *Deaf Gain: Raising the Stakes for Human Diversity* (1st edn, Vol. 1, pp. 341–355). Minneapolis: University of Minnesota Press.

Reis, F. (2015) Os Professores Surdos na Educação Superior. Tese de Doutorado, Programa de Pós-Graduação em Educação, Universidade Federal de Uberlândia. Uberlândia.

UNESCO (1994) *Declaração Mundial de Educação para Todos e Plano de Ação para Satisfazer as Necessidades Básicas para Aprendizagem*. Conferência Mundial para as Necessidades Especiais, Salamanca, Espanha.

17 Legal Recognition and Regulation of Catalan Sign Language

Maria Josep Jarque, Marta Bosch-Baliarda and
Menchu González

Introduction[1]

Catalan Sign Language (*llengua de signes catalana*, hereafter LSC) is the primary means of communication of deaf and deafblind signers in Catalonia. Politically, Catalonia is an autonomous community within Spain with an independent legislative mandate in culture, language policies and educational issues, among others. Catalonia has a strong national identity and a long tradition of advocating for the Catalan language and culture. Geographically, LSC is used within Catalonia only. This differs from the geographical distribution of the coexisting official spoken languages, namely Spanish and Catalan, which are also spoken outside Catalonia.

In 2010, the Catalan Parliament passed Law 17/2010 on Catalan Sign Language,[2] which legally recognised LSC from a language approach, as opposed to the Spanish State Law (27/2007),[3] which adopts an accessibility perspective. Very few studies have described the path to this legal recognition (cf. Muñoz, 2010; Quer, 2012) or its outcomes. This chapter discusses the legal recognition process of LSC within the context of general language policies in Catalonia, including the campaigners involved, and the effects it has generated. We also summarise the explicit and implicit legal status and policies regarding LSC in Catalan legal texts.

Our study adopts a qualitative approach based on semi-structured interviews with different government representatives responsible for language and education, and activists from the main deaf community organisations in Catalonia. The campaigners included members of deaf associations, educators of deaf children, governmental and private organisations for the study and promotion of LSC, teaching and learning of LSC and sign language interpreting. We also collected data from reports, statements, websites and videoblogs and other documents developed by both organisations and activists, as well as the parliamentary debates and appearances in several commissions leading to the enactment of the LSC Law.

The next section introduces the languages and language policies in Catalonia. This is followed by a section describing the legal recognition and regulation of LSC and the factors that enabled passage. The final section includes conclusions and future directions and challenges.

Languages and Language Policies in Catalonia

Catalonia is a multilingual region in Europe (population 7,546,522), where language policies constitute a complex and central political matter. On the one hand, Catalan is a minoritised minority language. It was persecuted and banned both as an official language and in education during the Francoist dictatorship in Spain (beginning in 1939) until the reinstatement of democratic rights and freedoms in 1975. On the other hand, Catalan is attributed as a key cultural value and is at the centre of the national identity. It is of utmost importance for social cohesion among the groups with diverse origins participating in Catalan society (May, 2012; Vila, 2016).

According to the last Survey of Language Uses of the Population developed by the Directorate General of Language Policy of the Catalan government (hereafter, DGPL) in 2013, the two majority official languages (Spanish and Catalan) coexist with hundreds of spoken languages and a few sign languages, due to migration flows at the turn of the 21st century (Departament de Cultura, 2015). There are currently more than 300 different languages used in Catalonia including more than 40 language groups with over 2000 speakers (Boix-Fuster, 2015; Comellas *et al.*, 2010; Junyent ed., 2005). The Group for Endangered Languages (GELA) from the University of Barcelona has identified 11 different foreign sign languages in use in Catalonia.[4] Multilingualism is thus an important characteristic of 21st-century Catalan society. This new social reality poses new challenges for language management and social cohesion, and for language policy in education (Arnau & Vila, 2013; Boix-Fuster, 2015; Strubell & Boix-Fuster, 2011; Vernet & Pons, 2011).

In past decades, the conceptualisation of multilingualism in Catalonia has shifted from a 'language conflict' approach to a 'language establishment and minorisation' approach (Vila, 2016). The latter predicts the behaviour of migrant foreign languages from a political and economic perspective in which languages have value as cultural capital in modern industrialised states (Boix-Fuster, 2015; Vila, 2016). Hence, while Québec was the model for Catalonia in early language policies, according to Vila (2016: 213) the new benchmark comes from northern European societies such as Denmark, Finland or the Netherlands in which language 'normality' is not associated with social monolingualism, but rather with multilingualism. In the new model, bilingualism is regarded as contributing towards language death whereas multilingualism assists language maintenance (Boix-Fuster, 2015; Comellas *et al.*, 2010; Vila, 2016). The challenges are 'to ensure the sustainability of Catalan and manage multilingualism within a framework of social policies that are equality and reality bound' (Vila, 2016: 213).

This multilingualism approach provided the right sociolinguistic context for the passage of a sign language law within a language rights model. Apart from that, there were other sociopolitical factors that positively influenced the passage of the sign language law. First was the enactment of Aranese language rights in 2010, which set an important precedent. Compared to LSC users, official numbers from the DGPL point to Aranese having a smaller number of speakers (between 5000 and 8000) and it is used in a geographically smaller area. According to the Federation of Deaf People of Catalonia (hereafter FESOCA), the number of LSC deaf signers is around 12,000, 25,000 being the total number that would include hearing relatives and professional users, such as interpreters, speech therapists and communication support workers (Muñoz, 2010).

A second sociopolitical factor positively influencing the passage of the LSC Law was the new Statute of Autonomy that the Catalan Parliament passed in 2005 and that was ratified by a referendum. It was later modified by both the Spanish Senate and the Constitutional Court as a result of the appeal presented by the Spanish Popular Party. The modifications erased all reference to Catalan national identity in the text, and to Catalan as a preferred language in the regional public agencies and public media. This act boosted the social movement in defence of Catalan identity and self-determination, comparable to the movements in the province of Quebec in Canada or Scotland in the UK. This sociopolitical context helped to create a cognitive framework for the defence of other groups' own identities.

Even though Catalan deaf identity finds it roots in the American and European deaf movements (e.g. McIlroy & Storbeck, 2011; Krausneker, 2015), it is also inspired by this Catalan sociolinguistic context (Gras, 2008; Morales-López, 2008a, 2008b; Morales-López *et al.*, 2002). Within the Catalan deaf community, LSC started to be regarded as a symbolic instrument with some social power achieving symbolic capital status in terms of Bourdieu (Morales-López, 2008b).

Deaf community members in Catalonia culturally regard themselves as Catalan and Deaf (Morales-López, 2008b). There is transference of ideas from the Catalan social movement 'we are a nation, we decide' which aims for an independence referendum, to the Catalan deaf community's campaign on sign language recognition. This is illustrated by the logo of LSC Now!, the platform for the linguistic and cultural rights of LSC users, (est. 2003) (Figure 17.1). This logo encompasses the hybrid nature of the Catalan deaf community identity. It uses the handshape of the LSC sign for Catalonia and the four red stripes of the Catalan flag and the words LSC ARA! meaning LSC NOW!

Figure 17.1 Platform LSC Now! logo

As detailed in the next section, LSC policymaking is embedded in this sociolinguistic context, which is complex and strongly politicised.

Path towards Legal Recognition and Regulation of LSC

LSC only started to be recognised as a true language by the deaf community in the early 1990s, as a result of the participation of a group of Catalan deaf leaders in the international culture and arts festival, *Deaf Way I* in July 1989 at Gallaudet University in Washington, DC. Catalan participants attended presentations on sign language linguistics, deaf culture and identity, and arts performances in different sign languages. This helped them realise their own communication system was a distinct linguistic system, with the features of natural languages and different from other national sign languages worldwide. Before that, deaf people in Catalonia referred to their communication as mime, or using similar expressions (Frigola, 2010). In fact, 'mimics' was the official name given to LSC as a subject at the school for the deaf.

Following this experience in the USA, the main leaders of the Catalan signing community in collaboration with academics started to advocate for their culture and language rights. Over the last 30 years, the political demands of this campaign have primarily focused on (1) legal recognition of LSC; (2) accessibility to information and training; (3) schooling of deaf children in a cross-modal bilingual model; (4) teaching and dissemination of LSC; and (5) creation of language materials for teaching and sign language interpreting.

Towards legal recognition of LSC

The leading organisation behind the campaign was FESOCA (est. 1979), a non-profit organisation representing around 30 local deaf clubs.

FESOCA is an associate member of the Spanish State Confederation of Deaf People (CNSE) and the Catalan Committee of Representatives for People with Disabilities (COCARMI).

In 1992, FESOCA organised a workshop on the 'Language of the Signs', in which there was a round table on 'Aspects of the Official Status of Mime Language'. FESOCA invited several speakers, including parliamentary representatives. This round table led to the creation of a parliamentary commission 'for the study of the difficulties in the use of sign language' (Muñoz, 2010: 22). This commission included representatives of deaf organisations such as FESOCA – with the support of the Platform on Behalf of Bilingual Education (est. 1992) – the local deaf association of Sabadell, and several sign language teachers and experts on deafness.

Following the Catalan legal tradition, the commission then created a report that resulted in Resolution 163/IV on the Promotion and Dissemination of Catalan Sign Language, which the Parliament of Catalonia passed with unanimous consent on 30 June 1994. This type of parliamentary non-binding resolution aims to: (1) urge the government towards a specific action; (2) show the majority public opinion and/or parliamentary option on a specific topic; and (3) establish the principles of public administration actions.

Although it was a non-binding resolution and does not specifically tackle the legal status of LSC, it is regarded by the Deaf community as the first step towards legal recognition. The resolution is a milestone as the first public recognition of the 'existence' of sign language in Catalonia, the first legal text on LSC and the first parliamentary text on a sign language in Spain. At that point, there was not any research study on the language status of LSC, and the only existing documentation was a dictionary (Perelló & Frigola, 1987).

Resolution 163/IV only acknowledges 'the importance of sign language and the need to be learned by profoundly deaf people for their personal, educational and social development in Catalonia' and recognises 'bilingualism in education as a priority for the participation of the hearing-impaired in society, workforce and culture'. Finally, the text urged the Executive Board to 'progressively introduce bilingualism, spoken language/sign language, in Catalan education'.

Progress on the other demands began in 1994. The first cross-modal bilingual educational projects began in Tres Pins School and in two special schools: Josep Pla and the Centre of Hearing Rehabilitation (CRAS). Alongside this, the first language learning materials for LSC were created and different groups of people within the deaf community started to mobilise. Moreover, during the next decade, several organisations that became active campaigners and language advocates were established to support and further FESOCA's demands towards the legal recognition of LSC. Among these organisations were the deaf parents of deaf children association, named Visual Communication and Sign Language of

Catalonia Association (est. 1994), LENCOVIS; the Association of Parents of Deaf Children of Catalonia (est. 1996), APANSCE; the Sign Language Teachers' Association (est. 1996), APROLS; and the Institute for the Study of the Sign Language in Catalonia (est. 1998), ILLESCAT Association.

2006 marked the next milestone, when the new Statute of Autonomy of Catalonia included LSC and the need to protect, promote and guarantee sign language rights. The Statute is a law hierarchically located under the constitution and overrules any other legislation, including organic laws. This recognition is thus akin to constitutional recognition within the region. The core campaigners that strived towards the inclusion of an article that legally recognised LSC in the new regional/national statute were FESOCA, APANSCE and the Platform LSC Now! The platform comprised individual members and associate members from deaf associations, professional associations and academia including different academics specialising in education, linguistics, law, interpreting and language teaching.

The campaigners held several meetings with the different parliamentary parties and members of the parliamentary commission. Initially, FESOCA worked towards the inclusion of LSC within chapter 5 of the law, which included regulations on accessibility and social rights. Platform LSC Now! however, advocated a language approach and strongly defended the inclusion of LSC in chapter 3 on language rights. Additionally, the platform campaigners wanted the text to mention *language users*, instead of deaf signers, to include non-deaf and deafblind signers (Gálvez, personal communication March 23rd 2018; Segimon, personal communication March 25th 2018). The academics on the platform provided a list of research studies that supported the language status of LSC and its users. Finally, all deaf organisations' perspectives converged and they advocated for a language rights approach. Representatives from FESOCA and APANSCE appeared at the parliamentary commission on social policies on 12 April 2005.

Consequently, LSC recognition was included in Article 50 on Promotion and Dissemination of Catalan. Article 50.6 reads: 'Public authorities must guarantee the use of LSC and the conditions that allow the equality of people with deafness to opt for this language, which must be subject to education, protection and respect'.[5] The Catalan Statute and the Valencian Statutes are the first legislations to regulate the protection of a sign language in Spain. While the 2006 legal recognition did not specify any financial benefits, it was legally binding, and also a symbolic milestone because it was the first legal recognition of the language using its proper name, *LSC, llengua de signes catalana* (CSL, Catalan Sign Language) and not its previous denomination *llenguatge de signes* (verbatim: language of signs).

After legal recognition, the campaigners and parliamentary groups in the commission agreed that, following the Catalan language legal tradition, further recognition and language regulation was needed. More specifically, they argued for the regulation of the use and promotion of LSC in different domains such as education, the public domain, teaching and learning. The model for this was to be found in the vast regulatory legal texts existing for Catalan and Aranese in Catalonia as minority languages to be protected and promoted.

To achieve this goal, on 8 March 2007 the vice-president of the Catalan government called a meeting with FESOCA and Platform LSC, Now! representatives to initiate the implementation of Article 50.6. A month later, on 11 April 2007, the Parliament passed with unanimous consent, Resolution 32/VIII to support the government and initiate a bill on the recognition, promotion and regulation of LSC. Oral language and speech support for deaf people would be included in an accessibility bill to be developed simultaneously. The first meeting to start drafting the Catalan bill on sign language was held on 23 April 2007, the national day of Catalan language and literature. It was organised by the DGPL of the Catalan government who invited representatives of the deaf organisations to create a working group to elaborate the bill's draft, now formally also including Institute for Catalan Studies (IEC), APANSCE and the Association of Interpreters and Guide-Interpreters of Catalonia (ACILS, 1991), (Muñoz, 2010). No deafblind organisation representatives were invited at this point (Gálvez, personal communication March 23rd 2018).

While the Catalan working group was drafting the bill, the Spanish Courts passed Law 27/2007 'by Which Spanish Sign Languages Are Recognized and Means of Support for Spoken Communication by Deaf People Are Regulated' as an extension of the general accessibility law (Law 51/2003). The law recognises the existence of two Spanish sign languages, namely *Lengua de Signos Española* (LSE, Spanish Sign Language) and LSC. The text only regulates LSE and other communication accessibility means for deaf, hearing impaired and deafblind people, within a disability model.[3] (See Muñoz (2010) and Quer (2012) for details on the process towards achieving legislative recognition.)

Negotiations between the Catalan and Spanish deaf associations, led by FESOCA and Plataform LSC, Now! with the support of IEC was crucial to guaranteeing the inclusion of a sign language other than LSE in the federal law. Initially, it only included recognition and regulation of LSE and mentioned other language rights should be regulated within each autonomous community. Hence, the federal law could not regulate LSC within the Catalan territory. The fact that the state law would also regulate the use of LSE within Catalonia was regarded negatively, because it was seen as opening the possibility for introducing LSE into Catalan schools and thus affect the distinct grammar and vocabulary of LSC. The deaf community feared that this would impose further minorisation of LSC and eventually lead to language substitution. The campaigners sought to incorporate legal recognition of LSC within the federal law to be further regulated within the Catalan laws. Towards this goal, Catalan representatives appeared before the Spanish Courts in April and May 2006 and presented more than 50 amendments (Gálvez, personal communication, March 23rd 2018). Academics of the University of Barcelona and IEC demonstrated the distinct language status of LSC. Hence, Law 17/2007 is the first federal legal text to include official recognition of LSC, although it transfers responsibility to regulate the language to the Catalan government.

Towards legal regulation of LSC

During the campaign in Madrid, a working group of the Catalan government, led by DGPL, continued developing the preliminary bill on LSC in Catalonia. In May 2007, the final version of the preliminary bill was concluded and in July 2009 the government approved the bill for submission to the Catalan Parliament, which was accepted on 1 September. Later in September 2009, the parliamentary commission was established and the period for amendments started. On 11 November 2009 there was a parliamentary debate on the law.

As per the LSC campaigners' demands, the bill was strictly language-oriented. From the beginning, it was aimed at being modelled on the Aranese language minority law and the campaigners advocated for a language rights discourse, as described in Murray (2015) and Wilcox *et al.* (2012) for other sign languages. This is similar to the influence that legal recognition of spoken regional minority languages, such as Sámi and Gaelic, has had on the recognition of sign languages in the same countries (De Meulder, 2017a, 2017b).

However, oralist campaigners attempted to duplicate provisions of the federal law in Catalonia into the LSC Law to include oral language support and accessibility through print (such as captioning, subtitling or speech-to-text technologies) and technologies that enhance hearing (such as hearing aids, cochlear implants or induction loop systems) (for similar opposition against sign language legislation from oralist campaigners, see Geraci & Insolera, this volume, Chapter 11, on the case of Italy).

The oralist groups were represented by ACAPPS (Federation of Catalan Associations of Parents and Deaf People) with the support of the research group GISTAL (Center for Research on Deafness and Disorders in Language Acquisition) from the Autonomous University of Barcelona and several speech-therapist organisations. The oralist pressure group feared that the LSC Law would impose the learning of LSC for all deaf children, which would, according to them, be against the freedom of language choice.

Their main argument was what we consider a quantitative fallacy. Oralist groups argued that among all deaf populations, signers purportedly represent only 10% and non-signers represent the 90% majority of the deaf. Consequently, they argued that a sign-language-only law was not in the best interests of the more general deaf populations; they wanted a broader legal text that represented the interests of their 'deaf majority', that is the oralists. Had they succeeded in their demands, this would have meant that the dominant oralist group could have used the law as a mechanism to continue a hearing hegemony, as pointed out by Bryan and Emery (2014).

During the bill's drafting period, and continuing through the amendments period and the parliamentary review, the LSC working group, the government representatives and some parliamentary members had to explicitly present arguments for a language-only perspective and against the adoption of a disability model approach to stop pressures from the aforementioned organisations adhering to an oralist ideology and medical discourse. Especially relevant in emphasizing the value of LSC as a cultural heritage and as a minority language were the contributions of both nationalist parties: the Republican Left of Catalonia (ERC) and the right wing Convergence and Union (CiU). For example, the former President Carles Puigdemont, representative of the CiU in the parliamentary commission at that time, stated:

> Today we do an act of justice, and it is an act of reparation against the intolerance and prohibitions against which the sign language has been victim in its historical course. It is an act of defence of the language heritage of Catalonia of which we, Catalonians, signing or non-signing, have to feel particularly proud. (Sessions Record of the Parliament of Catalonia, 26 May 2010: Series P, no. 122, 8)

In response to this pressure from oralist groups, the government and parliamentary groups agreed to a compromise: a language bill for LSC with explicit reference to the freedom of language choice and educational modality, as well as a reference to non-signing deaf people as *oral deaf* (Preamble of the Law 17/2010: 45011). Additionally, they committed to later regulate on communication accessibility for deaf, hearing-impaired and deafblind people in a disability-oriented law. In so doing, the government assumed deaf signers *dual category status* (De Meulder, 2017b; De Meulder & Murray, 2017). Deaf signers celebrated this decision because they benefited twofold.

Finally, on 3 June 2010, Law 17/2010 on Catalan Sign Language was enacted by the Parliament.[2] It draws on a language rights model and recognises LSC as a Catalan heritage language. It also lays the basis for its regulation, teaching, learning, professional accreditation and interpreting. The DGPL within the Department of Culture is designated to promote its regulation, normalisation, protection and dissemination, whereas the IEC is designated as the language research institution. For differences between the Spanish state law and the Catalan autonomous law, see Quer (2012).

The law urges the government to guarantee the freedom of choice of educational modality including bilingual or cross-modal educational programmes for deaf children, in which both LSC and Catalan are used as teaching languages. Article 5 of Law 17/2010 reads 'public education services shall guarantee information to parents or guardians of deaf and deafblind children on the various education programmes available, to allow a free choice' and establishes 'the learning of LSC shall be guaranteed in the bilingual education programme'.[2] It finally adds that LSC shall be disseminated through the general curriculum along with respect and promotion of the values of language diversity.

While the passage of Law 17/2010 on LSC was a huge step forward for the signing deaf community, the promulgated final version departed from the first versions presented by the coalition of campaigners. The legal text only partially fulfilled their expectations. The main barriers faced during the campaign were ideological and economic.

Regarding education, the deaf community advocates a move from the rehabilitation approach to the right to use LSC (Morales-López, 2008a), as described for other sign language communities (Plaza-Pust, 2017; Reagan, 2010). On the economic side, the budget shortfall was regarded as the most important barrier. The LSC Law was passed in the midst of the southern European economic crisis. It was clear from the beginning that the law would be enacted without any attached budget. However, campaigners celebrated the accomplishment of legal recognition and regarded it as a necessary step to later demand a budget allocation within the different governmental departments for their legally recognised rights.

Since then, LSC has been further regulated in other social legislation on accessibility and education. In 2014, the passage of the Catalan Law on Accessibility (13/2014) promoted accessibility as an instrument to achieve equality. The campaigners that represented the interests of deaf, deafblind and hearing-impaired people were FESOCA, ACCAPS, the Catalan Association for People with Deafblindness (est. 1999), ASOCIDE and the Federation of Spanish Associations of Cochlear Implanted (est. 2006), AICE. Law 13/2014 addresses the removal of communication barriers, architectural barriers and the promotion of technical aids to improve the quality of life and the autonomy of people with disabilities. Article 31 on the Rights of Hearing-Impaired People that Communicate in Sign Language acknowledges the role of LSC. Additionally, access in LSC is mentioned for broadcasting (Article 26.5), education (Article 32.5-6) and in public administration and public services (Article 33.2).

In education, Decree 150/2017 on Inclusive Schooling[6] 'aims to ensure that all non-university education schools supported by public funds are inclusive'. For instance, Article 5f indicates that the administration must 'guarantee the conditions of architectural and communication accessibility of the educational centres'. This part of the article entitles the provision of interpretation services and the use of sign language. Nonetheless, this regulation does not have a financial budget attached either.

In 2017, the Catalan Parliament passed Law 20/2017[7] on Transitional Jurisprudence and Foundation of the Republic, which the Spanish Constitutional Court overruled. This text was enacted to guarantee a new legal framework, as well as the orderly succession of the administrations and the continuity of public services, during the transition into an independent state. It was designed as a new constitutional framework for Catalonia that intended to replace the current Statute of Autonomy. This suspended law included the latest explicit legal reference to LSC. Article 24 on language rights includes the three official languages: Catalan, Aranese and Spanish, and mentions LSC. This article is based on non-discrimination and freedom of choice principles and supports former language policy laws in the country. In the first draft the legal text did not include LSC, but deaf activists detected this omission and urged FESOCA to contact the government and the parliamentary groups. Luckily, there was another amendment on the same group of articles and LSC was included along with the other languages.

To summarise the path to the legal recognition of LSC we provide Table 17.1 including both the timeline and the different legislations that have regulated the language during the past 25 years.

Right after the passage of the sign language Law 17/2010, a monitoring and evaluating committee was created to guarantee its enforcement. The committee included representatives from all the deaf community advocacy groups. The top-down planning actions were initiated with the passage of two decrees. Decrees are executive regulations created by the government that further develop laws; they have the force of law but are hierarchically lower than a legislative text. The decrees create new governing, executive and monitoring organs on language policy-making and language planning. Unfortunately, none of these regulatory texts, which were the first policy actions after the legal recognition, have any funding attached.

The DGPL is designated as the public organ in charge of language management and planning, interdepartmental coordination and language policy-making on LSC. The Technical Commission for Language Policy was appointed as the organ guaranteeing homogeneous application and cooperation in the implementation of interdepartmental language policies regarding LSC. A full-time permanent position for both Aranese and LSC language policies has been established.

Decree 142/2012 creates the Catalan Sign Language Social Board to parallel the Catalan Social Board and the Aranese Social Board. It is an advisory and consultation board that acts as the permanent organ for community engagement and social participation in the language policies promulgated or promoted by the Catalan government. The LSC Social Board includes seven representatives of the administration and seven representatives from the LSC community, all of them from different organisations participating in the campaign. The LSC Social Board has the functions of the former monitoring committee, namely: (1) to study and analyse, at the request of the government, questions related to the promotion and dissemination of LSC; (2) to advise the

Table 17.1 LSC legal recognition and regulation timeline

Year	Legislation	Legislative institution(s)	Type of legal text	Type of legal status
1994	Resolution 163/IV on promotion and dissemination of Catalan Sign Language	Parliament of Catalonia	Parliamentary Resolution on sign language	Parliamentary recognition (legally non-binding)
2006	Statute of Autonomy of Catalonia	Parliament of Catalonia Parliament of Spain (Congress of Deputes and Senate)	Organic Law	Legal regional/national recognition within the highest rank of autonomous community laws (akin to a constitution)
2007	Law 27/2007 by Which Spanish Sign Languages Are Recognized and Means of Support for Spoken Communication by Deaf People Are Regulated	Parliament of Spain	Accessibility Law on Sign language and other communication means	Legal state recognition (without regulation)
2010	Law 17/2010 on Catalan Sign Language	Parliament of Catalonia	Sign language law	Legal regional/national language recognition and regulation
2014	Law 13/2014 on Accessibility	Parliament of Catalonia	Accessibility law	Legal regional/national accessibility recognition and regulation
2017	Law 20/2017 on Transitional Jurisprudence and Foundation of the Republic	Parliament of Catalonia	Pre-constitutional recognition	Legal national language rights recognition

government on the appropriate planning actions to enforce Law 17/2010; and (3) to evaluate the objectives and results of public actions related to LSC planning.

Conclusions, Future Directions and Challenges

LSC has been promulgated by three common types of explicit legal recognition as distinguished by De Meulder (2015). It is recognised by a sign language law (Law 17/2010), and by a sign language law including other means of communication both at the state level (Law 17/2007), and in the Catalan Law on Accessibility (13/2014). More recently, it was further recognised by means of the general language article in the (overruled) proto-constitutional Law 20/2017[7] on Transitional Jurisprudence and

Foundation of the Republic. Additionally, there is explicit recognition by means of the Statute of Autonomy, which is the fundamental law defining the rights and obligations of the citizens in Catalonia. There is also implicit recognition in the Decree on Inclusive School and further explicit recognition in decrees implementing Law 17/2017. However, none of the legal acknowledgments grants official language status.

From a governmental point of view, the DGPL currently prioritises five top-down actions in the following areas: (1) creation of a LSC language corpus with IEC leading the technical management; (2) dissemination and promotion of LSC with the support of FESOCA; (3) promotion of LSC awareness among civil servants through an elementary training course on LSC; (4) the biennial LSC Awards recognising people, organisations and initiatives that contribute to the promotion, dissemination and prestige of LSC; and (5) definition of the LSC levels within the European Framework of Reference for Language with the support of University Pompeu Fabra, FESOCA and the University of Barcelona.

The immediate future direction for the DGPL is to obtain statistical data to quantify the LSC community. The DGPL wants to have data that can help designing language planning actions and evaluating the impact on the deaf community. This is a challenging enterprise, because traditional large-scale sociolinguistic survey designs (by telephone or writing) are not appropriate. Also, neither data related to the hearing-impaired population nor schooling census are sufficiently precise.

From the activists' point of view, the deaf community continuously endeavours to enforce full implementation of current laws, advocating for more investment in budgets and resources. As a measure to push enforcement, FESOCA wanted to appoint an external binding audit to analyse the current compliance with the LSC Law. Additionally, new campaigns have emerged which strive to achieve the highest legal status for LSC as the fourth official language in Catalonia. To achieve this goal, several deaf activists created the *Platform LSC in the Catalan Constitution*. At the time of writing, the Spanish and Catalan political situation is uncertain and changing rapidly, which means deaf advocates have to adjust their demands to changing political scenarios.

The main challenge the deaf community faces is language maintenance. On the one hand, language use is still constrained in diglossic terms, meaning in formal domains, predominantly Catalan or Spanish are used. On the other hand, LSC socialisation centres are weakened: deaf associations are becoming less active and schools no longer assemble a critical mass of deaf children. This causes a decreasing number of new members in the signing community and threatens intergenerational transmission of LSC. Parents of deaf children and deaf activists are conscious that the quality of life for their community relies on maintaining a critical mass of deaf signers. As for any cultural and linguistic minority this depends greatly on education (Gras, 2008; Hult & Compton, 2012; Wilcox *et al.*, 2012).

Concerning deaf education, FESOCA, APANSCE and, the recently created parents' of deaf children association, We Want to Sign and Hear (est. 2017) consider that although there are more resources for LSC interpreting in secondary education, there are still not enough measures towards educational language rights. Deaf children should have access to a rich signing environment, with a diversity of generational signers in functional contexts to promote successful sign language acquisition and enhance language maintenance. Family orientation in all resources and schooling programmes is vital in this regard. Sánchez Amat (2015) draws up a set of proposals, including both lines of action within the sign bilingual education institution and those issues which we consider should be promoted by the bodies managing cross-modal education for deaf children.

Despite the ongoing economic crisis, the Catalan deaf community still strives to advocate for language and social rights. The activists' vitality partly remedies the shortcomings of the different language planning actions. Although still scarce, budgets for LSC have been allocated in the Department of Education (for cross-modal bilingual programmes), the Department of Social Welfare (for accessibility) and the Department of Culture (within the DGPL for language planning).

On the whole, Law 17/2010 is still considered a valid legal framework even though there is no regulation yet for fundamental areas such as the media, higher education and research. A future interdepartmental plan could take sign language policies forward, parallel to the Catalan plan. A joint effort from both government and deaf community organisations can have the greatest impact on moving LSC status forward.

Notes

(1) The first author is part of the research group Grammar and Diachrony (GRADIA), University of Barcelona (AGAUR 2017SGR1337) and the research project FFI2016-77397-P (Spanish Ministry of Economy and Competitiveness). The second author is a member of the research group TransMedia Catalonia (2017SGR113, 2017) and her work is related to the research carried out on the European funded projects ImAC (Immersive Accessibility GA: 761974) and EasyTV (Easing the access of Europeans with disabilities to converging media and content GA: 761999). She is currently doing her research within the PhD programme in Translation and Intercultural Studies at the Department of Translation and Interpretation in the Autonomous University of Barcelona (UAB).

(2) The reference for the Catalan law is DOGC 5647, 10-6-2010. The full original text can be retrieved at https://www.parlament.cat/document/nom/TL118.pdf (in Catalan). The text is also available in Spanish at http://www.boe.es/buscar/doc.php?id=BOE-A-2010-10216 (in Spanish) or in English at https://www.parlament.cat/document/intrade/152430. (accessed March 23 2018).

(3) The legal text published in Spanish can be retrieved at https://www.boe.es/buscar/doc.php?id=BOE-A-2007-18476. An English version can be retrieved from http://sid.usal.es/idocs/F3/LYN11795/LEYLSE.pdf (accessed March 23 2018).

(4) See http://www.gela.cat/doku.php?id=llengues. (accessed March 23 2018).
(5) The full consolidated text of Organic Act 6/2006 (Statute of Autonomy of Catalonia) on can be retrieved in English at https://www.parlament.cat/document/cataleg/150259.pdf (accessed March 23 2018).
(6) The full educational decree 150/2017 can be retrieved at http://dogc.gencat.cat/ca/ pdogc_canals_interns/pdogc_resultats_fitxa/?action=fitxa&mode=single&docume ntIdhttp://dogc.gencat.cat/ca/pdogc_canals_interns/pdogc_resultats_fitxa/?action= fitxa&mode=single&documentId=799722&language=ca_ES (in Catalan) (accessed January 28 2019).
(7) The full text of Law 20/2017 can be retrieved in Catalan at https://portaljuridic. gencat.cat/ca/pjur_ocults/pjur_resultats_fitxa/?action=fitxa&mode=single&docum entId=796643&language=ca_ES) (accessed January 28 2019).

References

Arnau, J. and Vila, F.X. (2013) Language-in-education policies in the Catalan language area. In J. Arnau (ed.) *Reviving Catalan at School Challenges and Instructional Approaches* (pp. 1–28). Bristol: Multilingual Matters.
Boix-Fuster, E. (2015) Multilingualism in Barcelona: Towards an asymmetrical multilingualism. In E. Boix-Fuster (ed.) *Urban Diversities and Language Policies in Medium-Sized Linguistic Communities* (pp. 143–167). Bristol: Multilingual Matters.
Bryan, A. and Emery, S. (2014) The case for deaf legal theory through the lens of deaf gain. In H.D.L. Bauman and J.J. Murray (eds) *Deaf Gain: Raising the Stakes for Human Diversity* (pp. 37–62). Minneapolis, MN: University of Minnesota Press.
Comellas, P., Barrieras, M., Monrós, E., Cortès, M., Fidalgo, M. and Junyent, M.C. (2010) Descobrir les llengües de la immigració: ocultació, prejudicis i altres malentesos [Discovering the languages of immigration: Concealment, prejudices and other misunderstandings]. *Llengua, societat i comunicació [Language, Society and Communication]* 8, 54–62.
De Meulder, M. (2015) The legal recognition of sign languages. *Sign Language Studies* 15 (4), 498–506.
De Meulder, M. (2017a) Promotion in times of endangerment: The Sign Language Act in Finland. *Language Policy* 16 (2), 189–208.
De Meulder, M. (2017b) The influence of deaf people's dual category status on sign language planning: The British Sign Language (Scotland) Act (2015). *Current Issues in Language Planning* 18 (2), 215–232.
De Meulder, M. and Murray, J. (2017) Buttering their bread on both sides? The recognition of sign languages and the aspirations of deaf communities. *Language Problems & Language Planning* 41 (2), 136–158.
Departament de Cultura (2015) *Anàlisi de l'Enquesta d'usos lingüístics de la població 2013. Resum dels factors clau [Analysis of the Survey of Linguistic Uses of the Population 2013. Summary of the Key Factors]*. Barcelona: Departament de Cultura, Direcció General de Política Lingüística.
Frigola, S. (2010) La comunidad sorda de Catalunya [The deaf community of Catalonia]. In J. Martí and J.M. Mestres (eds) *Les llengües de signes com a llengües minoritàries: Perspectives lingüístiques, socials i polítiques [Sign Languages as Minority Languages: Linguistic, Social and Political Perspectives]* (pp. 29–54). Barcelona: IEC.
Gras, V. (2008) Can signed language be planned? Implications for interpretation in Spain. In C. Plaza-Pust and E. Morales-López (eds) *Sign Bilingualism: Language Development, Interaction, and Maintenance in Sign Language Contact Situations* (pp. 165–193). Amsterdam: John Benjamins.
Hult, F.M. and Compton, S.E. (2012) Deaf education policy as language policy: A comparative analysis of Sweden and the United States. *Sign Language Studies* 12 (4), 602–617.

Junyent, M.C. (ed.) (2005) *Les llengües a Catalunya: quantes llengües s'hi parlen?* [*The Languages in Catalonia: how many are spoken?*]. Barcelona: Octaedro.

Krausneker, V. (2015) Ideologies and attitudes toward sign languages: An approximation. *Sign Language Studies* 15 (4), 411–431.

May, S. (2012) *Language and Minority Rights. Ethnicity, Nationalism and the Politics of Language.* New York: Routledge.

McIlroy, G. and Storbeck, C. (2011) Development of deaf identity: An ethnographic study. *The Journal of Deaf Studies and Deaf Education* 16 (4), 494–511.

Morales-López, E. (2008a) Sign bilingualism in Spanish deaf education. In C. Plaza-Pust and E. Morales-López (eds) *Sign Bilingualism: Language Development, Interaction, and Maintenance in Sign Language Contact Situations* (pp. 223–276). Philadelphia: John Benjamins.

Morales-López, E. (2008b) La llengua de signes com a vehicle de comunicació i de capital simbòlic [Sign language as a medium of communication and symbolic capital]. In A. Massip (coord.) *Llengua i identitat* [*Language and Identity*] (pp. 29–36). Barcelona: Publicacions i Edicions de la Universitat de Barcelona.

Morales-López, E., Gras, V., Amador, J., Boldú, R.M., Garrusta, J. and Rodríguez-González, M.Á. (2002) Deaf people in bilingual speaking communities: The case of Deaf in Barcelona. In C. Lucas (ed.) *Turn-Taking, Fingerspelling, and Contact in Signed Languages* (pp. 107–155). Washington, DC: Gallaudet University Press.

Muñoz, E. (2010) El procés de reconeixement de la llengua de signes catalana des de la comunitat sorda [The process of recognition of Catalan Sign Language by the deaf community]. In J. Martí and J.M. Mestres (eds) *Les llengües de signes com a llengües minoritàries: Perspectives lingüístiques, socials i polítiques* [*Sign Languages as Minority Languages: Linguistic, Social and Political Perspectives*] (pp. 19–27). Barcelona: IEC.

Murray, J.J. (2015) Linguistic human rights discourse in deaf community activism. *Sign Language Studies* 15 (4), 379–410.

Plaza-Pust, C. (2017) *Bilingualism and Deafness.* Berlin: De Gruyter Mouton & Ishara Press.

Perelló, J. and Frigola, J. (1987) *Lenguaje de signos manuales* [*Manual Sign Language*]. Madrid: Inversiones Editoriales Dossat.

Quer, J. (2012) Legal pathways to the recognition of sign languages: A comparison of the Catalan and Spanish sign language acts. *Sign Language Studies* 12 (4), 565–582.

Reagan, T. (2010) *Language Policy and Planning for Sign Languages.* Washington, DC: Gallaudet University Press.

Sánchez Amat, J. (2015) Llengua de signes i llengua escrita en la modalitat educativa bilingüe i en la intervenció amb l'infant sord [Sign language and written language in the bilingual educational modality and in the intervention with the deaf child]. Unpublished PhD dissertation, Universitat Autònoma de Barcelona, Bellaterra.

Strubell, M. and Boix-Fuster, E. (eds) (2011) *Democratic Policies for Language Revitalisation: The Case of Catalan.* Basingstoke: Palgrave Macmillan.

Vernet, J. and Pons, E. (2011) The legal systems of the Catalan language. In M. Strubell and E. Boix-Fuster (eds) *Democratic Policies for Language Revitalisation: The Case of Catalan* (pp. 57–83). Basingstoke: Palgrave Macmillan.

Vila, F.X. (2016) Sobre la vigència de la sociolingüística del conflicte i la noció de normalitat lingüística [On the validity of conflict sociolinguistics and the notion of linguistic normality]. *Treballs de Sociolingüística Catalana* [*Working Papers in Catalan Sociolinguistics*] 26, 199–217.

Wilcox, S., Krausneker, V. and Armstrong, D. (2012) Language policies and the deaf community. In B. Spolsky (ed.) *Cambridge Handbook of Language Policy* (pp. 374–395). Cambridge: Cambridge University Press.

18 A Belgian Compromise? Recognising French-Belgian Sign Language and Flemish Sign Language

Maartje De Meulder and Thierry Haesenne

Introduction

Belgium is a small country, but a notoriously difficult one to understand, specifically with regard to its complex political system and the coexistence of different linguistic communities. This complexity, and the Belgian way of problem-solving, has given rise to a special internationally recognised expression, 'a Belgian compromise': complex issues are settled by conceding something to every party, with the resulting agreements often being so complex that they leave ample room for interpretation.

In this chapter, we argue that the recognition of the two Belgian sign languages, LSFB (French-Belgian Sign Language) and VGT (Flemish Sign Language), is an example of such a compromise: it allows for an agreement without unsettling the status quo, but also without granting any rights, and with no clarity about the scope and nature of the recognition.

Notwithstanding this, at least the recognition of VGT was reported in 2010 as 'perhaps the strongest recognition to be found in the EU at present' (Reagan, 2010: 159), because it goes well beyond mere recognition, creates a governmental advisory committee and recognises the need for research and funding. Despite the compromise on which it appears to be based, the cases of the legal recognition of VGT and LSFB are relevant for sign language planning scholarship primarily because of the specific Belgian context, which puts limits on the nature and scope of this recognition.

Before introducing the Belgian political and linguistic context, we clarify our positionality, since we come from both an academic and activist position. Both of us are deaf, were directly involved in the process leading to recognition and are still involved in the implementation phase.

Haesenne was involved in the recognition campaign and has been a member of the LSFB advisory committee. De Meulder was a founding member of Deaf Action Front (DAF, discussed later in the chapter) and has been a member of the VGT advisory committee for the last nine years (she was president of the committee between 2012 and 2016).

Belgium Political and Linguistic Context

Present-day Belgium has three official, constitutionally recognised, languages: Dutch, French and German. Since 1963, the federal state is flanked by a two-tier system of 'regions' and 'communities'. Geopolitically, Belgium is divided into three regions – Flanders in the north, Wallonia in the south (including the German-speaking community in the east) and Brussels, the capital region. Linguistically, Belgium is divided into three communities, which for Dutch and French largely overlap with the regions, and which are demarcated by official, fixed language borders according to a constitutional territoriality principle: the Flemish community, which is officially monolingual Dutch-speaking; the French-speaking community and the German-speaking community. The Brussels capital region is officially bilingual in Dutch and French. Each region and community has their own legislative and executive organs – in Flanders, the community and regional institutions were merged so there is one parliament and one government.

The territoriality principle means that language rights are applied differently according to the linguistic territory; public services in a region are only provided in the corresponding official regional language. The exception is the Brussels capital region, which has a bilingual regime and where a personality principle applies, which means language rights depend on the linguistic status of the person or persons concerned. This principle of territoriality coexists with the freedom of language, which puts limits on the territoriality principle in the private domain. The freedom of language means that Belgian residents may use the language of their choice in the broader private sphere.

This complex linguistic landscape also includes two legally – although not constitutionally – recognised sign languages: LSFB (French-Belgian Sign Language, *Langue des Signes de Belgique Francophone*), signed in the Walloon region and most of the Brussels capital region, and VGT (Flemish Sign Language, *Vlaamse Gebarentaal*), signed in the Flemish region. In the German-speaking community, LSFB is used with German mouthings (see Figure 18.1).

Belgium is a devolved state: while some matters are federal competences, others have been devolved to the regions, while the communities are responsible for individual or personal matters such as language, culture, early intervention, academic research and education. The communities can, in their corresponding linguistic regions, arrange language use

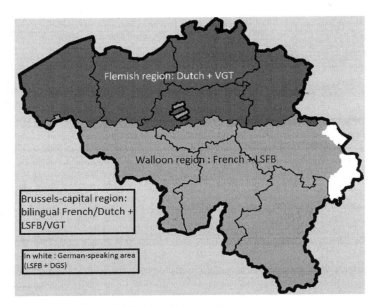

Figure 18.1 Use of VGT and LSFB in Belgium
Adapted from an original map © Stevefruitsmaak and used under a Creative Commons License CC-BY-SA.

through legislation (in Flanders, any legislation enacted by regions and communities are called 'decrees', which have the same force as a law). It is through such decrees that LSFB and VGT were recognised, by the Parliament of the French Community (2003) and by the Flemish Parliament (2006) respectively.

No provision in the Belgian constitution explicitly warrants the rights and freedoms of linguistic minorities. The definition of a 'national minority' in the Belgian context and the issue of whether linguistic minorities within the monolingual regions should be awarded special protection is a topical one (van der Jeught, 2016). This is also the main obstacle to the ratification of the Framework Convention for the Protection of National Minorities (Velaers, 2009), which Belgium has signed but not ratified. For similar (political) reasons, Belgium has not signed nor ratified the European Charter for Regional or Minority Languages.

This background helps to clarify that the Belgian political and linguistic context is not one that is very accommodating towards the position and rights of linguistic minorities. First, we introduce LSFB and VGT.

VGT and LSFB

LSFB and VGT are thought to descend from old French Sign Language (LSF) (Huvelle & Haesenne, 2006). This historical relation might partially explain why the signs of LSFB and VGT seem to show a high degree of similarity – anecdotal evidence points to a sharing of as much as 70% of the lexical items. However, due to the different spoken languages surrounding the respective sign language communities, the articulations of spoken words (mouthings) that accompany the signs are different; while the manual parts of LSFB and VGT are often similar, the mouthings are different and mutually unintelligible (Sáfar et al., 2015). In Belgium, nationalist and identity discourses seem to have historically played – and still play – a more significant role in Flanders (Blommaert, 2011). This is illustrated by the naming of the sign languages: Flemish Sign Language in Flanders and French *Belgian* Sign Language in Wallonia and Brussels (authors' emphasis).

When in the late 1980s and early 1990s linguistic researchers started to describe the sign languages used in Belgium, they felt the need for a name or label of some kind. At that time, Flemish researchers opted for the name 'Belgian Sign Language' (Loncke, 1986), while the first linguistic researchers in French-speaking Belgium for a while opted for 'French Sign Language' even though they knew LSF and LSFB were different (Nève & Martinet, 1996) or simply used 'Sign Language' or 'gestural language' (Huvelle, 1997).

In the 1970s, the Belgian deaf association had to split into a Flemish and a Walloon branch to be able to continue to receive (regional) government funding. In 1977, this led to the establishment of two separate deaf associations with different political identities: FENEDO (Federation of Dutch-speaking Deaf People), which became Fevlado and in 2017 became *Doof Vlaanderen* (Deaf Flanders) in Flanders and FFAS (Francophone Federation of Deaf Associations), which became FFSB (Fédération Francophone des Sourds de Belgique) in 1992 in the French-speaking part of Belgium (Wallonia and part of Brussels). The name of the deaf associations also clearly reflect nationalist and regional identity discourses.

From the 1990s onwards, it became clear that there was not enough linguistic evidence to know whether the differences between the sign languages used in Flanders and Wallonia were significant enough to talk about two different languages. In 1997, Fevlado organised a debate about the name of the sign language and chose to adopt 'Flemish Belgian Sign Language' because there was no linguistic reason (yet) to talk about Flemish Sign Language, and to emphasize the similarities rather than differences between Flemish and French-Belgian variants. The course of the next few years brought a political climate in which there was a gradual increase of the electoral market share in Flanders for parties advocating Flemish independence (Blommaert, 2011). The name of the language became a fiercely debated issue; Fevlado's monthly magazine even received letters in favour or against the label 'Flemish Belgian Sign Language' (Van Herreweghe et al., 2015). Also, the Fevlado board saw an increasing number of (younger) members with Flemish nationalist aspirations. In

2000, a debate and voting round was organised among association members and an overwhelming majority chose 'Flemish Sign Language', which has since been used to refer to the sign language in Flanders.

An example of a typical Belgian compromise can be found in the acronym LSFB. The reasons this acronym does not match the full name *Langue des signes de Belgique francophone* (French-Belgian Sign Language) are somewhat paradoxical. Prior to the LSFB decree, there had been no official consensus and no official statement by the FFSB about the name of the sign language in French-speaking Belgium. Most deaf people referred to their language as 'Sign Language' or 'Signs'. Some were using 'Belgian Sign Language' or 'French Sign Language', but these were the exception rather than the rule. Therefore, when the report on the feasibility of LSFB recognition was written (as explained later in the chapter), the authors had to decide on the name of the sign language. 'Walloon Sign Language' was not an option because LSFB is also used in Brussels, which is not Wallonia. Finally, 'langue des signes de Belgique francophone' – French-Belgian Sign Language – was chosen. 'Langue des signes belge francophone' – Francophone Belgian Sign Language – remains tolerated but its use is not encouraged because a sign language cannot be 'francophone'. The acronym LSFB was chosen over LSBF to emphasise that LSFB comes from the old LSF used in the early 19th century and that both sign languages remain to some extent, anecdotally, mutually intelligible.

Pre-recognition

LSFB

In French-speaking Belgium, several initiatives paved the way for the official recognition of French-Belgian Sign Language during the 1980s and 1990s. In 1992, 2000 deaf people marched the streets of Brussels demanding sign language interpreters on television. The 1980s and 1990s saw the establishment of sign language interpreter training, LSFB classes for adults (1993), a 'Resolution on the Charter of the Deaf'[1] (1994), the establishment of interpreting services (1995) and a decree on linguistic immersion that would become instrumental for the organisation of immersion education in LSFB (1998).

The 1988 and 1998 European Parliament resolutions encouraging EU Member States to recognise their sign languages were instrumental in initiating the process. Immediately after the second resolution, in 1999, the four major political parties of the Parliament of the French Community unanimously adopted a resolution aiming at the official recognition of LSFB. This was motivated by deaf activism, the aforementioned EU resolutions and the support of the Green Party.[2]

It was decided that the Minister of Youth and Health would submit a decree. In 1999, a first proposal was submitted to the government of the

French community. This was the result of a coalition of organisations including FFSB, the Centre Francophone de la Langue des Signes, APEDAF (parent organisation), the deaf clubs in Liège and Tournai and a sheltered work enterprise near Liège with many deaf employees. The government wanted to vote on the decree before the 2004 elections, but the funding for the feasibility research was only released in December 2002, which left very little time to write up a full report.

An inter-university group consisting of two hearing psycholinguists of the Free University of Brussels and two linguists (deaf and hearing) of PROFILS, an LSFB research centre within the Institut libre Marie Haps, was appointed to work on the report, which was submitted to the government in March 2003, after approval from FFSB (PROFILS & Université Libre de Bruxelles, 2003). The report identified four priorities: (1) encourage initiatives regarding bilingual education; (2) support the professionalisation of sign language interpreters; (3) increase the number of deaf professionals in deaf-related professions; and (4) promote sign language research, especially in the fields of comparative linguistics, and contained 75 recommendations. There was one instance when friction arose between the group writing the report and the FFSB, concerning LSFB standardisation. The working group argued that forced LSFB standardisation was not necessary and would even be harmful, while FFSB required them to remove any reference to regional LSFB variation. Indeed, the FFSB had been working closely with the CFLS (Francophone Centre of Sign Language), a stand-alone centre to promote a standardised variety of LSFB, while voluntarily excluding regional variation, which led to increased linguistic insecurity among LSFB signers (Haesenne et al., 2006). The feasibility report drew attention to this issue and in the end, the government followed the experts' view and even acknowledged regional variation in the comments of the 2003 decree. This effectively halted the forced standardisation of LSFB.

On 21 October 2003, the 'Decree on the recognition of sign language' (Décret relatif à la reconnaissance de la langue des signes)[3] was approved unanimously by the Parliament of the French Community. The responsible minister made clear that the recognition was only a first step in the recognition of the right to use sign language and that the decree had to be seen as a framework for every minister to be able to take action within their domain. This would then hopefully lead to concrete outcomes in the form of additional decrees and laws following the recommendations from the feasibility report. The reality turned out to be different, as we will discuss further in the chapter.

VGT

While VGT was only legally recognised in 2006, the demand and action for recognition is much older than that, and mainly concerns bottom-up language planning efforts by deaf community members and organisations such as a national conference on the theme, meetings with policymakers and marches during the 1990s and early 2000s. All these events coincided with changing language attitudes within the Flemish deaf community, the setting up of the first interpreter training programme in 1981, the further development and dissemination of linguistic research on VGT, the setting up of 'deaf awareness' courses by Fevlado and an increasing number of international exchanges (for an overview, see Van Herreweghe *et al.*, 2015).

The eventual legal recognition in 2006 was the result of momentum created by the previous developments, in addition to a combination of further bottom-up and top-down language planning, which enabled campaigners to overcome the final hurdle. This came in the form of the petition of DAF and political action led by deaf MP Helga Stevens, who was elected to the Flemish Parliament in 2004. DAF was a small organisation of deaf and hearing young people established in 2004, whose prime aim was the recognition of VGT. Because lobbying the Flemish political parties did not yield the desired results, DAF decided to use the Flemish right to petition, which means that any person can request the Flemish Parliament to discuss a proposal to change policy or a decree. When such a petition is signed by at least 15,000 people, the parliament has to discuss it and hear the first signer.

The petition ran for four months and when DAF submitted it to the Flemish Parliament in January 2005, 71,330 people had signed it, which made it the most successful petition ever submitted to parliament. Reflecting on how this achievement was possible, we identify several factors. One is that DAF was a pressure group operating outside of a traditional organisation such as Fevlado. DAF was not a conveniently independent offshoot for political reasons, but involved a slightly different demographic of activists from both the deaf community (younger, more educated) and larger society (hearing lay people who had never heard of Fevlado), and reframed the discourse around recognition claims. While the actions of Fevlado were perceived by many deaf community members as tardy and time-consuming, the DAF petition was a very concrete action that helped to garner support. This support created a climate in which some deaf people felt emboldened to 'come out' about their deaf identity with their families; for many deaf people, the demand of the petition was not just to recognise their language, but also to recognise *them*. DAF members had a significant nation-wide network, which made it possible to mobilise widespread support. Social media such as Facebook and Twitter were not yet widely used at that time in Flanders, which avoided 'slacktivism' and meant people had to go out of their way to collect signatures on paper (see Jarque *et al.*, Chapter 17, this volume, for example, on the Platform LSC Now! in Catalonia).

The petition was then discussed in the parliamentary commission for Culture, Youth, Sports and Media, and a public hearing was organised to inform MPs. At the same time, an explanatory document was drafted that came with the petition (Adriaenssens *et al.*, 2005), jointly written by DAF, Fevlado, the Flemish Sign Language Centre (VGTC) and Helga Stevens. Stevens, together with MPs from other political parties, took the initiative to draft a decree proposal for which they extensively negotiated with all stakeholders. In February 2006, a decree proposal was submitted by Stevens and colleagues and discussed in the parliamentary commission, after which the majority political parties came to an agreement. After voting in the commission, the decree proposal was discussed on 26 April 2006 in the plenary session of the Flemish Parliament, which unanimously voted in favour of the 'Decree on the Recognition of Flemish Sign Language' (*Decreet houdende de erkenning van de Vlaamse Gebarentaal*).[4]

The Decrees on LSFB and VGT Recognition[5]

The LSFB and VGT decrees are quite similar, although the VGT decree is more extensive. Both decrees have their legal basis in article 4,1° of the special law of 8 August 1980 for reform of the state institutions (communities and regions), which makes the communities responsible for 'the protection and the lustre of the language' ('lustre' is an archaic formulation that can also be translated as 'splendour' or 'glory' of the language). This entails recognition of language as a cultural means, not the protection of the people using it (le Maire, 2016).

LSFB decree[6]

The LSFB decree has five articles, of which most are linked to the establishment of the advisory committee. Article 1 reads:

> French Belgian Sign Language (LSFB), hereafter named 'sign language', is recognised. This language is the visuo-gestural language of the deaf community of the French-speaking community of Belgium.

The parliament stated that, through recognising sign language as the language 'of' the deaf community ('*propre à la communauté des sourds*'), it recognised a minority group based on its language and culture, not based on a disability (le Maire, 2016). According to the explanatory notes of the decree, the 'deaf community' does not only include people who have a hearing loss but also people who are not deaf, that is people who: (1) have mastered sign language; (2) are surrounded by family members who are deaf; (3) have gone to or are going to a school with one or more deaf pupils; (4) participate in deaf community life; (5) are involved in advocacy for rights of deaf people; (6) have followed sign language training; and (7) use sign language in the context of work.[7]

Articles 2, 3 and 4 concern the establishment, composition and functioning of a governmental advisory committee on sign language, with as its task 'to release advice and proposals to the Government concerning all issues related to the use of sign language' (Article 2). The committee consists of a maximum of 15 members nominated by the government for a period of four years, which can be renewed once. For each effective member, an alternate member is named. The government decides on the composition of the committee, which has to include:

(1) Representatives of associations of deaf people, parents of deaf children and cultural, sports or leisure organisations.
(2) Representatives of special schools, mainstream schools, deaf-specific social services, social support services, accommodation centres or day centres.
(3) Sign language teachers, sign language interpreters and sign language specialists.

Other regulations contained in the articles are that the committee has to convene a minimum of three times per year, that the government decides on a meeting honorarium for committee members per meeting, on the modalities for the disposal of sign language interpreters for the meetings and that the committee needs to issue a yearly report on its activities.

Article 5 states that 'Within the limits of budgetary credits, the Government fixes, after consultation with the advisory committee mentioned in Article 2, the implementing measures necessary to enable the use of sign language in the various domains of its competence.' The LSFB decree has no earmarked budget attached, apart from a budget (€6000) for the operation of the committee.

VGT decree

The VGT decree (2006) was mainly inspired by the LSFB decree. It entails a symbolic recognition and the establishment of an advisory committee, but also two additional measures: structural funding for research on VGT and for projects that contribute to the 'societal anchoring' of VGT. Article 2 reads:

> The Flemish Sign Language, abbreviated VGT, is the visual-gestural natural language used by deaf and hearing VGT signers in the Flemish Community and the bilingual region Brussels-Capital. VGT signers belong to the linguistic-cultural minority group for which the Flemish Sign Language plays an identifying role. The Flemish Sign Language is hereby recognized.

It is explicitly stated that deaf and hearing VGT signers belong to a linguistic-cultural minority group for which VGT plays an identifying role. VGT is not merely seen as the language 'of the deaf community'; it is a language used by both deaf and hearing signers.

The VGT decree differs from the LFSB decree in three aspects:

- It explicitly states that VGT is also being used by people in the bilingual region of the Brussels capital.
- It uses the full name of the sign language.
- The decree does not use 'national minority' but 'linguistic-cultural minority group', which has no definition either, but does not open up the 'national minority' discussion.

The recognition contained in Article 2 avoids any suggestion that VGT would have equal status with Dutch, and nowhere does the decree make explicit reference to Dutch. It only recognises VGT by confirming it is a language and has an identifying role for a specific group of people who use it. The obligations of the Flemish government in the Flemish community and the bilingual region the Brussels capital are thus limited to those three meanings: (1) the Flemish government affirms that VGT is a language being used by deaf and hearing signers in Flanders; (2) it accepts the existence of this language also in a judicial sense and treats it accordingly; and (3) it expresses its appreciation for the language (le Maire, 2016). The application of the decree is thus limited to the recognition of the *language* and does not entail recognition of the *right* to this language for the linguistic-cultural minority group of deaf and hearing VGT signers.

Articles 3, 4 and 5 discuss the establishment and functioning of the advisory committee, with a similar task as the LSFB committee. It consists of a minimum of 10 and a maximum of 15 members, appointed by the Flemish government for a four-year term that can be extended. The Flemish government decides on the composition of the committee, which needs to include a minimum of one member of the following categories:[8]

(1) Associations of deaf VGT signers.
(2) Parents who use VGT with their child.
(3) People with expertise on the education and raising of deaf children in VGT.
(4) VGT teachers.
(5) Experts linked to interpreting VGT-Dutch and Dutch-VGT.
(6) VGT researchers.
(7) Deaf studies researchers.
(8) Experts on the artistic use of VGT, Deaf culture or sign language media.

A notable difference with the LSFB decree is that the VGT decree states that a minimum of half of the committee members must be deaf VGT signers. In case not enough appropriate candidates can be found, a new call must be launched. A maximum of two-thirds of the members can be of the same sex. The committee needs to issue a yearly report of its activities to the Flemish government and the Flemish parliament.

Article 6 regulates the recognition of an association that needs to contribute to knowledge about and development of VGT through scientific research.

Article 7 states that the Flemish government can grant funding to projects that contribute to the 'societal anchoring'[9] of VGT (an alternative to the phrase 'promoting the status', found in other sign language laws), among other things the organisation, joint organisation or support of awareness-raising activities.

Article 8 is similar to Article 5 of the LSFB decree, and states that the Flemish government, within the limits of budgetary credits, in consultation with the committee, takes all initiatives useful and necessary to enable the use of VGT in the different domains of its authority. Indeed, as with the LSFB decree, the authors of the decree considered it to be a first step, or at least a point of reference for further legislation.

Post-recognition/Implementation Phase

Over 10 years have passed since the adoption of the LSFB and VGT decrees, which makes it possible to discuss challenges and opportunities regarding implementation. We do this with specific reference to the working of the advisory committees in both regions.

Implementation of LSFB recognition

Governmental advisory committee

In August 2004, the government appointed the first members of the LSFB advisory committee. It is unknown how many deaf and hearing people applied, but only five deaf members were appointed (all signing deaf people) while the other 10 members were hearing people of whom half could barely sign or not sign at all. Among the alternate members there were even fewer deaf people: there were four, among them two late deafened people who could not attend meetings in LSFB without an interpreter present. During the first meeting, a motion was tabled proposing a right for deaf members to have a veto because of the majority of hearing members. Hearing members rejected this motion, arguing for equality between members. This led to friction. Indeed, because most hearing members were not fluent in LSFB or could not sign at all, and had little contact with the grassroots deaf community, deaf members felt they were treated unfairly, even though the president of the committee was deaf and had the right to decide in case of equality in the votes.

The advisory committee consequently created four working groups, each focusing on a specific topic: (1) LSFB interpreting; (2) early intervention and childhood; (3) education; and (4) LSFB on TV. Between 2005 and 2008, the committee published yearly reports that can be found online.[10] The advisory reports the committee issued were mostly on education, early intervention and interpretation.[11]

On 21 May 2008, the members of the next advisory committee were appointed. Some had been members of the first committee and this time there were even fewer deaf members: three deaf to 12 hearing members (with six deaf alternate members and nine hearing alternate members).

Since 2008, there have been no yearly reports of activities available online, even though the committee's members still convene from time to time. In 2015, the advisory committee was transferred from the Department of Health to the Department of Culture. In October 2017, the composition of the new board was announced. This time, there were more deaf members: six were deaf, one hard-of-hearing and the other six were hearing. At least three members are on their third term, even though the recognition decree mentions a maximum of two terms.

Immersion education in LSFB

In 1998, a decree on education by linguistic immersion in the French-speaking community was adopted in Belgium. The original decree only envisaged immersion in the official languages, but a few members of parliament, with the support of the FFSB and the parent organisation APEDAF, submitted amendments to include LSFB. The funding for sign language teachers and bilingual classes in primary education was only made available in February 2009, after adoption of a new decree that allowed regular schools to offer immersion education in LSFB. The explanatory notes of this decree also make reference to the recognition of LSFB, which demonstrates the impact of this decree on the right to immersion education in LSFB (le Maire, 2016). Up till now, only one school has organised immersion education in LSFB, the Sainte-Marie School in Namur (Ghesquière et al., 2015; Meurant & Ghesquière, 2017).

Implementation of VGT recognition

Project funding

Following Article 7 of the decree, the Flemish government has since 2007 funded projects that contribute to the 'societal anchoring' of VGT for the amount of €30,000 per year. The funding is allocated by the Ministry of Culture on advice of the VGT advisory committee. The funding, although limited, has been important for both existing and new organisations. However, the number of applying organisations has decreased, which means that currently most of the funding goes to the national Deaf organisation that has greater staff capacity to write project applications than many of the smaller organisations, which are the main target of the provision. Also, because the funding is limited to one year, many of the projects have ceased to exist, which calls into question the long-term benefits of the funding.

Funding for the Flemish Sign Language Centre

Following Article 6, the Flemish Sign Language Centre[12] (which already existed before the recognition but did not receive any structural funding), became an official recognised organisation funded by the Flemish government. Since 2007, they have received yearly funding to conduct research on Flemish Sign Language. Up till the time of writing, this was €96,000 per year.

Advisory committee on VGT

In 2008, an advisory committee for VGT was established and is now in its third term. It has been used as a model for the establishment of the NZSL board (see McKee & Manning, Chapter 14, this volume). Following the VGT decree (and in contrast to the LSFB advisory committee), the majority of the VGT advisory committee members have always been, and continue to be, deaf VGT signers. Since 2008, the committee has issued various advisory reports related to sign language interpreting, sign language in the media, sign language in education and so on, which are all publicly available on its website.[13] The yearly budget for the committee (€14,537) is spent on member's fees, interpreter fees and website translations into VGT. It comes directly from the Department of Culture and is not earmarked to the VGT decree. The committee has a secretariat (equivalent to one part-time staff member) to communicate the committee's advice, write reports of committee meetings, administratively follow up project funding and so on. The secretary from the department always attends meetings.

Since its establishment, the committee was confronted with various challenges illustrative of those confronted by other sign language boards and councils (see the De Meulder, Murray & McKee, Epilogue of this volume).

One of the first challenges concerned the language in which meetings would take place. Originally, most hearing members spoke Dutch in meetings (including the first chairperson), even though they all knew VGT, while deaf members signed. Despite requests from some of the deaf members during the very first meeting, there was initial reluctance from most hearing members to sign. They claimed it was not their mother tongue, they were not proficient enough in VGT or found it disturbing to hear the interpreters at the same time. Deaf members continued to request for a change in language policy, later also supported by some hearing members, and after two years, the committee decided that VGT would be the language of meetings, and that being able to attend meetings in VGT was a prerequisite to applying for membership. This practice of using VGT has been maintained, although interpreters are still present at all meetings because the department secretary does not sign.

The dominant language within government structures being Dutch can place barriers on maximal participation of some deaf members who, while all multilingual, are not all equally familiar with government and policy jargon (also noted by McKee & Manning for the NZSL board, Chapter 14, this volume). Visibility of the committee is another issue – after eight years, interaction is still primarily unidirectional, with the committee issuing advisory reports to the government – reports that often have minimal impact.

The most significant challenge appears to be finding a critical mass of suitable deaf members for the committee. This has been a problem from the start, and it appears now that most of the deaf committee members come from within the Flemish deaf association. This places constraints on the neutrality of the VGT committee, can lead to (perceived or actual) conflicts of interest and can have an impact on the capacity for independent influence on policy. For example, in other advisory committees, staff and board members of deaf organisations cannot apply (which is problematic for different reasons, see Lawson et al., Chapter 4, this volume). This also demonstrates the paradox that quota (on the minimum number of deaf members) are not always sufficient to realise effective participation. The result was that certainly for the first committee, the elected deaf members were mostly starting from a position of little political experience about language rights or campaigning. Also, while the first and second committees had a number of hearing members (most of them linguistic researchers and/or interpreters/interpreter researchers), none of them except one, applied to be a member of the current, third, committee. Motivations given were lack of time, a perceived (by them) sufficient number of deaf applicants, high workload and the rather minimal impact of the committee.

Going Forward

In 2016, the Flemish Minister of Culture, on the initiative of the VGT advisory committee, asked the University of Leuven to carry out an investigation into the judicial status and possibilities for VGT. Indeed, the committee noted that even after 10 years, the legal recognition of VGT remained merely symbolic, and that Flemish signers were confronted with the decree's limitations. This investigation resulted in a research report (le Maire, 2016), which discusses whether it is necessary to ground VGT signers' rights in an additional (constitutional or other legal) provision, as a 'second step' after status recognition, also because the rights that are currently granted on a federal and Flemish level are incompatible with the level of commitment resulting from the UN Convention on the Rights of Persons with Disabilities (CRPD). Constitutional recognition, however, would still be hard to achieve, not in the least because it would entail a debate about the definition of 'national minorities', a debate that the Belgian government is reluctant to re-open. Also, it might not be desirable at all, since constitutional recognition is not always a guarantee for linguistic rights (e.g. see Dotter et al., Chapter 13, this volume, for the case of Austria). Another option would be a legal provision on the federal level. This would be limited however, since the federal level cannot regulate on the responsibilities of the regions and communities. Also, there is no constitutional provision on the protection of linguistic minorities, so there would be no constitutional basis. Nevertheless, le Maire (2016: 84) states, 'it would be quite inconceivable that the recognition of the rights of VGT signers would be limited to the community level', following international obligations of the Belgian government, primarily the UN CRPD and Article 27 of the International Declaration of Civil and Political Rights. She states there would be a limited possibility for the federal government to regulate for the use of VGT and LSFB in public services and courts. Both the Flemish and the Walloon governments can adopt further legislation and could in their provisions point explicitly to situations where VGT and LSFB must be used in the public sphere. The Flemish and Walloon legislators could provide for the use of VGT and LSFB in three domains: administrative matters, education and broadcasting.

Le Maire (2016) also discusses three possibilities for organising education in VGT. Since the 1963 educational language law states that the official language of education in the Dutch language territory is Dutch, there would need to be an exception to this law which allows for education in VGT (as well). The first possibility would be to amend the 1963 educational language law. Although feasible, the process to do so is quite complex. The Flemish community has the capacity to regulate for the languages to be used in education, which could allow for the use of VGT as a language of instruction – at least if this can happen without provoking debate about the use of French in the Flemish community. A second option is an amendment to the Primary Education Decree to organise immersion education in VGT and Dutch for specific classes of deaf *and hearing* VGT signing children. Le Maire (2016) stipulates that the judicial system of the French-speaking community can be used, without copying the whole system; that is, it does not necessarily entail mixed classes with hearing non-signing and deaf signing pupils in a regular school. A third option would be the use of existing legal provisions that allow educational institutions to organise projects or to (partially) deviate from the official curriculum; for example, changes to the use of teaching hours. At the moment of writing, *Doof Vlaanderen* is working with parents and the government to set up bilingual VGT/Dutch classes for deaf and hearing children in regular schools.

Conclusion

It remains quite remarkable that the LSFB and VGT decrees were passed unanimously, in a Belgian context where any legislation related to language is incredibly sensitive and hard to achieve. Analysis of the process points to a few factors which enabled passage: direct bottom-up action, top-down support in various forms, an 'embedded' change agent in the form of a deaf MP (in Flanders) and EU and UN measures. It also points to the decrees being an example of a Belgian compromise; indeed, while they recognise LSFB and VGT as languages and establish advisory committees, they do not go beyond that, do not lead to any instrumental rights and do not change the linguistic status quo. Also, LSFB and VGT signers already use French and Dutch as their written languages and only use LSFB or VGT in a limited number of domains and then mostly through interpreters. The decrees do not change that fact. Furthermore, the laws have negligible financial implications. When adopted, the decrees were considered to be a first step and a point of reference for further legislation, but 10 years later, it appears that their legal and practical impact has been minimal. The Belgian sign language communities will continue to work for sign language rights and meaningful recognition.

Acknowledgements

We would like to thank Delphine le Maire and Helga Stevens for their comments on earlier drafts of this chapter. The writing of the VGT sections has benefited from conversations with Jan Adriaenssens and Isabelle Smessaert, over the years.

Notes

(1) See http://www.pfb.irisnet.be/documents/compte-rendu-de-la-seance-pleniere-du-27-mai-1994/document (last accessed 27 January 2019).
(2) See http://www.pfwb.be/le-travail-du-parlement/doc-et-pub/documents-parlementaires-et-decrets/dossiers/000204839 (last accessed 27 January 2019).
(3) See http://archive.pfwb.be/100000000000ce6 (last accessed 27 January 2019).
(4) See http://www.ejustice.just.fgov.be/cgi_loi/change_lg.pl?language=nl&la=N&cn=2006050537&table_name=wet (last accessed 27 January 2019).
(5) All translations between French/Dutch and English by the authors.
(6) For all documents concerning the LSFB decree, see http://www.pfwb.be/le-travail-du-parlement/doc-et-pub/documents-parlementaires-et-decrets/documents/000361514 (last accessed 27 January 2019).
(7) Projet de décret du 17 septembre 2003 relatif à la reconnaissance de la langue des signes, *Parl. St.* Communauté française, 2002–2003, nr. 446/1, p. 4.
(8) The categories were changed following the decree amendment in 2014.
(9) This is a direct translation of the original '*maatschappelijke verankering*' used in the decree.
(10) See http://www.langue-des-signes.cfwb.be/.
(11) See http://www.langue-des-signes.cfwb.be/index.php?id=ccls_lesavis000&no_cache=1.
(12) See http://www.vgtc.be/ (last accessed 27 January 2019).
(13) See http://adviesvgt.be/ (last accessed 27 January 2019).

References

Adriaenssens, J., De Meulder, M., Smessaert, I., Van Herreweghe, M., Van Mulders, K., Vermeerbergen, M., Heyerick, I. and Verstraete, F. (2005) *Toelichting erkenning Vlaamse Gebarentaal* [Explanatory notes Flemish Sign Language recognition]. See http://www.sociaalcultureel.be/doc/Doc_GEBAAR/vgt%20verzoekschrift.pdf (last accessed 27 January 2019).
Blommaert, J. (2011) The long language-ideological debate in Belgium. *Journal of Multicultural Discourses* 6 (3), 241–256.

Ghesquière, M., de Halleux, C. and Meurant, L. (2015) Bilingual education by immersion in Namur, Belgium: Principles and pedagogical issues. *Proceedings of the 22nd International Congress on the Education of the Deaf*, 6–9 July, Athens, Greece.

Haesenne, T., Huvelle, D., Sonnemans, B. and Gerday, C. (2006) Les signes officiels: Schizoglossie en langue des signes de Belgique francophone? In Apedaf (ed.) *In-Ouïs. Pot-pourri sur la surdité* (pp. 38–42). Bruxelles: APEDAF (Les Cahiers de la Salamandre, 2).

Huvelle, D. (1997) Le langage des sourds revisité. In J. Giot and J.-C. Schotte (eds) *Surdité, différences, écritures: Apports de l'anthropologie clinique* [Deafness, differences, writings: contributions from clinical anthropology] (pp. 115–142). Brussels: De Boeck.

Huvelle, D. and Haesenne, T. (2006) Conséquences et enjeux de la reconnaissance officielle d'une langue: Le cas de la langue des signes en Communauté française de Belgique. [Consequences and issues of official language recognition: The case of sign language in the French community of Belgium]. In Conseil Supérieur de la langue française et Service de la langue française de la Communauté française de Belgique (eds) *Langue française et diversité linguistique. Actes du Séminaire de Bruxelles (2005)*, (pp. 195–201). Brussels: De Boeck-Duculot.

le Maire, D. (2016) *Onderzoek naar juridische status en mogelijkheden voor Vlaamse Gebarentaal. Onderzoeksrapport in opdracht van de Vlaamse overheid Beleidsdomein Cultuur, Jeugd, Sport en Media* [Research into judicial status and possibilities for Flemish Sign Language. Research report by order of the Flemish Government Department of Culture, Youth, Sports and Media]. KU Leuven Faculteit Rechtsgeleerdheid.

Loncke, F. (1986) Belgian Sign Language. In J. Van Cleve (ed.) *The Gallaudet Encyclopedia of Deaf People and Deafness* (pp. 59–60). New York: McGraw-Hill.

Meurant, L. and Ghesquière, M. (2017) Co-enrolment of hearing, deaf and hard of hearing pupils in a mainstream school. The bilingual classes of Sainte-Marie in Namur (Belgium). In K. Reuter (ed.) *UNCRPD Implementation in Europe – A Deaf Perspective* (pp. 202–212). Brussels: European Union of the Deaf.

Nève, F.-X. and Martinet, A. (1996) *Essai de grammaire de la langue des signes française* [Grammar test of French sign language]. Liege: Bibliothèque de la Faculté de philosophie et lettres de l'Université de Liège.

PROFILS (Institut Libre Marie Haps) & Université Libre de Bruxelles (2003) *Etude de faisabilité de la reconnaissance de la langue des signes en Belgique Francophone* [Feasibility study of the recognition of sign language in French-speaking Belgium]. Bruxelles: Communauté française de Belgique. (unpublished report).

Reagan, T. (2010) *Language Policy and Planning for Sign Languages* (Sociolinguistics in Deaf Communities Series, Vol. 16). Washington, DC: Gallaudet University Press.

Sáfár, A., Meurant, L., Haesenne, T., Nauta, E., De Weerdt, D. and Ormel, E. (2015) Mutual intelligibility among the sign languages of Belgium and the Netherlands. *Linguistics* 53 (2), 353–374.

Van der Jeught, S. (2016) Territoriality and freedom of language: The case of Belgium. *Current Issues in Language Planning* 18 (2), 1–18.

Van Herreweghe, M., De Meulder, M. and Vermeerbergen, M. (2015) From erasure to recognition (and back again?): The Case of Flemish Sign Language. In M. Marschark and P.E. Spencer (eds) *The Oxford Handbook of Deaf Studies, Language, and Education* (pp. 45–61). Oxford: Oxford University Press.

Velaers, J. (2009) Het kaderverdrag tot bescherming van de nationale minderheden: Een 'non possumus' voor Vlaanderen? [The Framework Convention for the Protection of National Minorities: A 'non possumus' for Flanders?] In A. Alen and S. Sottiaux (eds) *Taaleisen Juridisch Getoest* [Judicial Testing of Language Claims] (pp. 103–185). Leuven: Kluwer Uitgeverij.

Epilogue: Claiming Multiple Positionalities: Lessons from the First Two Decades of Sign Language Recognition

Maartje De Meulder, Joseph J. Murray and Rachel L. McKee

In this closing chapter, we reflect on evidence presented in the individual chapters. We look at the concept of the legal recognition of sign languages from a macro-level, going beyond individual countries.

The Concept of 'Recognition'

The concept of 'recognition' is central to sign language communities' demand for legal status of their languages. This is a unique aspect of sign language laws and the campaigns that drive them – campaigns for the legal status of spoken minority languages tend not to use 'recognition' as a concept because in most cases there is no need to prove that they are bona fide languages. The centrality of the 'recognition' concept is rooted in language ideologies about the normativity of the spoken modality (Hill, 2013; Senghas & Monaghan, 2002), which has motivated the need to 'recognize', in law, that signed languages are languages 'in their own right'. Discourses on the recognition of sign languages thus invoke specific language ideologies about sign languages as (real) languages (see also Kusters *et al.*, forthcoming), making claims for independent language status. For example the campaign for the Korean law used 'Sign language is a language' as a slogan (Hong *et al.*, Chapter 2, this volume).

Several laws contain in their preambles information on sign languages as languages, and specific provisions (often in one of the first articles) that either confirm or recognize sign languages' linguistic status; for example, 'Austrian Sign Language is recognized as a fully-fledged language' (Article 8(3) of the Austrian Constitution). Some laws define sign languages through nationalist or linguistic descriptions or a combination of these; for example, 'sign language is recognized as the natural means of communication of the Deaf community' (Chile), 'the official language of Korean deaf people', 'the visual-gestural language used by deaf and hearing VGT signers in the Flemish Community and the bilingual region Brussels-Capital', 'the linguistic system of signing deaf and deaf-blind people in Catalonia' and 'the sign language used by the majority of the deaf community in the State' (Ireland). Some laws contain more elaborate definitions of the specific sign language and make reference to the existence of other languages (signed or spoken); for example, the Libras Law Article 1

> Libras is recognized as a legal means of communication and expression, as well as other means of expressions associated with this language. The term Brazilian Sign Language is understood to mean – Libras, the form of communication and expression in which the visual-kinetic linguistic system, with its own grammatical structure, constitutes a linguistic system for the transmission of ideas and facts, originating from communities of deaf persons in Brazil.

Another example is the Act on the Status of the Icelandic Language and Icelandic Sign Language (ITM), which positions a spoken and signed language in parallel, defining ITM in Article 3 as 'the first language of those who rely on it for expressing themselves and communicating with others. It is also the first language of their children'.

Sometimes, legislators consider it necessary to 'define' a sign language in the course of the legislative process. The sixth paragraph of Law 20.422 (the 'Disability Law'), which mentions Chilean Sign Language, stipulates that 'the State and the Deaf community will define Chilean Sign Language within a period of three years'. After protest movements united under the slogan, 'Chilean Sign Language exists, there is nothing to define', the sixth paragraph of the law was abolished (González et al., Chapter 8, this volume). This definition of the language can be found in US state level legislation as well (Murray, Chapter 7, this volume).

That misconceptions about sign languages (and specific attitudes towards deaf people) still exist only emphasizes the need for recognition. Throughout the campaigns described in this volume, we see legislators and policymakers lack knowledge about how sign languages emerge, evolve and exist. In a debate in the Italian Senate, MPs stated Italian Sign Language (LIS) is 'less expressive' than Italian, is not a language because it has 'too many varieties and no standard', even going so far as to saying that International Sign should be used because this would allow for global communication and not just among the small group of deaf Italians (Geraci & Insolera, Chapter 11, this volume). These misconceptions are sometimes reflected in legislation; for example, in Turkey, where Article 15 of the Disability Act 2005 states 'Turkish Sign Language System is to be created in order to provide the education and communication of the hearing disabled' (İlkbaşaran & Kubus, Chapter 5, this volume). In Korea, the Basic Plan of the Framework Act on Korean Language, which preceded the KSL Act, mentioned KSL and braille as 'special Korean languages' (Hong *et al.*, Chapter 2, this volume).

Naming and Defining Sign Languages

This volume concerns the legal recognition of sign languages, which have been given names relatively recently, often as a first step towards a claim for recognition. For example, in 1979, the term '*langue des signes française*' (LSF) was adopted to designate what deaf people then called 'gestures'. The name was introduced by a linguist and a sociologist (Cantin *et al.*, Chapter 9, this volume). Some laws use the specific name of the sign language, while others just use 'sign language'. Some laws also recognize the tactile (deafblind) form of a sign language; for example, the BSL Act Scotland and the proposed LIS Bill.

Some sign languages did not have an official name until the legislative process for recognition, and the decision on which name to select can be a contentious part of the legislative process. Mori and Sugimoto (Chapter 6, this volume), Hong *et al.* (Chapter 2, this volume) and De Meulder and Haesenne (Chapter 18, this volume) discuss debates about naming sign languages in Japan, Korea and Belgium respectively. Naming national sign languages can also have perceived ideological advantages in specific contexts. For example, by identifying itself as the unifying sign language of the Turkish nation and an extension of the Turkish nationalist identity in a new modality, Turkish Sign Language (TİD) bypassed prevalent nationalistic protectionist instincts regarding minority languages at the core of Turkey's nation-state identity (İlkbaşaran & Kubus, Chapter 5, this volume). The argument for national affinity was also made in Iceland, where language policy has traditionally been driven by linguistic purism and protectionism, and a history of homogeneity (Stefánsdóttir *et al.*, Chapter 15, this volume). This can be seen as the flip side of arguments that emphasize the distinctiveness of sign languages from spoken languages. The argument seems to be that sign languages are distinct, but indigenous, and thus a part of the national cultural heritage. For example the Irish campaign referred to Irish Sign Language (ISL) as Ireland's second indigenous language, alongside Irish (*Gaeilge*).

Another unique aspect of sign languages is that the natural languages developed by deaf communities over time exist alongside artificial sign codes created by educators to be manual representations of the spoken language. These ideological contestations sometimes end up in legislation, specifically the issue of whether laws overtly distinguish between the natural sign language and an artificial code, and the relative status these forms achieve in the process of recognition. For example Mori and Sugimoto (Chapter 6, this volume) and Hong *et al.* (Chapter 2, this volume) express regret that this distinction was not stated in the legislation in Japan and Korea, respectively. Mori and Sugimoto outline the ideological considerations involved in determining a national sign language in Japan, while in Korea there are sign language linguists who regret that the KSL Act does not distinguish between Korean Sign Language (KSL) as a fully-fledged and independent language and Signed Korean, which is an artificial sign system. İlkbaşaran and Kubus (Chapter 5, this volume) state the creation of a 'Turkish Sign Language system' aimed for in the Turkish Disability Act 2005 falsely equated TİD with Signed Turkish and misleads agencies responsible for implementation. Then again, it would be unusual for any other language legislation to 'define' the language in question by excluding or including particular varieties or dialects, and deaf communities would likely resist having the profile of those artificial forms raised by legally codifying them.

Claims to Intersectional Rights

In the introduction to this volume we stated that deaf signers claim intersectional rights as both linguistic minorities and people with disabilities. Following these intersectional claims, strategic gains for sign language recognition often materialize under a disability rights framework, and in some cases, recognition is advanced on the coat-tails of disability rights legislation; for example, in Turkey. In France, the legal recognition of LSF was the result of an amendment of a larger disability law. LSF activists, while not being directly consulted in the formulation of the law, took the opportunity to advocate for recognition of LSF within it, something that was not initially envisaged by the government (Cantin et al., Chapter 9, this volume). Campaigns often also entail (necessary) alliances between leading deaf and disability rights NGOs, for example in Korea, or involve a certain kind of horse-trading, such as in Austria. Korean activists sought support from other disability groups for the KSL Act because policymakers saw it as a disability issue and wanted to ensure that it was supported by the disability community as a whole, not just deaf people (Hong et al., Chapter 2, this volume). In Austria, following an informal agreement between activists and politicians, the parliament voted in favour of the Federal Disability Equality Act while at the same time approving the constitutional amendment that recognized Österreichische Gebärdensprache (ÖGS) (Dotter et al., Chapter 13, this volume). A similar progression occurred in New Zealand, where a national disability strategy provided the administrative platform for work towards NZSL legislation (McKee, 2007).

The blending of language and disability perspectives is a double-edged sword. İlkbaşaran and Kubus (Chapter 5, this volume) assume that in Turkey, the adoption of a disability rights framework to recognize TİD has led to TİD gaining more direct legal recognition and status in the past decade than any other minority language in Turkey, including educational linguistic rights. They further state that the protectionist and charity culture around disability in Turkish and Islamic traditions may also have augmented the extent to which government bodies took ownership of the recognition. Quadros and Stumpf (Chapter 16, this volume) discuss how a disability framework, in which Libras is interpreted as a language accessible for deaf people, allows deaf university students in Brazil to submit dissertations exclusively in Libras, with optional subtitles or audio in Portuguese, thus circumventing existing frameworks that enshrine the place of Portuguese as the dominant state language. Invoking concepts of inclusion, exclusion and access clearly points to the interpretation of language legislation through a disability rights framework, and this can be used to advance instrumental rights for sign language users in ways not commonly found in minority language laws.

However, the blending of language and disability rights frameworks also has significant limitations. The Malta Act is limited by 'reasonableness' (of provision) as set in the Equal Opportunities (Persons with Disabilities) Act 2000 (Azzopardi-Alexander et al., Chapter 3, this volume). The BSL Act Scotland (2015) has to stay away from matters regulated in the Equality Act 2010 (Lawson et al., Chapter 4, this volume). Collaborations with other disability groups can also have drawbacks. İlkbaşaran and Kubus (Chapter 5, this volume) mention that members of other disability groups are generally more literate, better educated and are more politically active than deaf people in Turkey, and their relative dominance may diminish the agency of deaf leaders to advocate for their own claims.

Several chapters in this volume show another implication of blending language and disability perspectives; namely political manoeuvrings from outside pressure groups associated with deafness, not all of whom support the promotion of signed languages (e.g. in Italy, Scotland and Catalonia). This can spur the involvement of groups that are for and against legislation; for example, parents' organizations, charitable and scientific organizations 'for the deaf' and organizations of non-signing deaf people. Such 'stakeholder' groups may seek to undermine the status of sign languages; for example, by saying that 'there is no deaf community thus also no language' (Italy), that audiological interventions should be given priority (Ireland, Scotland, Spain, Italy), by advocating for inclusion of regulations on accessibility in spoken language and via technological aids (Catalonia), by pointing to the small number of signers among deaf people (several countries) or by claiming that a sign language law would be against the freedom of language choice (Catalonia). In some countries, these political manoeuvrings have been effective and the resulting law is a compromise between the two perspectives. In Catalonia, the government agreed to enact a language law for *llengua de signes catalana* (LSC), which included explicit reference to the freedom of language and educational modality as well as reference to non-signing deaf people. The government also committed to later regulate on communication accessibility in a disability-oriented law. Jarque *et al.* (Chapter 17, this volume) state that in doing so, the Catalan government explicitly attributed deaf signers a dual category status, which Catalan deaf signers celebrated 'because they benefited twofold'.

Barriers and Challenges in Campaigns

Finding allies among legislators

The case studies presented here reveal several barriers and challenges in campaigns for the legal recognition of sign languages. One of the challenges was to find allies among legislators sympathetic to the cause. This is common across most countries, and serves to bring in allies as well as raise awareness among legislators on the nature of sign languages. Bills are often introduced by legislators who have been cultivated by deaf community networks. In Ireland, the first bill was proposed by a member of the opposition who had been elected with the support of the Irish Deaf Society. The Scottish Bill was introduced by a legislator with deafblind grandparents. In Malta, however, the initial bill was written without deaf community involvement, despite an alliance with another legislator who was the minister of disability issues. Some countries had the benefit of deaf legislators. Flanders, Belgium had the specific advantage of a deaf MP (Helga Stevens) prepared to submit a bill and do this in close consultation with activist groups and the national deaf association. A deaf member of the Icelandic parliament (Sigurlín Margrét Sigurðardóttir) also submitted a bill, although in the end this was not adopted. Helene Jarmer's role as a deaf MP in Austria was crucial for raising awareness among fellow legislators.

Expectations of deaf communities versus political realities

Another common and recurring challenge was the expectations brought by deaf community members versus the political realities of legislative processes. As noted elsewhere (De Meulder & Murray, 2017), deaf communities' aims for sign language recognition have often been threefold: status recognition, the accordance of instrumental rights, often via interpreting services, and linguistic rights in education, particularly for deaf children. In some countries such as Norway and the Netherlands, many instrumental rights are accorded in separate laws and recognition campaigns are therefore explicitly status-oriented. In the Netherlands, this has also led to criticism from within the deaf community that the (long ongoing) debate on the formal recognition of *Nederlandse Gebarentaal* (NGT) only detracts attention from resolving practical issues regarding the guaranteeing of instrumental rights, primarily the provision of sign language interpreters (Meereboer *et al.*, 2018), issues that would not be solved by a status-oriented recognition. A common pattern has been that the first goal of status recognition has been relatively easy to achieve, whereas results are more mixed for the latter two goals. As a general rule we can see that campaigns often sought more from formal legal (symbolic) recognition than legislators were prepared to give.

Territoriality arguments

The nature of sign languages as indigenous minority languages used by a group spread throughout the country, has been interpreted in different ways in different countries. As noted above, in Turkey and Iceland, this 'native' language discourse has lent itself to arguments that the sign language is a part of the national cultural heritage. The existence of minority language legislation can be an asset in some countries; for example, in Finland, Norway and New Zealand, with deaf people claiming a role for sign languages alongside other national minority languages. On the flip side, the absence of minority language legislation (e.g. Belgium) or legislation specifying national or official languages per se (USA) can be a barrier to achieve legislation for sign languages. In some cases, minority languages are identified with specific territories and granted rights on that basis. This is where sign languages are often excluded. LIS has been excluded from minority language legislation in Italy and in Austria deaf people are not considered a minority (*Volksgruppe*) because they have no specific territory. Frisian in the Netherlands is recognized as a territorial minority language but NGT is not. Remarkably, this territorialization has not been an obstacle in the three peninsular Nordic countries, even though Sami is generally identified with the far north in those countries.

Access to literacy and participation in political advocacy

In general, members of deaf communities have poor access to literacy in the national written language and thus to participation in higher education and democratic institutions. Azzopardi *et al.* (Chapter 3, this volume) mention that in Malta, few of the deaf campaigners actually could read and fully understand the text of the Act. In Chile, structural inequalities mean deaf people have had limited social capital, something reflected in the long campaign towards recognition. In the UK, the Scottish Parliament has made accommodations towards this through allowing deaf people to share their views in British Sign Language (BSL) on the Parliament's Facebook group, and by allowing responses to consultation questions in BSL. The Scottish Parliament also published various key documents in BSL, including the call for views and other briefing material. Although this introduced deaf people in Scotland to the parliamentary process and the details of the BSL Bill in BSL, Lawson *et al.* (Chapter 4, this volume) report that viewing statistics remained low. Because of the small pool of experienced activists with the requisite literacy, representation falls on the shoulder of few people, making individual and organization advocates more vulnerable to the interference of other groups. This has an impact on political representation in many countries.

Linguistic human rights for deaf children

The lack of linguistic human rights for deaf children as a result of sign language recognition legislation is recurring and much-lamented phenomenon. This is partially a result of the way the laws were written, and partially due to resistance to a sign language medium education even when the legislative text creates linguistic rights in education. In New Zealand, campaigners sought educational language rights for deaf children, but these were not included in the law. Campaigners for the BSL Bill in Scotland identified language rights for deaf children and their families as a key priority. In Ireland, the Act contains references to the right of families of deaf children to learn ISL, among other references to deaf children, but the impact of these clauses remain to be seen. In Brazil, the right to use Libras in education exists, but is only realized at postsecondary level, due to the opposition of the inclusive education lobby to bilingual education of deaf children at elementary and secondary levels. In the USA, state-level recognition has predominantly supported the learning and teaching of American Sign Language (ASL) by hearing people who want to learn ASL as an additional language rather than first language acquisition by deaf children.

Sign Language Legislation and Interpreting Services

Another recurring issue in this volume is that sign language legislation which goes beyond status recognition often starts and stops at providing sign language interpreters, and the right to (use) sign language is often by default equated with the right to access public services in sign language with interpreters. In some laws this equation is made explicit, for example in Ireland, where the Act states 'The State recognizes the right of Irish Sign Language users to use Irish Sign Language as their native language and the corresponding duty on all public bodies to provide Irish Sign Language users with *free interpretation*' (our emphasis). The Korean Law states 'The government shall provide sign language interpretation to deaf people and foster sign language professionals to facilitate deaf people's access to public facilities, public events and judicial proceedings as required' (the meaning of 'sign language professionals' is not specified).

Chapters demonstrate that the provision of sign language interpreting services are important to start campaigns at all because they are needed for advocacy work and dialogue with policymakers, as noted in New Zealand, for example. In some countries, the training of interpreters has also been instrumental for raising deaf people's critical awareness about the status of sign language as a language. For example, Icelandic deaf people became aware of the status of ITM as a language as a result of the training of interpreters for a Nordic festival. Legislation often provides regulations for sign language interpreters, setting competency standards for interpreters, keeping a register of interpreters (e.g. Malta, Turkey) or establishes professional qualification and university education for interpreters (Catalonia).

However, legislation also often stops short at providing these services, or legislation may be seen as impossible to implement (or even pass) without interpreting services in place. In 2013, the Irish Sign Language Act did not pass because the then Minister for Disability said that 'we need to put the service in place before we put the legislation in place' (Conama, Chapter 1, this volume). In Malta, the 2016 Act can only be fully implemented after the first cohort of formally trained sign language interpreters will graduate in 2020. In the UK, during the legislative process for the BSL (Scotland) Act, the House of Lords Select Committee on the Equality Act 2010 opined that 'we wonder whether this very significant cost (the £6 million estimated for writing and reviewing plans under the Act) might not be better employed in directly training more BSL interpreters and increasing their availability where they are needed' (Lawson *et al.*, Chapter 4, this volume). The right to interpreter-mediated service provision overruling the right to direct services in a signed language sometimes leads to paradoxical situations. In Austria, for example, deaf people have the option to use ÖGS interpreters in school but do not have the right to learn, use or develop ÖGS in school (Dotter *et al.*, Chapter 13, this volume). Some countries mention sign language training for frontline staff of public services. Malta, for example, might make it mandatory for a percentage of frontline staff to attend *Il-Lingwa tas-Sinjali Maltija* (LSM) training, particularly those working in healthcare settings.

Implementing Bodies

Legal recognition of a national or minority language commonly entails assigning implementation oversight to a government sanctioned language agency (Spolsky, 2009). Eight chapters in this volume describe the existence of a body with a designated role in the implementation of sign language recognition legislation. In many cases, these entities transition some members of the campaigning group into authorized roles as language 'managers' (Spolsky, 2009). The implementation bodies described are of three types: (1) governmental advisory boards (Wallonia, Flanders, Chapter 18, Scotland, Chapter 4, New Zealand, Chapter 14); (2) sign language councils (Iceland, Chapter 15, Malta, Chapter 3, Turkey, Chapter 5); and (3) representation in an existing national languages council or institute (Norway, Chapter 12, and Korea, Chapter 2). No sign language bodies closely fit the model of a language commission or academy, although Turkey's agency is called a Commission.

Aims and functions of implementation bodies

Sign language bodies vary in their aims and scope: some mainly give strategic advice to the governmental sector concerning the language, while others also manage research associated with corpus planning, and some allocate project funding to external language promotion initiatives. Administrative hosting arrangements for sign language management bodies reflect the dual frameworks in which recognition has transpired: advisory boards are administered by government departments responsible for health and/or disability (e.g. New Zealand) or culture (e.g. Flanders, Belgium), whereas sign language councils come under national institutes or councils on language and culture (e.g. the Language Council of Norway or the Icelandic Language Council). The implications of affiliation are not neutral in terms of their operational relationship to branches of government and perception of their purpose. In Korea, for example, Hong *et al.* (Chapter 2, this volume) report that whereas campaigners wanted an independent Sign Language Research Institute, parallel to the National Institute of Korean Language, this was not realized in the KSL Act.

Both language agencies and language services (chiefly translation and interpreting) are key components of language management at government level (Spolsky, 2009: 248). Sign language agencies take on the remit of monitoring language services because sign language interpreting provision is essential to realizing participation in wider society. For example, in its first five years the Icelandic Sign Language Council addressed acquisition planning, attitude planning and cultural promotion, as is typical for a language management body; however, it has recently turned its focus to the collection of data on services and use of Icelandic Sign Language to inform future policy recommendations (Stefánsdóttir *et al.*, Chapter 15, this volume). Similarly, the work of the NZSL Advisory Board includes a strand on 'Use/Access', which focuses on access via interpreting and other measures (McKee & Manning, Chapter 14, this volume). Other bodies have given support to formal grievances about language accessibility barriers (e.g. the VGT Board regarding the right to sign language in education).

Membership of implementing bodies

The process of appointing sign language advisory bodies usually includes collaboration between a government authority, deaf organisation(s), and in some cases other another authority (e.g. Association of Local Authorities in Iceland). The size of sign language boards and councils reportedly ranges from five (Iceland) to 15 (Flanders), while a complete list of members of the 'TİD Science and Approval Commission' in Turkey is not known (İlkbaşaran & Kubus, Chapter 5, this volume).

The membership composition of implementing bodies reflects the politics of representation vis-à-vis stakeholders in sign language management; that is, who is deemed to have authentic speaker status, has investment in the language and has expertise relevant to guiding decisions about it. Unlike minority languages whose stakeholders are identifiable by ethnicity or territory (in addition to speaker status), stakeholders for sign languages include not only deaf sign language users, but also non-deaf people in categories such as parents of deaf children, professionals serving deaf people (e.g. interpreters, teachers, audiologists), and academics (usually linguists). Moreover, the disability status ascribed to deaf people has historically authorized clinical and educational professionals as de facto managers of institutional language policy affecting deaf people, and this legacy is apparent in some of the contention and compromise in determining membership of implementation bodies. In Belgium (Wallonia), for example, appointees to the LFSB governmental advisory committee established in 2004 (earlier than most others) comprised five deaf members and 10 hearing members, of whom only half were proficient signers; the subsequent 2008 board had an even lower ratio of three deaf to 12 hearing members. This imbalance meant deaf members felt disenfranchised in a body purporting to promote their linguistic and cultural interests (De Meulder & Haesenne, Chapter 18, this volume). On a smaller scale, the Icelandic Sign Language Council (established 2011) comprises just five members, with no regulated deaf to hearing ratio, of whom two are deaf (currently, a deaf organization leader and a deaf education professional) along with three hearing professionals.

In each of these (and many other countries), meetings are interpreted, since not all members have sufficient proficiency or willingness to conduct business meetings in sign language, yet this dual-language operation in itself can create a dynamic of participation inequity, particularly if deaf members are outnumbered and spoken language interaction norms are allowed to prevail. An alternative approach that aligns with language promotion goals is to prescribe a majority of deaf members and require fluency in sign language as a membership criterion so that business is conducted by default in that medium (e.g. in New Zealand and Flanders, although interpreters are still present at every meeting for government officials). The potential for inappropriate selection of language managers is highlighted by the case of Turkey İlkbaşaran and Kubus (Chapter 5, this volume). It is apparent that identity politics and internal language practices within these bodies can impede their efficacy and face validity as language promotion agencies.

Conclusion

This book is not intended to be a handbook on how to achieve sign language recognition. Indeed, the volume shows considerable variation between countries in the progress of their campaigns and the resulting legislation. While international aspirations for sign language recognition appear to be quite similar across countries, the practical achievement of it is contingent on each country's particular situation; sign language legislation necessarily needs to be achieved, implemented and understood through national legislative processes and taking into account local language ideologies. With this in mind, the book can be a useful guide for campaigners in those countries still advocating for sign language legislation and working towards meaningful implementation. It can be used as a reference tool for examples of good practice, a guide for pitfalls to avoid and provides a realistic perspective on the likely scope of the impact resulting from the legislative recognition of sign languages.

References

De Meulder, M. and Murray, J. (2017) Buttering their bread on both sides? The recognition of sign languages and the aspirations of deaf communities. *Language Problems & Language Planning* 41 (2), 136–158.

Hill, J. (2013) Language ideologies, policies, and attitudes towards signed languages. In R. Bayley, R. Cameron and C. Lucas (eds) *The Oxford Handbook of Sociolinguistics* (pp. 680–697). Oxford: Oxford University Press.

Kusters, A., Green, M., Moriarty Harrelson, E. and Snoddon, K. (eds) (forthcoming) Introduction: Sign language ideologies: Practices and politics. In A. Kusters, M. Green, E. Moriarty Harrelson and K. Snoddon (eds) *Sign Language Ideologies in Practice*. Berlin: De Gruyter Mouton.

McKee, R. (2007) The eyes have it! Our third official language – New Zealand Sign Language. *Journal of New Zealand Studies* 4–5, 129–148.

Meereboer, S., Meereboer, K. and Spijkers, O. (2018) Recognition of sign language under international law: A case study of Dutch sign language in the Netherlands. *Netherlands Yearbook of International Law 2017*, 411–431, Den Haag: T.M.C. Asser Press.

Senghas, R.J. and Monaghan, L. (2002) Signs of their times: Deaf communities and the culture of language. *Annual Review of Anthropology* 31, 69–97.

Spolsky, B. (2009) *Language Management*. New York: Cambridge University Press.

Index

Note: 'n' refers to chapter notes.